Studies in Medieval Philosophy

Studies in Medieval Philosophy

ÉTIENNE GILSON

Translated by
JAMES G. COLBERT

CASCADE *Books* • Eugene, Oregon

STUDIES IN MEDIEVAL PHILOSOPHY

Cascade Books
An Imprint of Wipf and Stock Publishers
199 W. 8th Ave., Suite 3
Eugene, OR 97401

www.wipfandstock.com

PAPERBACK ISBN: 978-1-5326-5527-2
HARDCOVER ISBN: 978-1-5326-5528-9
EBOOK ISBN: 978-1-5326-5529-6

Cataloguing-in-Publication data:

Names: Gilson, Étienne, author. | Colbert, James G., translator.

Title: Studies in medieval philosophy / Étienne Gilson ; translated by James G. Colbert.

Description: Eugene, OR: Cascade Books, 2019. | Includes bibliographical references and index.

Identifiers: ISBN 978-1-5326-5527-2 (paperback). | ISBN 978-1-5326-5528-9 (hardcover). | ISBN 978-1-5326-5529-6 (ebook).

Subjects: LCSH: Philosophy, Medieval. | Thomas Aquinas, Saint, 1225?–1274. | Joannes de Jundun, –1328. | Descartes, René, 1596–1650.

Classification: B721 G450 2019 (print). | B721 (ebook).

Manufactured in the U.S.A. JUNE 11, 2019

Études de Philosophie Médiévale
Étienne Gilson, Imprimerie Alsacienne, Strasbourg, 1921
Strasbourg, Commission des Publications de la Faculté des Lettres

Contents

Preface

The studies that are collected in this volume all bear directly or indirectly on medieval philosophy. The first four fit into the chronological framework traditionally assigned to the period. The subsequent ones study the prolongation of medieval through the Renaissance or the beginnings of the modern period. Each of these studies has been undertaken for its own sake, without any concern to make it conform to a general hypothesis. The facts themselves make the studies cluster around two central figures, St. Thomas Aquinas and Descartes. In the measure in which we tried to define the historical conditions within which Thomistic thought developed, it has seemed to us that St. Thomas Aquinas is the first modern philosopher in the full sense of the word. It is not that he created the principles and invented the attitudes within which we live. Not all the tendencies by which the thirteenth century prepares the modern period are compressed into Thomas's work, but he is the first Westerner whose thought is not prisoner of a dogma or a system. Situated within the general history of philosophy, St. Thomas continues Arab and Jewish speculations. But in regard to us he is truly the first link by which our chain is connected to that of Oriental and Greek philosophers. He was able to inherit and pass on to us a legacy that he developed and with which he enriched us. The common conclusion of the first four studies, therefore, is that, until Thomism, there was no philosophy in the Middle Ages in the modern sense of philosophy. This apparently paradoxical conclusion will become trivially evident; that it appears extraordinary is characteristic of truths to which we are not yet accustomed. When the necessary research has established that just as Albert the Great and St. Thomas restored the idea of philosophy for us, and Robert Grosseteste and Roger Bacon reinvented empiricism for us, perhaps we will give up the dangerous practice of making the history of modern philosophy begin in the seventeenth century. From that moment, the French and English will grasp the history of their own intellectual development in a more exact perspective. Auguste Comte saw perfectly that the introduction of positive sciences into Europe by Arab scholars is the living germ from which modern thought developed. We are more convinced of the truth of that affirmation each day. Furthermore, we think with Comte that the consequences for the appreciation of our past that could be drawn from this affirmation are not just theoretical. A people and a continent do not deny half their intellectual and moral history without paying for such a great error with inner distortion and strife.

The studies related to the influence of medieval thought on René Descartes do not attempt to modify traditional perspectives on history in any serious way. They deliberately approach Descartes on that side of his personality where he is not really himself and, to be completely explicit, through one of his defects. What is still medieval in Descartes is not Cartesian, but if the failures of a great philosopher are part of his complete story, and if we need to know why his reason could not accomplish the whole task his genius projected, studies of this kind will perhaps be useful. In Descartes's desire to merge physical and metaphysical truths in a single block, he ran the serious risk of not revising sufficiently the theses of Scholastic metaphysics or of received theology that seemed to be adapted to the general plan of his project. The uncertainties in the doctrine of human freedom that we have indicated elsewhere come from there. From there also stems the unfinished character in which the doctrine of innate ideas, as we interpret it in this volume, has come down to us. But, in a different aspect of Descartes's thought, he was exposed to external influences without possessing the means to assimilate them. From the outset of his philosophical reflections, Descartes had to choose between two procedures to master the truth, experiment and deduction. Seduced immediately by the clarity and evidence that arithmetic and geometry offer, Descartes opted for deduction. In the flash of genius by which he raised mathematics to the dignity of regulatory science, he was unable to foresee what difficulties it would cost later to apply mathematics to the real. In the second *Rule for the Direction of the Mind*, Descartes considers experiment alone as a source of error, and one of the principal reasons that explain the certainty of mathematics and geometry according to him is precisely that one never does experiments there. Nothing could ever modify the initial orientation given the whole system by mathematics. Cartesian thought remains a deduction that flows naturally along the track of the facts and flows with such abundance that it can cover all the facts, true or false indistinctly. Its possibilities of explanation are such that it was never embarrassed by factual criticism, and there lies the reason that this physics, so novel in its inspiration, remains dependent on Scholastic physics. Apparent facts appeal to Cartesian deduction as irresistibly as real facts. As will be seen in this volume's last two studies, Cartesian deduction engaged itself in luminous explanation of facts that do not exist. That is why we owe Cartesian deduction many more explanations than proofs, and French physicists of the group to which Blaise Pascal belonged already perceived this clearly. It remains no less true today that the type of Cartesian explanation corresponds to one of the deepest needs, perhaps even the deepest need, of scientific thought. It is appropriate to recall this when we establish that Scholastic physics itself left lasting traces of its influence within the Cartesian system.

ONE

The Meaning of Christian Rationalism

Nisi credideritis, non intelligetis.

ISAIAH 7:9

The expression *Christian rationalism* designates the movement that brings dialectic to the very heart of the deepest theological speculation. Its characteristic stages are marked by the works of SS. Anselm and Abelard. What precisely was this rationalism? Can these thinkers be seen as precursors of modern rationalism in any degree and as initiators of philosophy liberated from theology? To answer this question it is necessary to take up the very delicate problem of the relations their systems establish between reason and faith.

Let us first consider John Scotus Eriugena, whose ill-famed doctrine was condemned during his own lifetime and again after his death, to the point that in the thirteenth century Honorius III would still curse *De Divisione Naturae*, where the worms of heresy proliferate.[1] For some, Eriugena was a pantheist and "the father of anti-Scholasticism." For others, he was a rationalist who more or less consciously subordinated revelation to reason. One might ask in what sense and in what measure Eriugena was really a pantheist, but for the moment we only want to examine his attitude toward faith. That attitude is extremely difficult to comprehend when we try to define it starting simply from a direct interpretation of

1. *Chartularium*, Honorius III, 1:106–7: "Nuper . . . est quidam liber, qui *Perifisis* titulatur, inventus, totus scatens vermibus heretice pravitatis."

the scattered passages in which he formulates it. Even partial success in understanding his attitude is achievable only on condition of making a considerable effort to picture reality from the vantage point where John Scotus Eriugena himself perceived it. The obstacle is not what we fail to know, but what we do know. We might manage to learn what men knew in the ninth century but we no longer know. However, we never are able to forget what we know and they did not know. In the mind of a theologian of our time, there are at least two representations of the universe, which are intermingled or superposed and arranged hierarchically: that of religion and that of science. It is certainly true that God created the world with a view to his glory and made humans in his image and likeness. It is certain that the central fact of world history is the drama of Adam's fall and the redemption by Jesus Christ. Yet, it is equally true that the content of this religious interpretation of the universe is defined by science. Earth, as well as the humans that the earth contains, has another meaning and another definition for our reason than fall and redemption. However firmly an anatomist may believe the dogma that humans are the image and likeness of God, if he is asked to define human, such a definition will not be what first comes to mind. Today things have a certain reality and a certain existence by themselves. They are, first of all, what science and observation teach, and we can add a mystical or religious symbolic meaning to stable systems of phenomena controlled by necessary laws.

This is precisely what we must be able to forget for an instant if we want to have some hint of the way in which Eriugena views the universe. For a theologian of his period, the universe has only one meaning, its religious meaning. The theologian's doctrine may be rationalist, but we are sure beforehand that the reason whose rights this doctrine proclaims will have to move in a world whose profound content is identical with the world of faith. God is found at the origin and heart of every existence. We cannot say that God is an existence or even a being. He is beyond existence and being. All that can be put forward with certainty is that all reality and being hold their positive perfection only from God. Therefore, God escapes human reason. He even escapes the angelic intellect, whose purely spiritual nature is superior to ours. God is not directly knowable by any created thought, and if he wants to make himself known through the beings that depend on him, he has to be translated and expressed in a figurative language that puts his infinity within the reach of the intellects or reasons whom he addresses. The angels glimpse God through invisible and incorporeal signs that theology calls *theophanies*. The angelic intelligences, detached and freed from the burden of the flesh, are thus the creatures least far from God. But for human minds, which are still held in the bonds of the flesh, purely spiritual signs remain unintelligible. We need material and sensible symbols that we can use as so many rungs to elevate us closer to God. Consequently, human revelation is still lower than angelic revelation, and from our point of departure, we can measure how incapable we are of attaining the depths of reality through the effort of our reasons alone.[2]

Since God is the real, and since God is not directly accessible for us, it turns out that any human knowledge of the real presupposes revelation. Therefore, reason will always work on revelation, and the pretension to know anything other or more than what this revelation contains can be considered once and for all to be absurd at its very root. Our thought works in a ray of light that comes from above. It cannot see anything beyond what this light shows us or exceed its source. This is why the paradigmatic definition of God that we find in Pseudo-Dionysius, in Eriugena, and that will constantly issue from St. Bonaventure's pen, is that of the Epistle of St. James: "The Father of Lights." "Every good gift and every perfect gift is from above, coming down from the Father of Lights . . ." Considered in relation to us, God is essentially light and the source of light. Each of his acts is a self-manifestation proportioned to the capacity of our intellect. God acts only to reveal himself[3] in the following form.

A first light that emanates from the Father of all lights is that of Scripture. God's sacred books reveal him to humans in the form that is the simplest and most easily accessible possible. Therefore, it is necessary to begin there, and all reasoning should take its point of departure from Scripture.[4] Scripture's authority is unshakable, and we must admit the

2. Eriugena, *Super Hierarchiam Caelestem Sancti Dionysii*, I, col. 141, and *Expositiones in Mysticam Theologiam Sancti Dionysii*, I, col. 272: "Ac brevi sententia beatus Dionysius docet nos, incunctanter non solum humanos animos adhuc in carne detentos per sensibilia symbola, verum etiam angelicos intellectus omni carnali gravitate absolutos, per invisibiles significationes, quas theologia *theophanias* nominat, ipsam veritatem cognoscere, quoniam per se ipsam nulli creaturae seu rationali seu intelligibli comprehensibilis est."

3. Epistle of St. James 1:17. "Omne datum optimum et omne donum perfectum desursum est, descendens a Patre Luminis."

4. Eriugena, *De Divisione Naturae*, II, 15, col. 545: "Ratiocinationis exordium ex divinis eloquiis assumendum esse aestimo.—Nil convenientius, ex ea enim omnem veritatis inquisitionem initium sumere necessarium est."

reality of what it tells us, even when what it tells us exceeds our reason's capacity.[5] Only thanks to it are we assured of triumphing over the traps of the enemy of humankind. Scripture is the pledge of our future happiness, and our salvation can be said to originate in faith.[6] From that stems the vehemence of Eriugena's attacks upon Gotteschalk's heresies. Let us not forget that before being the victim of orthodoxy, Eriugena was its zealous defender.

The total and absolute truth of the revelation contained in Scripture is thus placed once and for all beyond dispute as a consequence of the very conception Eriugena formed of truth and reality. The role reserved for reason is also defined by the nature of revelation, in which every human science is contained virtually. Scripture makes us know God but, precisely because it is revelation and an accommodation of the supreme reality to our finite minds weighed down by matter, it does not give us God's nature. Even if our minds had not been clouded and blinded by sin, our knowledge would have to be founded upon revelation; we are naturally sensitive to light; we do not produce it.[7] With even more reason, we must receive an illumination proportioned and adapted to our state after the fall. This is why Scripture, whose authority must prevail in all things, does not use the words or names it employs in their own direct sense when it tries to suggest to us what divine nature is. Scripture always proceeds through analogies and transpositions, making allowances for our weakness, Scripture uses them with us as we use them with children, and it strives to translate the supreme reality into language that is intelligible to us.[8] Therefore, symbols are revelation's natural language and necessary means of expression, and all revelation is symbolic by definition.

5. Eriugena, *De Divisione Naturae*, III, 17, col. 672: "Inconcussa itaque auctoritas divinae Scripturae nos compellit credere, totius creaturae universitatem in Verbo Dei conditam esse, ipsiusque conditionis rationem omnes intellectus superare, solique Verbo, in quo condita sunt omnia, cognitam esse."

6. Eriugena, *De Praedestinatione*, I, 4, col. 359: "Quoniam igitur antiqui hostis miseria humane beatitudini semper invidet insidias nostrae saluti preparare non cessat. Salus autem nostra ex fide inchoat."

7. Eriugena, *In Prologum Evangelii secundum Ioannem*, col. 290: "Sed iste, sensus moralis, Physica vero horum verborum theoria talis est. Humana natura, etsi non peccaret, suis propriis viribus lucere non posset. Non enim naturaliter lux est, sed participes lucis. Capax siquidem sapientiae est, non ipsa sapientia, cujus participatione sapiens fieri potest. Sicut ergo aer iste per seipsum non lucet, sed tenebrarum vocabulo nuncupatus, capax tamen solaris luminis est; ita nostra natura, dum per seipsam consideratur, quaedam tenebrosa substantia, capax et particeps lucis sapientiae . . ."

8. Eriugena, *De Divisione Naturae*, I, 64: "Sacrae siquidem Scripturae in omnibus

A symbol is an intermediary employed by divine providence to allow us to penetrate more and more into the intimate knowledge of intelligible realities. Without degrees of this kind, our gradual ascent toward higher realities would be impossible. What allows symbols to play the roles of intermediaries is precisely their sensible, material character. They are accessible to minds like ours, whose activity is still tied to the corporeal senses, but also the symbols inevitably betray the pure intelligibles that they translate. Accordingly, they are at the same time similar and different.[9] They are similar to us and dissimilar in relation to their objects.

Perhaps we might ask why in these conditions, God did not keep to just one symbol or a small number of appropriately chosen symbols. If a translation was necessary, would it not have been better to adopt just one instead of perplexing us unrestrainedly by the multitude of interpretations of the divine nature that Scripture presents to our understanding? Such is not the case. Under the pretext of clarifying things better for us, this would proceed in opposition to God's plans. The point is not to give us symbols of the intelligible in which our slothful imagination can easily find rest. Symbols are means for us and not ends. We grasp images only to go beyond them and to allow our understanding to raise itself up to purely spiritual realities that the imagination does not attain. A single symbol or a small group of symbols would chain our mind rather than liberate it, since we would not escape the illusion that God is essentially and in himself the way the symbols represented him. To avoid this danger, revelation has taken care to represent God and heavenly things to us under a multitude of different symbols, even contradictory ones, which correct each other, and whose opposition prevents any of them from passing itself off as an exact representation of its object. As in certain modern doctrines metaphors as different and varied as possible facilitate the effort that goes beyond them and leads to intuition, so also,

---

sequenda est auctoritas. Non tamen ita credendum est, ut ipsa semper propriis verborum seu nominum signis fruatur, divinam nobis naturam insinuans, sed quibusdam similitudinibus variisque translatorum verborum seu nominum modis utitur, infirmitati nostrae condescendens, nostrosque adhuc rudes infantilesque sensus simplici doctrina erigens."

9. Eriugena, *Super Caelestem Hierarchium*, II, col. 143: "At vero quoniam noster animus . . . ad ipsam intimam intelligibilium rerum speculationem non continuo, nulla mediante intercapedine potest ascendere, pulchre divina Providentia dissimilia symbola interposuit, similia quidem nobis adhuc corporeis sensibus detentis, dissimilia vero puris intellectibus, ad quorum contemplationem per illa noster dicitur intellectus."

the multiplicity of scriptural symbols permits us better to discard them and to lead to the contemplation of the intelligible.[10]

If matters stand thus, the necessity of interpreting Scripture is forced upon us, and the philosopher's particular task will be to elaborate the interpretation. The function of reason is to interpret and go beyond the symbols of revelation to lead us to the goal that these symbols designate. The contents of philosophy and religion are exactly the same, and the proof of this is that those who do not share doctrine with us do not share our sacraments either. Therefore, what is philosophy's task, if not to expound the rules of true religion? Religion teaches us to humbly adore God, sovereign and cause of all things, and to scrutinize him by means of our reason. From that it follows that true religion is true philosophy and that in turn true philosophy is true religion.[11]

Consequently, reason and authority are defined within the limits of revelation and in relation to the elements it furnishes to us. Reason necessarily comes first. We see it appear at the creation itself. It is exactly contemporary to nature and to the first instant of time, and as soon as revelation is given to us, the task of rational interpretation of revealed symbols begins. The effort at clarification starts there and also the purification that must prevent simple minds, nourished in the cradle of the church, from having unworthy beliefs and thoughts about God, for example, believing that everything that Holy Scripture tells us about the first cause of the universe must be taken literally. If reason did not intervene to explain symbols, simple minds would believe not only that God

10. Eriugena, *Super Caelestem Hierarchiam*, II, col. 145: "Haec enim sunt dissimilia symbola in propheticis visionibus, in eorum prophetarum spiritu administratione angelica plasmata [that is, the symbols formed in the minds of the prophets are aroused by the ministry of angels] ad nostram eruditionem et introductionem ad purissimas caelestium essentiarum in semetipsis, remota omni phantastica plasmatione, cognitiones. Quae prophetica figmenta si quis incaute cogitaverit, ita ut in eis finem cognitionis suae constituat, et non ultra ea ascendat in contemplationem rerum intelligibilium, quarum illa imagines sunt, non solum ipsius animus non purgatur et exercitur, verum etiam turpissime polluntur et stultissime opprimitur."

11. Eriugena, *De Praedestinatione*, I, 1, col. 357–58: "Sic enim, ut ait Sanctus Augustinus, creditur et docetur, quod est humanae salutis caput, non aliam esse philosophiam, id est sapientiae studium, et aliam religionem, cum hi, quorum doctrinam non approbamus, nec sacramenta nobiscum communicat. Quid est aliud de philosophia tractare, nisi verae religionis, qua summa et principalis omnium rerum causa, Deus, et humiliter colitur, et rationabiliter investigatur, regulas exponere? Conficitur inde veram esse philosophiam veram religionem, conversumque veram religionem esse veram philosophiam."

is life or virtue, but also that he is sun, light, and star. We might not even necessarily keep to moral qualities or the most perfect parts of the world. If we wanted to follow the letter of Scripture, we would have to descend even more. Does not Scripture symbolically say that God is breath, a luminous cloud, thunder, dew, rain, water, river, earth, stone, wood vine, olive, cedar, hyssop, lily, man, lion, ox, horse, bear, panther, worm, and many other things, giving the names of created nature to creative nature by a kind of figurative meaning and transposition? But Scripture goes still further. It not only attributes nature to God, but even what is contrary to nature like madness, intoxication, forgetfulness, anger, fury, hatred, concupiscence, and similar vices. Taking things correctly, simple souls are less exposed to be deceived when they encounter such comparisons than when they encounter the previous ones. No rational soul, however simple it may be, hearing properties contrary to nature attributed to God, fails to judge that these things do not belong to God or concedes that they are only attributable in a figurative sense. The error that is still possible in the first case would become so crude that it is practically impossible in the second.

When reason has found the interpretations of the symbols, they give birth to authority. Therefore, reason is prior in time to authority, whose source is reason. The explanations of Scripture discovered by the Fathers of the Church by means of reason and committed to writing by them, play a very important role in relation to the mass of the faithful. Thanks to the authority of these Fathers, when this reason has crystallized, the study or intelligence of true religion cannot be lacking in any soul. There is no faith so crude or so simple that nourishment by true doctrine cannot develop it, or that is not capable of victoriously repelling the enemies of faith thanks to the arms that true doctrine has furnished it. But it is quite evident that authority has its first source in reason. We must always opt for reason when it is in conflict with authority. Any authority that contradicts reason is null, while true reason does not need any authority's help to be confirmed and is always self-sufficient. It is never true, but false authority that can be opposed to reason. Right reason does not contradict true authority, and true authority does not contradict right reason, because it is certain that both flow from the same source, which is divine wisdom.[12] Consequently, John Scotus Eriugena energetically

12. Eriugena, *De Divisione Naturae*, I, 66–67, col. 511–12: "Nulla itaque auctoritas te terreat ab his, quae rectae contemplationis rationabilis suasio edocet. Vera enim auctoritas rectae rationi non obsistit, neque recta ratio verae auctoritati. Ambo siquidem

revindicates and defends reason only against human authority and not at all against God's. Everything is in Scripture, but it remains for us to find it there, and it is the role of reason to discover it. But woe to him who dares to say something he himself invented of God, to believe or think of God something other than what the Holy Scriptures tell us, to appeal to other symbols or other images than those that God himself inspired in his prophets![13] Reason can only pretend to recapture the true sense of revelation.

What is true about scriptural revelation is equally true of the other revelation that we find inscribed in the book of creation. God does not speak to us through the Bible alone but also through all of nature and, without distorting reality, it can be said that all knowledge is revelation for us. Everything that our bodily senses suggest or that we discover by the pure intellect, everything that we perceive or know clearly in the universe of created things, is only known and revealed to us by the Father of Lights. This is true whether we are dealing with the properties of natural

---

ex uno fonte, divina scilicet sapientia, manare dubium non est. Una quidem [*scilicet*, auctoritas] de natura incomprehensibili ineffabilique pie quaerentibus multa concessit ac tradidit et cogitare et dicere ne verae religiones studium in omnibus sileat, ut et rudes adhuc in fidei simplicitate doctrina nutreat et catholicae fidei aemulis instructa armataque divinis propugnaculis munita respondeat. Altera vero [*scilicet* ratio], ut simplices adhuc in cunabulis Ecclesiae nutritos, pie casteque corrigat, ne quid indignum de Deo vel credunt vel aestiment, nec omnia quae sacrae Scripturae auctoritatis de causa omnium praedicat proprie praedicari existiment."—Eriugena, *De Divisione Naturae*, I, 69, col. 513: "Non ignoras, ut opinor, majoris dignitatis esse quod prius est natura quam quod prius est tempore. Rationem esse priorem natura, auctoritatem vero temore didicimus. Quamvis enim natura simul cum tempore creata sit, non tamen ab initio temporis atque naturae coepit esse auctoritas. Ratio vero cum natura ac tempore ex principio rerum orta est.—*Discipulus*: Et hoc ipsa ratio edocet Auctoritas siquidem ex vera ratione processit, ratio vero nequaquam ex auctoritate. Omnis enim auctoritas quae vera ratione non approbatur infirma videtur esse. Vera autem ratio, quoniam suis virtutibus rata atque immutabilis munitur, nullius auctoritatis adstipulatione roborari indiget. nil enim mihi videtur esse vera auctoritas, nisi rationis virtute reperta veritas et a sanctis Patribus at posteritatis utilitatem litteris commentata."

13. Eriugena, *De Divisione Naturae*, I, 64, col. 509: "In hoc enim student divina eloquia, ut de re ineffabili, incomprehensibili, invisibilique aliquid nobis ad nutriendam nostram fidem cogitandum tradant atque suadeant. Siquidem de Deo nil aliud caste pieque viventibus, studioseque veritatem quaerentibus dicendum vel cogitandum, nisi quae in sacra Scriptura reperiuntur, neque aliis nisi ipsius significationibus utendum his, qui de Deo sive quid credant, sive disputent. Quis enim de natura ineffabili quippiam a seipso repertum dicere praesumat, praeter quod illa de seipsa in suis sanctis organis, theologis dico [*scilicet*, inspired men] modulata est."—Eriugena, *De Divisione Naturae* I, 65, col. 509: "Videsne quemadmodum [Dionysius] universaliter prohibet, ne quis de occulta divinitate, praeter quae in sacris eloquiis dicta sunt dicere audeat?"

substances or perfections of grace; the Father of lights is the heavenly Father, the inner, first light from whom his Word, the true light, is born, by whom everything has been made, and in whom everything subsists. From him and from his only Son, the Word who is coessential to the Father, proceeds the light that is the Holy Spirit, spirit of the Father and of the Son, in whom and by whom all the gifts of grace are spread everywhere. This triple light, this triple goodness, these three substances in one essence, Father, Son, and Holy Spirit, constitutes the single light spread throughout everything that is, serves as the essential foundation of substances, and arouses in all souls the thought and love of its beauty.[14] We can say with complete rigor that each creature, visible or invisible, is a light created by the Father of the lights. If the supreme goodness, which is God, an invisible, inaccessible light exceeding all sensation and all intelligence, has made everything that it wanted to make, with the intention of descending down to the range of intelligent rational creatures; if the supreme goodness wanted to make itself known by the intelligent, rational creatures through the means of figures and artifices, are we not right to consider everything to be a kind of light that shines upon our souls, that brings them closer to the knowledge of their creator, and that makes him less inaccessible to them? Viewed from this standpoint, everything in the world is light. Let us use an example taken from the lowest levels of nature. This stone and bit of wood are light for me, and they are light, because, by considering them, many thoughts occur to me that illuminate my mind. Each thing is a substance that possesses certain beauty, certain perfection, and a certain kind of being. Each thing is classified in a certain genus and a certain species. It is distinguished from other genera and other species by its difference. Finally, it possesses its numerical identity, its peculiar order, and occupies the place that corresponds to its weight. For me, all these things and everything of this kind that I see in this stone are so many lights that illuminate me.[15] Because, when I see them, I ask

14. Eriugena, *Super Caelestem Hierarchiam*, I, col. 128: "Quodcumque enim seu sensu corporeo internuntiante, seu puro intellectu investigante, in universitate condita ad liquidum percipitur atque cognoscitur, in substitutionibus naturae et perfectionibus gratiae, non aliunde nisi a Patre luminum procedit." Eriugena, *Super Caelestem Hierarchiam* I, col. 128: "unum lumen diffusum in omnia quod sunt ut essentialiter subsistant . . ."

15. Eriugena, *Super Caelestem Hierarchiam*, I, col. 120: "Est et alia ratio quae luculenter edocet, omnino creaturam visibilem et invisibilem lumen esse conditum a Patre luminum. Si enim summa bonitas quae Deus est, omnia quae volunt, propterea fecit, ut, quoniam per seipsam invisibilis et inaccessibilis lux est, omnem sensum et

myself why these things have all these properties. I immediately grasp that they can get them from no creature, visible or invisible, and my reason raises me above them to the first cause from whom all things have their place and order, number, species and genus, goodness, beauty, and essence, in a word, all goods that they have received. The same goes for all creatures from the most perfect to the most humble, that is to say, from the angels to material beings. For a mind that relates everything to the glory of the creator and that ardently seeks to find God, each thing is an introductory light. It suffices for the soul to consider the thing's properties exactly and cast a pure gaze upon it. Finally, this is why the order of the entire universe in its turn is only an immense light composed of a multitude of partial lights that are like so many torches, an immense light destined to reveal, to make us see directly the pure appearance of intelligible things, as occurs in the soul of a philosopher who is also a believer, by the help and cooperation of divine grace and reason.

From such a concept of the universe it follows that reason, considered insofar as it studies nature, is in exactly the same situation as when it studies Scripture. Therefore, there can only be one total wisdom whose two main branches deepen this double revelation, physical and scriptural. The seven liberal arts that philosophers study and that, in their turn, are only the symbol of beatific contemplation, form a single body inside which is found all that is necessary for us to interpret Scripture. We cannot do without the liberal arts to explain the sacred texts, but the liberal arts tend toward the deep meaning of Scripture as their natural goal. As numerous brooks, which are from different springs, follow toward the

---

intellectum superans, per ea, quae ab ipsa facta sunt, veluti per quasdam lucubrationes in notitiam intellectualis et rationalis creaturae possit descendere, quid mirum si omne quod inaccessibilem lucem quodam modo, ut accessibilis sit, puris intellectibus introducit, lumen illuminans animos, et in cognitionem Creatoris sui eos revocans, nulla ratione obstante intelligatur? Verbi gratia, ex infimis naturae ordinibus paradigma sumamus: Lapis iste vel hoc lignum mihi lumen est, et si quaeris quomodo, ratio me admonent, ut tibi respondeam, hunc vel hunc lapidem consideranti multa mihi occurrunt, quae animum meum illuminant. Haec horumque similia dum in hoc lapide cerno, lumina mihi fiunt, hoc est, me illuminant. Similiter de omni creatura, a summo usque ad deorsum, hoc est, ab intellectuali usque ad corpus ad laudem Creatoris referentibus eam et se ipsos, et Deum studiose quaerentibus, et in omnibus, quae sunt, eum invenire ardentibus, et super omnia quae sunt, eum laudare diligentibus lux introductiva est, suis rationibus consideratis, liquidoque mentis contuitu perspecuis. Hinc est quod universalis huius mundi fabrica maximum lumen fit, ex multis partibus veluti ex multis lucernis compactum, ad intelligibilium rerum puras species revelandas et contuendas mentis acie divina gratia et rationis ope in corde fidelium sapientium cooperantibus."

bed of a single river and are mixed there, so philosophical and natural sciences are mixed to form the single symbol of this inner contemplation that Christ, highest source of all wisdom, unceasingly invites us to contemplate. All the liberal arts, which means all philosophy with the whole of Scripture that it contains and interprets, are gathered in a single river and in a single science, whose end point is the typical signification of Christ.[16] In upholding this thesis, as astonishing as it may seem to us today, Eriugena remains faithful to the idea of a single Wisdom as St. Augustine conceived it. What makes it more difficult for us to understand this thinking is that, even if we admit that reason and philosophy can and should also be used in the interpretation of Scripture, they would appear to us at the very least as having another function to accomplish, that of knowing and explaining nature. But we know that there is nothing of the kind. With Eriugena, we are in the realm of universal symbolism. The natural world, where we live, belongs to exactly the same order as Scripture, and the meaning of things belongs to exactly the same order as that of the psalms or prophets. Let us add that the profound reality of one is identical to the profound reality of the other. Things do not have a certain nature plus their mystical, symbolic meaning. They *are* that same symbolic meaning. Visible forms, whether they are the ones that Scripture reveals or those that we discover in nature, have not been made for themselves; they are not desirable for themselves and have not been announced to us for themselves. They are only images of the invisible beauty by means of which divine Providence calls human minds back toward the pure beauty of the Truth, last end of all who love, even when it remains unknown.[17] Accordingly, the theory of knowledge developed

16. Eriugena, *Super Caelestem Hierarchiam* I, cols. 139–40: "Septem disciplinas, quas philosophi *liberales* appellant, intelligibilis contemplativae plenitudinis, qua Deus et creatura purissime cognoscitur, significationes esse astruit. Ut enim multae aquae ex diversis fontibus in unius fluminis alveum confluunt atque decurrunt, ita naturales et liberales disciplinae in una eademque internae contemplationis significationes adunantur quam summus fons totius sapientiae, qui est Christus, undique per diversas theologiae speculationes insinuat. Et fortassis hoc est, quod per Psalmistam de beato viro dicitur: 'Et erit tanquam lignum, quod plantatum est secus decursus aquarum,' hoc est, sicut Christus erit, in cujus significationem typicam, omnes naturales artes, intra quarum terminos tota concluditur Scriptura, concurrunt. Nulla enim sacra Scriptura est, quae regulis liberalium careat disciplinarum."

17. Eriugena, *Super Caelestem Hierarchiam* I, cols. 138–39: ". . . visibiles formas, sive quas in natura rerum, sive quas in sanctissimis divinae scripturae sacramentis contemplatur, nec propter seipsas factas, nec propter seipsas appetendas seu nobis promulgatas, sed invisibilis pulchritudinis imaginationes esse, per quas divina Providentia

by Eriugena cannot be understood independently of the theory of the real that gives its true meaning; and when we look at the doctrine in its totality, we see immediately what can be thought about so many interpretations that simply fix upon one or another particular text. Furthermore, denominations are merely conventional here, and nothing forbids us to declare that Eriugena's doctrine is rationalist, because it places reason about the patristic tradition or because its rational interpretations of dogma are often unfortunate. Everyone is a rationalist for someone. However, it is legitimate to wonder whether this label still means anything when it is applied to a man whose primary concern is to combine philosophy and theology under the indisputable authority of Scripture, and who conceives natural, philosophical knowledge as a particular case of revelation.

Moreover, it is a fact that the synthesis attempted by John Scotus Eriugena was infelicitous, and the reason is not hard to see. Because of the influence of Pseudo-Dionysius, what primarily concerned Eriugena is the problem of scriptural symbolism. Evidently, reason alone is qualified to determine the allegorical sense or senses of images employed by the prophets or comparisons contained in the Psalms, but Scotus Eriugena has no criterion or fixed rule to determine what ought to be taken in the literal sense and what ought to be understood in the allegorical sense. Properly speaking, since no name is applicable to God in its human sense, everything Scripture tells us about God must be interpreted rationally. It has been quite correctly noted that for an Augustinian like Scotus Eriugena, all knowledge results from an illumination of the soul by God and thereby is closely related to revelation. "Theophanies," which are the normal mode of angelic knowledge and an accidental mode of knowledge in a soul purified and illuminated by grace,[18] are all invitations addressed to each of us to consider ourselves prophets inspired by God. These are not special difficulties, in our theologian's view, and we are going to see analogies with them arise in St. Anselm's doctrine.

Whatever the differences that separate the "father of Scholasticism" from the "father of anti-Scholasticism," there is at least a point on which their two doctrines are close, and that is the relation between reason and faith. Like John Scotus Eriugena, St. Anselm remains faithful to the

---

in ipsam puram et invisibilem pulcritudinem ipsius veritatis, quam amat, et ad quam tendit omne quod amat, sive sciens sive nesciens, humanos animos revocat."

18. Eriugena, *De Divisone Naturae*, I, 7, col. 446; I, 9, col. 449; II, 23, col. 577. Cf. Eriugena, *Super Caelestem Hierarchiam*, VII, 2, col. 182.

notion of a single Wisdom inside of which reason and revelation find their places naturally, and again, like Eriugena, St. Anselm holds that all philosophical speculation ought to start from revelation and end up in intelligence. But while Eriugena seems concerned and mesmerized by the letter of revelation, St. Anselm worries much less about scriptural symbolism than about the content of the faith. Except for this difference, the attitudes of the two theologians are very similar.

For St. Anselm, faith is the necessary point of departure for all investigation: necessary first in the sense that it is the only place from which we may start, and also in the sense that it is necessary to start from it. God is the ultimate object, who alone can satisfy our reason and our love. When we shall see him face to face in the beatific vision (*species*), every need of our mind and our heart will be satisfied. At present, this clear vision of God is denied us, but we have revelation and faith in place of the object toward which we tend, as a permanent encouragement to direct ourselves toward it. By faith we adhere to formulas that take the place for us of the object that is inaccessible at present. We firmly grasp a reality to which we hold but do not see. No effort can lead the human intellect to penetrate the depths of the divine essence. The disproportion is too great between our thought and such an object. But as soon as our reason believes in the hidden truth of faith, it fixes upon it and our heart loves it. From there comes this effort to understand what we believe, which is at the origin of all philosophy. We do not seek to understand in order to believe, but it is necessary for us to believe first in order to have something to understand, and if we did not believe first, we would not understand.

Philosophy is born of faith that seeks to obtain understanding of its own content and that has the duty to obtain it for itself.[19] But this understanding is far from having absolute rights and from being able to criticize the faith from which it issues. In the first place, the understanding of which St. Anselm speaks is nothing like that demonstrative reason, whose evidences, taken in the Cartesian fashion, present it with an entirely intelligible content. The issue is never to comprehend faith

19. Anselm, *Proslogion* I, col. 227 (Migne, Patrologia Latina 158): "Non tento, Domine, penetrare altitudinem tuam, quia nullatenus comparo illi intellectum meum, sed desidero aliquatenus intelligere veritatem tuam, quam credit et amat cor meum. Neque enim quaero intelligere, ut credam, sed credo ut intelligam. Nam et hoc credo, quia nisi credidero non intelligam."—St. Anselm, *Cur Deus Homo*, I, 2, col. 362 (*Patrologia Latina* 158): "Sicut rectus ordo exigit ut profunda fidei prius credamus priusquam ea praesumamus ratione discutere, ita negligentia, mihi videtur, si postquam confirmati sumus in fide, non studemus quod credimus intelligere."

fully, but to comprehend it in some measure—*aliquatenus intelligere.* The understanding that faith can obtain is not an end in itself, nor is it knowledge that is satisfactory enough for our mind to be able to rest in it. The *intellectus* sought by faith is a simple intermediary between faith and beatific vision. The more we advance in the understanding of the mysteries that revelation proposes to us, the more we also approach, in this life, the beatific vision to which we aspire.[20]

Moreover, this is why the acquisition of understanding is not a simple matter of natural reason. It is not good, and therefore not recommendable, to start the search for understanding without taking a certain number of precautions. It is negligence on our part not to seek to attain understanding when we are already confirmed in faith, *postquam confirmati sumus in fidei,* and there is no reason to reproach anyone who does his best, provided that he undertakes the search after previously having been *fide stabilitus.* But it is evident that we would be hugely mistaken if we tried to subject the insufficient resistance of a still uncertain faith to the proof of reason. Scripture says: *Nisi credideritis, non intelligetis* (Isa 7:9). We must believe precisely that it is necessary to believe in order to understand. But first it is necessary to believe truly and firmly, and a pure heart is also necessary to undertake this search and divine grace to permit us to bring it to a good conclusion.[21]

From this we perceive that the area of exploration that St. Anselm grants to reason is both vast and rigorously determined. It is vast to the point of being practically infinite. Since its object is the faith whose content exceeds us and must always escape us in this life, we are guaranteed that reason will never lack new objects of investigation. The cumulative labors of the apostles, fathers, and doctors have not sufficed to exhaust it. The days of humans are short, and they have been unable to say all they would have said had they lived longer, but even then they would not have said everything, because the truth is too vast and too deep for mortal minds to be able to exhaust it. Furthermore, we know that the understanding, in relation to faith, does not proceed without the help of grace, and God unceasingly heaps new gifts upon his church. Consequently, faith will always seek understanding.[22] But it is equally true

20. Anselm, *De Fide Trinitatis,* preface, col. 259: "Denique quoniam inter fidem et speciem intellectum quem in hac vita capimus esse medium intelligo, quanto aliquis ad illum proficit, tanto eum propinquare speciei (ad quam omnes anhelamus) existimo."

21. Anselm, *De Fide Trinitatis,* I, col. 264.

22. Anselm, *De Fide Trinitatis,* preface, cols. 260–61.

that understanding has no object to pursue other than that of faith. At the beginning of those works that seem to us to be most philosophical in the modern sense of the word, St. Anselm does not fail to recall it. In the measure in which philosophy, for us, corresponds to a search that starts and ends in rational premises, we can say that Anselm did not write a single work of philosophy. Even when he intends to prove the Trinity by giving reasons, he knows that revelation was what directed the first sign to reason. Reason is capable of furnishing necessary, purely rational demonstrations of objects that can only be furnished to it by faith. Reason demonstrates after it is prepared and informed about what it is possible to demonstrate. No one could doubt that this is the case when we are dealing with rational proof of the existence of the Trinity or the necessity of the incarnation. But it is exactly the same when the issue is proving the existence of God or the nature of his attributes. In Anselm's mind, the two treatises that have occasioned the expression *Christian rationalism*, the *Monologion* and the *Proslogion*, are just mediations on faith.[23] The famous proof known by the name *ontological argument* began by being just that. The issue was above all to discover a rational proof of God's existence starting from belief in the existence in God and in a certain idea of God; the proof was to be rapid and direct enough to bring us close to that vision of God's existence to which we all aspire. Therefore, *fides quaerens intellectum* is not the way Anselm conceives the relations between reason and faith. It is the title he initially wanted to give the *Proslogion* in which the ontological argument is set forth.[24] Nothing is worse than the habit acquired by historians of suppressing the proof's first three lines, precisely where it affirms the desire to find understanding of the faith: "Grant me therefore, oh Lord, you who give understanding to faith, grant me, in the measure in which you judge it useful, that I may understand that you exist, as we believe, and that you are what we believe. Now, we believe that you are a being such that nothing greater can be conceived."

23. Anselm, *Proslogion*, preface, col. 225: "Unicuique suum dedi titulum ut prius [*scilicet, Monologion*], exemplum meditandi de ratione fidei, et sequens [*scilicet, Proslogion*] fides quaerens intellectum diceretur."

24. The ontological argument initially circulated under the title *Fides Quaerens Intellectum*, without a signature. Anselm, *Proslogion*, preface, col. 225: "Sed cum iam a pluribus cum his titulis [see the previous note] utrumque transciptum esset, coegerunt me plures, et maxime reverendus archiepiscopus Lugdunensis, Hugo nomine, fungens in Galia legatione apostolica, qui mihi hoc ex apostolica praecepit auctoritate, ut nomen meum illis praescriberem. Quod ut aptius fieret, illud quidem *Monologion*, id est *Soliloquium*; istud vero *Proslogion*, id est *Alloquium* nominavi."

Accordingly, this proof by rational evidence is first of all the effort of a soul that asks grace to instruct it on the object of its faith and that thanks divine goodness for having illuminated it: "Thanks be to you, my good Lord, thanks be to you. Because what you have first given me to believe, you now illuminate me, so that I understand it to such a degree that, even if I no longer wanted to believe that you exist, I could no longer fail to understand it."[25]

All of St. Anselm's works are simply the rigorous application of this conception of reason. Only the pagan has to search for faith by means of reason. Let him do his best, since he cannot do otherwise in order to arrive at the same truth as we do. But he seeks reason because he does not believe; we seek it because we do believe. Rationalism is good for unbelievers. Real wisdom belongs to the Christian. The Christian ought to go from faith to understanding and not from understanding to faith. With even greater reason, the Christian does not acknowledge a right to depart from faith in the pretense that he cannot understand it. If he succeeds in understanding what he believes, he is filled with joy, but what he does not manage to understand remains for him to venerate. That is the Christian's true attitude,[26] and it is Anselm's attitude. Here we meet exactly the same

25. Anselm, *Proslogion*, II, cols. 227–28: "Ergo, Domine, qui das fidei intellectum, da mihi, ut quantum scis expedire, intelligam quia es, sicut credimus: et hoc es quod credimus. Et quidem credimus te esse aliquid quo nihil majus cogitari possit. An ergo non est aliqua talis natura [The text of the argument follows.] . . ."—Anselm, *Proslogion*, IV, col. 229: "Qui ergo intelligit sic esse Deum, nequit eum non esse cogitare. Gratias tibi, bone Domine, gratias tibi; quia quod prius credidi, te donante, jam intelligo, te illuminante, ut si te esse nolim credere, non possim non intelligere."—Anselm, *Proslogion*, preface, col. 223: "Considerans illud [*scilicet, Monologion*] esse multorum concatenatione contextum argumentorum, coepi mecum quaerere si forte posset inveniri unum argumentum, quod nullo alio ad se probandum quam se solo indigeret, et solum, ad astruendum quia Deus vere est, et quia est summum bonum nullo alio indigens, et quo omnia indigent ut sint et bone sunt, et quaecumque credimus de divina substantia sufficeret."—In order to answer Gaunilo's objections, St. Anselm constrains the fool who does not admit this idea of God in the name of faith, to admit it in the name of his conscience, *Liber Apologeticus*, I, col. 249: "quod quam falsum sit, fide et conscientia tua pro firmissimo utor argumento," and *Liber Apologeticus* VIII, col. 258: "sic itaque facile fefelli potest insipiens, qui sacrum auctoritatem non recipt, se negat quo majus cogitari non valet, ex aliis rebus conjici posse. At si quis Catholicus hoc neget, meminerit quia invisibilia Dei a creatura mundi, per ea quae facta sunt, inellecta conspiciuntur, sempiterna quoque ejus virtus et divinitas."—Anselm, *Epistola ad Falconem*, col. 1193. Connecting this last phrase with the refusal to argue with Roscelin, one only argues with pagans.

26. Anselm, *Cur Deus Homo*, II, col. 364: "Ut cum nostrae fidei rationem studemus inquirere, ponamus objectiones eorum, qui nullatenus ad fidem eandem sine

doctrine that John Scotus Eriugena taught in the ninth century: *Lux in tenebris fidelium animorum lucet, a fide inchoans, ad speciem tendens.* We cannot imagine a less rationalist use of reason.[27]

It is absolutely remarkable that this need to discover an intelligible meaning under the formulas of faith was sufficiently intense to exert a decisive influence on minds most naturally inclined to purely philosophical speculation. Anselm was, and had always been, a theologian. Consequently, there is nothing surprising in his taking on the exploration of mystery as his own particular task. But the case of Peter Abelard is perhaps still more instructive, because he shows us clearly what an irresistible fascination theology exerted upon the most deeply independent minds. It is well known that Abelard began as, and always remained, a fervent dialectician. After wielding dialectic like a sword and having spent his whole life amid the most acrimonious conflicts, old and worn out, having abandoned all vanity and ambition, astonishing Peter the Venerable and the monks of Cluny with the depth of his renunciation, Abelard was not yet detached from philosophy.[28] As the discourse he left us on the question of the universals testifies, Abelard had not only been a learned and acute dialectician,[29] but also was a devotee of dialectics from cradle to grave. Logic made him odious to the world,[30] but nothing could turn him away from logic. Yet, it was absolutely impossible for Peter Abelard to remain a mere dialectician. As much as he loved dialectic, he was equally convinced that it was not an end in itself, and his audience and his disciples pressed him to go on to higher studies. To fail to make

---

ratione volunt accedere. Quamvis enim illi ideo rationem quaerant, quia non credunt, nos vero, quia credimus, unum idemque tamen est quod quaerimus."—St. Anselm, *Epistola ad Falconem*, col. 1193: "Nam Christianus per fidem debet ad intellectum proficere, non per intellectum ad fidem accedere, aut si intelligere non valet a fide recedere. Sed cum ad intellectum valet pertingere, delectatur, cum vero nequit, quod capere non potest, veneratur."

27. Eriugena, *In Prologum Evangelii secundum Johannem*, col. 290.

28. Abelard, *Petri Abelardi Opera*, Letter from Peter the Venerable to Heloise, 1:713–14: "Et quid multa? Mens ejus, lingua ejus, opus ejus, semper divina, semper philosophica, semper eruditoria meditabatur, docebat, fatebatur."—Abelard, *Introductio ad Theologiam*, prologue, 2:3: "Ad has itaque dissolvendas controversias cum me sufficere arbitrarentur, quem quasi ab ipsis cunabulis in Philosophiae studiis, ac praecipue dialecticae, quae omnium magistra rationum videtur, conversatum sciant atque experimento, ut aiunt didicerint . . ."

29. Geyer, *Abaelards philosophische Schriften*, 9–32.

30. Abelard, *Epistola ad Heloïssam*, 1:680: "Soror mea Heloïssa, quondam mihi in saeculo cara, nunc in Christo carissima, odiosum me mundo reddidit logica."

God, to whom everything must be related, the end point of his study of philosophy, was to condemn himself to leave the course in philosophy unfinished. That meant failure to arrive at the end to which everything tends and, in a word, failure to harvest any fruit. The faithful are allowed to read pagan books and study profane sciences only in order to give them the means and knowledge necessary to defend and maintain the truth of Holy Scripture.[31] But these reasons and all the reasons that were added to them would not have been enough to establish Abelard's vocation as a theologian if an overriding inner need had not swept him along.

This necessity was just what had produced Anselm's whole doctrine. There are two kinds of humans, who are in very different situations: pagans, who have only their reason, and the others, who have their reason plus revelations. The pagans live under the regime of natural law. Jews and Christians have the Scriptures—*scripturas habent*.[32] This is a fact, which ought to have a decisive influence on the use that they can and must make of reason. The Christian who believes in a divine revelation can certainly know that a philosophy entirely based on natural reason has been and is still possible, but it has been and is possible only for pagans. The Christian can conceive the distinction between the realms of reason and faith theoretically, but it is impossible for him to act as if revelation had not taken place. From the moment that we believe, it is completely useless to pretend that reason is going to continue to behave as if we did not believe. In a believer's soul, faith takes precedence, and Peter Abelard has the soul of a deeply convinced believer. He wrote to Heloise:

> I was credited with an acute mind, but the purity of my Christian faith was disputed. But it seems to me that their judgment expresses an opinion rather than being based on experience. I do not want to be a philosopher, if it makes me contradict St Paul. I do not want to be an Aristotle, if I must be separated from Christ. In heaven there is no other name than his in which I must achieve my salvation. I adore the Christ who reigns at the right hand of God the Father. I embrace him by faith when his divinity works marvels in the virginal flesh that he takes on by the work of the Holy Spirit. And, in order that the trembling anxiety, in order that all doubts may be calmed in your heart, learn from me who have based my conscience upon that rock

31. Abelard, *Introductio ad Theologiam*, prologue, 2:2: "Addebant etiam ne me aliter philosophiae cursum consummare, nec ad ejus pervenire metam, aut aliquem ex ea me fructum colligere, nisi ejus studium ad Deum, ad quem omnia referri convenit."

32. Abelard, *Dialogus inter Philosophum*, II, 644.

> upon which Christ build his church. If storms are unleashed, I will not be shaken. If the winds rage, I will not be moved. I am build upon the unshakable rock.[33]

Evidently, this indestructible faith cannot remain inactive. It must entice, move, and ultimately shake up reason. Faith is the assent of thought to realities it does not perceive. Accordingly, this reality constitutes a truth hidden to us and presently inaccessible to our thought. And yet, the very certainty that strict knowledge of this object is denied us does not completely discourage our reason. On the contrary, our faith is like a call and continued invitation to philosophy.

A faith that might be reduced to a pure formula without content would not be viable or even possible. Normally, and almost necessarily, faith is accompanied by understanding. To say that we have understanding of our faith, or even seek to acquire it, does not at all mean that we have or that we wish to have comprehension of it. It simply means that we manage to give a certain meaning to the formulas in which faith is expressed. Consequently, the question is simply to know whether the act of faith can only fall upon the words. If it falls upon any content that is defined or suggested by the words, it is accompanied by understanding. The answer to this question is clear. It would be useless to utter words that had no meaning for us; we could not believe something we did not understand at all; and it would be ridiculous to preach a doctrine to others that signified nothing to our own understanding. When Abelard calls

33. Abelard, *Epistola ad Heloïssam*, I, 680–81: "Aiunt enim perversi pervertentes, quorum sapientia est in perditione, me in logica praestantissimum esse, sed in Paulo non mediocriter claudicare. Quumque ingenii praedicent aciem, Christianae fidei subtrahunt purities. Quia at mihi videtur, opinione potius traducuntur quam experientiae magistratu. Nolo sic esse philosophus, ut recalcitrem Paulo, nolo sic esse Aristoteles, ut secludar a Christo. Non enim aliud nomen est sub coelo, in quo oporteat me salvum fieri. Et hoc de me teneto, quod super illam petram fundavi conscientiam meam, super quam Christus aedificavit ecclesiam suam. Haec itaque est fides in qua sedeo, ex qua spei contraho firmitatem. In hac locatus sum salubriter, latratus Scyllae non timeo, vertiginem Charybdis rideo, mortiferos Sirenarum modulos non horresco. Si irruat turbo, non quatior. Si venti perflent, non moveor. Fundatus enim sum supra firmam petram."—The report of Peter the Venerable, who was deeply edified by Abelard's attitude toward the end of his life, confirms the sincerity of those sentiments. See the entire letter of Peter the Venerable to Heloise, I, 710–14, especially: "concessum tamen est de illo tuo, de illo inquam, saepe et semper con honore nominando servo ac vere Christi philosopho magistro Petro, quem in ultimis vitae suae annis eadem divina dispositio Cluniacum transmisit. Nisi enim fallor, non recolo vidisse me illi in humilitatis habitu et gestu similem, in tantum ut nec Germanus abjectior, nec ipse Martinus bene discernenti pauperior appareret."

for understanding of the faith, he primarily contrasts *intelligi* with *dici*, and he claims first of all that the dogmatic formulas mean something for the one who believes them.[34] If the letter of revelation cannot be a pure and simple *verborum prolatio*, which would amount to making all beliefs practically equivalent, it certainly is necessary that a rational interpretation should come to be added to this. In this regard, let us observe that the meaning of the revelation does not necessarily have to be apparent to the prophet or the inspired person by whose mediation God reveals it to us. If it were so, the meaning of Scripture would be given to us at the same time as the letter, and understanding would be mixed up with reading. But revelation is like miracles. God does not will them in the interest of the prophet or the miraculously cured person, but for the greater good of all the faithful. A kind of division of labor occurs here. Some have the grace of the word and others that of understanding as their share. But while waiting for divine providence and the merits of certain doctors to bestow upon humans the interpretation of the texts, authority must remain in force. It is extremely important that the words of revelation should have been pronounced before they were understood. To hear things said about God that the understanding does not grasp is a powerful stimulus to search. If the hearer does not listen to them being uttered, he cannot seek to find their meaning. Search easily engenders understanding, provided that devotion accompanies it.[35]

Accordingly, Peter Abelard naturally comes to join St. Anselm and John Scotus Eriugena on the road that leads the great medieval doctors from faith to philosophy. It is quite true that Abelard's paradigmatic labor

34. Abelard, *Historia Calamitatum*, 1:18: "Accedit autem mihi ut ad ipsum fidei nostrae fundamentum humanae rationes similitudinibus disserendum prius me applicarem, et quemdam theologiae tractatum de Unitate et Trinitate divina scholaribus nostris componerem, qui humanas et philosophicas rationes requirebant, et plus quae intelligent quam dici possunt efflagitabant, dicentes quidem verborum superfluam esse prolationem quam intelligentia non sequeretur, nec credi posse aliquid nisi primatus intellectum, et ridiculosum esse aliquot alias praedicare quod nec ipse, nec ill quod doceret intellectu capere possent."

35. Abelard, *Theologia Christiana*, 2:461: "Sed fortasse inquirunt, quid eam veritatem dici attinet ab aliquo quam ipse non valet explicare, ut intelligi possit? Multum equidem respondeo. Cum enim auditur de Deo quod non intelligitur, excitat auditorem ad inquisitionem; quod nec fieret nisi audiretur. Inquisitio vero facile intelligentiam parit, si devotio adsit."—Abelard, *Theologia Christiana*, 2:462: Further on we find the same contrast that defines *intelligi* by relation to *dici*: "Aliis itaque dicendi gratia data est, aliis intelligent enervator quousque opus sit secundum divinae consilium providentia . . . Interim autem dum ratio latet satisfaciat auctoritas . . ."

is the application of dialectic to theology. It is certain that Abelard knows what a rational demonstration is, even better than his predecessors, and distinguishes the posture of a philosopher from that of a believer. But Abelard is in agreement with his predecessors in admitting that the highest value of philosophy resides in what it allows us to understand about our religion. He is a dialectician who is obliged to become a theologian to do something with his dialectic. Taken in itself, his philosophy is empty of all content and his dialectic would serve for nothing. That is why we see him settle within dogma to try to find its meaning. The question here is no longer to comprehend but, within the realm of what we comprehend, to discover examples, analogies, and resemblances that provide intelligible content to the letter of revelation.[36] The errors for which Abelard is blamed are contained in explanations that are taken to be exhaustive, but which in his mind were provisional and approximate interpretations. For example, he absolutely must give a meaning—*intellectus*—to the term *Trinity*. When he speaks of generation to designate the relation of the Son to the Father, the word must not be a simple *flatus vocis*; in conformity with what Abelard teaches in his dialectic, a signification should be added to the word and interpret it.[37] He offers the all too famous comparisons between the three persons of the Trinity and bronze from which a seal is made, that engenders this seal as the Father engenders the Son. The bronze and the seal together constitute "what seals" as the Holy Spirit proceeds from Father and Son. Again, there is the comparison of the Trinity to Socrates. As the grammarian understands it, Socrates speaks or understands in one person, is spoken to in the second person, and is spoken about in the third person. Yet he remains as one single substance.[38] This is ultimately why Abelard maintains that the pagan philosophers naturally had a kind of knowledge of the Trinity. Plato knew God, as everyone agrees, but he also knew the Word, since he refers

36. Abelard, *Theologia Christiana*, 2:450: ". . . aliquas vel ex nobis, vel ex philosophis similitudines . . ."—Abelard, *Theologia Christiana*, 2:464: "Quidquid itaque de hac altissima philosophia disseremus, umbram non veritatem esse profitemur, et quasi similitudinem quamdam, non rem."

37. Geyer, *Abaelards philosophischen Schriften*, 20–21; Abelard, *Tractatus de Intellectibus*, 2:735–36.—Cf. Abelard, *Introductio ad Theologiam*, 2:92: "De quo siquidem aliqua similitudine de creaturis ad creatorem vocabula transferimus, quae quidem vocabula omnes instituerunt ad creaturas designandas quas intelligere potuerunt, cum videlicet per illos intellectus manifestare vellent."

38. Heitz, *Essai historique*, 27, notes. [Translator: I have made the example of Socrates and the Trinity clearer than it is in the original.]

to the *Noym* [*sic*], Wisdom born of God, who is co-eternal to God, and lastly he knew the Holy Spirit, whom he designates in the clearest way by the name *soul of the world*.[39] Peter the Venerable was not wrong to call Abelard a true philosopher of Christ—*vero Christi philosopho*. Despite all the efforts Peter made to moderate and hold back the great dialectician's reason, it set forth to discover the whole realm of revelation.

It is rather odd that precisely because of the passionate appetite to understand the divine, Abelard has been made out to be a rationalist. He is not a rationalist either by intention, since he declares the mystery to be impenetrable, nor in fact, since he never maintained that his comparisons were exact equivalents of the dogma's reality. He does not claim to discover the meaning of revelation to us, but a meaning of revelation, exactly what is necessary for the formula not to be reduced to words without a sense when we pronounce them. Abelard cannot explain the comparisons he employs without appearing to want to explain the dogma itself. Yet his reason does not absorb his faith, when he works to discover within the human realm realities analogous to what dogma reveals. His faith, on the contrary, absorbs his reason and pushes it toward tasks for which reason is not made.

Once more, it is the same urgent need to satisfy the demands of faith that leads Abelard to suppose that there was some knowledge of the mysteries among the pagan philosophers. Abelard emphatically affirms that Plato knew the mystery of the Trinity and had a premonition of the mystery of redemption, and that the Sybil announced the incarnation in more exact terms than the holy books themselves.[40] Yet, this does not prove that Abelard submitted the mystery to human reason in intention or in fact. Needless to say, in no case could the pagans have a perfect comprehension of the mystery of the Trinity, which is still denied to us today. What is true is that Plato, for example, rose to a concept of God in agreement with what dogma defines. Evidently, Plato knew the three persons of the Trinity and their relations, though that does not mean he comprehended them. How did he know them? Divine inspiration revealed them to him. The philosophers are the prophets of the pagans.[41]

39. Abelard, *Theologia Christiana*, 2:379: "Nunc autem illa Platonis verba de anima mundi diligenter discutiamus, ut in eis Spritum Sanctum integerrime designatum esse agnoscamus."—Moreover, this natural knowledge comes from a kind of natural revelation (*Theologia Christiana*, 2:361).

40. Abelard, *Theologia Christiana*, 2:406–7.

41. Abelard, *Theologia Christiana*, 2:361: ". . . quam quidem divina inspiratio et per

They merited this divine inspiration because of the purity of their morals and the perfection of an already Christian life. Between the great pagan philosophers and Christians there is little or no difference. Their lives were exemplary. Their very name of *philosophers* shows that they loved the wisdom of God the Father whom we call *Christ*. Lastly, they had faith, hope, and charity, because, like us, they acted by love of eternal things not by fear of punishments or hope of temporal rewards. This is why the faith in the Trinity was revealed to them and why they preached it at the same time as the hope of immortality and the expectation of eternal reward. The only knowledge missing for the pagans to be as well-instructed as Christians was knowledge of the resurrection, the incarnation, and lastly, the sacraments. For the rest, we can say that thanks to the revelation with which God favored the philosophers, there is really agreement between philosophy and the gospel.[42] Thus, the Christianity Abelard bestows upon the pagans is not explained by a rationalization of revelation but by an anticipated revelation whose beginnings would be prior to Christ's coming, and which Christ would only have clarified and completed.[43] Therefore, the issue is not at all to substitute reason for revelation but simply to know the moment at which revelation began.

Finally, let us add that if the notion developed by Abelard surprises us, it is because we have forgotten what the universe was in the eyes of a twelfth-century theologian. Revelation is not necessarily the abrupt and radically new discovery of that about which reason could have no suspicion, or about what the order of things does not permit us to guess. Revelation can be inscribed in things and laid out before an eye that cannot see it. To lead the philosophers' reason to knowledge of the Trinity, divine inspiration had only to direct the gaze of those whose heart was pure

prophetas Judeis, et per philosophos gentibus dignata est revelare."

42. Abelard, *Theologia Christiana*, 2:414: ". . . reperiemus ipsorum tam vitam, quam doctrinam maxime evangelicam seu apostolicam perfectionem exprimere, et a religione Christiana eos nihil aut parum recedere, quod nobis tam rationibus mirum quam nomine ipso juncti reperiuntur, quibus, ut diximus, et Fides Trinitatis revelata est, et ab ipsis praedicata, et spes immortalis animae, et aeternae retributionis expectata. Hinc quidem facilius evangelica praedicatio a philosophis quam a Judaeis suscepta est, cum sibi eam maxime invenirent adfinem. Unde cum tanta, ut dictum est, evangelicae ac philosophicae doctrinae concordia pateat . . ."

43. Abelard, *Theologia Christiana*, 2:361: "Sed prius hanc divinae Trinitatis distinctionem, non a Christo incoeptam, sed ab ipso apertius ac diligentius traditam esse ostendamus . . ."—This is evident regarding the Jews through the prefiguration of the prophets, and it is what Abelard wants to demonstrate concerning the philosophers.

toward the hidden meaning under the appearance of visible things. Did not St. Paul say expressly *invisibilia enim ipsius a creatura mundi per ea quae facta sunt, intellecta conspiciuntur* (Rom 1:19)? Accordingly, divine inspiration did not reveal the Trinity to the philosophers by the transmission of dogmatic formulas or symbolic images; it did so by permitting them to read the Trinity in things in which it was already inscribed.[44] Their opened eyes perceived in the universe the Power, the Wisdom, and the Goodness that are reflected in creatures as the triple image of Father, Son, and Holy Spirit. From there it is a short distance to discovering the comparisons that permit us to imagine their relations, and the philosophers traversed it.[45] Therefore, here again, the traditional notion of a universe intimately penetrated by the triple divine perfection and bearing its creator's typical likeness is what allows the claim of a revelation without Scripture to the pagan philosophers and to pure reason.

Despite the nuances of their thinking and deep differences of their doctrines, all these alleged rationalisms end by coming together and agreeing on at least one point: true wisdom does not go from reason to faith but, on the contrary, from faith to reason. Not human beings but God is the Father of lights. Like salvation, the highest knowledge takes its point of departure in faith, and because it always starts from a conscious or unconscious revelation, nothing ever keeps it from speaking its word on the deepest mysteries. The universe and the Scriptures constitute so many enigmas for us. The peculiar task of our reason is to seek the word about them. For all these thinkers, reality is so permeated by mystical and religious meaning that it is impossible for them to sharply distinguish the natural from the supernatural. From that comes the curious and contradictory impression they make on us today, and also the different interpretations that their historians offer. Seeing them passionate about dialectic and argumentation, we have difficulty resisting the impression that their reason proposes to absorb dogma. Exactly the opposite happens. What prevents them from being confused with rationalists in the modern sense is, therefore, not their conception of knowledge but their conception of

44. Abelard, *In Epistolam ad Romanos*, 2:172–74.

45. Abelard, *In Epistolam ad Romanos*, 2:172–74: "Verum est dicere eousque [sic] per similitudinem corporalium rerum humanam rationem conscendisse, ut ipsam Dei unitatem, atque in eo personarum Trinitatem, et quomodo ipsae personae invicem se habeant congruis similitudinum exemplis assignare valeret . . ."—The example about the bronze statue symbolizing Father and Son follows. The subsequent commentary only seems to direct the famous *haec ut sint inexcusabiles* against ignorance of the one God (*In Epistolam ad Romanos*, 2:174).

reality. These thinkers certainly have reason, but they do not have nature. They go straight to the supernatural, for which what we call the real is only a figure in their eyes and a pale imitation. They provide a point of departure to dialectic that dialectic's own powers would not permit it to reach. They require of it the interpretation of a reality for which it is not suited. We always see the syllogism put at the service of the most elusive and least perceptible analogies and see them continually beseech heaven for lights with which the dialectic is not equipped. There could be no rationalisms as long as Aristotle's example did not demonstrate to medieval thought that things have a certain existence by themselves and that the elements of an exhaustive interpretation of what they are can be found within them. In a word, there will be no rationalism as long as nature has not re-conquered its reality and natural reason its content.

TWO

The Handmaiden of Theology

Si egressus fueris ad pugnam contra inimicos tuos . . . et videris in numero captivorum mulierem pulchram . . . introduces eam in domum tuam, quae radet cesariem et circumcidet ungues . . . et postea intrabis ad eam, dormiesque cum illa, et erit uxor tua.

DEUTERONOMY 21:1–13

The thinkers who enclose philosophy within the boundary of revelation are much more alien to our modern mentality than is generally supposed. Yet it is not from them that we must start if we wish to measure exactly the road taken by medieval thought and the progress that the great Scholastic doctors accomplished on it. The theologians who were haunted by the recollection of a mystic version of the universe were philosophers in their fashion. We perceive that they were inspired by a lively taste for rational speculation, and the tenderness with which an Abelard speaks of Plato or other pagan philosophers shows us that a secret affinity brings them together over the distance of centuries and the radical difference of civilizations. To get an exact idea of the obstacles to the constitution of a purely rational philosophy, and to appreciate how it suits the work of those who let it flow around them or over them, we must know what the attitude of intransigent theologians was. Indeed, a whole series of doctors exists in whom we see Christianity embodied in its pure state. After the disorders of the tenth century, at the moment when the church undertakes a movement aimed at internal reform and sees a rebirth of the life of the hermit in the Camaldolese monasteries, notably under the influence of Romuald (956–1027), it is natural to find theologians who completely distrust any philosophy. Humans must work out their salvation, and they do so by renouncing the world completely. We do not renounce the world completely, unless we renounce philosophy. There we have, with minimal simplification, the elementary reasoning from which they started and to which they constantly returned. Let us add that at the same time, very serious problems perturbed the church. The issue was to discover what the relations ought to be between the spiritual and temporal powers. Hildebrand, who later became Gregory VII, struggled equally to forbid bishops from receiving their investiture from princes and to maintain the law of ecclesiastical celibacy in its entirety. It surely is no accident that the professed enemies of philosophy were gathered around the supreme leader of Christianity in this struggle. Peter Damian, Manegold of Lautenbach, and Bruno of Segni were not just rigorist theologians who believed they ought to repeat the invectives against dialectic that the Fathers of the Church had heaped upon dying paganism. They were, at the same time, staunch, active partisans of Gregory VII in his struggle against Henry IV. Whether they entered the battle on behalf of priestly celibacy or to demand the use of force against heretics or on the question of the investitures, politically, these theologians were always Gregorians.[1] The observation is all the more important, because, if they upheld the doctrine of the papacy in political controversies, their thought is what would inspire the papacy's attitude in regard to philosophy. This alliance predetermines the character that Gregory IX will strive to give the University of Paris, and that his successors will work to preserve.

The most typical representative of the strict theologians is certainly St. Peter Damian (Petrus Damiani), and in his writings we find the clearest expression of the fundamental hostility toward any purely rational speculation. For a mentality of this kind, the only issue is to know whether the Christian religion is or is not the whole truth. If it is, as we believe, we have no need of anything else. Let us say more; if the Christian religion is the whole truth, everything that is not it, or absorbed into it, can only be an error. Choosing between theology and philosophy is choosing between God and the devil, and we cannot escape these alternatives.

One February 14 when St. Peter Damian had to give a homily for the feast of St. Eleuchadius, he took advantage of the occasion to explain

1. Mirbt, *Die Publizistik*, 450–56, 478–90.

to his audience what a Christian ought to think about philosophy. Eleuchadius had been a philosopher before he was converted to Christianity and embraced the doctrine of truth. Accordingly, in this conversion Plato's wisdom was vanquished by a disciple of the fisherman: *superata est ergo sapientia Platonis a discipulo piscatoris*. He threw his net into the briny depths of the sea of Ravenna and bought his golden net toward the shore of faith.[2] The disciples of this fisherman became the masters of the orators of the world and as St. Paul prevailed over Dionysius the Areopagite, the wisdom of the world was conquered by the simplicity of Christ: *sapientia mundi victa est a simplicitate Christi*.

Moreover, we can learn from Scripture what a Christian ought to make of the philosophers' false wisdom. When Moses saw the Hebrews adore the golden calf, he seized it, put it into the fire, beat it into powder, and put this powder into water that he made the children of Israel drink (Exod 32:20). If we know how to read the deep meaning under the facts that are only an allegory, we will see that the calf represents the whole body of pagan society given over to idolatry. Moses plunges the calf into the fire because the Redeemer will light the fire of his charity in pagan hearts and because the fire will destroy the bestial form of idolatry in their thinking. Moses beat the golden calf into dust, because the pagan society, whose origin is diabolical (*illa societas diabolicae conspirationis in unum arte conflata*), must one day be shattered and broken up under the hammer of the divine word. Lastly, this powder is put into water that the Israelites drink because the holy preachers of the gospel, who are really the Israelites, assimilate into their limbs and, so to speak, drink those who are converted to the body of the Lord, his church. Why is this calf golden? Because, as has been proven, before the grace of the new faith, the wise of the world were the founders of the worship given the devil.

The apostle speaks of them (Rom 1:21–23) when he condemns those who did not recognize God and are misled in vain reasoning. Called wise, they have lost their reason. They represent the glory of the incorruptible God by human images or even images of birds, four-footed animals, and serpents. Confused by the vanity of this insane science, the poets, philosophers, magicians, astrologers, and lastly all those who subject themselves to the discipline of the liberal arts, were worshipers of the devil. The philosophers, so to speak, have established idolatry.[3] Therefore,

2. Damian, *Opera*; see vol. 144, col. 535.

3. Damian, *Opera*, vol. 144, col. 536: "Aureus itaque fuit vitulus, quia mundi sapientes ante novam gratiam fidei demoniacae culturae fuisse probantur auctores . . . Per

let us smash the idol of this false wisdom. Let us reduce it to powder, and let us absorb it in order to transform into our substance what was to transform us into members of the devil.[4]

If we had the illusion that St. Peter Damian might have conceived this absorption and assimilation in the form of a dialectical and philosophical interpretation, the advice he gave his monks is enough to correct us. His point of view always remains the rigorous perspective of the monk who renounces the world to save his soul. Indeed, what is a monk who toys at frequenting the grammarians, scorns spiritual studies, and delights in the nonsense of the science of this world? There are monks who pay little attention to St. Benedict's rule and prefer Donatus's rule [translator: presumably Aelius Donatus, the Roman rhetorician and grammarian]. They neglect to be initiated into the ecclesiastical sciences and only cultivate profane science. What is this but to desert a chaste spouse on the bed of faith in order to kiss the prostitutes of the theater? It might be said that, seduced by the courtesans' charms, they want to repudiate the free women and break the conjugal pact in order to be joined to slaves. They abandon the spouses of Laban to take prostitutes as concubines.

Moreover, we hear such monks object that, if they devote themselves to the vanities of sciences alien to the faith, it is to be able thereafter to approach the study of divine things with greater profit. Certainly, Jacob only tolerates the concubines' embraces at the request of his wives. Without them, the children that resulted would never have obtained their part in the inheritance. Consequently, these monks search. They subtly consult the authority of the fathers. They want to prove that Scripture at least allows the study of the liberal arts, as a spouse hands over a maidservant to her husband for him to obtain descendants. But in reality, Gregory, Jerome, and the other holy doctors absolutely deny that this study is licit, and those who intend to give themselves up to them lead an obstinate and illicit conflict against the sanctity of the conjugal pledge. It is not only forbidden to us, to those of us who are monks, to devote ourselves to the study of these vain doctrines after we have received holy orders, but it is also mandated for us to eliminate from then on everything superfluous

---

hanc itaque vesanae sapientiae vanitate, poetae, philosophi, magi, siderum rimatores, omniumque disciplinarum liberalium instructi peritia, prodigiosa demoniorum solebant adorare figmenta."

4. Damian, *Opera*, vol. 144, col. 537: "Sic, sic, ille vitulus per ignem zeli, et aciem verbi, aquamque baptismi ab eis potius absorptus est quos conatus est absorbere: in eos enim transfusus est, quos in sua, hoc est diabolica tentaverat membra transferre."

in what we had previously learned. This is why the law of Moses decrees that the victor must remove everything superfluous from the body of the captive woman he wants to make his wife: "[If thou] seest in the number of captives a beautiful woman and lovest her, and will have her to wife, thou shalt bring her into thy house; and she shall shave her hair, and pare her nails, and shall put off the raiment in which she was taken, and shall remain in thy house, and mourn for her mother and father one month, and after that thou shalt go in unto her, and shalt sleep with her, and she shall be thy wife" (Deut 21:11–13). We shave this woman's hair when we suppress the useless theories of philosophy. We cut her nails, when we knock down all the dead works of superstition. She abandons the garments in which she was taken, when she sheds the covering of fables and fictions in which she is arrayed in order to let the solid core of truth appear. She mourns for her father and her mother, because our thinking considers the inventers of the liberal arts to be dead and compassionately deplores those who have perished in errors. Lastly, there is the order in which the woman's blood purges her body each month. Therefore, it is mandated for us to wait for each of these sciences to be purified of any mixture of superstition before we make it our spouse in any way. Only then, having become an Israelite herself, will she be worthy of an Israelite, and will she be able to give him a fertile decadence of spiritual works.[5]

Accordingly, philosophy appeared to St. Peter Damien as only able to be the captive and handmaiden of theology. This expression and the comparisons that illustrate it do not at all mean that theology can leave

5. Damian, *Opera*, vol. 145, *De Perfectione Monachorum*, ch. 11, cols. 306–7: "Ut autem cum stomacho loquar, ex istorum numero sunt ii, qui grammaticorum vulgus adeunt, qui relictis spiritualibus studiis, addiscere terrenae artis ineptias concupiscunt: parvipendentes siquidem regulam Benedicti, regulis gaudent vacare Donati. Hi porro fastidientes ecclesiasticae disciplinae peritiam et saecularibus studiis inhiantes, quid aliud quam in fidei talamo conjugem relinquere castam, et ad scenicas videntur descendere prostitutas? Sed fortassis objiciunt, quia ad hoc exteriorum artium nugis insudant, ut locupletius ad studia divina proficiiant . . ."—But they are mistaken—"Nam non solum prohibemur post acceptum sacrum ordinem vanis hujusmodi doctrinis intendere, sed ex iis quoque quae ante didicimus, superflua quaeque principium detruncare. Unde per Moysen lege decernitur, ut mulieri in bello captae, et in conjugem victoris electae, corporis superfluitas abscindatur. 'Quae radet, inquit cesariem et cicumcidet unques, et deponet vestem in qua capta est, sedensque in domo tua flebit patrem et matrem uno mense; et postea intrabis ad illam, dormiesque cum illa, et erit uxor tua' (Deutronomium 21: 11–13). Mulieri quippe caesariem radimus, cum rationali disciplinae sensus superfluos amputamus. Haec autem adversus monachos nugis exteriorum artium implicatos diximus, ut eorum vanitas quam procul a linea rectitudinis exorbitet, monstraremus."

it up to philosophy to take care of certain needs, even inferior ones. To the contrary, they mean that theology must have no confidence in philosophy and very distrustfully keep it in a state of strict servitude. Never should natural reason under any circumstances take the initiative in research or presume to decide what is true. It is not an easy task to adapt the reasoning of dialecticians or rhetoricians to the dogmas revealed by God. So it is a grave error to dare to submit revelation to the rules of the syllogism; for example, to claim that it is impossible for God to make what took place not to have taken place, because that is contradictory for reason. Philosophy does not precede theology. It follows it, because, if philosophy desired to precede theology, by following the consequences of the terms that it enunciates, philosophy would lose sight of the inner light that illuminates us and of the straight path of truth. Therefore, philosophy must not seize the right to teach about revelation but rather make itself its slave and serve it as a handmaiden serves her mistress.[6]

In St. Peter Damian's famous phrase, the idea of slavery predominates over that of utilization, and by a great deal. Strictly speaking, we can achieve salvation with faith alone, whereas with science alone we certainly hasten to damnation. Let us compare so many pious hermits who saved their souls while hardly knowing more than the Psalms, with that Gauthier, who traveled through Germany, Gaul, and Spain for thirty years to amass a treasure of science. When he wanted to instruct others in his turn, his enemies murdered him, and to his last breath he could only cry, "Alas, what a catastrophe!" They talked to him about confession, about penance, but he could only repeat continually, "Alas, what a catastrophe!"[7] Such people are like that astrologer who dropped into the bottom of a well, while he attempted to read the stars.

Moreover, it is easy to understand why the study of the sciences is useless for the true believer. It can serve neither to win souls for God nor even to understand the truth to which the believer adheres. To conquer

6. Damian, *De Divina Omnipotentia*, vol. 145, ch. 5, 603: "Haec plane, quae ex dialecticorum et rhetorum prodeunt argumentis, non facile divinae virtutis sunt aptanda mysteriis, et quae ad hoc inventa sunt in syllogismorum instrumenta proficiant vel clausulas dictionum absit ut sacris legibus se pertinaciter inferant et divinae virtuti conclusionis suae necessitates opponant. Quae tamen artis humanae peritia, si quando tractandis sacris eloquiis adhibetur, non debet jus magisterii sibimet arroganter arripere, sed velut ancilla dominae quodam famulatus obsequio subservire, ne si praecedit oberret, et dum exteriorum verborum sequitur consequentias, intimae virtutis lumen et rectum veritatis tramitem perdat."

7. Damian, *De Sancta Simplicitate*, vol. 145, 699.

souls, indeed, dialectic is absolutely useless. God does not need our grammar to take over the human heart. If God had judged such means necessary, he ought to have appealed to them at the very beginning of the work of redemption, when it was important to scatter the seeds of the new faith as widely as possible. Now, God did not send philosophers or orators to evangelize humans. Rather he sent simple, humble fishermen. The example of a holy life showing faith in action is what can sweep souls up, and the effect of this lived preaching is much more powerful than any possible word.[8] Let those who fear to fail in their preaching through lack of science, think of the simple jawbone of an ass with which Samson killed a thousand Philistines.

If science does not help us to comprehend other people, it is also does not help us to comprehend ourselves. It would be completely mistaken to imagine that we renounce knowing ourselves and that we sacrifice learning about ourselves by turning away from profane knowledge. At the instant when the believer carries out this sacrifice, almighty God, dispenser of merit, can confer on the believer's mind subtlety, perceptiveness, and agility that are tokens of his future reward. In our new mental perspicacity is there not often compensation for the learning that we have renounced for the love of God? This is all the easier to believe since there is more in faith than in learning and someone who embraces the first instead of the second truly possesses everything. He has really renounced nothing. The humanities are born of sense; sense does not arise from the humanities; the humanities are useless for one who has sense. More complete and deeper knowledge thus opens up before the mind that knows how to renounce itself. By that very thing it acquires a holy ignorance, more luminous than all profane learning. Let us not become so ridiculous as to light a lantern to see the sun better.[9]

8. Damian, *De Sancta Simplicitate*, ch. 3, vol. 145, 697: "Tu quoque valentius provocas videntes te properare post Christum, quam promovere potueras audientes qualibet multiplicate verborum. Nec enim Deus omnipotens nostra grammatica indigent, ut post se homines trahat, cum in ipso humanae redemptionis exordio, cum magis videretur utique necessarium ad conspergenda novae fidei semina, non miserit philosophos et oratores, sed simplices potius ac pescatores."

9. Damian, *De Sancta Simplicitate*, ch. 4, vol. 145, 698: "Quid enim scis utrum dispensator meritorum, omnipotens Deus ad hoc tibi subtilioris ingenii perspicaciam agilitatemque contulerit, ut jam tibi, quodammodo signum futurae remunerations ostenderet, et occidentem illam scientiam, quam pro illius amore sprevisti, vivacis mentis acumen compensaret? Nam cum litterae oriantur ex sensu, non sensus procedat ex litteris, cui sensus incolumnis est, litteras non requirit. In litterario quippe ludo, ubi pueri prima articulatae vocis elementa suscipiunt alii quidem abecedariii,

So, St. Peter Damian's intentions are clear. The scope of the expressions he employs cannot be diminished by explaining his attitude as a reaction against the excesses of dialecticians. No doubt such excesses took place. But the condemnation promulgated by this merciless monk has quite another scope. It evidently transcends that particular concern and envisages all of philosophy. It is a declaration of distrust of all profane learning. God, who is authentic Wisdom, is also the end of every search, the sole object of our intelligence. As for what is called learning, it is the beginning of all errors and vices. We have said that the pagan philosophers were the founders of the cult of the devil, but we can add that it is the devil himself who subjected them to the seductions of their false learning.

> God knows, he had declared to our parents in the earthly paradise, that on whatever day you shall eat of this fruit, your eyes will be opened, and you will be like gods, knowing good and evil. Behold our first grammar teacher, and the first lesson he gives to us is to teach us to decline *God* in the plural. Since the devil wished to introduce the horde of all vices into the world, he wondered what leader he might give this army, and he chose the desire for learning. This *cupiditas scientiae* has marched in the van the multitude of iniquities and led them to the conquest of our unhappy earth.[10]

With different shades of leniency or rigor we meet similar declaration from the pens of the monastic reformers or the intransigent theologians. But the violence of Gauthier of St. Victor and his frenetic curses against the "four labyrinths of France," Peter Abelard, Gilbert of la Porrée, the Master of Sentences himself, and Peter of Poitiers would not add any new characteristics to what we already know.[11] By contrast, what matters

---

alii syllabarii, quidam vero nominarii, non nulli etiam calculatores appellantur, et haec nomina cum audimus ex ipsis continuo quis sit in pueris profectus agnoscimus."—St. Peter Damian, *De Sancta Simplicitate*, ch. 5, vol. 145, 698–99: "Cum vero per donum Sancti Spritus intellectus peritur, quia per conceptum vigorem vivacis ingenii cuncta facile comprehendit, his ad discendum gradibus magnopere nos egebit."

10. Damian, *De Sancta Simplicitate*, I, vol. 145, 895–96: "Porro, qui vitiorum omnium catervas moliebatur inducere, cupiditatem scientiae quasi ducem exercitus posit, sicque per eam infelicii mundo cunctas inquitatum turmas invexit."

11. Endres, *Forschungen zur Geschichte*, ch. 4, 50–113; Grabmann, *Geschichte der scholastischen Methode*, vol. 2, ch. 4, 94–127 [Gilson omits the title here. Given the date of the present work and the fact that Gilson cites a two-volume work, we are probably dealing with *Geschichte der scholastischen Methode*, Freiburg im Breisgau: Herder,

extraordinarily for us to know is that the protests of these fanatic theologians became formidable in the church at the point when they crossed the threshold of their monasteries to be adopted by the papacy. Indeed in the closing years of the twelfth century we see how something takes place that will have decisive importance for the future of French thought and perhaps for the future of European thought. This conception of the overriding, absolute value of faith was everywhere but dispersed, floating, as it were, throughout the church. It is going to take root in a place from which it will be proclaimed throughout the earth and incarnated in an institution especially charged with maintaining it. The University of Paris is established, and the popes decided to make it the citadel of the faith.

Its advent had been prepared for many years, and to explain the prestige that Paris enjoyed from this period on, we would have to appeal both to doctrinal and philosophical reasons and to various geographical and historical causes. It is a fact that, in all of Europe, from the second half of the twelfth century, the residence of the kings of France was considered a center of philosophical and theological studies to which no other could be compared. The sweetness and urbanity that foreigners appreciated in its inhabitants,[12] the abundance of foodstuff that particularly surprised English travelers,[13] the beauty of the city and of its surroundings, the intense commerce that was developing there, all contributed to make it the great city whose appearance drew admiration from visitors and whose reputation attracted those who had not yet seen it.[14] Rich and beautiful among cities, at the same time Paris was the most vibrant of all the centers of study. The schools had not yet crossed the Petit Pont to establish themselves on the left bank of the Seine, but the logicians had already acquired the habit of walking along it while they disputed, and

---

1909 and 1911]; Geyer, *Die Sententiae Divinitatis*, spec. 175*–199*.

12. John of Salisbury, 1167, in *Chartularium*, I, 21: "Francia omnium mitissima et civilissima nationum."

13. Letter of Petrus Cellensis, 1164, in *Chartularium*, I, 24: "Quis praeter te alius sub coelo, Parisius non estimavit locum deliciarum, hortum plantationum, agrum primitiarum? Ubi exuberat plus quam in patria panis et vini copia?"—Cf. likewise *Chartularium*, texts 51, 52, 53, I, pp. 50ff.

14. Letter of the student Guy de Bazoches to a friend (1175–1190), in *Chartularium*, I, 55: "Status itaque meus hic est . . . Sum quidem Parisius, in urbe regali, que non solum dulciflua naturalium dotum retinet oblectatione presentes, sed etiam remotos allicit, invitat absentes. Sicut enim luna splendidioris speculi majestate sidereum sepelit jubar, non aliter urbs praefata super ceteras urbes diademate regie dignitatis imperiosum caput attolit."

three of the four faculties whose union would constitute the University of Paris had already developed on the island. Although the term *faculty* was not in use during this period, it is obvious that the thing already existed. A first group of masters and students devoted themselves to the study of the seven liberal arts. A second group studied ecclesiastical decrees and laws. Lastly, a third cultivated theological science and worked upon the doctrine of salvation.[15] By the twelfth century, public opinion considered the Paris masters to be a kind of body whose opinion was authoritative.[16] Difficult questions had to be brought to them, if one desired to get a solution.[17] All the science of the times was concentrated in them. Thus, a kind of aureole had already formed around Paris, drawing everyone's attention. Yet, how many anxieties did the name awake in pious souls! People boasted of having gone to Paris, but the boasting could only be about having acquired genuinely valuable science there.[18] In the imagination of those who guided souls, Paris already appeared in the Romantic guise of a city at the same time holy and infernal, where one's soul was lost as easily as saved, where all the vices of the heart and all intellectual disturbances ruled no less than salvific virtues and sciences.[19] But if some rigorist theologians feared for those who gave in to the snares of evil and the arrows of hell, in the eyes of the larger number, the great city remained the home of the sacred and profane sciences and the intellectual center of Christendom. Even before the university's establishment, people hastened along the roads that led to Paris, as if toward the citadel

15. Letter of Guy de Bazoches, in *Chartularium*, I, 56: "Pons autem parvus [as distinct from the Great Bridge] aut pretereuntibus, aut spatiantibus, aut disputantibus logicis didicatus est . . . In hac insula regale sibi solium ab antiquo philosophia colocavit . . . In hac insula perpetuam mansionem septem pepigere sorores, artes videlicet liberales, et intonante nobilioris eloquentiae tuba decreta leguntur et leges. Hic fons doctrina salutaris exuberat, et quasi tres rivos ex se limpidissimos ad prata mentium irriganda producens, dividit tripliciter intellectum sacrae pagine spiritalem, in historicam, allegoricam et morale."

16. Thomas Becket to G. de Sens, November 1169, in *Chartularium*, I, 23: ". . . vel judicio ecclesie gallicane, aut scolarium Parisiensium."

17. Pierre de Blois, 1175, in *Chartularium*, I, 35: "qui interrogant interrogent Parisius, ubi difficilium questionum nodi intrincatissimi resolvuntur."

18. Letter of Guy de Bazoches, in *Chartularium*, I, 54–55: "Non enim Parisius fuisse, sed Parisius honestam scientiam acquississe honestum est."

19. Letter of Petrus Cellensis, in *Chartularium*, I, 24: "O Parisius, quam idonea es ad capiendas et decipiendas animas! In te retiacula vitiorum, in te malorum decipula, in te sagitta inferni transfigit insipentium corda."

of the Catholic faith.[20] John of Salisbury, who was on a mission to France in 1164, could not resist the urge to go to see Paris, and the spectacle he found there struck him with admiration. Seeing the abundance of provisions, the cheerfulness of the populace, the respect that surrounded the clergy, the glory and majesty of the whole church, and the variety of philosophical studies, John believed he was witnessing Jacob's ladder, one end of which reached heaven and upon which a double line of angels ascended and descended. John of Salisbury exclaimed, "In truth the Lord is in this place, and I did not know it."[21]

Consequently, it is a fact that in the last years of the twelfth century, thanks to the number and renown of the masters who imparted their teaching in Paris, the city had become the most important place of study in Europe and "the citadel of the Catholic faith." Hence, it is not surprising that at the start of the thirteenth century the papacy conceived the project of officially recognizing the *de facto* status Paris had won, and of making it something like the intellectual capital of Christendom for the greater good of the whole church. The idea must have imposed itself all the more urgently since some of the masters of the several faculties felt themselves united by common interests and threatened by common dangers and were thinking of organizing into a single body including the totality (*universitas*) of the masters and students of Paris. This amorphous, disorganized crowd, which included men of all nations, felt lost and defenseless in the midst of a foreign and frequently hostile populace. Like everyone in the Middle Ages, it needed privileges to protect it and its own justice to remove it from the justice of its neighbor.[22] France provided the framework and the intellectual environment, but France was evidently incapable of nourishing such a home for studies alone. The special significance and unique situation of the Paris schools stemmed from

20. Peter of Blois, *Chartularium*, I, 39: "Parisius quasi ad catholicae fidei arcem festinantes."

21. John of Salisbury, 1164, *Chartularium*, I, 18–19: "Sic ergo discessi, instructus a vobis, ut Parisius sedem figerem, et me studerem omnino scolaribus conformare . . . Ubi cum viderem victualium copiam, letitiam populi, reverentiam cleri, et tutus Ecclesiae majestatem et gloriam, et varias occupationes philosophantium, admirans velut illam scalam Jacob, cujus summitas celem tangebat, eratque via ascendentium et descendentium angelorum, lete peregrinationis urgente stimulo coactus sum profiteri, quod vere Dominus est in loco isto, et ego nesciebam. Illud quoque poeticum ad mentem rediit: Felix exilium, cui locus iste datur!"

22. October 2, 1255, *Chartularium*, I, 292: ". . . illud unum in ea nobis intolerabile et letale periculum continetur, ut cum simus alienigenarum multitudo inhermis, quibus ab indigenis atroces et corporales injurie frequentius irrogantur . . ."

their international character. When the foreigners no longer felt secure, they went home or threatened to do so, all the more willingly because the sovereigns of certain neighboring countries did not hesitate to offer the freedoms they lacked at Paris.[23] The papal policy precisely encouraged the corporative sense that had already developed among the Paris masters in order to crystallize it in the form of a regularly constituted social institution. In addition the policy aimed at furnishing the newly constituted body with all the privileges that might ensure its vitality and duration, and finally, included careful vigilance about its functioning in order to harness it closely to the goals that papal policy had directly assigned it.

The project of establishing an educational center at Paris, which would then be utilized by the church, seems to have been first conceived by Pope Innocent III. He had studied theology at Paris himself under Peter of Corbeil. Therefore, he knew the environment through personal experience that made him aware of its lights and shadows. The corporative sense had already developed sufficiently by the period of his stay in Paris so that, once seated upon the papal throne, he sometimes adopted the tone of an old colleague.[24] But he knew that the Paris ferment could certainly corrupt the mass of the church as well as elevate it. Everything was taught at Paris, but everything was subject to dispute there. The mysteries of the divine essence and the incarnation of the Word were interpreted and commented there. The indivisible Trinity was dissected even on the street corners, in such a way that there were as many errors as doctors, as many scandals as classrooms, and as many blasphemies as public places. Education in the liberal arts, or as they were already called, the faculties of arts, were invaded by impudent youths who wanted to be masters before being students and shamelessly installed themselves in the chairs their elders occupied.[25] Consequently, it was important to act

23. *Chartularium*, I, 118, 119, 126, 139. See the case of five English masters who returned to England and the invitation of King Henry III of England directed to the masters and students of Paris to leave France, where they were oppressed, for England, where they would be free.

24. Innocent III, January 20, 1212, in *Chartularium*, I, 73: "Cum igitur tempore quo vacavimus Parisius studio litterarum, nunquam viderimus scolares sic tractari . . ."

25. See the complaints and imprecations against Paris addressed to the pope by Stephen of Tournay, in *Chartularium*, I, 43: "Vel ad Parisienses secularium scolas et venditores verborum mittendo . . ." 1192–1203 *Chartularium*, I, 47–48: "Disputatur publice contra sacras constitutiones de incomprehensibili deitate; de incarnatione verbi, verbosa caro et sanguis irreverenter litigat. Individua Trinitas et in triviis secatur

as quickly as possible in this environment, and the first thing to do, if one hoped the action would be fruitful, was evidently to organize it.

The name itself of the University of Paris, as designating the totality of masters who lived in Paris and taught theology, law, and liberal arts there, begins to appear in the first years of the thirteenth century in the letters of Innocent III. The pope establishes it in the same documents that impose duties and confer privileges on it.[26] He immediately becomes its protector and head, and he strives to obtain all the temporal privileges from the king of France that he himself is not in a position to grant. Accordingly, the University of Paris is the work of the church. Obviously, in constituting the university, the church simply utilizes skillfully a *de facto* situation it has not created. But although the foundation is not a creation *ex nihilo*, Innocent III's decision to take it in hand and bend the spiritual forces it represented to his will, would exert a profound influence upon the university's future and on the future of French philosophy. Innocent's university policy, which would remain that of his successors for a long time, was to support the University of Paris in order to make use of it. The development of modern philosophy cannot be understood nor can a clear idea be formed of its origins, if one does not pay constant attention to the consequences of this event.

The first of these consequences is that the faculties that made up the University of Paris had different importance. Standing above the others, dominating them, and directing them from on high was the faculty of theology. It is impossible to insist enough that the crude formula, *philosophia ancilla theologiae*, does not represent the thought of the great Scholastics concerning the relations of reason and faith. But it must be added that it represents the church's and the papacy's conception very exactly. One of Innocent III's first concerns was to put in their places *quidam*

et discrepitur, ut tot jam sint errores quot doctores, tot scandala quam auditoria, tot blasphemie quot platee . . . Ve duo predicta sunt, et ecce restat tertium ve: facultates quas liberales appellant, amissa libertate pristina in tantam servitutem devocantur, ut comatuli adolescentes earum magisteria impudentes usurpent, et in cathedra seniorum sedeant imberbes, et qui nondum norunt esse discipuli laborant ut nominentur magistri. Conscribunt et ipsi summulas suas pluribus salivis effluentes et madidas, philosophorum sale nec conditas . . ." etc.

26. Innocent III, 1208–1209, in *Chartularium*, I, 67: "Universis doctoribus sacre pagine, decretorum, et liberalium artium Parisius commorantibus . . ." *Chartularium*, I, 67, ". . . universitati parere contempneret magistrorum . . ." *Chartularium*, I, 67: ". . . universitati resisteret magistrorum." *Chartularium*, I, 68: "universitati vestre presentium auctorite mandamus . . ."

moderni doctores liberalium artium, who did not follow the customary order in their disputes and their lectures.[27] Every faculty but especially the Arts Faculty was always more or less tempted to consider itself as being its own end, but Innocent III and Gregory IX continually brought it back within its natural limits, and recalled that it owed deference and submission to the Faculty of Theology. Accordingly, the University of Paris was a Faculty of Theology that subjugated the Faculty of Arts and Law.

No pope was more clearly aware of this particular conception of the University of Paris than Gregory IX. The vehement letter in which he forbids the masters of theology who teach at Paris to let themselves be drawn into teaching profane sciences and to introducing the philosophers' fictions into the word of God is one of the most typical expressions of this point of view. For Gregory, also, philosophy is only a captive whom theology takes from its enemies by conquest. Philosophy cannot claim to command and must be content with obeying as is appropriate for a subject. The theological spirit must dominate the different faculties as man dominates woman. It must exercise its authority over them as spirit over flesh. Consequently, it is a crime and genuine aberration to introduce profane novelties into the doctrine that the fathers have transmitted to us, or to allow oneself to be seduced by pagan philosophical systems and to want absolutely to employ them in the interpretation of the Holy Scriptures. Only vanity can induce the masters into these damnable machinations. The spirit of vanity inflates them like wineskins and incites them to make ostentation of their science rather than to seek their listeners' benefit. Their duty is to expound theology according to the tradition of the fathers. Their peculiar task is to mow down everything that rises up against the science of God and to reduce all minds to captivity under the law of Christ. But they must support themselves upon God himself to carry out this task, and they must not go to seek their arms among the pagans. To manipulate the sacred word that God himself inspired in order to make it agree with the doctrine of philosophers who do not know God, is to introduce idols into the temple of the Lord. Moreover, if we attempt to justify faith by natural reason more than is appropriate, we end by making faith useless and vain, because *fides non habet meritum,*

27. Innocent III, 1208–1209, in *Chartularium*, I, 67. Likewise, cf. the old ordinances of Alexander III, 1163, renewed by Robert of Courçon in 1213 and Innocent III in 1219, in *Chartularium*, I, 77, 90–92.

cui humana natura praebet experimentum.[28] It is precisely because faith of itself possesses value incommensurable with the value of any other knowledge that all other sciences must be considered handmaidens of theology: *Cum sapientiae sacrae paginae reliquae scientiae debeant famulari, eatenus sunt a fidelibus amplectandae, quatenus obsequi dinoscuntur beneplacitis donantis.*[29] We must devote ourselves to other studies only in the measure in which they are useful to theology.

Whatever notion contemporary masters at the University of Paris may have formed about the role they had to play and the relations between reason and faith, it is obvious, that the popes had their conception and that it was very clear. Theology is the only absolutely good science, necessary in itself. In the view of the popes, who protected and presided over the university, the latter was the center of theological studies, where masters would come to be taught, who would then spread sound doctrine throughout the whole universe. Alexander IV compares it to the radiant light that illuminates the Lord's house and to the tree of life planted in the middle of the garden of Eden. In this university, mankind is cured of the blindness of its original ignorance and recovers sight through the

28. Gregory IX to the theology masters of the University of Paris, July 7, 1228, in *Chartularium*, I, 114–16: "Puella etiam de hostibus capta, que pilis rasis et ungulis circumcisis viro Israelitico jungitur, dominari non debet eidem, *sed obsequi potius ut subjecta*. Et quidem theologicus intellectus quasi vir habet preesse cuilibet facultati, et quasi spiritus in carnem dominium exercere, ac eam in viam dirigere rectitudinis ne aberret . . . Sane tacti dolore cordis intrinsecus amaritudine replete sumus abscinthii, quod sicut nostris est auribus intimatum, quidam apud vos spiritu vanitatis ut uter distenti, positos a patribus terminos prophana satagunt transferre novitate ad doctrinam philosophicam naturalium inclinando, ad ostentationem scientiae, non profectum aliquem auditorum, ut sic videantur non theodocti, seu theologi, sed potius theophanti. Cum enim theologiam secundum approbatas traditiones sanctorum exponere debeant, et non carnalibus armis, sed Deo potentibus destruere omnem altitudinem extollentem se adversus scientiam Dei et captivum in obsequium Christi omnem reducere intellectum ipsi doctrinis variis et peregrinis abducti redigunt caput in caudam et *ancille cogunt famulari reginam*, videlicet documentis terrenis, celeste quod est gratie tribuendo nature . . . Nonne dum ad sensum doctrine philosophorum ignorantium Deum, sacra eloquia divinitus inspirate extortis expositionibus, immo distortes inflectunt, juxta Dagon arcam federis collocant, et adorandam in templo Domini statuunt ymaginem Antiochi? Et dum fidem conantur plus debito ratione astruere naturali, nonne illam reddunt quodammodo inutilem et inanem, quoniam fides non habet meritum, cui humana ratio praebet experimentum?" Note the extremely vehement tone of this whole letter.—Cf. likewise, Gregory IX, April 13, 1231, in *Chartularium*, I, 138: "Magistri vero et scolares theologie in facultate quam profitentur se studeant ladabiliter exercere, nec philosophos se ostentent."

29. Gregory IX, April 23, 1231, in *Chartularium*, I, 143–44.

knowledge of truth.[30] There, in this supreme dispensary of Wisdom, in this illustrious city of the arts, holy and venerable theology reigns. It commands, and other sciences obey it. It is the mistress, and the other sciences are close by like handmaidens.[31] Paris is the inexhaustible source from which the waters of truth flow through the world,[32] the fountain of wisdom that spreads through the four faculties of theology, law, medicine, and philosophy, as if by the four rivers of Paradise, throughout the whole world, which it irrigates and makes fertile with its waters for the greatest spiritual and temporal benefit of Christendom. Or again, the University of Paris is the river by which, after the grace of the Holy Spirit, the whole paradise of the church is irrigated and made fertile.[33] Consequently, since that was the church's official conception, it is understood, that the university was never its own mistress and that it never belonged to itself. It is because the university was first of all the most powerful instrument of which the pope disposed to guarantee the spread of Christian truth, that the popes imposed the involvement of Dominicans and Franciscans upon the body of the Parisian masters, favored the establishment at Paris of all existing religious orders, strove to promote in it the study of Eastern languages that were needed to permit a wider propagation of the faith among the infidels, and would even have liked to introduce Jews and pagans into the university as auditors. Finally, it is why the popes watched

30. Alexander IV, 1255, in *Chartularium*, I, 279–80: "Quasi lignum vite in paradiso Dei et quasi lucerna fulgoris in domo Domini est in sancta Ecclesia Parisiensis studii disciplina . . . Ibi humanum genus originalis ignorantie cecitate deforme et cognitionem veri luminis, quam scientia pietatis assequitur, reddita visionis specie reformatur."

31. Alexander IV, November 10, 1256, in *Chartularium*, I, 343: "Haec [Parisius] est igitur egregia litterarum civitas, artium urbs famosa, eruditionis scola precipua, summa sapientie officina et potissimum gymnasium studiorum. Hic conversantur et degunt scientie . . . inter quas sacra et venerabilis theologia locum obtinet altiorem. Preest enim reliquis sicut superior, et tanquam inferiores cetere subsunt, imperat aliis ut domina, et *ille sibi ut famule obsequuntur*; gubernat alias ut prelata, et ipse sibi tanquam subidite reverenter intendunt. Ad hanc singule in viis suis levant et habent intuitum, ut juxta permissum ejus se metientes inoffense incedant, et gressum aliquod inconveniens non impingant."

32. John XXII, March 8, 1317, in *Chartularium*, II, 234–36.

33. Cf. *Chartularium*, I, first part, text 230, and Gregory IX, 1227, in *Chartularium*, I, 127: "Fluvius profecto est litterarum studium, quo irrigatur et fecundatur post Spiritus Sancti gratiam, paradisus generalis Ecclesia, cujus alveus Parisiensis civitas ex eo, quod idem studium Parisius viguit hactenus noscitur extitisse." Gregory IX, 1230, in *Chartularium*, I, 133–34: "Parens scientiarum, Parisius . . . civitas litterarum, etc." See also Gregory IX, 1231, in *Chartularium*, I, 136–37; November 26, 1229, I, 128–29; and February 1233, I, 148–50.

over the university with jealous care. To be authentically great and powerful, the university had to be at Paris and to remain united there. Even if the university had wished to, it would not have had the right to divide and be fragmented, because by fragmenting, it would diminish itself, close the heaven of Scripture, and destroy the keystone of science.[34] A doctor from Paris with no other title could step into a chair in any other European university, but a doctor of another university, although he had obtained his degrees in the most famous universities, even at Oxford, had to pass a new examination to have the right to teach at Paris. Oxford requested a similar privilege from the papacy several times, but in vain. The church's university policy required that the University of Paris should remain the brain of Christendom.[35]

This fundamental fact lets us effectively understand and appreciate the general attitude of church authorities toward philosophy in general and Aristotle's doctrine in particular. The popes never considered Aristotle's philosophy *qua* philosophy. It could never enter their minds that a purely rational explanation of the universe elaborated by a pagan could have exceptional value precisely because it did not know dogma and appealed only to the lights of reason. Popes are not philosophers, and they do not for an instant bother about favoring the development of an independent philosophy. The peculiar task with which they felt themselves to be charged by God and the church was to achieve the union of humanity under the law of Christ. The West was already beginning to be covered by universities and schools in which masters formed at Paris taught theological truths, sound interpretations of Scripture, and the rules of canon

34. Gregory IX, 1229, in *Chartularium*, I, 127: "Unde quod nostris temporibus illud [studium] alibi transferatur non debemus equanimiter tolerare ne forsan ex hujusmodi translatione per plura loca divisum ad nichilum redigatur, et claudatur celum scripture . . ." Also, ". . . iidem magistri [Parisienses] cum scolaribus damnis et injuriis lacesciti a Parisiis discesserunt, studium alibi transferendo, per quod videntur clavem tullisse scientie, ac ante homines celorum claudere velle regnum, et ipsi non intrantes, volentes intrare nolle sincere introire."

35. See the recommendations and regulations of Innocent IV, in *Chartularium*, I, 212, and I, 213, and the exhortation of Humbert of Romans, General of the Order of Preachers, June 1256, in *Chartularium*, I, 318, on the study of Eastern languages, for emphasizing whose utility Roger Bacon is usually praised. The privilege *docendi regendique ubique terrarum sine ullo praevio examine*, which had already been recognized de facto, was officially conferred by Nicholas IV, March 23, 1292, in *Chartularium*, II, 54–55. See *Chartularium*, II, 213, for the requests from Oxford. One of their arguments is: "Galicanum studium ab Anglicanis nostris orignale traxisse principium . . ." Cf. *Chartularium*, II, 269.

law thanks to which the body of the universal church could be constructed—all according to the order, procedures, and doctrine of Paris. That is the great task, and the popes hover over the University of Paris with concerned attention, because it is the forge where this great task was to be accomplished by the fusion of the French, Picards, Normans, English, Germans, and Italians, who were mingled in the university. The future church already squeezes into the classrooms on Rue de Fouarre or the slopes of Mount St. Genevieve. Those students are the future masters; they are also the future doctors and pastors of Christendom. The cosmopolitan character of the University of Paris is only the particular expression and a sort of reduced image of the church's own Catholicity. What hopes the popes placed in this conservatory of the Christian faith and what fears it inspired in them! Paris can cause the world to be lost as well as save it. If error were introduced into Paris, if the paganism of the Greek philosophers managed to contaminate the waters of theological truth at their very source, the whole universe would be poisoned. Error in questions of faith is dangerous and worthy of condemnation everywhere else, but it only constitutes a local danger that can be easily contained and whose development can be suffocated. In Paris, by contrast, heresy would immediately threaten to become a universal evil. There the disease would be situated in the church's very brain, and it will lead the whole body down into the depths. *Puritas studii quae hactenus Parisius viget*—the popes had the responsibility for that treasure, and they wished to preserve it at all costs.

When we are capable of placing ourselves in their vantage point, we easily understand that the official church never felt the least respect or the least kindness toward Aristotle before he was baptized. The first apparition and condemnation of his physics and metaphysics are inseparable in the texts of Amaury of Bène and David of Dinant.[36] Because Toulouse is only a regional university, Aristotle's physics can still be studied there publicly, when it can no longer be studied at Paris.[37] It is on the occasion of the prohibitions leveled against Aristotle's doctrine that Gregory IX compares philosophy to a handmaiden who owes respect and submission

36. Decree of Peter of Corbeil, 1210, in *Chartularium*, I, 70–72: "Quarternuli magistri David de Dinant infra natale episcopo Parisiensi afferantur et comburantur, nec libri Aristotelis de naturali philosophia nec commenta legantur Parisius publice vel secreto, et hoc sub pena excomnunicationis inhibemus."

37. *Chartularium*, I, 130–31. Likewise, the teaching of civil law is prohibited at Paris and permitted at Orleans, *Chartularium*, I, 92, and I, 156.

to her mistress, theology. This pagan's doctrine is exactly the captive of Scripture, and the theological mind can be united to it, but as man is united to woman, by directing and commanding her. Therefore, the church never took interest in Aristotle for his own sake, or in philosophy for its own sake. It always had simply utilization of Aristotle in mind. This is why Gregory IX saw the *Physics* and *Metaphysics* as books like any other, texts that could easily be expurgated and trimmed. Instead of conceiving the necessary work of adaptation in the Albertine-Thomist form of interpretative commentaries, Gregory simply anticipated a censored version of this dense text and doctrine.[38] It is useless to add that this impossible project was never carried out. The illusion that dictated such prescriptions is, nonetheless, instructive and revealing about the authentic mindset of the pope. Accordingly, modern philosophy was born in an institution desired by the church, with a view to specifically religious goals, and in large measure against the spirit of the institution at the heart of which it was developing. The first European university was not founded to benefit reason and science, but to benefit faith and religion. We will have to start there if we want to understand how theology, after remaking the philosophical education of the Western world, despaired of agreeing with its handmaiden, renounced her services, and by separating itself from her, set the captive of Scripture free forever.

38. Gregory IX, April 23, 1231, in *Chartularium*, I, 143–44: "Ceterum cum sicut intelleximus libri naturalium, qui Parisius in Concilio provinciali fuere prohibiti, quedam utilia et inutilia continere dicantur, ne utile per inutile vitietur, discretioni vestre, de qua plenam in Domino fiduciam obtinemus, per apostolica scripta sub obtestatione divini judicii firmiter percipiendo mandamus, quatinus libros ipsos examinantes sicut convenit subtiliter et prudenter, qui ibi erroronea scandali vel offendiculi legentibus inveneritis illativa, penitus resecetis, ut que sunt suspecta remotis incunctanter ac inoffense in reliquis studeantur."

THREE

The Doctrine of Double Truth

Scholars have been rightly concerned about explaining in complete detail how the Western Middle Ages came to possess Aristotle's thought. The date and attribution of the oldest translations of the *Physics*, *De Anima*, and *Metaphysics* have been debated. Researchers have tried and still try to retrace the path from the Eastern circles where the texts originated to the learned men who translated them and the philosophers who employed them. It is self-evident that these studies are an indispensable condition of any interpretation of the thirteenth-century Aristotelian movement. The interpretation itself has already been thoroughly developed, and studies of the first order, like those of Fr. Mandonnet, describe three definite attitudes within Scholastic circles in regard to the new philosophy. The first position is that of the Augustinians who let themselves be influenced only superficially by Aristotle. Second come the Albertine-Thomists, who deliberately include Greek doctrine in their philosophical syntheses. The third attitude is that of the Averroists, who adopt all of Aristotle as the Arab commentators saw him and attempt to leave it at that. These results have been acquired by patient work and lucid analysis of the materials. They seem definitive to us. We would simply like to base ourselves on them to draw out solutions to some more general historical problems. If these solutions are possible, they would permit us to return subsequently to the facts from which we began and clarify their interpretation. The problem is the following: exactly what conflict was stirred up by the medieval discovery of Aristotle's philosophy?

It can escape no one that the advent of Aristotelianism posed weighty problems and entailed many difficulties. It is known, and often cited as a kind of curiosity, that the teaching of Aristotle was prohibited at Paris for a long time; that St. Thomas Aquinas had to overcome strong resistance to get his viewpoint adopted; that certain Aristotelian theses adopted by St. Thomas were swept up in the general condemnation at Paris of Averroist errors that St. Thomas combated. These events are well known, but they are very often recalled only as picturesque episodes within a development whose outcome was fixed beforehand. St. Thomas's official triumph in the church has been so complete and its effects are still so easily recognizable, that we no longer perceive what a historical paradox such a triumph constituted. That is a very natural illusion but an illusion nonetheless. Far from having been negligible incidents devoid of deep meaning, the opposition with which St. Thomas collided reveals the radically revolutionary character of the movement St. Thomas inaugurated. It is important to go beyond the events themselves to the fundamental states of mind that provoked and explained them.

Aristotle's dialectics nourish medieval thinking from the start. The Middle Ages did not need to possess Aristotle's complete works to have great admiration for him. The discovery of his metaphysics and his physics produced such an impression on thirteenth-century minds that Aristotle rapidly came to be identified with philosophical reason. A certain effort of imagination is necessary to judge and interpret this historical fact appropriately. For us, medieval Aristotelians are conventional thinkers who admit the alien doctrine that philosophical thought was discovered once and for all time, and who absurdly opposed new investigation. More or less consciously, we continue to accept the criticisms of Descartes and Molière against the Scholastics of their time. The criticisms were necessary and, moreover, justified, but they have much more force against later academic Aristotelianism of teachers and textbooks than against the position adopted by the thirteenth-century Aristotelians. Before Aristotelianism became an undisputed authority and an intellectual routine, it was a living philosophy whose triumphal march is not explicable without the great superiority, youthfulness, and novelty that characterized it at its apparition. Aristotle simply sweeps over the thirteenth century in the fashion in which a Descartes or a Kant sweep over their times. Aristotelianism's ascendency was not based on mystical respect for a name or an ancestral habit. Its deep impact on medieval thinking was due first of all to the enthusiasm thinkers of the time felt for the wealth and fecundity of its doctrine. These men had nothing to bridge the gap between their sterile dialectics and risky speculations about dogma. They abruptly saw that vacuum filled by a comprehensive explanation of the universe. In our days a philosophical doctrine can still seduce minds, brilliantly conquer the place occupied by old doctrines, and force itself on everyone's attention, because it satisfies more completely the intellectual needs of our period. How can we reproach either these doctrines or their time for their successes? Their authority was a product of their superiority. Yet, the new philosophies to which we give our allegiances or that drag it out of us are only systems that follow systems. We only change explanation. The case of the thirteenth century was quite different. The system of the world proposed in Aristotle's books had nothing to replace. It followed nothing. The system simply seemed to rest in the absolute, like a sort of revelation. It had to succeed, as a new philosophy succeeds in the thought of young generations that it initiates into philosophical life. At that point Aristotelianism was not a philosophy; it was *the* philosophy.

But we must add that if Aristotle's doctrine was a revelation, it was a completely peculiar revelation, rather troubling in nature. For centuries the best minds lived the sweet and consoling illusion that the sum of our beliefs and knowledge constitutes a kind of unique system. A single wisdom, which is God, suffices both as rational philosophy and doctrine of salvation. Starting from the revelation of the dogmatic expression of divine mysteries, human thought can and should descend toward the speculations of human reason without having to cross over any real break in continuity. That is why the difference is not so great between the philosophers or sibyls of paganism and the prophets and theologians of the true religion. Both can be considered brethren who march toward the same goal and are separated only by more or less great distances. When one is not a Christian who goes from faith to intelligence, said St. Anselm, one is necessarily a pagan who goes from intelligence to faith. If we seek the reason, it is either because we believe or else because we do not believe. But in any case, philosophical speculation spontaneously directs itself toward the same object as faith. *Quamvis enim illi ideo rationem quaerant, quia non credunt, nos vero, quia credimus, unum idemque tamen est quod quaerimus.*[1]

Clearly, one of the first effects of discovering Aristotle had to be to dispel brutally this illusion. For the first time an authentic pagan presented himself. The reach of the finest human reason, when abandoned by God to its own powers, could be measured experimentally. The result

1. Anselm, *Cur Deus Homo*, II, 364.

of this gripping experience presented by history, is that a yawning gap appeared between so-called natural revelation and genuine revelation. To discover Aristotle was first of all to discover that human reason does not spontaneously move toward revelation. Whether the Aristotle discovered in the Middle Ages was the real Aristotle or only an Aristotle deformed by Arab speculation is something that we still argue about today. The interest of the discovery does not lie in this problem of history of philosophy. It resides solely in the divergence between revelation and reason that abruptly appeared. What St. Jerome and St. Gregory proclaimed and St. Peter Damian recalled was confirmed in the most resounding way: the syllogism does not lead to the true God.

Who was this God of the philosophers? What universe was he the God of? For Aristotle, God is pure act, pure thought who thinks himself eternally. This is to say that God knows nothing outside himself, from which it follows that he knows neither singulars nor future contingents. Therefore, the details of things, the actions that stem from human wills, escape God, and that very fact negates the fundamental dogma of Providence in the most radical way. In the presence of this God who is not providence, stands a universe that is coeternal with him. Nothing in either an immutable God or in essences whose definition is indifferent to time permits us to suppose that the world could have begun to exist. If the world is, it has always been, and the species that populate the world have always existed with it. Adam disappears at the same time as the first chapter of Genesis. There was no time before creation nor was there a first human. Placed in this world, humans are composed of matter, which is their body, and a soul, which is the form of the body. Therefore, it is evident that when death occurs, the soul perishes with the body, whose form it is. Only human intelligence survives the death of the body, although that is because it is not the form of the body. There is a single intelligence of the whole human species. This intelligence comes into contact with the body and touches it, at the instant when the operation of knowing is produced. So, the intelligence's immortality stems precisely from its being the nature of the species, permanent and indestructible. Individual souls, as such, cannot aspire to immortality. If we admit a viewpoint like this, God himself cannot make our corruptible soul immortal. We no longer have rewards to hope for or punishments to fear in a future life, and human last ends are definitively abolished.[2] In the face of such contradictions that suddenly appear between the conclusions of natural reason and

2. For the details of these doctrines, see Mandonnet, *Siger*, see vol. 1, ch. 7.

the teaching of revelation, how was one not to despair ultimately about their agreement?

Something like this must have been the initial response of some medieval philosophers, and notoriously it was the settled attitude assumed by the philosophers we call Averroists. The position called the "doctrine of double truth," which is usually attributed to the Averroists, simply states the divorce between revelation and reason. In reality, this customary designation of the Averroist attitude is infelicitous, and these philosophers did not choose it themselves. Their adversaries imposed it upon them. At the University of Paris, the Averroists occupied a well-defined position. The great majority of them belonged to the Arts Faculty. They are the thirteenth-century successors to those dialecticians who, at least in theory, were supposed to restrict their teaching to the truths defined by the seven liberal arts. The domain reserved to them is that of natural reason, and their teaching can only be considered to be the initiation and preparation required for a higher teaching, namely theology. The discovery of Aristotle's philosophy could not fail to transform completely the intellectual, moral, and religious position held by the masters of liberal arts. Whereas Abelard had nothing further to say when he had ended his teaching of dialectic and had to become a theologian if he wanted to confront other problems, the most insignificant thirteenth-century master of arts found himself in possession of a vast domain that, beside the old dialectic, included psychology, ethics, and metaphysics. Early on, the University of Paris Arts Faculty had to regulate the teaching of the new sciences whose proprietor the faculty had become, and to establish the order in which Aristotle's treatises containing the new sciences were to be read and commented. The *Ethics* was to be covered in twelve weeks, if one studied it along with another book, or in six weeks if one studied it alone. Each work had its place and date, fixed in the plans of study that the faculty statutes had organized.[3] The situation of a master of arts

3. *Chartularium*, I, 278 (text 246), Statutum Facultatis Artium de modo docendi et regendi in artibus: "Veterem logicam, videlicet librum Porphirii, praedicamentorum, periarmeneias, divisionum et topicorum Boetii, excepto quarto, in festo Annunciationis beate Virginis, vel ultima die legibili precedente; Priscianum minorem et majorem, topica et elenchos, priora et posteriora dicto tempore vel equali terminare teneantur. Ethicas quantum ad quatuor libros in XII septimanis, si cum alio legantur; si per se non cum alio, in medietate temporis . . . Physicam Aristotelis, metaphysicam et librum de animalibus in festo sancti Johannis Baptiste; librum celi et mundi, librum primum metheorum cum cuarto in Ascensione; librum de Anima, si cum naturalibus legatur, in festo Ascensionis, si autem cum logicalibus, in festo Annunciacionis beate

who imparted such teaching was manifestly very different from that of the old dialecticians. He was led to consider from the viewpoint of pure natural reason some problems that he previously considered as reserved to theology and theologians. Central questions like Providence, nature, and immortality of the soul were among them, and the student in arts saw his masters examine them from the viewpoint of reason not yet illuminated by the light of faith. The masters of arts may have the scruples to approach such problems philosophically. They may have accepted it as a duty not to do so, as they were afterwards required to do. Even supposing that, their hearers could not fail to draw the necessary conclusions of the teaching they received. It was not necessary to make the comparison between dogma and Aristotle's philosophy. It forced itself on those students.

Their *de facto* situation obliged Arts Faculty masters to adopt an ambiguous stance, close to what the Averroists seem to have held. Since physics and metaphysics had been added to dialectic, they taught a doctrine about whose truth they were not supposed to pronounce themselves. As masters of arts, they could say that Aristotle had taught this or that solution to such and such a problem and that, consequently, those solutions are the results to which we arrive when we are situated in the standpoint of pure reason. But they were unable to say whether Aristotle's philosophy is true or not, because the touchstone of the truth of philosophical doctrines was in the hands of theologians. The most prudent and submissive among the arts masters willingly resigned themselves to this situation. The decree emitted by the Faculty of Arts on April 1, 1272, following imprudent actions of certain of its members, precisely defined all kinds of reservations to which the majority of its members bound themselves. They were never to resolve or even discuss purely theological questions like the Trinity, the incarnation, or other similar matters. That would exceed the boundaries assigned to them, and violate Aristotle's precept against disputing with a geometer without knowing geometry. Those who commit such an infraction must retract publicly within three days after the faculty's notice, and in the same place where they committed the infraction, under pain of permanent exclusion from the faculty. Every master or bachelor of arts at Paris who permitted himself to discuss

---

Virginis; librum de Generatione in cathedra sancti Petri; librum de causis in septem septimanis; librum de sensu et sensato in sex septimanis; librum de sompno et vigilia in quinque septimanis; librum de memoria et reminiscentia in duabus septimanis; librum de differentia spiritus et anime in duabis septimanis, Librum de morte et vita in una septimana."

a question involving both philosophy and faith, and to resolve it contrary to the teaching of faith, was to be permanently excluded from the faculty as a heretic. Likewise, it was forbidden to deal with difficult texts or problems concerning matters of faith without resolving them. Every argument contrary to faith must be refuted. Every text contrary to faith had to be interpreted. Those incapable of doing so had to avoid engaging with this sort of difficulties and pass them over in silence, or just pronounce the errors they could not refute to be simply false and totally erroneous.[4]

Consequently, it was not enough for a master of arts to keep away from dogma strictly speaking in order to avoid all difficulty. Anyone who was satisfied to interpret Aristotle as an Averroist and as an Aristotelian committed a very grave imprudence and could not avoid directly ending in heresy. To stay on the straight path, it was not enough to refrain from any incursion into the realm of the Trinity or the incarnation. It was also necessary for the master of arts to keep his eye constantly on the rule of theological truth. Those masters of arts who refused to go so far and simply claimed to affirm that, according to Aristotle and reason, the world is eternal and the individual soul perishable, or that the God whom pure philosophical reason reaches is not a providential God, found themselves immediately implicated in the oddest difficulties. These philosophers in no way taught that there are two simultaneous and contradictory truths. Siger of Brabant always declared that truth is on the side of faith. Since he was not a theologian, his only goal was to explain the doctrine of the philosophers, especially Aristotle, but it was still understood that truth can be difficult, and that, for example, revelation may teach us truths about

4. *Chartularium*, I, April 1, 1272, 499, text 441: "Universis ac singulis presentibus ac futuris sancte matris ecclesie filiis . . . omnes et singuli magistri logicalis scientie seu etiam naturalis Parisius professores, salutem in omnium Salutari. Statuimus et ordinamus quod nullus magister vel bachellarius nostre facultatis aliquam questionem pure theologicam, utpote de Trinitate et Incarnatione sicque de consimilibus omnibus, determinare seu etiam disputare presumat, tanquam sibi determinatos limites transgrediens, cum sicut dicit Philosophus non Geometram cum geometra sit penitus inconveniens disputare. Statuimus insuper et ordinamus quod si quaestionem aliquam, que fidem videatur attingere simulque philosophiam, alicubi disputaverit Parisius, si illam contra fidem determinaverit, ex tunc ab eadem nostra societate tanquam hereticus perpetuo sit privatus. Superaddentes iterum quod si magister vel bachellarius aliquis nostre facultatis passus aliquos difficiles vel aliquas questiones legat vel disputet, que fidem videantur dissolvere, aliquatenus videatur, rationes autem seu textum, si que contra fidem, dissolvat vel etiam falsas simpliciter et erroneas totaliter esse concedat, et aliter hujusmodi difficultates vel in texto vel in auctoritatibus disputare vel legere non presumat, sed hec tanquam totaliter erronea pretermittat."

the soul that natural reason would be incapable of acquiring by its own powers.[5] The decision of the Catholic faith must take precedence over Aristotle's doctrine each time that they are in opposition, and the fact that philosophy or philosophers reach a conclusion must not prevail against the truth of faith that is infallible and cannot deceive.[6] With greater reason, this must be so when philosophy leaves us in doubt concerning the solution of a difficult problem. At such times, faith, which surpasses all human reason, indicates to us in the surest fashion the alternative in which truth is found.[7]

Siger of Brabant did not teach the simultaneous existence of two contradictory truths. The adversaries of Siger and of the other Averroists attributed this theory to them as a necessary consequence of the Averroist position. For example, St. Thomas decided that the necessary conclusions of reason are necessarily true, that the opposite of these conclusions is necessarily false and impossible, and that to oppose reason to faith is to say that what faith affirms is false and impossible. Perhaps we have there the preambles of Étienne Tempier's condemnation of 1277, which gave the Averroist conception of the relations between reason and faith a label it still bears today. By accusing the Averroists of maintaining as true according to philosophy theses that were not true according to faith, the bishop of Paris forever saddled Averroism with the doctrine of the double truth.[8] Today it is very difficult for us to know with certainty what exactly

5. Mandonnet, *Siger*, 2:153–54: "Quaerimus enim hic solum intentionem philosophorum et praecipue Aristotelis, etsi forte Philosophus senserit aliter quam veritas se habeat, et per revelationem aliqua de anima tradita sint, quae per rationes naturales conclude non possunt. Sed nihil ad nos nunc de Dei miraculis, cum de naturalibus naturaliter disseramus."

6. Mandonnet, *Siger*, 2:164: "Certum est enim secundum veritatem quae mentiri non potest, quod animae intellectivae multiplicantur mutiplicatione corporum humanorum. Tamen aliqui philosophi contrarium senserunt."—Cf. 2:157.

7. Mandonnet, *Siger*, 2:169: "Et iterum Philosophus vult intellectum esse in potentia ad species intelligibiles, et receptivum specierum, et denudatum a speciebus, quod si sit unus, erit semper plenus speciebus et destruetur intellectus agens. Et ideo dico propter difficultatem praemissorum et quorumdam aliorum, quod mihi dubium fuit a longo tempore, quid via rationis naturalis in praedicto problemate sit tenendum, et quid senserit Philosophus de dicta quaestione, et in tali dubio fidei adhaerendum est, quae omnem rationem humanam superat."

8. Aquinas, *De Unitate Intellectus*, ch. 7: "Ergo sentit quod fides sit de aliquibus quorum contraria de necessitate concludi possunt. Cum autem de necessitate concludi non possit nisi verum necessarium, cujus oppositum est falsum et impossibile, sequitur secundum ejus dictum, quod fides sit de falso et impossibili, quod etiam Deus facere non potest."—*Chartularium* I, 543, text 473: "quod nonnulli Parisius studentes

these philosophers really thought. It is evident that the circumstances imposed great reserve on someone like Siger of Brabant, but the fact that he would not have expressed himself any differently if he had simply desired to protect himself from persecution does not prove that this is the reason why he effectively adopted the language he did. In the always very measured expressions he uses, nothing permits us to deny that he simply wanted with total sincerity to expound the conclusions to which natural reason led, all the while referring the more certain conclusions of faith to those of purely natural reason.

But it must be added that not all Averroists had Siger's moderation and perhaps his sincerity. If we trust the expressions St. Thomas uses in *De Unitate Intellectus* and certain theses condemned by Bishop Étienne Tempier, several Averroists, who perhaps did not write or whose writings are now lost, may plausibly have taken the side of reason against faith. It is not Siger of Brabant who declared: *Latini pro principiis eorum haec non recipiunt, scilicet quid sit unus intellectus tantum, quia forte lex eorum est in contrarium*. He never doubted the genuine teaching of his faith on this point, and he never spoke of Christian faith or the faith of Catholics, as if he did not include himself among the Catholics and the partisans of this faith.[9] By contrast, we can hardly doubt that other Averroists wrote or said what Siger of Brabant did not teach. St. Thomas argues against an adversary who declares himself a Christian and yet speaks of the law of Christians or Catholics as if he no longer had anything in common with them from the instant he became a philosopher. This adversary is evidently someone real. These are not invented phrases any more than the propositions condemned by Étienne Tempier in which the pure thought of Averroes is expressed: that no state of life is more excellent than cultivating philosophy; that the only wise men in the world are philosophers; that nothing is to be believed but what is known of itself or can be directly deduced from what is known of itself; that in order to be certain about a

---

in artibus propie facultatis limites excedentes quosdam manifestos et execrabiles errores, quasi dubitabiles in scolis tractatre et disputare presumunt. Dicere enim ea esse vera secundum philosophiam, sed non secundum fidem catholicam, quasi sint due contrarie veritates."

9. Evidently the expressions *lex eorum* and *Catholici* are what anger St. Thomas. These expressions just like the *forte* that precedes them, are not found in the texts of Siger to which Fr. Mandonnet remits (1:152n1). It seems to us that Fr. Mandonnet clearly goes beyond what it is allowable to conclude from these comparisons of texts, when he connects the refutation undertaken by St. Thomas back to Siger of Brabant alone.

question humans must not be satisfied with authority; that the Christian law prevents being educated; that there are fables and errors in the Christian law as in other religions; that we know no more by knowing theology; that the arguments of theologians are founded on fables; that what is impossible according to philosophy is absolutely impossible.[10] But by the very fact that these freethinkers discovered authentic Averroism and accepted its doctrine to its ultimate consequences, they manifestly refused to adhere to a doctrine of double truth. For them as for Averroists, there is only one truth, and it is the truth of philosophy. Religion presents this same truth in a crude pictorial way that is suitable for ignorant minds, but the philosopher has nothing to do with it, and we can really say of him: *quod plus nihil scitur propter scire theologiam.*

Consequently, if we compare the attitudes of these different philosophers, none of them ever held the doctrine of the double truth. Perhaps Siger of Brabant did not hold it simply out of prudence, but perhaps also because he preferred the truths of faith to the conclusions of reason. It is indisputable and must be maintained that Siger of Brabant thought differently as a philosopher than as a Christian,[11] but to then declare that such a position is contradictory is to speak as a dogmatic philosopher rather than as a historian. The position became contradictory only when, with St. Thomas or Étienne Tempier, we add that the necessary conclusions of philosophy are necessarily true. This is something Siger of Brabant never told us. It is not contradictory to hold that certain conclusions are philosophical and that others are true, when we explicitly admit that philosophy's conclusion can be false, *etsi forte Philosophus senserit aliter quam veritas se habeat.* Therefore, we have no sufficient reason to affirm that Siger's religious faith "was at least rather feeble if not entirely fictitious." To conclude that, we would need to know that Siger lied when he situated the whole truth on the side of faith. In the present state of the texts, Siger does not provide the slightest indication that he dissembled or joked.

If we can say that Siger of Brabant did not teach the doctrine of double truth out of lack of confidence in reason, we can likewise maintain that others did not teach it out of lack of firmness of their faith. Those who admitted *quod nihil est credendum nisi per se notum, vel ex per se notis possit declarari* and that *sapientes mundi sunt philosophi tantum* are

10. *Chartularium*, I, 153ff., propositions 40, 154, 37, 150, 175, 174, 153, 152, 146.

11. Mandonnet, *Siger*, 2:153n1.

thinkers who openly admitted Averroes's genuine doctrine and mercilessly drew all of its conclusions. For the Arab philosopher, the absolute truth was the philosophical truth. He considered that it constituted the object of an esoteric teaching reserved to the minds capable of receiving it. As for the faith, it constituted the equivalent of philosophy for the use of simple folk. Its content is philosophical truth translated into symbolic formulas by prophetical inspiration. Between the teaching of rational truth and the teaching of philosophy falls a mixed teaching, that of theology. It is adapted to minds that are incapable of pure philosophy but that are not satisfied with pure and simple faith. Averroes did not hesitate at all about where truth was to be found.[12] For the philosopher the only authentic truth is philosophical truth and rational speculation. While piously preserving religion for popular consumption, the philosopher must never hesitate to subordinate revelation.[13]

That there were partisans of this attitude in the period of Siger of Brabant seems to be proven by the formulas condemned by Étienne Tempier. Like Averroes, these thirteenth-century Averroists put the whole truth on the side of philosophy. To the doctrine of Averroes they added only a rather brutal disregard for the established order. No thirteenth-century document lets us directly study the thought of any of these unbelievers, but the beginning of the fourteenth century amply compensates for this gap. The work of the Averroist John of Jandun, who fled to the court of Louis of Bavaria and assisted him in his struggle against the papacy, offers us a fairly good specimen.[14] As it is easy to foresee, John of Jandun does not openly proclaim the absolute value of philosophy and the superiority of reason over faith. On the contrary, he declares that the realm of philosophy, which is his, must not be confused with the domain of truth, which is that of faith. Like Siger of Brabant, John of Jandun assumes no other task than to slavishly repeat what Aristotle and Averroes say. He presents

12. Gauthier, *La théorie d'Ibn Rochd*, 177–82.

13. Gauthier, *La théorie d'Ibn Rochd*, 109.

14. A colleague of Marsilius of Padua, John of Jandun taught in the Faculty of Arts of the University of Paris at the start of the fourteenth century. In 1324 they composed together the *Defensor Pacis*, which proclaimed that sovereignty resides in the people. In 1326 they took refuge at the court of Louis of Bavaria, where Michael of Cesena and William of Ockham were to seek asylum in 1328. John XXII excommunicated John of Jandun in 1327, and he died in 1328. We quote the commentary *Super Tres Libros De Anima* according to the Venice, 1544 edition and the *Quaestiones de Physica Auditu* by the 1501 edition that gives no indication of the place of publication.

himself simply as Aristotle and Averroes's monkey,[15] an attitude that does not keep him from exhibiting a rather naïve delight when he happens to find something completely on his own.[16] He is certainly an imitator of Averroes with whose authority he occasionally associates that of Siger of Brabant.[17] For him, St. Thomas is only an *antiquus doctor*. Though the *melior expositor inter latinos*,[18] his constant failing is to wear himself out vainly contradicting Averroes.[19] Besides, many Latins have made the mistake of losing sight of philosophy in their old age and forgetting it for theology,[20] but that is not a sufficient excuse for us to commit the same mistake in our turn. Only one foundation of philosophical truth exists, *ratio sensata*, which means the agreement between the testimony of our senses and the conclusions of our reason.[21]

15. According to Wulf, *Histoire de philosophie médiévale*, 451.

16. John of Jandun, *De Anima*, bk. III, questions 1 and 6 at *rationes*. See particularly *De Anima*, III, q. 9 at *His visis*, and particularly: "et in hac declarationis ordinatione gaudebat animus meus cum laude Dei, quia a nullo doctore extrinseco existente, nec sonante, nec scriptura eam suscepi, sed a vero doctore qui mentem illuminat et veritatem ostendit. Quod si haec declaratio non est completa, erit aliis principium perscrutandi."

17. On Averroes, see John of Jandun, *De Anima*, III, 38, near the end: "Nullus enim in rebus physicis inventus est illus subtilem perspicacitatem excedere, imo nec ei aequipari." Cf. *Physica*, VIII, 21 at *Istam quaestionem*, and VI, 2 at *rationes*.—*De Anima*, III, 5: "Et debes scire quod istam solutionem hujus rationis qualiter homo intelligit quantum ad aliquid posuit reverendus doctor philosophiae magister Remigius de Brabantia [*sic*, for *Sigerus*] in quodam suo tractatu de intellectu qui sic incipit: cum anima sit aliorum cognoscitiva." This is the *incipit* of Siger's *De Anima Intellectiva*.

18. John of Jandun, *Physica* II, 5 at *Tunc dico*; I, 3, at *De ista quaestione*; IV, 6, at *istam quaestionem*; IV, 46 at *ista quaestio*.

19. John of Jandun, *Physica*, VII, 2 at *questionem*: "Et intelligendum quod sanctus Thomas qui in omnibus aut pluribus in quibus potuit, conatus fuit contradicere Commentatori."—Ibid.: "Sed revera, salva reverentia hujus hominis ipse inaniter laborat contra Commentatorem, sicut et in omnibus aliis philosophicis in quibus ei objicicit."—Ibid., at *auctoritatem*: "Dico quod ego non credo ei in hoc sicut nec in aliis conclusionibus philosophicis in quibus contradicit Commentatori, sed magis credendum est Commentatori in illis quae debent probari demonstratione, et hoc dictum sit."

20. John of Jandun, *De Anima*, III, 23, near end: "Vel dicamus expositores latinos non expressisse hunc modum necessitatis intellectus agentis; quod non provenit ex ignorantia, nec eo quod illi non crediderunt illum esse unum entium, sed hoc contigit multis ex eo quod ipsi in sua senectute magis fuerunt intenti circa theologica quam circa philosophica, et ideo multas conclusiones philosophiae naturalis praetermiserunt sine sufficienti declaratione."

21. John of Jandun, *Physica*, preface: "Conditio necessaria veris demonstrationibus est ut illud quod apparet ad sensum non differat ab eo quod videtur secundum

These tendencies evidently let John of Jandun find permanent disagreement between philosophy and theology. He is a rigorous and, if we may say so, classic Averroist. Just one distinction enables him to resolve every conflict between faith and reason. The domain of reason is also the domain of the natural, the normal. Consequently, what reason concludes necessarily expresses what must naturally exist. But the domain of faith corresponds to the supernatural and the miraculous. Through his omnipotence, God can do what reason represents as naturally impossible. Therefore, it is legitimate to admit the truth of the conclusions of faith, even if they are rationally contradictory, because miracles are things that an omnipotent God can do.

No matter what our reactions may be to John of Jandun's tenets, nothing allows us to doubt his sincerity, if our only reason is the mediocrity of the method he uses to reconcile philosophy and theology. No *a priori* limit can be set to human credulity in matters of justificatory sophistry. What is troubling in John of Jandun is not only what he says, but the tone in which he says it. He is not satisfied with regretfully observing the oppositions between reason and faith; in some manner he provokes them.[22] And when the occasion presents itself, he never fails to recall complacently the whole parade of rational absurdities to which faith obliges us. For example, if he must conclude that faith forces us to believe in the existence of a rational soul that is the form of the human body and to deny the philosophically necessary doctrine of the separate intellect, John of Jandun resolutely declares that, although the latter is the opinion of Aristotle and Averroes, that one must express oneself otherwise. It must be said that the rational soul is the substantial form that confers being on the human body and that it is really united to the body. The soul is a substantial form that does not owe its origin to any particular agent that draws it from the matter's potency, but to the universal agent that is the cause of the total being, namely the supreme God who created it by a pure and simple production without movement on his part and without the transmutation of any preexisting object. Moreover, God created everything else this way. This substance will be permanently maintained in existence by God's power alone, which will confer immortality on it,

rationem. Ergo rationis sensatae, id est sensibilibus concordantis veritas est experta . . . ratio autem sensata, id est sensibilibus concordans indubitanter haberi non potest sine notitia rerum sensiblium quibus debet ratio concors esse."

22. For example, John of Jandun seems to make freedom of indifference an article of faith. Cf. *De Anima*, III, 41.

although it is naturally corruptible. "I say moreover, and I firmly hold" that this substance has natural faculties that are not acts of corporeal organs, but have their immediate foundation in the essence of the soul. They are the possible intellect, the agent intellect, and the will. These faculties are superior to the capacity of corporeal matter, and they are only present in humans by reason of the soul whose substance cannot be completely included in matter. Although the soul is in matter, it still retains a certain action in which the body does not participate. All these attributes of the soul really belong to it according to our faith, and it is absolutely necessary to grant them to our faith. It is also necessary to grant that the soul can suffer from corporeal fires after death, although it is incorporeal itself, and that it can be reunited to the body by order of God, its creator. "I do not intend to furnish the demonstration of all that, but I believe it" on simple faith like many other things that must be believed without demonstrative reason, on the pure authority of Scripture, and on the proof by miracles. It is in this faith without reasons that merit is found, because *fides non habet meritum ubi ratio humana praebet experimentum.*[23] It is impossible for an Averroist to heap up more absurdities in fewer words.

John of Jandun not only expounds the contradictions between faith and reason, but with visible complacency he further finds ironical expressions to show us he is not taken in. If he admits the truth of an otherwise philosophically indefensible dogma, he declares he admits it with all the contradictory consequences that can also be drawn from it by demonstrative reason. Better to admit it without discussion than to deny it, but that is also better than to seek to refute the philosophical reasons invoked against it, because the insufficiency of the refutation would have the effect of weakening this truth instead of upholding it.[24] If the issue is the infinity of time, Jean of Jandun declares it eternal in the philosopher's eyes, but limited in the eyes of the believer. That time had a beginning and has to have an end must be believed. Doubtless, this is not an evident truth or a humanly demonstrable conclusion, but it must be believed on the authority of revelation, and the habit of our hearing it since childhood greatly helps us to believe it, like a number of other things of the same kind.[25] He believes what faithful Catholics say on the subject of immortality, but he is incapable of demonstrating it. If

23. Cf. appendix, text 1. [Translator: there are no quotation marks in Gilson's text here.]

24. Cf. appendix, text 2.

25. Cf. appendix, text 13.

there are people who can, so much the better for them; *gaudeant qui hoc sciunt*. John knows that God can make the soul immortal miraculously, but he adds: "How, I have no idea; God knows."[26] John of Jandun prefers to say that souls are not immortal philosophically speaking, rather than to attribute to philosophers a doctrine they do not hold, because it is reprehensible to lie. "If someone can demonstrate the soul's immortality," he adds, "I congratulate him and do not envy him, but I confess he is more able than I." Again, if the issue is creation, John of Jandun declares: "It must be admitted simply and with Christian faith that God himself creates the world from nothing and without any pre-existing matter." Pagan philosophers did not know this manner of producing something. There is no reason to be surprised by this because the idea cannot be conceived starting from sensible things nor can demonstrations be provided that match with sensible things. This is why pagans, all of whose knowledge is based on reasoning in agreement with facts, never possessed knowledge of creation. Much more so because this manner of production is rare, because it only happened once, and that leaked out much later.[27] In the face of such an accumulation of indications, the hypothesis of irony is more economical than the hypothesis of naïveté, and it certainly seems that John of Jandun resolutely sacrifices faith to reason as a good disciple of Averroes.

The doctrine of double truth has never been held. It is simply a reduction to the absurd attempted by orthodox theologians against heterodox philosophers. However, it can be said that even discharged from this absurdity with which Latin Averroism was sometimes unjustly encumbered, Latin Averroism testifies to a crisis whose solution it does not provide. Evidently, such an attitude does not correspond to the requirements of theology. Even in the case where the sincerity of certain Averroists can be acknowledged, it is impossible that the church should recognize a formal contradiction between faith and reason. The spread of such a thesis could only expose faith to the gravest dangers. Faith can live without demonstration; indeed it must not be demonstrable if it is to remain faith. However, without being demonstrable, faith must remain at least believable, and the faith of the Averroist was difficult to believe. From there come the condemnations handed down against Averroism in general in 1276 and 1277 and the later condemnation of the leaders of

26. Cf. appendix, text 4.

27. Cf. appendix, text 14.

Averroism in particular.[28] But this doctrine opens up no perspective of development for philosophy itself. The Averroists certainly observed that purely rational speculation had been possible, but they believed or professed to believe that such rational speculation was insufficient of itself to judge its own truth. If we suppose a sincere Averroist, philosophy must necessarily appear to him as ending in innumerable errors. If, on the other hand, we consider only those Averroists who dissemble real incredulity, under their apparent submission to dogma, we observe that they were no better endowed. Indeed, at the start of the movement, the acceptance of Aristotelianism by the Averroists, even when it contradicted dogma, could constitute an act of philosophical freedom. But the very condition in which their adherence had seemed possible to them definitely bound them to the letter of the doctrine they claimed to accept. The thesis they believed they had to maintain from the start was that their philosophy was identified with Aristotle. They only dared to set philosophy and reason in conflict with dogma on the condition of regarding themselves as simple echoes of the philosopher's voice. For the Averroists, seeking the truth is reduced to seeking Aristotle's intention and the meaning of his doctrine. They boasted of inventing nothing and of simply being spokesmen of the master whose doctrine was identical to reason. That is why we have no example, possibly excepting Epicureanism, of a philosophical school that is more bound to routine and more sterile than Averroism. It was forever enclosed in a certain interpretation of a certain system, from which nothing summoned them to emerge, since Averroism did not wish to attempt the slightest effort to adapt philosophy to dogma, and from which it could not have emerged without being exposed to the reproach of dogmatizing on its own account. The Averroist School will traverse the centuries without learning anything, and Galileo himself will collide with the irreducible opposition of these hardened Aristotelians. Latin Averroism was not the point of departure of a new philosophical era, but the witness to a violent crisis that the recent discovery of Aristotle's philosophy had precipitated, and from which a new philosophy would come forth.

28. Mandonnet, *Siger*, 1:276.

APPENDIX TO CHAPTER 3

Texts of John of Jandun on the Relations between Reason and Faith

Agent intellect

1. *De Anima*, book III, question 5

Nec est aliquid inconveniens quod ipsius hominis sit duplex forma propria, quarum una det ejus corpori esse substantiale, et alia esse intrinsecum operans, a qua denominatur intelligens modo supradicto, praecipue quia homo est ens nobilius et perfectius omnium quae sunt hic. De hoc tamen inquiretur inferius seorsum et divisim ubi quaeretur an anima sensitiva et intellectiva in homine sint una sola substantia animae an diversae Sed attendendum est quod licet ista fuerit determinatio Aristotelis et Commentatoris, praecipue et hoc non revoco in dubium, tamen dico et firmiter aliter esse dicendum assero, scilicet quod ipsa anima intellectiva est forma substantialis dans esse et unita secundum esse corpori humano, et est talis forma substantialis quae habet initium esendi non quidem ab aliquo agente particulari educente eam de potentia materiae, sed ab agente universali quod est causa totius esse, seu a Deo supremo, producente eam simplici productione sine motu et transmutatione ex nullo subjecto, sicut et omnia alia creavit, et ista quidem substantia virtute divina perpetuabitur in futurum quamvis sit annihilabilis de se. Dico etiam et teneo firmiter hanc substantiam habere virtutes quasdam naturales quae non sunt actus aliquorum corporalium organorum, sed fundantur immediate in essentia animae, et sunt intellectus possibilis et agens et voluntas. Istae quidem virtutes sunt elevata supra materiam, et capacitatem materiae corporalis superexcellunt, et facultatem ejus supergrediuntur ratione substantiae animae quae non potest totaliter includi a materia, et quamvis ipsa sit in materia, tamen remanet ei aliqua actio in qua materia corporalis non communicat, et omnia talia attributa ei secundum fidem nostram verissima sunt simpliciter et omnino. Et quod ipsa pati potest ab igne corporali et reuniri corpori post mortem jussum creatoris Dei. Horum autem demonstrationem inducere non intendo, sed simplici fide haec puto esse credenda, ut et alia muta quae credenda sunt sine ratione demonstrativa, sola auctoritate sacrae Scripture et divinis miraculis approbata. Et sic recipiendo talia nos meremur. Dicunt enim Doctores fidem non habere meritum ubi ratio humana praebet experimentum.

Rationes autem philosophorum quae contra istam viam esse videntur, solvendae sunt secundum praemissa. Omnes enim procedunt si poneretur animam rationalem esse factam a generante particulari, et per extractionem de potentia materiae, sed quia non est ita, immo ipsa est creata a Deo immediate, ideo multa potest habere quae aliae formae naturales habere non possunt, scilicet quod ipsa remaneat post mortem secundum suam substantiam, non autem inquantum forma, et quod ipsa non sit extensa secundum extensionem corporis, et quod recipiat non individualiter sed universaliter, et quod sit intellectiva per se et quod possit recipere species intelligibiles et intelligere, et tamen ipsum corpus non recipiet istos actus neque etiam aliqua pars corporis, et omnia talia. Quod si alicui primo aspectu non videretur sufficere ad solutiones rationum, non tamen propter hoc debet conturbari, quia certum est quod auctoritas divina majorem fidem debet facere quam quaecumeque ratio humanitus inventa, sicut auctoritas unius philosophi praevalet alicui debili rationi quam aliquis puer induceret.

2. *De Anima*, book III, question 7

Sed quamvis haec opinio sit Commentatoris et Aristotelis et quamvis etiam haec opinio non possit removeri rationibus demonstrativis, tamem ego dico aliter et dico quod intellectus non est unus numero in omnibus hominibus, immo ipse est numeratus in diversis secundum numerationem corporum humanorum, et est perfectio dans esse simpliciter. Hoc autem non probo aliqua ratione demonstrativa, quia hoc non scio esse possibile, et si quis hoc sciat, gaudeat. Istam autem conclusionem assero simpliciter esse veram et indubitanter teneo sola fide, et ad rationes contra istam opinionem responderem breviter concedendo tanquam possibilia apud Deum omnia illa ad quae illae rationes deducunt tanquam impossibilia. Quod enim aliqua forma dans esse materiae precipue sine quacumque alia forma substantiali non sit extensa secundum extensionem corporis, hoc non video nisi ex solo miraculo divini contingere posse, et quod aliqua forma individuata individuatione materiae corporalis recipiat comprehensionem universalem diversam a comprehensione sensitiva, hoc non video possibile nisi solum per divinum miraculum, et hujusmodi similia. Unde secundum eamdem radicem qua teneo conclusionem, teneo omnia illa quae ad illam conclusionem necessario consequuntur, et non aliter imo si ex illa positione virtute argumentationis necessario aliquis contradictoria concluderet, adhuc magis vellem ea concedere quam istam positionem negare. Et puto quod qui per alium modum nititur solvere rationes quasdam contra istam positionem, ipsa ex insufficientia solutionis magis redderet hanc positionem improbabilem quam sustineat eamdem, et ideo non plus de isto ad praesens.

3. *De Anima*, book III, question 7

Ex positione catholica conceditur quod Deus immediate agit in corpus humanum de novo, et creat animam intellectivam de nihilo, et quod eo ipso quod aliquod agens particulare aliquam dispositionem inducit in materia, licet per actum deformem et non placentem Deo, creat de novo animam infundendo eam corpori, et omnia ista dicit Commentator ficta, quia non sunt per se nota, nec possunt sufficienter demonstrari, et ideo sine dubio parum possunt gloriari deducendo Commentatorem ad inconventientia contra theologiam, quia ad multo plura et majora deducerentur quae in philosophia inconvenientia reputantur et quae solum tanquam mirabilia recipiuntur ut vera.

Immortality of the Soul and Resurrection

4. *De Anima*, book III, question 12, at *Tunc diceretur*

Sed quamvis Aristoteles et Commentator sic dicerent et non possent aliud ponere secundum principia concordantia rebus sensatis, tamen ego dico aliter, scilicet quod anima intellectiva hominis est forma communicans esse suum corpori humano, et indivisibilis omnino, et inextensa et per se et per accidens, et perficit totum corpus humanum et omnes ejus partes sine omni alia forma substantiali inhaerente materiae; et ista anima intellectiva incepit esse de novo postquam non erat, non quidem per generationem, sed per creationem ex nihilo, et ista perpetuabitur a parte post virtute divina; et omnia talia quae dicunt fideles catholici ego dico simpliciter esse vera sine omni dubitatione, sed demonstrare nescio; gaudeant qui hoc sciunt; sed sola fideo teneo et confideor. Rationem in oppositum dissolvo secundum eamdem viam. Quamvis enim omnis forma inhaerens materiae esset corruptibilis, tamen dico quod Deus potest eam perpetuare et praeservare a corruptione in aeternum. Modum tamen nescio; Deus scit.

5. *De Anima*, book III, question 30, near end

Sed dico et indubitanter assero quod anima intellectiva humana non est aeterna a parte ante, sed incipit esse de novo, non quidem per generationem ab aliquo agente particulari, sed per creationem ab ipso Deo creatore omnium, et tamen erit aeterna in futurum Dei voluntate, et tandem reunietur corpori eidem numero in quo fuit Dei voluntate; sed istas veritates demonstrare, aut verbis, aut principiis philosophorum concordes esse ostendere non presumo nec credo esse possibile. Melius autem reputo dicere eos deceptos quam falso aliquid eis imponere cujus contrarium intellexerunt. Per se enim mendacium pravum est et fugiendum, secundum Aristotelem *Ethica*. Has ergo conclusiones assero simpliciter esse veras sola fide, quia credo potentiam Dei omnia posse facere. Et eodem principio responderem ad omnes rationes quibus contra illam veritatem arguitur. Concedo enim omnia quae ex eis necessario sequuntur esse possibilia divinae potentiae. Quod si quis demonstrare sciat et principiis philosophorum concordare, guadeat in illo; et ego ei non invideo, sed eum dico meam capacitatem excellere.

6. *Physica*, book V, question 14, at *de quaestione*

Ex omnibus his manifestum videtur quod impossibile est aliquid corruptum regenerari idem in numero, et prima ratio forte est effacior inter omnes. Considerandum tamen quod licet sic dicerent philosophi, tamen secundum fidem nostram debemus dicere, et ita confiteor et assero simpliciter, quod homo postquam fuerit corruptus vel mortuus, iterum redibit idem numero simpliciter, sed hoc non erit per regenerationem et per agens naturale, et sic procedunt rationes philosophorum; sed per resurrectionem, aut per iterationem, aut per aliqam hujusmodi viam praeternaturalem, et ab agente universali quod est causator omnium nullo praesupposito subjecto, et hoc non improbant rationes adductae.

7. *Physica*, book V, question 14, at *Ad rationes*

Sicut lapis potest manere durior, neque mollior, sed habens duritiem eamdem et eodem gradu, ut dicit Philosophus in 8 hujus. Et tamen non sequitur quod ejus durities eadem numero permaneat in aeternum, quamvis hoc agere posset Deus supremus qui est benedictus in saecula saeculorum, Amen.

8. *De Anima*, book III, question 7

Dicunt ergo catholici quod ex anima intellectiva, non obstante quod sit subsistens, et humano corpore fit unum, et similem modum, immo veriorem poterit assignare Commentator. Dico *veriorem* quia veriori modo fit unum ex forma quae non potest omnino esse sine corpore et ex ipso corpore, quam ex forma quae potest existere sine omni corpore. Nunc autem, secundum catholicos anima Socratis potest existere essentialiter sine omni corpore, et essentialiter existeret sine corpore, nisi accideret miraculum valde magnum ad hoc quod uniatur scilicet resurrectio.

9. *De Anima*, book III, question 30, at *ad quaestionem*

Et occurrit unum dubium mirabile, si quilibet homo habeat suum proprium intellectum qui remanet post mortem, cum sit incorporeus, non distinctus loco et subjecto a phantasmatibus hominum remanentum quare non immutatur ab ipsis phantasmatibus, praecipue cum phantasmata hominum remanentium sint ejusdem speciei cum phantasmatibus ejus qui mortuus est, vel earundem rerum. Et si dicatur quod intellectus hujus hominis sit per naturam individualem appropriatus ad hoc ut recipiat a phantasmatibus hujus hominis, quaeratur de illa natura individuali quid sit, utrum sit substantia vel accidens, et utrum remanet post mortem, et audies mirabilia responderi. Item multi eorum, ut frater Thomas qui ponit animam intellectivam esse formam, et datum esse homini, et quod multiplicatur et numeratur, posuerunt quod omnes virtutes animae praeter intellectum et voluntatem, sunt ejusdem speciei cum virtutibus aliorum animalium, et sic phantasmata, et universaliter species rerum individuales, sunt ejusdem speciei in homine et in bove. Quaeratur ergo ab illis, sicut anima intellectiva Socratis immutatur ab albedine existente in phantasia Socratis, quare non immutatur, post mortem Socratis, a phantasmate albedinis existente in phantasia bovis, et hoc est difficile multum. Item, ponatur quod post mortem Socratis, per multas transmutationes materia quae fuit sub intellectu Socratis iterum disponatur ad hoc quod ex ea generetur homo, quare non requiretur intellectus Socratis ipsi materiae cum fuerit disposita sufficienter? Forte hoc pro tanto est quod dispositiones non erunt eadem cum praecedentibus sed in resurrectione, cum intellectus suus reunietur suo corpori, recipiet dispositiones corporis quae fuerant corruptae. Hoc itaque est omnino supra naturam, et nulli principio philosophiae conveniens, quod corruptum redeat idem numero.

Plurality of Forms

10. *Physica,* book VIII, question 10, at end.
Cf. *Physica*, book VII, question 8

Et tu dices: ergo concedis gradus formarum et pluralitatem in eodem individuo; certo dico quod hoc est verum, et alias probavi seorsum, et dixi ad ea quae in contrarium huic objiciuntur, et puto istam fuisse intentionem Aristotelis et Commentatoris, ut ibidem patuit. Immo illa positio aliquando fuit famosa apud omnes antiquiores, sed post tempus Alberti et Thomae aliquantulum facta est improbabilis propter eorum famositatem, et propter quasdam rationes eorum superficiales, quas ipsi adduxerunt contra istam positionem. Et forte iterum revertetur probabilitas ejus, cum visa fuerit efficacia rationum ejus et debilitas rationum ipsam improbantium.

Freedom

11. *De Anima,* book III, question 41. On astrological determinism, see *De Anima,* book III, question 29

Ad rationem dico breviter quod libertas hominis non consistit in hoc quod voluntas possit non velle bonum judicatum ab intellectu pro illo tunc pro quo stat tale judicium, sed in hoc quod homo possit per intellectum ratiocinari de ordinatis in finem, et per rationem sumptam ex fine potest intelligere quid melius sit de diversis ordinatis in finem. Et quamvis ita diceret Aristoteles, ut credo, tamen dico et simpliciter assero quod voluntas humana sic est libera quod ipsa potest non velle bonum quod sibi ipsi praesentatur per intellectum practicum, et praesentatis majori et minori bonis, adhuc voluntas pro illo tunc potest velle minus bonum et dimittere majus bonum omnibus circumscritis sufficienter. Et hanc conclusionem nescio demonstrare, sed simplici fide teneo esse veram.

Creation and Eternal Movement

12. *Physica,* book VIII, question 3, at *Ad istam quaestionem*

Et est considerandum quod licet Aristoteles et Commentator sic dicunt motum semper fuisse, tamen dico quod secundum fidem et veritatem, et hoc simpliciter determino et indubitanter confiteor, quod motus incepit esse et terminabitur, et non solum motus habuit initium essendi sed etiam omnia alia entia ab ipso primo principio quod est Deus fuerunt facta postquam non erant, non quidem factione proprie dicta et univoca cum factionibus quae nunc contigunt, scilicet per transmutationem et motum, sed factione omnino aequivoce dicta, sine motu et transmutatione sine subjecto praeexistente. Et sic ante primum motum non fuit aliquis motus, quia productio ipsius mobilis non fuit motus, ut frequenter sumitur, nec sequens motum, nec habuit subjectum prius nec illi potentiae productivae praesupponitur aliqua potentia receptiva, idea ratio Aristotelis non procedit. Motus etiam terminabitur, et remanebit motor et mobile in aeternum, propter hoc quod ipsum movens primum movet per voluntatem, et ideo potest destruere motum sine omni innovatione sui et mobilis.

Istam autem conclusionem non probo ratione demonstrativa, sicut nec alias quas fide tenemus et quas credendo movemur; nec puto quod sit possibile homini demonstrare eam ex principiis sensibilibus vel assumptis ex sensibilibus.

Ratio etiam de tempore solvitur . . . Et cum dicitur quod dispositio quae inest pure per accidens insit omnibus individuis illius speciei praeter duobus, hoc est impossibile; et dico quod nihil est impossiblile apud Deum omnipotentem, et multa apparent hominibus impossibilia quae sunt possibilia secundum Deum summum et benedictum.

13. *Physica*, book VI, question 11, at *ad quaestionem*

Considerandum est quod licet Aristoteles ita diceret, ut praemissum est, tamen dico secundum fidem et veritatem quod totum tempus est terminatum a parte ante, ita quod aliquod instans sic fuit initium temporis quod non fuit terminus alterius; et terminabitur a parte post, ita quod erit aliqod instans quod sic erit ultimum temporis praecendentis quod non erit initium alterius temporis sequentis. Hoc autem quamvis non sit per se notum, tamen non est demonstrabile aliqua demonstratione ab homine, sed sic esse credimus sola auctoritate divina et scriptura sanctorum. Et ad hujusmodi et similem credulitatem multum facit consuetudo audiendi a pueritia hujusmodi dicta.
Cf, *Physica*, book VIII, question 4 at *ad quaestionem*.
Sed aliqui profundi perscrutatores de secreto divinae voluntatis dicunt . . .

14. *Physica*, book I, question 22, at *ad quaestionem*

Tenendum est tamen simpliciter et cum fide christiana, quod ipse Deus produxit omnia de novo, ex nullo praeexistente subjecto. Sed illa productio non fuit facti nec fieri, nisi aequivoce, quantumcumque terminus ejus fuerit univocus cum termino factionis naturalis, sed dicitur *creatio* et simplex *emanatio*. Hanc igitur modum ignoraverunt philosophi gentiles. Nec mirum, quia non potest cognosci ex sensibilibus, nec convinci ex aliquibus quae cum sensibilibus concordant. Et ideo illi qui sumpserunt cognitiones suas ex rationibus concordantibus sensatis non pervenerunt ad notitiam hujusmodi factionis. Praecipue quia raro contingit iste modus et nunquam fuit nisi semel, et est valde longum tempus praeteritum postquam fuit.

Illi autem qui istum modum productionis cognoscunt dicuntur per aliam viam cognoscere, scilicet per auctoritates sanctorum et per revelationes et hujusmodi. Per illam autem distinctionem productionis quae facta est, solvuntur argumenta Aristotelis et Averroïs. Probant enim sufficienter quod ex nihil simpliciter non possit aliquid produci productione quae est modus et transmutatione naturalis, sed productione quae est creatio et supernaturalis bene potest.

FOUR

The Historical Significance of Thomism

The very essence of Thomism has long been deemed to be reducible to a naïve confusion between philosophy and theology. It is starting to be acknowledged that Thomism is nothing of the sort. But the first error disappears only to make room for a subtler one for which certain defenders of Thomism are as responsible as its adversaries. St. Thomas's labor, they tell us, did not consist in randomly mixing the data of reason with those of revelation, but in disingenuously seeking out the data of reason in order to orient them in the direction of revelation. In short, St. Thomas elaborated less philosophy than apologetics. If this interpretation of Thomism is sound, the opus of St. Thomas sprang from fundamentally religious concerns, and consequently dogma must play the strictly determining role in it. Accordingly, it is foreseeable that St. Thomas, sacrificing the requirements of philosophical thinking to those of religious faith, will always consider true the philosophical theses most favorable to the requirements of faith. Inversely however, if we observe that the works of Albertus Magnus and his great disciple consisted above all in restoring the integrity of what they considered rational truth, and if it is proven that their philosophy speaks as loudly and firmly in its domain as theology does in its, then we would have to recognize that Thomism is one of the most significant manifestations of human reason's independence. Is this doctrinal synthesis the result of reason being subverted by religious feelings or of an effort by reason to impose itself upon religious feeling? Such is the problem we will ask history to solve.

The Illuminative Way

Patet quam amplia sit via illuminationis et quomodo in omni re quae sentitur, sive quae cognoscitur, interius lateat ipse Deus

St. Bonaventure, *De Reductione Artium ad Theologiam*, number 26

To gauge the scope of the Albertine-Thomist movement exactly and to understand the decisive progress it brings to Western philosophy, it is necessary to begin with St. Bonaventure as a witness to faith and traditional philosophy.

Of all the masters whom the popes' university policy imposed upon the Parisian educational scene, no one seemed better adapted to his task than Brother Bonaventure of the Order of Friars Minor. He had received the Augustinian tradition from his teacher Alexander of Hales as a sacred legacy. His spirit found complete satisfaction of all its needs there, drawing at the same time from St. Augustine's writings the doctrine of salvation as the fathers had transmitted it and the demonstration of the intimate harmony between the witness that faith bears to God and that which the universe and our reason give him. Against the flood of new doctrines, in the face of the triumphs of Aristotle's pagan philosophy, Brother Bonaventure simply sought refuge in his master's teaching and in tradition. For Bonaventure, it suffices to draw from the treasure of Christian philosophy to reestablish the doctrine of the faith in all its purity.[1] Therefore, we may be sure in advance that the notion of erecting an unbreakable wall between our different kinds of knowledge never entered Bonaventure's mind. Like St. Anselm, and perhaps even more, Bonaventure knows perfectly that reason is not faith. He very clearly distinguishes between what is believed and what is known. He is aware that a point comes very soon at which the reason that set out toward God feels its powers failing. But he also knows that help from on high is never denied to tottering reason, and that it can ultimately reach its goal. The goal is intuition of the infinite good that is God. In him alone our soul

1. Bonaventure, *In Sententiarum II*, Praelocutio, p. 1 (in *Opera Omnia*, vol. II): "At quemadmodum in primo libro sententiis adhaesi et patris nostri bonae memoriae fratris Alexandri, sic in consequentibus libris ab eorum vestigiis non recedam. Non enim intendo novas opiniones adversare, sed communes et approbatas retexere. Nec quisquam aestimet, quod novi scripti velim esse fabricator."

can find rest and happiness.[2] We direct ourselves to this goal by means of our reason and our faith. Reason pushes its search as far as its powers allow, and when reason is forced to stop, faith comes to its aid to permit it to go further. Faith certainly does not enrich reason with completely formulated supplementary knowledge, but it permits reason to acquire it. Between the understanding of the real that reason gives us and faith that Scripture's authority gives us, there is room for a quite particular order of knowledge, the credible. The credible comes from an authority added to reason and tends toward the intelligible. Between pure faith and pure reason, there is room for faith to become intelligible to reason.[3] Above evident knowledge acquired by the normal effort of our natural reason, there is a place for another use of reason, no less natural and more elevated than the preceding one. Thanks to the gifts of science and understanding, reason raised above itself by faith, becomes capable of penetrating into the new object in some measure. Faith permits reason to accept it; science and understanding allow reason to find the meaning of what it accepts and consequently to go beyond itself without ceasing to be reason. This mode of knowledge, where faith enlightens us and reason explains to us, is not only the noblest knowledge accessible to us; it is also the most delightful. The combination of faith and intelligence is also what gives St. Bonaventure the deepest inner satisfaction. There is no greater joy for the soul than understanding what it believes. St. Bernard already said so, and St. Bonaventure further refines what St. Bernard said. The sweetness of comprehending what we believe is such that it is always necessary to make an effort to penetrate reason with love and faith even when sheer rational evidence would be possible. When we accept a truth because of its rational demonstration, it is evidently impossible to believe it. We cannot at the same time know and believe, and reason tears assent from the human soul by a kind of violence. This purely scientific adherence to truth is dry and without merit. The adherence that takes its origin in faith is very different, where faith is based upon the love of the object to which it adheres. For, faith that loves its object seeks reasons that allow

2. Bonaventure, *In Sententiarum*, I, 3, 2, body of article: "Nata est anima ad percipiendum bonum infinitum, quod Deus est: ideo in eo solo debet quiescere et eo frui."

3. Bonaventure, *In Sententiarum*, I, 2, reply to obj. 4: "Quaenam ergo sacra scriptura est de credibili, ut credibile, hic est de credibili ut facto intelligibili, et haec determinatio distrahit. Nam quod credimus debetur auctoritati et quod intelligimus rationi."—*In Sententiarum*, I, 1 at the conclusion: "Possumus et unico vocabulo nominare, et sic est credibile, prout tamen credibile transit in rationem intelligibilis, et hoc per additionem rationis; et hoc modo propie loquendo credibile est subjectum in hoc libro."

it to acquire understanding of the object, and reason that responds to faith's appeal does not diminish its merit; it only increases its sweetness.[4] This very particular realm, in which knowledge is never separated from piety and which properly constitutes the realm of Wisdom, is St. Bonaventure's preferred domain, the one where his thought seems to have willingly situated itself.

Here we encounter Augustinianism's traditional viewpoint with the single modification that St. Bonaventure is even better informed than his predecessors about the dangers of an independent philosophy and that the example of Aristotle leads him to draw the most extreme consequences from his premises. We have only one teacher, who is not Aristotle but Christ: *unus est magister vester, Christus* (Matt 23:10). Consequently, there is only one wisdom for us, *Sapientia Christiana*. Likewise, there is only one order that permits us to reach this wisdom. The order requires that we begin with stability in faith, that we advance through serenity of reason to reach the sweetness of contemplation. It is the path that Christ indicated to us, when he said, "I am the way, the truth and the life" (John 14:6). Thereby, the phrase of Proverbs 4:18 is fulfilled: "But the path of the just, as a shining light, goeth forwards and increased even to perfect day." This is also the order the saints followed and that Isaiah (7:9) prescribes when he declares, *Nisi credideritis, non intelligetis*. By contrast, the philosophers have ignored this order. They have preferred to neglect faith and base themselves entirely upon reason. The result is that they never reach contemplation.[5]

4. Bonaventure, *In Sententiarum*, I, 2 reply to obj. 5: "Et quod objicitur quod credible est super rationem, verum est super rationem quantum ad scientiam acquisitam per rationem evidentem; sed non supra rationem elevatam per fidem et per donum scientiae et intellectus. Fides enim elevat ad assentiendum; scientia et intellectus elevant ad ea, quae credita sunt, intelligendum."—*In Sententiarum*, I, 2, reply to obj. 6: "Quando assentitur propter se rationi, tunc aufertur locus fidei; quia in anima hominis dominatur violentia rationis. Sed quando fides non assentit propter rationem, sed propter amorem ejus cui assentit, desiderat habere rationes; tunc non evacuat ratio humana meritum, sed auget solatium."—That is an elegant solution to the problem posed by the phrase of St. Gregory: "Nec fides habet meritum cui humana ratio praebet experimentum."

5. Bonaventure, *Sermo Anecdota*, 79: "Ordo enim est, ut inchoetur a stabiltate fidei, et procedatur per serenitatem rationis, ut perveniatur ad suavitatem contemplationis . . . Hunc ordinem ignoraverunt philosophi, qui, negligentes idem et totaliter se fundantes in ratione, nullo modo pervenire potuerunt ad contemplationem."—This whole sermon is devoted to demonstrating that Christ is our only teacher. It has no meaning if we interpret it as a declaration of principle against pure philosophy.

It is easy to see that without the light of Christ we could not direct ourselves with security upon the way of truth. Of the three decisive actions in our inner ascent to God, it is evident that the first and last would be impossible for us without divine illumination. To begin with faith and end in mystical contemplation is something that comes directly from Christ and his grace. But we ought to go further, and the second effort that is required of us must be considered as impossible without divine help as the others are. This serene reason, this philosophical speculation by which we pass from faith to contemplation, is a gift of God, the gift of understanding, so that Christ is not only our teacher in matters of faith or mystical illumination, but also in rational knowledge.[6] By the fact that true wisdom is defined as an application of rational reflection to the data of reason, it immediately follows that pure philosophy can only be a teacher of error and that, in the most favorable hypothesis, it is incapable of leading us to certainty. For knowledge to be certain and scientific, two conditions are necessarily required: infallible certainty on the side of the knowing subject and immutable truth on the side of the known object. All true knowledge must be certain and deal with what is necessary. To know something is to know its cause and to know that it cannot be other than it is. If scientific knowledge requires immutable truth on the object's part, this truth cannot be created truth that is subject to change. It can only be immutable creative truth, which alone is exempt from change. Things have three different ways of existing. First, they exist in themselves, that is according to their peculiar nature and the created existence that has been imparted to them. Next, they exist in our thought as particular objects of our knowledge. Lastly, they exist in the eternal reason where their archetypes are found, which are their exemplar and the first

6. Bonaventure, *In Sententiarum*, III, 35, 1, 3 at the conclusion: "Cognitio de Deo sub ratione veri potest haberi secundum triplicem modum: uno modo habetur cognitio Dei per simplicem asensum; alio modo per rationis adminiculum; tertio modo per simplicem contuitum. Primum est virtus fidei, cujus est assentire; secundum est doni intellectus, cujus est credita per rationem intelligere; tertium est beatitudinis munditiae cordis, cujus est Deum videre."—*Sermo Anecdota*, 73–74: "Secundum hoc apparet, quod triplex est modus cognoscendi, quorum primus est per credulitatem piae assentionis, secundus per approbationem rectae rationis, tertius vero per claritatem mundae contemplations. Primus spectat ad habitum virtutis, quae est fides, secundus ad habitum doni, quae est intellectus, tertius ad habitum beatitudinis, quae est munditia cordis. Cum igitur triplex sit cognitionis differentia, videlicet creditiva, collativa et contemplativa omnium harum est Christum principium et causa, et ita quod primae est principium in quantum via, secundae in quantum veritas, et tertiae in quantum vita."

origin of their existence. It is only in the Eternal Word that things can enjoy immutable existence. Accordingly, if scientific knowledge (*cognitio scientalis*) requires its object's immutability, we are left with the fact that nothing can render things perfectly knowable to us but the presence of Christ, the Son of God and our teacher. We reach the same conclusion if we place ourselves in the standpoint of the knowing subject. Knowledge is not certain if it belongs to a mind that can be mistaken, or if it comes from a light that is capable of being darkened. Such a light cannot be that of a created intelligence, but only the light of uncreated Wisdom, who is Christ. By itself, the created intellect's light is insufficient to guarantee the certain comprehension of anything without the light of the eternal Word: *lux ergo intellectus creati sibi non sufficit ad certam comprehensionem rei cujuscumque absque luce Verbi aeterni.*[7]

If this is the case, every philosopher whom the light of faith does not illuminate is destined to fall into error.[8] In the absence of full, completely and absolutely grounded knowledge, which would only be available to us if we had a direct vision of the divine ideas, clear and certain knowledge is possible to us here below.[9] However, it is only possible with the help of God. The greatest philosophers have not been able to discover the truth, and the only philosophy that is completely true is not the work of a pagan but of a Christian and a believer. For example, let us consider the teaching of the ancients about the origin and nature of our knowledge. We

7. Bonaventure, *Sermo Anecdota*, 75–77: "Cum igitur res habeant esse in proprio genere, habeant etiam esse in mente, habeant esse et in aeterna ratione, nec esse earum sit omnino immutabilis primo et secundo modo, sed tantum tertio, videlicet prout sunt in Verbo aeterno; restat quod nihil potest facere res perfect scibiles, nisi adsit Christus, Dei filius et magister."—The passages of St. Augustine upon which this doctrine is based are *De Libero Arbitrio*, XII, 33, *De Trinitate*, XV, 21, *De Vera Religione*, 30–31, *De Musica*, VI, 12, and *Retractationes*, ch. 4.

8. Bonaventure, *In Sententiarum*, II, 18, 2, 1, reply to obj. 6: "Necesse est philosophantem in aliquem errorem labi, nisi adjuvetur per radium fidei."

9. Bonaventure, *De Humanae Cognitionis Ratione, Anecdota*, 61 and 69, reply to obj. 22: "Item, se quidquid cognoscitur, cognoscitur rationibus aeternis, aut ergo velate, aut sine velamine. Si velate, ergo nihil clare cognoscitur. Si sine velamine, ergo omnes vident Deum et exemplar aeternum absque omni aenigmate; sed hoc est falsum secundum statum viae: ergo, etc. Ad illud . . . dicendum, quod in statu viae non cognoscitur in rationibus aeternis sine velamine et aenigmate propter divinae imaginis obscurationem. Ex hoc tamen non sequitur, quod nihil certitudinaliter cognoscatur et clare, pro eo quod principia creata, quae aliquo modo sunt media cognoscendi, licet non sine illis rationibus, possunt perspicue et sine velamine a nostra mente videri. Si tamen diceretur, quod nihil in hac vita scitur plenarie, non esset magnum inconveniens."

will immediately see that neither Plato nor Aristotle found the problem's real solution but only St. Augustine. The Christian doctor knows that our soul is in close relation to the eternal laws that reside in God. In some fashion, the soul attains the higher light through the extreme point of its agent intellect and the highest part of its reason. It is unquestionably true, on the other hand, as Aristotle said, that knowledge is found in us by means of the senses, memory, and experience. Plato made all of our certain knowledge depend just upon the intelligible world, which is the world of ideas, and Aristotle rightly criticized him. It is not that Plato was mistaken in affirming the existence of ideas and eternal reasons, because Augustine explicitly praised him for it. But Plato was wrong to scorn the sensible world and make all certainty of knowledge rest upon the ideas. By doing this, Plato might seem to affirm the passage that leads us toward wisdom through the eternal reasons. However, at the same time, he destroyed the road to science that passes through created essences, just when Aristotle was consolidating science and compromising wisdom. It seems as though, among the philosophers, speaking the language of science was reserved to Aristotle, and speaking the language of wisdom to Plato. But to Augustine, by the grace of the Holy Spirit it was given to speak both languages. After Paul, Moses, and Jesus Christ, Augustine is our teacher and doctor.[10]

All true science comes from Christ; all light comes from the Father.[11] The excellent things we receive and every perfect gift comes to us from above, descending from the Father of lights. The Apostle James designates the first origin of every illumination in these terms. At the same

10. Bonaventure, *Sermo Anecdota*, 80–81: "Postremo, si esset [Deus] ratio totalis [intelligendi], non indigeremus specie et receptione ad cognoscendas res, quod manifeste videmus esse falsum, quia amittentes unum sensum, necesse habemus amittere unam scientiam. Et ideo videtur quod inter philosophos datus sit Platoni sermo sapientiae, Aristoteli vero sermo scientiae. Ille enim principaliter aspiciebat ad superiora, hic vero pricipaliter ad inferiora. Uterque autem sermo, scilicet sapientiae et scientiae, per Spiritum Sanctum datus Augustino, tanquam praecipuo expositori totius scripturae sicut ex scriptis ejus apparet."

11. Bonaventure, *Sermo Anecdota*, 81: "Excellentissime autem fuit [uterque sermo] in Domino nostro Jesu Christo, qui fuit principalis legislator et simul perfectus viator et comprehensor, et ideo ipse solus est principalis magister et doctor."—Here, of course, we meet again the *omne datum optimum et omne donum perfectum* of the Epistle of St. James. It is a kind of connecting thread that continually recurs in the writings of Bonaventure, for example, *Itinerarium*, prologue, 1, *Breviloquium*, prologue, 2, *De Reductione Artium ad Theologiam*, 1 and 5. This last little book is nothing but a sort of commentary on the fundamental passage in St. James on the first source of all illumination.

time, he suggests the multiplicity of channels by which this generous emanation of light reaches us from its source. When we define God as the Father of lights, in the first place we naturally think about illumination of knowledge. But things themselves are what they are only by light, that most perfect body of all, whose perfection borders upon the perfection of the spiritual. The form of light is never in a body as an imperfect disposition that must receive its perfection from the ultimate form of this body. On the contrary, it is in each body as the conservator of all the other corporeal forms. Light makes them capable of acting, and the dignity and excellence of all other corporeal forms can be measured in function of their participation in light.[12] If it were otherwise, we could not understand how sense knowledge would be possible. We cannot dispute that all knowledge, even the most inner sort, is a certain illumination. All knowledge supposes a certain proportion between the knowing subject and the known object. The light of sense knowledge requires the presence of an object that participates in its fashion in the nature of light. It is because there is a certain luminous principle in bodies and a degree of luminosity proper to each element, that all corporeal elements are perceptible by our senses. Even the division of our sensible faculties into five senses is based on this very particular property of the elements. The sensitive mind participates in the nature of light and resides in the nerves, whose substance is easily penetrated and transparent. The totality of things results from the mixture of five simple bodies: the four elements and the quintessence or substance out of which the heavenly bodies are made. The distinction of these different elementary sensations is explained in turn by their degree of participation in light: *natura luminis elementorum*. Therefore, for humans to be able to perceive all corporeal forms they need five corresponding senses, whose nature is such that each species of corporeal form finds in humans an appropriate sense upon which it can act. We have sight, which is sensitive to the most eminent properties of light and perceived in its purity. It is the sense corresponding to the quintessence. Beneath sight comes hearing, which is sensitive to light mixed with air; odor, which perceived light mixed with vapor (fire); taste, sensitive to

12. Bonaventure, *In Sententiarum*, II, 13, 2, 2: "Forma lucis, cum ponitur in eodem corpore cum alia forma, non ponitur sicut dispositio imperfecta, quae nata sit perfici per ultimam formam, sed ponitur tanquam forma et natura omnis alterius corporalis formae conservans et dans ei agendi efficaciam, et secundam quam attenditur cujuslibet formae corporalis mensura in dignitate et excellentia."

light mixed with humor (water); and lastly touch, sensitive to light mixed with the coarse element of earth.[13]

But things are not merely penetrated by corporeal light to the depths of their substance. They are also the reflection of spiritual light emanating from the creator. For one who knows how to look at them, things are so many vestiges of God, and the world is a vast mirror in which we see its author's face reflected. Anyone who wants to understand the great pilgrimage of the soul toward God must impart to his faculties part of the vigor and penetration that they enjoyed before original sin. Therefore, a person needs to pray, meditate, beg for grace, and not consider these preliminaries to speculation as optional conditions but as necessary. Prayer first, then holy life, finally turning toward the mirrors in which truth is reflected and rising gradually toward God: this is how we can climb this high mountain where the God of gods is found in Zion.[14] From the first moment in which well-prepared reason considers material conditions, it observes that some are, that others are and live, that others lastly are, live, and know. Reason further observes that some are purely corporeal, that others are part corporeal and part spiritual. From this it considers that some must be purely spiritual, nobler and more perfect than the previous ones. Again, reason sees that changing, corruptible bodies exist, earthly bodies. Other bodies change but are incorruptible, namely heavenly bodies. From this, reason concludes the existence of immutable, incorruptible things, which are the supercelestial realities. From the consideration of visible things, the soul rises to consider the power, wisdom, and goodness of the divine being, living and intelligent, purely spiritual, incorruptible, free from change.[15] These are not remote conclusions that our reason would only reach by complicated reasoning. Rather, they are evidences to which our sight cannot be befogged.

Someone whom the splendors of created things do not enlighten is blind. One must be deaf not to awake at the cries they utter. One must be mute not to praise God in presence of all these effects. Finally, one must be obtuse not to recognize the principle of so many indications.[16]

13. Bonaventure, *De Reductione Artium ad Theologiam*, 3. Cf. Augustine, *Super Genesi*, III, 4 and 5, numbers 6 and 7.

14. Bonaventure, *Itinerarium Mentis in Deum*, I, 8.

15. Bonaventure, *Itinerarium*, I, 13.—Cf. *Itinerarium*, I, 14, the sevenfold witness that things give to God's power, wisdom, and goodness, according to what we consider in them: origin, size, number, beauty, plenitude, operation, and order.—See also Bonaventure, *In Hexaemeron, Collatio IV*, 6ff.

16. Bonaventure, *Itinerarium*, I, 15: "Qui igitur tantis rerum creatarum

St. Bonaventure never wearies of insisting that sensible things are essentially *umbrae, resonantiae, picturae, vestigia, simulacra* or *spectacula*, in a word, signs, which God has given us in order to allow us to discover him there: *spectacula nobis ad contuendum Deum proposita et signa divinitus data*. Consequently the famous saying of St. Paul that those who do not know God are inexcusable is certainly correct. Between sacramental or prophetic signification and natural signification of things there is no difference of nature. There is only difference of degree. Every creature is already by nature a kind of likeness and image of the eternal wisdom. The creatures employed by the spirit of prophecy in Holy Scripture as prefigurations of spiritual reality are especially this likeness and image. Still more especially, so are the creatures under whose appearance wisdom has chosen to manifest itself by the ministry of angels. Finally, and very specially, so are the things wisdom has expressly instituted in order that they not be simply signs but also sacraments.[17] Consequently, there are two realities, one of which is expressed in the Scriptures and the other in nature. As creator, God expresses himself in the book of creation. He expresses himself as redeemer in the book of Scripture.[18] This is even the reason for being, the deep meaning of things that continuously take our minds back toward their author. God has created this sensible world with the very particular intention of making himself known and manifesting himself: *primum principium fecit mundum istum sensibilem ad declarandum se ipsum*. This is why we can read the creating Trinity in things in which it is more or less faithfully represented as so many vestiges, images, or resemblances. *Creatura mundi est quasi quidam liber, in quo relucet,*

---

splendoribus non illustratur caecus est; qui tantis clamoribus non evigilat surdus est; qui ex omnibus his effectibus Deum non laudat mutus est; qui ex tantis indiciis primum principium non advertit stultus est."

17. Bonaventure, *Itinerarium*, 11–12: "Omnis enim creatura ex natura est illius aeternae sapientiae quaedam efficies et similitudo, sed specialiter illa quae in libro Scripturae per spiritum assumpta est ad spiritualium prefigurationem; specialius autem illae creatura in quarum efficie angelico ministerio voluit apparere; specialissime vere ea quam voluit ad signficandum instituere, quae tenet non solum rationem signi secundum nomen commune, verum etiam Sacramenti."

18. Bonaventure, *Breviloquium*, II, 5, 2: "Cum primum principium reddat se nobis cognoscibile et per Scripturam et per creaturam, per librum creaturae se manifestat ut principium effective, per librum Scripturae, ut principium reparativum."—Cf. *Breviloquium*, II, 11, 2: "Et secundum hoc duplex est liber, unus scilicet scriptus intus, qui est aeterna Dei ars et sapientia et alius scriptus foris, mundus scilicet sensibilis."

repraesentatur et legitur Trinitas fabricatrix.[19] We can see it written in particularly visible characters in the image of God that is our soul.

It is completely evident that no knowledge is easier for us to attain than the knowledge of God's existence. When we seek to discover God in our soul, the issue is not so much constructing dialectical proofs as of rediscovering evidence. We do not see God, and moreover, our vision would be incapable of bearing the brightness of eternal light, but this light can still be said to penetrate us intimately. This light makes possible our knowledge of things in general and our knowledge of God necessary in particular.

We have already noted that all true knowledge deals with what is necessary and immutable. Our thought is subject to change. Therefore, it is incapable of attaining any truth by itself, and it is necessary that what makes us capable of attaining truth should be above us. Only God and eternal truth are above us. Accordingly, if we know necessary truth, it is only in divine truth and eternal reasons.[20] All certain knowledge is grounded in the eternal reasons, because it would not be enough to say that it rests *upon* them. It is genuinely grounded in them. Divine light certainly penetrates our understanding. It is diminished, attenuated, and adapted to our insufficiency, but still near enough to its origins to guarantee certainty in truth in us. St. Bonaventure would not say with Malebranche that we see all things in God, but with St. Augustine he says that we see the truth of all things in God's truth.[21]

19. Bonaventure, *Breviloquium*, II, 11, 2, and II, 12, 1.

20. Bonaventure, *De Cognitione Humana*, 4, reply to objection 17. *Sermo Anecdota*, 53: "Omne immutabile est superius mutabili, sed illud quo certitudinaliter cognoscitur est immutabile, quia verum necessarium; sed mens nostra est mutabilis; ergo, illud quo cognoscimus est supra mentes nostras. Sed quod est supra mentes nostras non est nisi Deus et veritas aeterna; ergo illud quo est cognitio est divina veritas et ratio sempiterna."

21. Bonaventure, *De Cognitione Humana*, 4, reply to obj. 3, *Sermo Anecdota*, 50: "Si tu dicas, quod ex hoc non sequitur quod in veritate vel in rationibus, sed quod a rationibus videamus, contra: Augustinus, duodecimo *Confessionum*: *Si ambo videmus verum esse quod dicis, et ambo videmus verum esse quod dico, ubi, quaeso, id videmus? Nec ego in te, nec tu in me, sed ambo in ipsa quae supra mentes nostras est incommunicabili veritate.*"—*De Cognitione Humana*, 4, body of article. *Anecdota*, pp. 62–63: "Ad certitudinalem cognitionem intellectus etiam in viatore requiritur, ut aliquo modo attingatur ratio aeterna ut ratio regulans et motiva, non tamen ut sola et in sua claritate, sed simul cum propria ratione creata et ut ex parte a nobis constituita secundum statum viae."—There is a slightly different passage in *De Scientia Christi*, q. 4, conclusion, *Opera* V, p. 22: ". . . sed simul cum propria ratione creata et ut in specula et aenigmate cognita."

St. Bonaventure's intention is to stay away from two errors about human knowledge. One consists of maintaining that an all-certain knowledge acquired by knowing the evidence of eternal light must contribute as the total, single source of our knowledge. According to this doctrine, there would only be knowledge of things in the Word, but the knowledge of things as we possess it here below would differ in no way from what we will have in heaven. To know things in the Word and to know them in themselves would be two identical knowledges. It would be necessary to conflate knowledge *qua* science with knowledge *qua* wisdom, knowledge by nature and knowledge by grace. This was Plato's theory. For Plato, we can only know anything with certainty in the eternal world of archetypes. Its error is that we would know absolutely nothing, because that intelligible world is impenetrable for our minds. In this sense, the First Academy engendered the Second, and Platonism led to skepticism, because a little error in the beginning is a great error at the end. But it would likewise be an error to reduce the eternal reason's contribution to simple influence, so that, in knowing, the person who knows would not attain eternal reason itself, but only its influence: *ita quod cognoscens in cognoscendo non ipsam rationem aeternam attingit, sed influentiam ejus solum*. Such a claim cannot be reconciled to the decisive authority of St. Augustine and would be manifestly false, because if human reason can know the truth by an influence that makes it habitually and normally capable of truth—*per habitum suae mentis*—by that very fact, intrinsically mutable and contingent human reason would become capable of attaining the immutable and necessary. This impenetrable boundary between the changeable and the immutable is what does not allow us to explain human knowledge without assigning it a stable foundation in God's immutability and necessity.[22]

A conception of our knowledge like this one necessarily implies that we can directly attain God's existence. Divine truth and eternal wisdom must be in us and speak in us for them continually to provide support for our knowledge of the truth. To hear God's voice we have only to listen. Nothing requires us to ask dialectical reasoning for a proof of his existence. Our soul is naturally empty and bare of the species that represent external things to us. It pertains to the senses to make us know what a stone is, for example, by transmitting a kind of painting of it. But another sort of species exists, species that are not expressions of things but of

22. Bonaventure, *Sermo Anecdota*, 60–61.

impressions produced in our souls by the supreme truth.[23] Accordingly to the thinking of all the doctors, Christ is our true inner doctor, and we can know any truth only through him. He is present and intimate in every soul, and he inundates our intellect's murky species with the luminous species of which he is full. In this way, their mixture with sensible phantasms illuminates these dark and obscure species in order that our intellect may know.[24] Therefore, the divine light is more intimate to the soul than the soul itself. This is why this light, whose direct vision is inaccessible to us, nevertheless makes itself known, felt, and experienced by us. We attain the image of God that he himself has impressed upon us in the fact that we know truths; and in each of these truths that we know, the presence of God is involved in any of our certainties and in the existence of human certainties in general.[25] This knowledge by presence is truer than knowledge by resemblance, such as we possess of sensible things. Therefore, the knowledge we have of God present and united to our soul is truer than the knowledge of sensible things.[26] It follows from this that the question of God's existence is not posed. Not only is St. Anselm's argument evidently true, but we can almost say that even such a

23. Bonaventure, *In Libros Sententiarum*, I, 7, 1, 4, body of article: "Species autem innata potest esse dupliciter, aut similitudo tantum, sicut species lapidis, aut ita similitudo, quid etiam quondam verities in seipsas. Prima species est sicut pictura, et ab hac creata est anima nuda. Secunda species est impressio aliqua summae veritatis in anima."

24. Bonaventure, *In Hexaemeron*, XII, 5: "Secundum sententiam omnium doctorum Christus est Doctor interius, nec scitur aliqua veritas nisi per eum . . . Ipse enim intimus est omni animae, et suis speciebus clarissimis refulget super species intellectus nostri tenebrosas; et sic illustrantur species illae obtenebratae, admixtae obscuritati phantasmatum, ut intellectus intelligat. Si enim scire est cognoscere rem aliter impossibile se habere, necessarium est, ut ille solus scire faciat qui veritatem novit et habet in se veritatem."—*In Hexaemeron*, XII, 11: "Haec lux est inaccessibilis, et tamen proxima animae etiam plus quam ipsa sibi. Est etiam inalligabilis et tamen summe intima."

25. Bonaventure, *In Libros Sententiarum*, I, 3, 1, 1, reply to obj. 5: "Ad illud quod ultimo objicitur de informatione, dicendum quod Deus est praesens ipsi animae et omni intellectui per veritatem; et ideo non est necesse ab ipso abstrahi similitudinem, per quam cognoscatur; nihilominus, dum cognoscitur ab intellectu, intellectus informatur quadam notitia, quae est velut similitudo quaedam, non abstracta sed impressa, inferior Deo, quia in natura inferiori. Est superior tamen animae, quia facit ipsam meliorem."

26. Bonaventure, *In Libros Sententiarum*, bk. I, dist. 3, q. 1, art. 1, at *Contra*: "Item, cum fiat cognitio aliquorum per praesentiam, aliquorum per similitudinem illa cognoscuntur verius quae cognoscuntur per praesentiam, ut dicit Augustinus (*Soliloquium*, I, 8): sed Deus est ipsi animae unitus per praesentiam; ergo Deus verius cognoscitur quam alia quae cognoscuntur per similitudinem."

simple argument is uselessly complicated. When the occasion calls for it, Bonaventure happily takes up all known arguments for God's existence, but, like his master St. Augustine, he does not seem convinced of the necessity to furnish a genuine demonstration of God's existence. St. John Damascene declares that the knowledge of God's existence is naturally imprinted upon us. What is naturally imprinted cannot be combined with its contrary. The truth of God imprinted upon the natural soul is therefore inseparable from it, and we cannot think that God does not exist.[27] Like Hugh of St. Victor, St. Bonaventure judges that God has balanced from the start the knowledge that humans possess in such a way that they can never fail to comprehend his essence or to be aware of his existence.[28] The rational soul is naturally aware of itself, because it is naturally knowable and always present to itself. God is still more internally present to the soul that the soul is to itself. Accordingly, the soul necessarily possesses innate knowledge of God: *inserta est animae rationali notitia sui, eo quod anima est ipsi animae et eo ipso cognoscibilis, ergo inserta est ipsi animae notitia Dei sui.*[29]

If we may attain knowledge of the Trinity starting from natural things, it is still more accessible to us starting from our soul. It is not that natural reason can rise to knowledge of one God in three persons without the help of faith. Philosophers never reached it, or if they reached it, that

27. Bonaventure, *In Libros Sententiarum*, I, 8, 1, 2: "Damascenus dicit quod cogntio essendi Deum nobis naturaliter est impressa, sed naturales impressiones non relinquunt nec assuescunt in contrarium; ergo veritas Dei impressa menti humanae est inseparabilis ab ipsa, ergo non potest cogitari non esse."

28. Bonaventure, *In Libros Sententiarum*, I, 8, 1, 2, body of article: "Convenit autem dupliciter esse cogitationem de aliquo ente, videlicet si est, et quod est. Intellectus autem deficit in cogitatione divinae veritatis quantum ad cognitionem quid est; tamen non deficit quantum ad cognitionem si est. Unde Hugo (*De Sacramentis*, I, 3, 1), Deus ab initio sic cognitionem suam in homine temperavit, ut sicut nunquam quid esset poterat ab homine comprendi, ita nunquam quia esset poterat ignorari. Quia ergo intellectus noster nunquam deficit in cognitione Dei si est, ideo nec potest ignorare ipsum esse, similiter non cogitare non esse."—Cf. likewise, *In Libros Sententiarum*, II, 3, 2, 2, reply to obj. 4: "Cognoscitur autem Deus per effectus visibiles et per substantias spirituales et per influentiam luminis connaturalis potentiae cognoscendi, quod est similitudo Dei non abstracta, sed infusa, inferior Deo, quia in inferiori natura, sicut dicit Augustinus (IX *De Trinitate*, capitulo 11, numero 16)."—In it, God's existence does not follow from a proof properly so-called. It is the immediate corollary of the principle that *veritas est proprietas divini esse*. From that comes the way in which St. Bonaventure posses the question: *an divinum esse sit adeo verum, quod non possit cogitari non esse*.

29. Bonaventure, *De Mysterio Trinitatis*, IV, 1,1, conclusion 10.

could only be because they received some illumination of faith. But they were able to know a number of attributes of the Trinity without knowing the Trinity itself. Divine attributes can be distinguished into common, appropriated common, and proper. Common attributes, strictly speaking, belong to the three divine persons indifferently; for example, being, life, and so forth. Appropriated common attributes are those that, although common to the three persons, are more specially attributed to one than to the others, for example, power to the Father, wisdom to the Son, and goodness to the Holy Spirit. Lastly, the proper attributes belong to each distinct person and to him alone. They are paternity, filiation, and spiration. Purely rational knowledge is incapable of acquiring knowledge of proper attributes, but it can acquire knowledge of common appropriate attributes. In fact, these attributes have their image in the three powers of the human soul, memory, intelligence, and will. We can say that these three powers have a single essence, the soul, and distinct acts that condition each other according to a certain order. Memory, in conserving species, disposes intelligence to know them. Intelligence, when the known object is good, disposes the will to love it.[30]

This natural aptitude of reason to discover appropriated attributes allows us to understand that proper attributes and the existence of the three distinct persons seem easily accessible to it when it is illuminated by faith. Once we are informed about the existence of the Trinity, we find its image everywhere. St. Bonaventure devoted one of his best known treatises to make us encounter the dogma of the Trinity inscribed in the core of our souls and each of its operations, in the fourfold light of the mechanical arts, sensible knowledge, philosophical knowledge, and knowledge of holy Scripture. The simple consideration of the mechanical arts and of the way in which the product emerges from the artisan's hands permits us to conceive the generation of the Incarnate Word, that is to say, the union of divinity and humanity and consequently the very

30. Bonaventure, *In Libros Sententiarum*, I, 3, 1, 1 at the conclusion.—See also *In Libros Sententiarum*, I, 3, sole article, 4: "Pluralitas personarum cum unitate essentiae est proprium divinae naturae solius, cujus simile nec reperitur in creatura, nec postest reperiri, nec rationabiliter cogitari; ideo nullo modo trinitas personarum est cognoscibilis per creaturam rationabiliter ascendendo a creatura in Deum. Sed licet non habeat omnino simile, habet tamen aliquo modo quod creditur simile in creatura. Unde dico, quod philosophi nunquam per rationem cognoverunt personarum trinitatem nec pluralitatem, nisi haberent aliquam habitum fidei, sicut habent aliqui haeretici; unde quae dixerunt, aut locuti sunt non intelligentes, aut fidei radio illustrati. Est alia trinitas appropriatorum, silicet unitatis, veritatis et bonitatis, et hanc cognoverunt, quia habet simile."

essence of faith.[31] We find the relation of Father and Son again in the relation of word to thought. We likewise find it in the illumination that is natural philosophy. Abstract intellectual reasons are in some measure intermediaries between seminal reasons and ideal reasons. Seminal reasons cannot be found in matter without engendering and producing forms. In the same way, intellectual reasons cannot exist in thought without the word being engendered in it. Consequently, it must be admitted that ideal reasons cannot exist in God's thought without the Divine Word being engendered by the Father because, if the suitability of such a relation corresponds to the dignity of a simple creature, with greater reason it corresponds to God's perfection.[32] The reasons that invite us to admit the Trinity are not merely reasons of convenience. They are reasons of necessity that force us to acknowledge that there must be three distinct persons in God, no more and no less. God's perfect simplicity only permits the distinction of persons according to the order of emanation. There are only two possible orders of emanation: generation and procession. Therefore, there cannot be more than three persons. But there cannot be less. Perfect beatitude requires love and harmony in that love just as supreme perfection supposes dual emanation one by nature and the other by free generosity. In either case, there must necessarily be three persons. Accordingly, reason taught by faith finds a way to be satisfied in the consideration of the mystery of the Trinity.[33]

When we bring together all the characteristic traits of the theory of human knowledge in order to compare them, we easily discover that they have been chosen and adjusted with a view to producing a single impression, that of God's nearness and how easily it can be discovered. At the end of one of his treatises, St. Bonaventure concludes:

31. See the whole comparison in Bonaventure, *De Reductione Artium ad Theologiam*, 12: "Considerantes igitur illuminationem artis mechanicae quantum ad operis egressus intuebimur ibi Verbum generatum et incarnatum, id est Divinitatem et humanitatem et totius fidei integritatem."

32. Bonaventure, *De Reductione Artium ad Theologiam*, 16 and 21: "Praedicat igitur tota naturalis philosophia per habitudinem proportionis Dei verbum natum et incarnatum, ut idem sit alpha et omega, natum scilicet in principio et ante tempora, incarnatum vero in fine saeculorum."

33. Bonaventure, *In Libros Sententiarum*, I, 2, sole article, 3: "Dicendum quod sicut fides catholica dicit, ponere est tantum tres personas, non plures nec pauciores. Et ad hoc sumitur ratio necessitatis et congruitatis. Ratio utique necessitatis, quare non possunt esse pauciores quam tres, est summa beatitudo et summa perfectio . . . item ratio necessitatis quare non possunt esse plures, est summa simplicitas . . ."

> It appears how the multiform wisdom of God, which is clearly transmitted to us in Sacred Scripture, is hidden under all knowledge and everything. We also see how all knowledge is put at the service of theology. This is why theology borrows examples and uses expressions that belong to all branches of knowledge. Finally, we se how broad the illuminative way is and how God hides within everything we feel and know. The fruit of every science is that faith be edified, that God be proved, that behavior be ordered, and that consolations be obtained there in the union of spouse and bride. This union is only consummated through charity, and all Holy Scripture tends toward charity. Accordingly, all illumination proceeding from above tends toward charity. Without it, all knowledge is vain, because we never come to the Son without passing thorough the Holy Spirit, who teaches every truth and who is blessed forever and ever, amen.[34]

Beneath his cardinal's *galero* and the dignity of being general of the Franciscan order, Fray Bonaventure certainly kept the Poverello's spirit, which "so rejoiced in all created things, inwardly and outwardly, that when he touched or saw them, his mind seem no longer to be on earth but in heaven."

It becomes clear that the intensity and depth of this religious feeling, the vehemence of the desire that pushed St. Bonaventure to seek and discover God everywhere, could not be accommodated with equal facility in just any philosophical system. St. Bonaventure was not the zealous defender and fervent propagator of traditional doctrines simply because they were traditional. He was attracted to them with his whole soul because they alone seemed to him capable of maintaining the contact between humans and God that his mystic piety needed. If we do not first feel the very particular demands of the Franciscan soul in devotion and interior life, we are condemned from the start to see only as disputes about terminology and as subtleties of school controversies where each doctrine is really a definite form of religious life and of the faith that seeks to justify and ground itself.

The Albertine–Thomist Reform and Religious Consciousness

Competit animis ut a corporibus et per corpora suam perfectionem intelligiblem consequantur, alioquin frustra corporibus unirentur.

34. Bonaventure, *De Reductione Artium*, 26.

Summa Theologiae, Part I, Question 55, Article 2

If we hold to outward appearances and literal expressions, nothing changes when we go from St. Bonaventure or the Christian rationalists to Albertus Magnus or St. Thomas. Like their contemporaries or their Augustinian predecessors, the two great Dominicans are above all and essentially theologians. They even gladly accept the expression whose elements St. Peter Damian had provided and that Gregory IX made the program of the new University of Paris: the end of theological science is not in other sciences. On the contrary, theology is the end of other sciences, and they must consider themselves its handmaidens. Like St. Bonaventure, Albertus Magnus thinks that we pursue theological knowledge through all other knowledge. Accordingly, only theological knowledge is free, and the other sciences serve theology. It is the mistress who always takes first place.[35] Like his teacher, St. Thomas Aquinas does not hesitate to assign other sciences to the role of handmaidens of theology: *Aliae scientiae dicuntur ancillae hujus. Proverbia 9:3, Misit ancillas suas vocare ad arcem.*[36] But it remains to be seen whether the official formula here and elsewhere refers to the same doctrine. That is what we are going to examine by defining the situation made by theology for philosophy in the systems of Albertus Magnus and Thomas.

We can say that the sense of a difference between philosophy and theology is not unknown before the intervention of Albertus Magnus. We know, and Anselm clearly affirms, that philosophy argues in the name of principles of reason while theology argues in the name of principles of revelation. But the common impression consists in believing that a necessary, rational demonstration still remains possible within problems whose whole data can be furnished only be revelation. Everything proceeds as if human reason were capable of proving knowledge that it is incapable of acquiring. This confusion, into which we have seen Anselm,

35. Albertus Magnus, *Summa Theologica*, I, 6 at *Solutio*: "Ad hoc dicendum, quod est finis intra et finis extra. Finis intra in ipsa scientia est, et finis extra in sciente. Et sicut probatum est in primis rationibus, impossibile est, quod haec scientia [*scilicet*, theologia] finem in illis scientiis habeat, sed ipsa finis aliarum scientiarum est, ad quam omnes aliae referuntur ut ancillae. Et hoc modo libera est: omnibus enim existentibus et suffragantibus nobis et ad voluptatem et ad necessitatem, ista post omnia habita et in omnibus habitis quaeritur: et ideo libera est, et domina est, et sapientia, et in omnibus potior."

36. Aquinas, *Summa Theologiae*, pt. I, q. 1, art. 5, at *Sed contra*.

Abelard, and Bonaventure fall, stems from the distinction between the realms of philosophy and theology being felt and guessed at, rather than defined. It cannot be rigorously described before a resolutely empiricist doctrine of knowledge closes off all the loopholes by which human thought perennially tries to escape in order to attain the intuition of the divine.

From Albertus Magnus forward, the problem is going to be posed in a completely new way. What tormented his predecessors was the fear of demonstrating so many theological truths that faith and its merits might be compromised. This is why their constant concern is to find a mixed knowledge and kind of formula of adherence in which reason and the will would share equally. By contrast, Albertus Magnus declares that faith and reason are mutually exclusive. We cannot believe what we know, and when one of these kinds of certainty is established, the other has no place. It is legitimate, and even necessary, as a general rule to begin by believing truths, but from the moment when we succeed in demonstrating some of them, we no longer believe them, we know them. A good philosopher does not believe that God exists; he knows it. As we know in advance that many truths of faith will never be demonstrated, because they are not rationally demonstrable, we no longer are afraid that the merit of faith will vanish. There will always be mystery and the unknowable. Consequently, there will always be merit to be gained.[37]

If matters stand thus, whatever the factual relations of philosophy and theology and their mutual assistance in certain cases, they must be considered completely different in kind. They are neither knowledge nor sciences of the same order. There are at least five differences between them, and we could assign a number of others. The first is in the relation of each of these sciences to the person possessing them. Natural, philosophic knowledge depends on reason. Knowledge by faith is superior to reason. A second difference resides in the principles upon which these two kinds of knowledge are based. In natural knowledge, we rest upon principles known by themselves; we do that, for example, when we declare that it is essential to a first principle not to have its being from anything else; that other things must have their being from it; that it has

37. Albertus Magnus, *In Libros Sententiarum*, III, 24, 9, at *Solutio* and reply to obj. 2: "Fides et scientia sunt de eodem, non secundum idem et ideo unum non evacuat aliud, et ideo concedo rationes primo inductas . . ." "Ad aliud dicendum quod hoc modo quo fides est de articulo illo non potest esse scientia vel ratio de eodem."—See the passages quoted by Heitz, *Essai historique*, 142nn1–3.

no beginning, because that would suppose it has a cause; that it cannot be moved by another, and other principles of the same order. In fact, by contrast, knowledge is based on an infused light, which is a gift of the Holy Spirit, or upon oral revelation like that of Scripture. The gift of the Holy Spirit inclines us and guides us toward God without reason having to justify this movement. As for revelation *ex auditu*, the very fact that its transmission is necessary shows clearly that we would never reach its content by means of reason. Someone can argue in order to facilitate our belief, but they will never succeed in proving it.[38] Accordingly, faith entails conviction rather by engendering love in the will than by furnishing proofs to reason. The third difference resides in the case of knowledge. The cause of rational knowledge is found in the essence of created things, to which reason applies itself. On the other hand, the cause of faith is the first truth, which is its origin and end. The fifth difference is found in the subject in which these two kinds of knowledge reside. Faith is founded upon the affective intellect, that is, upon the intellect insofar as its adhesion is decided primarily by affective and voluntary motives. The science of natural reason, by contrast, resides in the speculative intellect, in the intellect insofar as it exercises its function of pure knowledge.[39] Consequently, Albertus Magnus tells us, theology is a science separated from other sciences in regard to the principles upon which its reasoning is based.[40] It is all too evident that the reciprocal is true. This firm decision

38. Albertus Magnus, *In Libros Sententiarum*, III, 24 A, 1: "Quaedam fides est ex auditu et quaedam est charisma Spiritus Sancti: illa quae est ex auditu, potest habere rationem inductivam, non probativam; non ut quis consentiat, sed ut facilius consentiat ei, cui tamen per affectum est inclinatus et paratus consentire. Charisma autem est lumen infusum tendens in primam veritatem, et haec non habet rationem inducentem, ut ita dicam."

39. Albertus Magnus, *In Libros Sententiarum*, I, 3, art. 4 at *Solutio*: "An ista cognitio naturalis differt a cognitione fidei? . . . dicendum quod istae cognitiones in quinque differunt ad minus, etsi in multis aliis differentia possit assignari. Prima differentia est in comparatione scientiae ad scientem; quia processus naturalis subest rationi, fidei autem processus, est supra rationem. Secunda differentia est in principiis in quibus accipitur cognitio ipsa: quia illa in naturali cognitione sunt principia per se nota . . . sed in fide est lumen infusum quod informando conscientiam, rationem convincit magis ex amore quodam voluntatis, quam ex probatione rationis."—Cf *Summa Theologica*, I, 3, 15, 3, 1.

40. Albertus Magnus, *Summa Theologica*, I, 1, 4, at *Solutio*: "Utrum theologia sit scientia ab aliis scientiis separata? . . . Quod concedendum est, et dicendum, quod haec scientia separatur ab aliis subjecto, passione et principiis confirmantibus ratiocinationem . . . Principio vero, quia quod in ista scientia probatur, per fidem quae articulus est qui creditur, vel antecedens fidem, quod est Scriptura, vel per revelationem probatur

Albertus Magnus has just made delimits philosophy at the same time as theology, and this separation marks the first step of philosophy on the long road to liberation.

Accordingly, it is within the thought of a medieval theologian that for the first time reason is brought within its limits, and by that very act reason is reestablished in part of its rights. From the point of view of unshakable firmness of assent, no certainty is more solidly established than faith's. Faith is based on God's authority, and every affirmation that surely possesses such a guarantee can be deemed above all dispute. Yet, insofar as faith is human knowledge, it belongs to a lower order. It is a fact that we are animals endowed with senses and that we draw our knowledge properly speaking from our sensibility. Consequently, faith that imposes acceptance of what our reason cannot attain is the least satisfying knowledge possible.[41] In our present state, the beatific vision is the least certain of all. Therefore, it is a lively awareness of what rational certainty can be—*certitudo quasi arguentis*—that leads Albertus Magnus to consider philosophy and theology as two separate sciences. This is also why the argument from authority, sovereign and decisive in theology, seems to Albert to possess only mediocre philosophical value. God's authority is sovereign, and all theology rests upon it. But human authority is fallible, and all philosophy rests upon reason.[42]

Therefore, it is not surprising that any pretension to discover a necessary demonstration of the Trinity of divine persons vanishes definitively. Pagan philosophers were never able to know the existence of

---

ut principium. Quod autem in aliis scientiis probatur, probatur per principium quod est dignitas, vel maxima propositio."—See ibid., reply to the third objection, for the distinction between revelation by natural light and supernatural light: "primum [lumen] relucet in per se notis, secundum autem in fidei articulis."

41. Albertus Magnus, *Summa Theologica*, I, 3, 15, 2, at *Solutio*: "Certitudo autem quae est quoad nos, ex notioribus est quoad nos, secundum quod animales sumus enutriti sensibus, ut dicit Augustinus. Et hoc modo nihil prohibet cognitionem per naturales rationes esse certissimam, et post hoc cognitionem fidei, et minime certam eam quae est facie ad faciem."

42. Albertus Magnus, *Summa Theologica*, I, 1, 5, 2, reply to obj. 4: "Ad 4um dicendum, quod in theologia locus ab auctoritate est ab inspiratione Spiritus veritatis. Unde Augustinus in libro I *Super Genesim* dicit quod *major est scripturae auctoritas quam omnis humani ingenii perspicitas.* In aliis autem scientiis locus ab auctoritate infimus est, et infirmior caeteris, quia perspicacitati humani ingenii quae fallibili est, innitur. Propter quod Tullius in libro *De Natura Deorum*, deridens scholam Pythagorae dicit, quod *de nullo quaerebat rationem aliam nisi quod ipse dixit. Ipse* autem erat Pythagoras."

the Trinity merely by the resources of natural human lights.[43] Albertus Magnus is even more convinced of this than St. Bonaventure. At most, these pagans knew the common appropriated attributes.[44] No necessary reason of the Trinity is accessible to us. The philosophers did not know it, because knowledge by purely natural reason is based on certain evident principles and because knowledge of the Trinity is in opposition to those principles: *cognitio illa oppositionem habet ad principia quibus intellectus accipit scientiam.* For the philosopher, it is evident that a single numerically indivisible nature cannot have several subjects. For natural reason, it is equally certain that he who engenders of his own substance and he who is engendered of it cannot exist simultaneously; that everything engendered is in potency before being in act. All these principles, which are the foundation of science according to natural reason, are opposed to the distinction of persons in the Trinity.[45] As for the necessary reasons that St. Anselm, Hugh of St. Victor, and St. Bonaventure discussed, they certainly exist in God, but they are inaccessible to us. That the philosophers have known the common appropriated attributes hardly helps them. They certainly possess knowledge of the attributes and they would have been able to appropriate them if they had known the existence of the divine persons. But as they did not know that, these attributes remained impossible for them. Consequently, there are only virtually appropriated attributes for them. If they were fairly close to the Trinity, it was without knowing it. Appropriation of attributes to proper attributes is only possible through faith.[46] What is true of the knowledge of the attributes is true of all the reasons called necessary. They certainly are necessary, but they are likewise supernatural and divine. Therefore, these reasons remain unknown to us, and natural reason cannot attain them.[47] This amounts to saying that in relation to us, the necessary reasons of the Trinity do not exist.

St. Thomas remains faithful to his master, St. Albertus Magnus, on all these points. Thomas also thinks that philosophy and theology are

43. Albertus Magnus, *In Libros Sententiarum*, I, 3, F. 18 at *Solutio*. See also *Summa Theologica*, I, 3, 13, 3.

44. Albertus Magnus, *In Libros Sententiarum*, I, 3, F. 18, reply to obj. 1: "Aristoteles non intelligit Trinitatem nisi forte per appropriata."

45. Albertus Magnus, *In Libros Sententiarum*, I, 3, F. 18, at *Solutio*.

46. Albertus Magnus, *In Libros Sententiarum*, I, 3, F, reply to obj.; *Summa Theologica*, I, 3, 13, 3, reply to obj. 9.

47. Albertus Magnus, *Summa Theologica*, I, 3, 15, 3, 2 reply to obj. 3: Ad dictum Ricardi dicendum, quod licet rationes necessariae sint ad distinctiones personarum, tamen illae sunt supernaturales et divinae; et ideo solo lumine naturali invenire non possunt." Cf. *Summa Theologica*, I, 3, 15, 3, reply 2 to obj.

formally different sciences.[48] He likewise holds that it is impossible to believe and know the same thing at the same time and under the same regard.[49] Finally, he too teaches that the Trinity eludes the grasp of natural knowledge. Still, Thomas seems intentionally to avoid saying with Albertus Magnus that there is opposition between the dogma of the Trinity and principles of natural reason. His favorite argument is that we only know God by his effects. The three persons of the Trinity are undividedly the cause of created things. Accordingly, it is impossible for us to discover, starting from creatures, that one God exists in three distinct persons.[50] In this particular case, a rather odd comparison reveals what comparative certainty Thomas grants to rather different kinds of knowledge. Thomas has to respond to the inevitable passages taken from Richard of St. Victor. Are there necessary reasons that can be presented in favor of the Trinity? Thomas answers by distinguishing two orders of reasons. In certain cases, it is possible to offer a reason that sufficiently demonstrates a fundamental truth. Thus, in sciences of nature, sufficient reason can be furnished to prove that uniform movement animates the heavens. However, other kinds of reasons exist that are not sufficient demonstrations of certain fundamental truths but do show the agreement of the facts with an already established truth. Such is the kind of truth possessed by the theory of eccentrics and epicycles in astronomy. When these reasons are admitted, we can justify the sensible appearance that heavenly movements present and, nevertheless, we cannot say that such reasons are sufficient reasons, because it would perhaps be possible to account for the phenomena by means of other reasons. We can prove the existence of God or his unity by reasons of the first order. But the reasons offered in favor of the Trinity belong to the second order. That is, when the Trinity is already posited, these reasons agree with it, but the reasons do not permit us to posit the Trinity.[51] There are not demonstrative reasons that can be

48. Aquinas, *Summa contra Gentes*, bk. II, ch. 4.

49. Aquinas, *Quaestiones Disputatae de Veritate*, XIV, 9, body of article.

50. Aquinas, *In Boethii De Trinitate*, 1, 4, body of article. See also *Summa Theologiae*, 1, 32, 1, body of article.

51. Aquinas, *Summa Theologiae*, I, 32, 1, reply to obj. 2: "Alio modo inducitur ratio, non quae sufficenter probet radicem, sed quae radici jam posita ostendat congruere consequentes effectus: sicut in astrologia ponitur ratio excentricorum et epicyclorum ex hoc quod, hac positione facta, possunt salvari apparentia sensibilia circa motus coelestes; non tamen ratio haec est sufficienter probans; quia etiam forte alia positione fact salvari possent. Primo ergo modo potest induci ratio ad probandum Deum esse unum, et similia; sed secundo modo se habet ratio, quae inducitur ad manifestationem

offered in favor of the Trinity. We can only supply some reasons that are not at all necessary and that do not even seem to be very probably unless one is already a believer: *et nullo modo potest demonstrative probari, quamvis ad hoc aliquales rationes non necessariae, nec multum probabiles nisi credenti haberi possint.*[52]

Consequently, we are already very far from the naïve confidence of the Augustinians about the possibility of justifying dogmas naturally, but Albertus Magnus and Thomas go further. Their respect for the demands of reason in the matter of rational demonstration is so deep that they will not hesitate to transform into a truth of faith what everyone had considered a philosophical truth for centuries. It is an urgent duty to distinguish the two realms clearly where there is cause to distinguish them. To present an article of faith to believers as a demonstrated truth perhaps would not do great harm. The faithful Christian already believes, and he does not believe by virtue of a proof, since strict proof excludes faith. But the confusion is dangerous and can produce lamentable results when one perpetrates it among unbelievers. To direct oneself to a nonbelieving adversary and try to demonstrate articles of faith by reasons that are not compelling is to make oneself ridiculous. The unbeliever, in fact, is invited to think that our faith's only basis is reasons of this type.[53] *Cedit in irrisionem infidelium.* It is necessary to have worked through volumes of unperturbedly objective discussions written by Thomas to feel the indignation and silent anger this expression encloses. It is very significant and worthy of notice that Thomas the theologian is indignant with other theologians because they do not know what reason is. Evidently, Thomas does not feel this concern solely for the sake of reason. Above all, he worries about faith, compromised and exposed to ridicule because of ignorant apologists. But his fears and indignation cannot be explained

---

Trinitatis, quia scilicet, Trintate posita, congruunt hujusmodi rationes; non tamen ita, quod per has rationes sufficienter probetur Trinitas personarum." The end of the article responds to reasons presented by St. Bonaventure.

52. Aquinas, *In Boethii De Trinitate*, I, 4, body of article. Against Richard of St. Victor's authority, see ibid., reply to obj. 7. For multiple insufficiencies of appropriation to divine persons, see *Summa Theologiae*, I, 39, 8.

53. Aquinas, *Summa Theologiae*, I, 32, 1, body of article: "Cum autem aliquis ad probandam fidem inducit rationes, quae non sunt cogentes, cedit in irrisionem infidelium. Credunt enim, quod hujusmodi rationibus innitamur, et propter eas credamus. Quae igitur fidei sunt, non sunt tentanda probare, nisi per auctoritates his, qui auctoritates suscipiunt. Apud alios sufficit defendere non esse impossibile, quod praedicat fides."

without deep awareness and definite knowledge of the requirements of natural reason in regard to proofs.

Thomas's sensitivity on this point is so strong that we find threatening expressions and defiance in the *opusculum* he devotes to the problem of the eternity of the world. Its title is *De Aeternitate Mundi contra Murmurantes, On the Eternity of the World against the Malcontents.* Here again, it is important not to allow pious sophisms to be forced on us as if they were demonstrations. As to the particular problem of the world's eternity, we can legitimately admit that it has been settled for a long time. The question of finding out whether the world exists from all eternity or was created by God in time has been widely discussed by Arab and Jewish philosophers and theologians. Moses Maimonides reached an ingenious solution to the problem that respected the concerns of reason and faith alike. According to the Jewish philosopher, Aristotle's seven demonstrations in support of the eternity of the world are not demonstrations. Moreover, Aristotle acknowledged that he has not proven his thesis. On the other hand, neither can we demonstrate that the world was created in time. Therefore, the fact remains that the creation of the world is an article of faith whose truth we accept on the witness of revelation interpreted in its literal sense. On this point, Albertus Magnus adopts a position very similar to that of Maimonides. What particularly strikes him is the demonstration, which is experimental in some measure, provided by the history of philosophy regarding the impossibility of natural reason proving such a thesis. If the creation of the world were rationally demonstrable, the philosophers certainly would have discovered it, and the fact that philosophers did not possess the concept of such a truth certainly shows that it eludes our reason. The genuine philosophical position to which philosophical thought spontaneously recurs when it wishes to account for the apparition of things is that nothing comes from nothing. Such a principle is the radical negation of all creation. Accordingly, it must be acknowledged that we formulate not a rational truth but an article of faith, when we repeat with the Nicene Creed, "I believe in one God, the Father almighty, maker of heaven and earth." We can supply plausible reasons in favor of this thesis, but we cannot furnish sufficient demonstrations. The fact remains that no philosopher has ever demonstrated it.[54]

54. Albertus Magnus, *In Libros Sententiarum*, II, 1, 8 at *solutio*: "Nos autem videtur mirabile, eo quod non possumus in id, quia non subjacet demonstrationi rationis; et ideo etiam philosophi non cognoverunt ipsum, nisi forte aliquis ex dictis prophetarum;

In his turn, St. Thomas Aquinas takes up the same position and defends it still more vigorously. We cannot prove demonstratively either the creation of the world in time or its eternity. To demonstrate the creation of the world in time, we must seek out the first reason of such a creation either in God or in things. If we place ourselves in the standpoint of things it is impossible to demonstrate that they had a beginning. The principle of every demonstration related to a thing resides in the thing's essence. If we consider everything that exists from the point of view of its essence, it is indifferent to time. Species and definitions of species never include existence in this or that particular moment; essences as such are universally and eternally valid. Consequently, there is nothing in the definition of the heavens, of human, or of stone that allows us to demonstrate that it has not always existed. But the same holds if we situate ourselves in the point of view of the cause, when the cause is a voluntary agent. We can only assign reason to God's wishes in the case of what is absolutely necessary that God should want. God wills only himself necessarily, and his will in regard to creatures does not bear any stamp of necessity. Therefore, it is impossible to demonstrate that God wanted or did not want to create the world; the only way we can attain the knowledge of these wishes is revelation. For us to know whether God has willed or not willed what he is not obliged to want, God himself must say that he willed it. Accordingly, the creation of the world is an object of belief for us, not an object of demonstration or science. It is important to know this in order that, once again, we may not undertake to demonstrate a truth of faith by offering insufficient proofs and providing infidels with the occasion to hold us in derision for basing our faith on such reasons.[55]

---

sed per demonstrationem nullus unquam investigavit ipsum."—*Summa Theologica*, I, 13, 53, 1, reply to obj. 4: "Illi enim [Philosophi] non dicunt esse creatum, nisi quod ante se non praesupponit aliud, sicut ens et unum: quod autem ante se supponit aliquid, non dicunt esse creatum, sed factum per informationem; creationem autem secundum quod fit ex puro nihilo, per rationem cognoscere non potuerunt. Non enim cum sit entis creati, decurrit nisi de ente in ens, de principio, scilicet in principiatum, et non potest se fundare in non ente. Et ideo, ut dicit Aristoteles in primo *Physicorum*, omnes Philosophi convenerunt in hoc, quod ex nihilo nihil fit. Propter quod etiam non acceptio intellectus humani, sed articulus fidei est quod dicitur in symbolo Nicaeno: *Credo in unum Deum, Patrem omnipotenterm, factorem coeli et terrae.*"

55. Aquinas, *Summa Theologiae*, I, 46, 2, body of article: "Unde mundum incoepisse est credibile, non autem demonstrabile vel scibile. Et hoc utile est, ut consideretur, ne forte aliquis, quod fides est demonstrare praesumens, rationes non necessarias inducat, quae praebeant materiam irridendi infidelibus existimantibus nos propter hujusmodi rationes credere, quae fides sunt."—The answer provided by St. Thomas

But the consequences of the reform inaugurated by Albertus Magnus and brought to fruition by Thomas did not stop there. Not only did the reform forbid natural reason to undertake any demonstration in matters of fact, but also it even seemed to happily pile up difficulties about the reduced knowledge that we can attain about a creator. It is as if the overwhelming concern of Thomas were to shrink as much as possible the illuminative way whose breadth delighted the heart of a Bonaventure. If the first cause of this severity is sought, it is not found in some modification of the traditional conception of God. It is found in a profound modification of the Augustinian conception of human beings. God is always the Father of lights, and he has not become stingier with his illuminations, but humans have become more opaque. The soul has become less and less permeable by divine light, and the reason is that the soul has distanced itself more from God, to be bound more and more closely to the body. Albertus Magnus is the first to enter this path, not without much reticence and great hesitation. The relentless logic of the new philosophical orientation requires the sacrifice of too many consoling illusions for religious consciousness to resign itself to it immediately. But Thomas will do what Albertus Magnus did not dare to do. He will place the sensible world between the soul and God.

In a doctrine like St. Bonaventure's, the soul has maximum independence in regard to the body. In the first place, the soul is not a pure form, but composed of spiritual matter and a form. Consequently, it is self-sufficient according to the requirements of the strictest Aristotelianism. In a sense, the doctrine of hylomorphic composition of angels and human souls has the result of distinguishing them more radically from God. On the one hand, God is posited in his absolute simplicity, and on the other, the creature is posited with its dual composition of essence and existence, and of matter and form, as characterized by an inevitable multiplicity. This is why Bonaventure declares that, even if the doctrine of hylomorphic composition of angels is not true, it at least has the merit of being less dangerous.[56] But, in another sense, to consider the soul as

to the Augustinian objection that if the world always existed, it must have existed for infinity of years by now is remarkable and bold. It is situated in the context of the most explosive Averroist questions. *De Aeternitate Mundi contra Murmurantes*, conclusion: "Et praeterea adhuc non est demonstratum, quod Deus non possit facere ut sint infinita actu."

56. Bonaventure, *In Hexaemeron*, IV: "Minus est periculosum dicere, quod angelus sit compositus, etiamsi verum non sit, quam quod sit simplex; quia hoc ego attribuo angelo, nolens ei attribuere quod ad Deum solum aestimo pertingere, et hoc propter

composed of matter and form is to subject it to everything Aristotle requires of a genuine substance. As a simple form the soul would need to be united to an alien matter to achieve full substantiality. As composite of matter and form, the soul is complete in itself, substantial and independent of the body to which it is united.[57] Moreover, it immediately follows from this thesis that every composite is explained by the presence of a multiplicity of hierarchical forms. In beings like humans, there are at least two forms, that of the soul, which informs its spiritual matter, and that of the body, which organizes its corporeity. But in reality, there are many others. Since the body whose form is the soul, is already organized and capable of exercising its vegetative functions by itself, it is certainly necessary to attribute to it the forms necessary to accomplish those functions. When the soul is united to the body in order to penetrate it with its own life and form a new substance by the union of two substances, the soul subordinates those multiple forms, completes their action, and confers its last perfection upon the human composite. The point is not to compromise the unity of the human composite or even to render the union of body and soul less intimate, but the intimacy of this union, as Bonaventure conceives it and as his doctrine of forms allows him to conceive it, leaves the soul with all its independence, but placing all activity and all perfection on the soul's side. When the soul is united to the already organized body and gives it its highest form, the soul certainly yields to the desire to perfect and finish the body, but we are not in the presence of an incomplete substance, which would look to the body for the possibility of being completely realized. We are in the presence of an already complete and higher substance that intimately penetrates an already complete but lower substance, seizes it from within, and animates it in some measure as God animates the soul.[58] Accordingly, these two theories are closely associated in Bonaventure's mind. What forms the bond in this association is the desire to safeguard illumination and the soul's immortality. The higher unity of the human composite must obviously be maintained, but we must not forget that one day the composite will be dissolved into two elements of very different worth, whose destinies will be very different. The soul is destined to immortality and beatitude, and this end accounts for all the soul's properties: because the soul is destined

---

reverentiam Dei."

57. Bonaventure, *In Libros Sententiarum*, II, 17, 1, 2, 2.

58. Bonaventure, *In Libros Sententiarum*, II, 26, 1, 2, 4.

to beatitude, it is immortal; because it is immortal, it is separable from the body; because it is separable from the body, it is not only a form, but also a genuine substance: *ex his apparet qualiter finis beatitudinis necessitatem imponuit praedictarum conditionum ipsi animae ad beatitudinem ordinatae. Quoniam autem ut beatificabilis est immortalis; ideo, cum unitur mortali corpori, potest ab eo separari; ac per hoc non tantum forma est verum etiam hac aliquid.*[59] If the soul is a substance by itself, the body is one also. This keeps Bonaventure from affirming the unity of forms in the human composite at the very moment when he most strongly affirms the unity of the composite.

Albertus Magnus seems to have retained some of these scruples. He departs from the Augustinian tradition on the question of the soul's substantiality and doubts that the soul is composed of matter and form. But the soul is a creature and, therefore, it cannot claim God's perfect simplicity, and is metaphysically composed of essence and existence. *Quod est* is not identified with *quo est* in the soul. However, this composition does not necessarily entail hylomorphic composition. Albertus Magnus does not consider that some *materia* is indispensable to guarantee angels and souls a sufficient degree of substantiality,[60] but he certainly hesitated to admit the form's absolute unity in the human composite. Clearly, Albertus Magnus in no way admits the coexistence of several substantial forms in humans, but with Bonaventure he still admits that the soul is the form of an already organized body. As for discovering whether and how these forms subsist in the final composite, this is a point on which Albert does not inform us, no doubt because he does not come to a clear awareness of the problem and does not perceive all its complexity.[61]

By contrast, in St. Thomas Aquinas there is no longer any uncertainty, and the rupture between Albertus Magnus's disciple and tradition is complete. The *physical* character of the soul and the soul's role of *nature* in regard to the human body are now affirmed as rigorously as possible. The soul is no longer conceived as the form of an already organized body, but as the form of matter that the soul itself organizes into a body. The corporeity of any body, including the human body, is nothing but the

59. Bonaventure, *Breviloquium*, II, 9, 4–5.

60. Albertus Magnus, *In Libros Sententiarum*, II, 2, 2; and *Summa Theologica*, II, 4, 13, 1.

61. On the uncertainty that remains in Bonaventure's thinking about these questions, see Ziesché, "Naturlehre Bonaventuras," 168–69. Regarding Albertus Magnus's uncertainty, see Schneider, *Beiträge*, IV, 5, pp. 28–29.

substantial form that situates it in a certain genus and a certain species. Therefore, there cannot be different substantial forms in one and the same being, one making it a substance, the other making it a body or an animal, and another one situating it in the human or equine species. Once a substantial form has taken hold of certain matter to inform it, all subsequent forms can only be accidental forms and consequently incapable of engendering a genuine substance. What is true of substantial forms in general is true of the form of the body in particular. The human soul and it alone is what confirms in the body all its organization.[62]

Consequently, the only genuinely complete substance of which we can speak is the composite of soul and body. The soul taken in itself is evidently a substance, but it is not a complete substance. For St. Thomas Aquinas, the soul radically excludes matter as form radically excludes potency. Accordingly, it is impossible to conceive the soul, *qua* soul as composed of matter and form. It is form by definition.[63] Precisely because the soul is only a form it does not suffice to constitute a complete substance.[64] We cannot abstract from its union with the body when we want to give its definition. Something composite remains in the soul even when death separates it from the body. Far from rejoicing at finally being liberated from such servitude, the separated soul conserves a disposition and a natural inclination to be reunited with the body. In short, the human soul is only found in its state of natural perfection when it is united to the body: *anima non habet naturalem perfectionem, nisi secundum quod est corpori unita.*[65]

From this point of view, the soul no longer appears to us as a reality capable of being self-sufficient. It is only a part of human nature: *pars humanae naturae.* The only fully substantial reality is the human being.

62. Aquinas, *Summa contra Gentes*, IV, 81, at *Quod vero*. This single form takes the place of all others, because it contains them virtually, *virtute*.—Cf. *In Libros Sententiarum*, I, 76, 4, reply to obj. 4; and *Summa Theologiae*, I, 76, 4, body of article.

63. Aquinas, *Summa Theologiae*, I, 75, 5, body of article.

64. Aquinas, *Summa Theologiae*, I, 75, 2, reply to obj. 1: "Hoc aliquid potest accipi dupliciter. Uno modo pro quocumque subsistente, alio modo, pro subsistente completo in natura alicujus speciei. Primo modo excludit inhaerentiam acccidentis et formae materialis. Secundo modo excludit etiam imperfectionem partis; unde manus posset dici hoc aliquid primo modo, sed non secundo modo. Sic igitur, cum anima humana sit pars speciei humanae, potest dici hoc aliquid primo modo, quasi subsistens sed non secundo modo: sic enim compositum ex anima et corpore dicitur hoc aliquid."

65. Aquinas, *Summa Theologiae*, I, 90, 4, body of article. Cf. I, 76, 1, reply to obj. 6; also Ia IIae, 4, 5, reply to obj. 2.

Such a doctrine is troubling not only for the indirect consequences that could result, notably in what concerns the aptitude of this incorporeal substance to subsist after death. It is also troubling in itself and in the completely new situation in which it places the soul in regard to God. With Thomas, we are no longer confronted by a light soul, always ready to detach itself from the body to rise to God. We are dealing with a soul closely related to the body and heavily weighted down by matter. Perhaps their relation is no more intimate than in the doctrine of St. Bonaventure, but it is different. In Bonaventure, a soul that is already complete in itself, comes through a desire of pure grace to perfect the organized body and raise it to the dignity of a human body. In Thomas, a soul that by itself is not a complete substance seeks to be united to a body, because it needs the body in order to be realized in all its perfection. The soul is completed when it possesses the body. When it is separated, it misses the body. Accordingly, all the problems that we posed for the soul are going to be posed for the whole human from now on.

In the first place, there is the problem of knowledge. We need a theory of knowledge such that it is clearly the human being and not only the soul that knows. There are really only two options for the solution of this problem. Either our intellect possesses intelligible species within itself and therefore innate knowledge, or originally it is without such knowledge, and it must form it with the help of the senses. In the first hypothesis, the body is useless and does not contribute at all to the formation of our knowledge. On the contrary, we can even say that the body prevents us from knowing, and that the soul must turn away from it to perceive in all their purity the innate ideas of which the soul is naturally full. In the second hypothesis, the body is the necessary instrument that the soul must use to acquire knowledge. Far from being an obstacle to it, the body is an indispensable help for us, with which we cannot dispense. If the soul is naturally united to the body, and if the highest operation of the soul is intellectual knowledge, it would be truly odd that the soul should find an obstacle to its highest operation in a union that is natural to it and that in some measure is part of its definition.[66] The very nature and closeness of the bond that we have established between soul and body compels us to deny innate knowledge to humans and to locate the origin of our ideas in

66. Aquinas, *Summa Theologiae*, I, 84, 3, body of article: "Praecipue autem hoc videtur inconveniens si ponatur esse animae naturale corpori uniri, ut supra habitum est, quaestione 76, articulo 1. Inconveniens enim est quod naturalis operatio alicujus res totaliter impediatur per id quod est sibi secundum naturam."

sense knowledge. Here below, we only raise ourselves to the intelligible by the intermediary of the sensible. We must wait for the future life for another mode of knowledge to become natural to us. To attribute innate knowledge to humans is to identify them with angels. Platonism is the theory of the knowledge of separated intelligences.[67]

Applying this doctrine to our knowledge of God's existence, the difficulty of acquiring it appears to be considerably aggravated. The broad illuminative avenue that St. Bonaventure so liberally opened is immediately narrowed, and the ray of light that traversed it only arrives in refracted form, almost extinguished. Yet it still reaches us, and we can say that in a certain sense, the truth according to which our soul judges all things is the first truth. But we are far from the ease with which the Seraphic Doctor led us to God! Between angels and humans divine illumination undergoes profound modification. It is weakened and attenuated so that, in order to adapt to the sensible beings that we are, we can no longer read in it the intelligible species that the least of the angels discerns there. The divine ray reaches the angel rich in intelligible species that constitute so many instances of innate knowledge. When the divine ray reaches the human agent intellect, it provides no more than the empty light of the first principles, so uniformly transparent a light that we do not perceive it in itself, and its presence is discovered by the first conceptions that it allows us to form by abstracting the species of sensible things.

What is true of all our knowledge is true of our knowledge of God. We know all things thanks to the reflection of the first truth that reaches us, but we know nothing of the eternal reasons. The only innatism of which we can speak in connection with humans is virtual innatism that left to itself would be incapable of discovering content.[68] Consequently, we

67. Aquinas, *Summa Theologiae*, I, 84, 7: "Hujus autem ratio est, quia potentia cognoscitiva proportionatur cognoscibili. Unde intellectus angeli, qui est totalitar a corpore separatus, objectum proprium est substantia intelligibilis a corpore separata, et per hujusmodi intelligibile materialia cognoscit. Intellectus autem humani, qui est conjunctus corpori, proprium objectum est quidditas, sive natura in materia corporali existens . . . Et ideo necesse est, ad hoc quod intellectus actu intelligit suum objectum proprium, quod convertat se ad phantasmata, ut speculetur naturam universalem in particulari existentem, si autem proprium objectum intellectus nostri esset forma separata, vel si formae rerum sensibilium subsisterent non in particularibus, secundum Platonicos, non importeret, quod intellectus noster semper intelligendo converteret se ad phantasmata."—See also *Summa Theologiae*, I, 89, 1, body of article; and Ia IIae, 6, 1, reply to obj. 2.

68. Aquinas, *Quaestiones Disputate de Veritate*, X, 6, body of article: "Et secundum hoc, verum est quod scientiam a sensibilibus mens nostra accipit; nihilominus tamen

have no innate idea of God any more than we have one of anything else, and we must demonstrate his existence by his effects. But the Thomistic proofs of God's existence are not remarkable simply by their content and by the constant concerns they evince to take their point of departure in sensible reality. The mere fact of their existence is as significant as their content. We can hardly speak of proofs of God's existence in doctrines like those of Bonaventure and Anselm. For these doctrines, God is either already given through faith or else immediately evident to reason. By contrast, Thomas, following his master Albertus Magnus, refuses to start from faith and denies us any spontaneous knowledge of God's existence. Therefore we must now fight for that knowledge and demonstrate it by rigorous proofs. When the consequences of innatism are developed logically, it dispenses with any demonstration. Empiricism like that of Thomas excludes direct intuition and requires proofs.

The content of these proofs is well-known. Although interpretations may differ as to this or that detail, it is impossible not to agree upon the spirit that animates the proofs. Manifestly, in St. Thomas's mind, the proofs of God's existence have a limiting value. Each of them is based on two elements whose solidity and evidence are equally indispensable, a sensible experience that can be the observation of movement, causes, the contingent, the degrees of perfection in things, or the order that reigns in them, plus an application of the principle of causality that hangs movement upon the immobile, second causes upon the first cause, the contingent upon the necessary, the imperfect upon the perfect, order upon ordering intelligences. It remains no less true that Thomas's is a demonstrated God instead of an evident God like that of Anselm or Bonaventure. His idea is not a principle for us, it is a laboriously won conclusion thanks to the cooperation of first principles and sensible knowledge. The proof of the first mover, *prima et manifestior via*, itself only leads us to God's existence through the subtle and often delicate discussion that the *Summa contra Gentes* pursues through Aristotelian conceptions about causality

---

ipsa anima in se similitudines rerum format, in quantum per lumen intellectus agentis efficiuntur formae a sensibilibus abstractae intelligibiles actu, ut in intellectu possibili recipi possint. Et sic etiam in lumine intellectus agentis nobis est quodammodo omnis scientia originaliter indita mediantibus universalibus conceptionibus, quae statim lumine intellectus agentis cognoscuntur, per quas sicut per universalia principia judicamus de aliis, et ea praecognoscimus in ipsis."—This passage may be completed by *Quaestiones Disputate de Veritate*, XI, 1, body of article: "Primae conceptiones intellectus, quae statim lumine intellectus agentis cognoscuntur per species a sensibilibus abstractas." Cf. *Quaestiones Disputate de Veritate*, I, 4, reply to obj. 5.

and infinity. Thomas has immersed us in dialectic and, by denying direct illumination or innate ideas, he has burnt our ships. Since God does not make himself known to us by imprinted species or by natural evidence, it only remains for us to hope in the principle of causality. Therefore, the rational certainty of God's existence hangs upon the certainty of that principle and upon the legitimacy of the way Thomas uses it.

When we view this aspect of philosophical reform undertaken by Albertus Magnus and Thomas, we cannot help being astonished by the boldness these two Dominicans demonstrated and the ultimate success of their efforts. Their endeavor is very far from consisting, as is generally believed, in more or less consciously falsifying philosophy to enslave it to theology. It seems rather to have consisted in continually doing violence to the religious consciousness of their time in order to bend it to the requirements of philosophical thinking. In particular, for St. Thomas, everything transpires as if he always chose his philosophical solutions in the line of greatest theological resistance. Obviously, both theologians obeyed the watchword given by the popes to the University of Paris: *philosophia ancilla theologiae*. But we must admit that they supplied a completely new and quite singular interpretation of it. To better guarantee the services of the handmaiden, theology had just freed her.

Until then, the consoling illusion had been entertained that there existed Wisdom, a kind of common ground of philosophy and theology, and that reason guided by faith oversaw everything. Revelation was presented as so reasonable that the prophets and Fathers of the Church could legitimately consider pagan philosophers as their authentic precursors. The church's dream of universal expansion and proximate unification of humanity under the common doctrine of the faith were nourished in their turn by this illusion. If revelation is totally justifiable though not wholly intelligible, we can still hope to make it universally accepted. But now we know philosophy and theology do not overlap. Pagan philosophers did not rationally anticipate the content of revelation. We cannot even give an adequate account of revelation's mysteries, we who at least know the expression of that content. What is more serious, the greatest service we can give to faith in the face of infidels is not to make faith ridiculous by trying to demonstrate it. The *Summa contra Gentes* is precisely the model of this new apologetics that pushes rational demonstration as far as possible, while making it as difficult as possible, and that stops honestly where reason must yield to authority. Albertus Magnus and Thomas took the first step on the road the led to separating Augustinian wisdom into positive theology and independent philosophy. They ought to receive the honor for this, just as they bear the responsibility.

The content of the Albertine-Thomist doctrine must have been as disconcerting for thirteenth-century theologians as its spirit. It is immediately evident that, unlike John Scotus Eriugena or Bonaventure, Albertus Magnus and Thomas are men for whom the world around them exists, perhaps even more for the master than the disciple. In the view of Albertus Magnus, the universe interpreted by Aristotle has just become weightier and more real. For Albertus, things are no longer the transparent gauze that scarcely disguises the face of God. Nature is no longer simply a book analogous to Holy Scripture, a second system of symbols whose meaning is equivalent to revelation. Albertus Magnus is interested in what things are before being interested in what they represent. The mark of God certainly remains upon the surface of things, but is it only a mark? What can we conclude from such a light trace? The mark a human foot leaves in the dust is only a trace of the sole and toes of a foot. It does not represent the foot's upper service, inner structure, thickness, or its connection to the leg. It is even truer that the mark that the sole of a foot leaves in the dust does not teach us anything about the human to whom it belongs. Accordingly, God's mark in creatures is nothing more than a sign thanks to which we can form some probable knowledge about God.[69] But things in themselves already deserve to hold our attention.

This is why the contemporaries of Albertus Magnus and Thomas witnessed the spectacle, so natural for us but so new and perhaps even so troubling for some of them, of professional theologians tied to the study of pagan philosophy and lecturing upon the scientific explanation of natural phenomena. Albertus Magnus takes on the task of making Aristotle intelligible to the Latin readers and of offering continuous explanations that take the place of the original text. His work is an authentic restoration of Aristotelian philosophy, where we encounter not only the same number of Aristotle's known treatises with the same titles that the Greek philosopher had given them, but also reconstructed lost works,

69. Albertus Magnus, *Summa Theologica*, I, 3, 15, 1, 1 at *Solutio*: "Vestigium proprie est impressio pedis in pulvere vel via molli. Et quia omnis impressio secundum tactum fit, omnis autem tactus secundum ultimum tangentis, ideo vestigium similitudo est ad ultimum quod est in pede, et hoc est planta pedis et digitorum. Quia autem hoc imperfect repraesentat pedem et imperfectius eum cujus est pes; spissitudinem enim pedis non repraesentat, neque lineamenta et figuras superiorum pedis nec interiorum. Et secundum hoc dicitur vestigium Dei in creaturis, signum scilicet quo probabiliter aliquid Dei cognoscitur."—Cf. *In Libros Sententiarum*, I, 3, F. 14, at *Solutio*.

and even works that Aristotle did not have time to write.[70] If Albertus Magnus wants to give us a continuous exposition of Aristotle in the manner of Avicenna, Thomas wants to give us a literal and explanatory commentary in the manner of Averroes. Neither doctor wants to shake off the rudiments of dialectical techniques as quickly as possible and to plunge definitively into pure theology. They continued to study, comment upon, and explain Aristotle. St. Thomas Aquinas wrote his commentaries on *De Coelo* and *De Generatione* while he composed the *Summa Theologiae*.[71] If the lists of their complete works upset the modern reader because of the abundance of theological writings, the proportion of philosophical writings must have been no less astonishing for their contemporaries. Today, it seems very natural to us that two Dominicans, whose official function was to teach theology and transmit God's revealed truth, should have made the study and interpretation of a pagan philosophy the work of their whole lives. But it is quite easy to conceive that the vigilant guardians of theological tradition should have felt some unease at seeing the competition offered by Aristotle's text with the sacred text and that several of them should have been deeply scandalized by it.

Moreover, Albertus Magnus was not merely an erudite seeker of book learning. He was also informed and inquisitive about direct observations and things. Roger Bacon, who was so jealous of Albertus's reputation, acknowledged that Albertus had observed a great deal and spared no expense to learn. Albertus Magnus declared that he had taken long trips to find minerals with which he wanted to experiment, that he devoted himself to alchemy and studied its transformations to learn their nature and properties.[72] He insisted on the necessity of experience, which alone permits us to reach sure conclusions in natural sciences. No doubt Albertus Magnus's requirements for experimental verification are not yet very rigorous. He imprudently placed on the same level what scholars whom he considers worthy of trust have observed and what he himself observed. Some observations that he claims to have made are really surprising.[73] Yet, what is most surprising is not that Albertus

70. Albertus Magnus, *Physica*, I, 1, 1.

71. Mandonnet, *Chronologie sommaire*, 150–51.

72. Albertus Magnus, *De Mineralibus*, III, 1, 1: "Exul enim aliquando factus fui, longe vadens ad loca metallica, ut experiri possem naturas metallorum, ut ex his innotesceret et aliquatenus eorum natura et accidentia eorum propria."

73. Albertus Magnus, *De Animalibus*, Stadler edition, VIII, 1, 3, p. 581: "Similiter autem hahynoz [*sic*] and yboz [*sic*] quem supra *acontim* [*sic*] vocavimus, pugnant ad

Magnus committed errors but that he discovered some scientific truths. What is really truly new is the orientation itself of a scholar who devotes whole volumes to describe minerals, plants, animals, and humans, no longer considered as vestiges or images of God, but as realities that are interested in themselves. This theologian-naturalist must have appeared a living paradox to the Augustinian theologians. Thomas's curiosity was less broad and less lively than his master's. For Thomas, Aristotle replaces nature. Still, we must not forget that the opposition was drawn much less between bookish science and science of things than between the differing interests in the natural and supernatural. Above all, the issue was to establish whether we ought to prefer philosophy to wisdom and whether too strong a taste for earthly things risks weakening the taste for heavenly things.

Less disturbing than his teacher from the point of view of abuse of profane science, Thomas takes his revenge in metaphysical doctrine. Albertus Magnus always took care to recall at least the principle of divine illumination, without attributing to it any effect beyond the knowledge of first principles. Thomas makes no effort to hide the poverty and weakness of this illumination. For a transparent universe whose smallest parts are penetrated by divine meaning, for a soul intimately illuminated by God's light, Thomas substitutes an opaque universe and a darkened soul. The adherents of Augustinian Wisdom always had their God at hand. A glance at things or a sincere effort to enter into themselves permitted them to discover God or to encounter him. God made himself known directly by a special action that he exercised upon our intellect for this purpose. God's existence was demonstrated *a priori* by a brief reflection on the idea of his essence, and we possessed this idea naturally, as something born with us, a good owed us. In Thomas Aquinas, God absents himself from our intelligence. The illuminative way becomes narrower and more obscure. We must renounce the direct connection and innate knowledge that we erroneously imagined God had bestowed upon us. The human intellect must painfully form a deficient and impoverished idea of God by patiently interrogating sensible things. Why give up so

---

invicem, et tanta est inimicitia harum duarum avium sicut quidam fingunt, quod etiam sanguis mortuarum permisceri et conjungi non potest, sed unus retrahitur ab alio. Et talis est horror inter pennas aquilae et anseris, quod una aquilae penna conjuncta mutis pennis anseris consumit eas, et hoc jam sum expertus in pennis alarum, et forte similiter in aliis pennis dictarum avium. Et dicitur similiter sic esse inter pilos lupi et lanam ovis, sed hoc non sum expertus."

many beautiful dreams? In the name of what authority must religious consciousness be persuaded that mysticism's effusions and consolations are neither knowledge nor proofs? In the name of the pagan Aristotle, certainly a philosophical genius but someone who lived and thought in the shadow of the natural law; someone who, despite all his science, did not know what a humble thirteenth-century woman knew about God thanks to revelation. Everyone was aware of Aristotle's inferiority then, and Thomas did not hesitate to proclaim it loudly: *plus scit modo una vetula de his quae ad fidem pertinent quam quondam omnes.*[74] But Aristotle knew more philosophy than all the theologians, and accordingly, the masters charged with teaching divine wisdom modestly enrolled in his school, intending to overthrow on his authority, the very foundation of our inner life. We must adopt this perspective if we want to understand the profound meaning of the reform carried out by Albertus Magnus and Thomas and the dramatic crisis that their work initiated.

It is not enough to cite routine, the natural fear of new ideas, or the traditional character of all schools in order to explain the violent opposition that the two Dominicans met. We diminish its scope extraordinarily when we only want to see in the attacks against it the expression of petty jealousy of one order against another, as if the Franciscans were humiliated by the brilliant successes of the Dominicans. The character of the brief but extremely violent crisis set off by Thomism is completely different. Situated within the totality of Catholic thought, we can say that Albertine-Thomist philosophy constitutes the only modernist attempt that has ever succeeded.

Let us note first that Albertus and Thomas's philosophy was just as novel and unheard of for Dominicans as for Franciscans. Before this philosophy, Augustine reigned as absolute master in education. Since he had no competition, we can even say that strictly speaking no Augustinian school existed. The first Dominican masters, without establishing a doctrinal synthesis similar to Bonaventure's,[75] could still only be attached to the theoretical movement designated by the term *Augustinianism*. Once Thomism was constituted, it met as much resistance from Dominicans as from Franciscans. The Dominican Robert Kilwardby, Archbishop of Canterbury and Primate of England, directed the Augustinian movement at Oxford and condemned thirty Thomist propositions on March

74. Mandonnet, *Siger*, 1:109n1.

75. Martin, "Quelques premiers maîtres," 556–80.

18, 1277.[76] Yet, while it is certain that the struggle between Augustinianism and Thomism is not sufficiently explained by the opposition and rivalry of the two orders, it at least finds its particular and most striking expression there. If we set aside the violent diatribes of certain *spiritual* Franciscans, who were extremists even within their order,[77] the attitude of John Peckham, who succeeded Kilwardby as Archbishop of Canterbury, seems extremely instructive.[78] When we read the instructions that Peckham gives his clergy or the supplication he addresses to the pope, we cannot help being struck by the authentic, deep religious concern that they express and touched by their pained tone. We do not find wounded vanity or jealously here. We are faced with a person who fears that there are those who want to tear away his faith to put philosophy in its place. John Peckham obstinately holds the plurality of forms only because, in the last analysis, all philosophy and all Christian wisdom depend on the relation philosophy defines between soul and body. Before being a dialectician who argues, John Peckham is someone whose religious consciousness defends itself.

In his letters, Peckham in fact states that he does not want to sow discord between the religious orders; that he does not even want to compare them, although certain Dominicans proclaim their order to be more learned than all others; and that the Franciscan order has nothing to fear from the comparison.[79] He adds that the doctrine of the form's unity maintained by Friar Thomas Aquinas involves invincible theological difficulties.[80] Peckham declares to the cardinals of the Roman Curia,

> We write these things to you so that, if by chance your wisdom hears them spoken of, you may know the real situation with absolute truth. May the holy Roman church deign to consider that the doctrines of the two orders are in almost complete opposition on all questions about which dispute is permitted. The doctrine of one of these orders, abandoning and to a certain point scorning the doctrine of the Fathers, is almost exclusively based on the opinions of philosophers, so that the Lord's house

76. *Chartularium*, I, 558.

77. Mandonnet, *Siger*, 96n1.

78. *Registrum Epistolarum*; and Ehrle, "John Peckham," 172–93.

79. Ehrle, "John Peckham," 179, letter of December 7, 1284.

80. Ehrle, "John Peckham," 181, January 1285: "Alia etiam inconvenientia sequuntur innumera ex hoc ipso. Fuit revera illa opinio fratris Thomae sanctae memoriae de Aquino . . ."

> has been filled with idols and with the apathy that dispute engenders. Finally, may the holy Roman church consider what danger such doctrines constitute for the church's future. Is it not absolutely inevitable that the edifice crumble if its columns are broken? If the authentic doctrines are scorned, like those of Augustine and the rest, will not the Prince of Darkness sweep away the church?[81]

In another letter, directed to the bishop of Lincoln on June 1, 1285, John Peckham again declared:

> You know that we do not at all condemn philosophical studies insofar as they serve theological dogmas, but we condemn these profane novelties that were introduced into the heart of theology around twenty years ago, against philosophical truth and to the detriment of the Fathers, involving rejection and contempt for the doctrine of the Fathers. Consequently, what is the most solid and healthiest doctrine? Is it that of the sons of St. Francis, which is to say that of Friar Alexander of Hales of blessed memory, of Friar Bonaventure, and others like them, whose works are above all suspicion and based both on the Fathers and the philosophers? Or is the most solid doctrine this new one that is almost totally contrary to the first and that devotes its powers to destroying or shaking up everything that St. Augustine teaches on the eternal ideas and the unchanging light, the soul's powers, seminal reasons innate in matter, and on numberless other questions, propagating controversy throughout the whole world in this way? May our elders, they who dwell in wisdom, see it; may God in heaven see it and correct it. Therefore, we pray insistently in the name of vigilant concern that you owe your flock, [that you] lead in the path of truth by faithfully communicating the content of this letter to those whom an unworthy writing may have made fall into an error of law and fact. Since the doctrine of one of these orders is almost completely contrary to that of the other, except for the data of faith, and since the contrary of the true can only be false, I beg you to meditate upon the seriousness of the danger the obstinate defenders of these many errors constitute, errors that have spread almost throughout the

81. Ehrle, "John Peckham," 181: "et ut sacrosancta Romana ecclesia attendere dignaretur, quod cum doctrina duorum ordinum in omnibus dubitabilibus sub pene penitus hodie adversetur, cumque doctrina alterius eorumdem, abjectis et ex parte vilipensis sanctorum sententiis, philosophicis dogmatibus quasi totaliter innitatur, ut plena sit idolis domus Dei et langore."

> whole world, some of whose defenders refuse to submit to the correction of the prelates of the church and of Catholic doctors.

Peckham calls upon God to direct the Supreme Pontiff's heart to be concerned about the danger and to separate the tares from the good grain: . . . *et utinam ille, in cujus manu cordis sunt regum, summo Pontifici parasset vaccandi spatium et hoc ejus animam inclinasset, ut vellet ipse zizania a tritico distinguere.*[82] We know what John Peckham and the Augustinians were losing or afraid of losing. After comparing the doctrine of Bonaventure and Thomas, we can no long interpret these words as expressing normal philosophical impatience about being disturbed or of petty antagonism between rival orders. They primarily express all the anguish of religious consciousness that trembles for the very foundations of faith.

But if matters certainly stand thus, we see how inaccurate it would be to interpret the work accomplished by St. Thomas as a vast apologetic endeavor. In him, apologetics is only derivative, the result of prior philosophical elaboration. Thomas does not first seek to tie up in a bundle or even organize in a system the philosophical theses most satisfactory for his time's religious consciousness. Everything transpires as if he wanted to do exactly the opposite. Instead of systematically yielding to the entreaties of faith, his whole effort consists first of installing philosophy in faith, in a domain where reason will be no less independent of Averroist literalism than of religious dogma. Once this realm is defined, Thomas situates human beings within it and with nature as understood in Greek speculation, weighed down with matter and reality burdened with temporal interests, possessing indisputable existence and meaning by themselves. Obviously, Thomas remains a theologian, and his interpretation of the universe remains religious and Christian. However, what is completely

82. Ehrle, "John Peckham," 186: "Praeterea noverit ipse quod philosophorum studia minime reprobamus, quatenus mysteriis theologicis famulantur; sed profanas vocum novitates, quae contra philosophicam veritatem sunt in sanctorum injuriam citra viginti annos in altitudines theologicas introductae, abjectis et vilipensis sanctorum assertionibus evidenter. Quae sit ergo solidior et sanior doctrina, vel filiorum sancti Francisci . . . vel illa novella quasi tota contraria, quae quidquid docet Augustinus de regulis aeternis et luce incommutabili, de potentiis animae, de rationibus seminalibus inditis materiae et consimilibus innumeris, destruat pro viribus et enervat, pugnas verborum inferens toti mundo . . . Et cum doctrina unius ordinis sit tota pene contraria doctrinae alterius, exceptis fidei fundamentis, nec potest esse vero contrarium nisi falsum, pensetis, quantum sit periculum, tam multiplicem falsitatem habere pene per orbis spatium improbos defensores, quorum nonnulli correctioni praelatorum ecclesiae et doctorum catholicorum despiciunt subjacere."

transformed by this novelty is the conception of the nature that the supernatural is to fulfill and transfigure. What is new in Thomism is that in the concern to lead human beings to their highest last ends, the doctrine never argues as if their last ends must already be more than half achieved in order to be subsequently achievable. Accordingly, the doctrine begins by accepting the real as it is given, and its first step is in the philosophical, not the religious, order. From this moment, Thomism is developed as a philosophical system whose field of investigation, at least in its intention, extends to all nature. If it is developed according to the direction that we see him taking, it is not at all that this seems religiously comfortable, but (despite being extremely uncomfortable) simply because Thomas believes it true. His philosophical truth is certainly one with his religious truth, but the more deeply philosophical truth is pursued for its own sake from the outset, the deeper will be the point of connection that will have been established from the outset, and the more convincing the verification of this agreement will be. Therefore, true philosophy goes freely to its own completion and therefore verifies as a fact its encounter with religion. In no way does it follow that the religious consciousness of Thomas had shallower needs than those of John Peckham or Bonaventure, nor that his philosophy is less Christian than theirs. It simply follows that just as the natural is a necessary moment of the supernatural, philosophy taken in itself becomes a necessary moment of religion. In the human being of Thomas there is more of the philosopher. Yet there is not less of the Christian. Evidently, the philosopher cannot make a place for himself without giving the Christian the impression of intruding upon his place. However, Thomas does not believe that religious susceptibilities are respectable, if they are not rationally based. He has the sense of only divesting religious consciousness of its illusions. What is deepest and most original in Thomas is the very attempt at philosophical honesty, of complete acceptance of the demands of the real and of reason. Perhaps some theologians will show us that this is what constituted the originality of his thinking. As historians of philosophy, we must see in his work the first system of purely rational truths that Western speculation established, and one of the direct sources of modern philosophy.

FIVE

Reasoning by Analogy in Campanella

Te perducam de similitudine in similitudinem
sub ducatu scientiae et fidei.

Realis Philosophiae Epilogisticae

There are numerous and tenacious prejudices against Renaissance philosophies. Evaluations of the authors of these philosophies are generally unkind. We can say that Campanella is plausibly the worst treated thinker of the period. Leafing through Campanella's work, we initially seem to discover a foggy mind, an unbalanced imagination, and a multitude of whimsical deductions. Francisque Bouillier gives a fairly good summary of the impression Campanella produces, remarking: "It would be difficult to imagine the queerness and childishness of the proofs he piles up and the credulity with which he accepts the crudest popular beliefs to come to the conclusion that the world is a living animal, that it is completely life, soul, and feeling."[1] While we await the revision of unjust judgments against Renaissance philosophers, we would like to show that the apparent oddness of Campanella's system, upon analysis, resolves into a vision of the world that has coherence and that the queerness and childishness of the proofs suppose a logic by which the proofs are explained. Campanella's conception of human knowledge allows us to discover that.

1. Bouillier, *Histoire de la philosophie cartésienne*, bk. 1, 18.

All human knowledge originates in sensation, according to Campanella's philosophy. This thesis is set up against the Aristotelian deduction of different powers of the soul. It is based on the affirmation of a corporeal spirit that circulates throughout all the animal's organs and assures all its functions.[2] The soul's absolute unity is the foundation of this theory of knowledge. It is helpful to establish this first for the external sense. Each *sensorium* does not suppose a distinct informing power. The sensorial organs are simply indications of different ways by which sensations can be introduced. What does not reach the sentient mind by a coarse part of the body arrives by a finer and more tenuous part. What does not traverse an opaque part will traverse a translucent part. But the same spirit always perceives everything through different organs. Thus, the same man writes with a pen, cuts with a sword, and digs with a mattock.[3]

Every sensation is the perception of a passion. It is necessary not to say just "every sensation is a passion." The animal's spirit does not feel everything it suffers, but only that which determines a change of state in the spirit itself, the judge of actions that modify it. When this change does not occur, there is no longer any sensation.[4] A sleeping person or someone very attentive to a given object no longer perceives sensations that he perceives in a normal state.[5] Similarly, in a passion like anger, a multitude of little passions are hidden and remain unperceived.[6] Accordingly, sensation is the perception of a passion. But we must always add, "and a judgment about the felt object." According to Aristotle and the Scholastics, sensation requires information from the soul in such a way that the spirit informed by the object would undergo a total transmutation, at least for a time.[7] That is absurd, however. For this doctrine to be true, the form of the object would have to be momentarily separated from it, come to the sensing power, and be imprinted on it. During this

2. According to the fundamental distinction posited by Telesius and adopted by Campanella, we call *spirit* the bodily principle from which sensation and reasoning come and *soul* the immaterial and immortal principle of human beings. *Spiritus* and *mens* should not be confused.

3. Campanella, *De Sensu Rerum et Magia*, bk. II, ch. 17.

4. Campanella, *Realis Philosophia Epilogisticae Partes IV* (Frankfurt, 1623; which also contains the *Civitas Solis*), bk. I, ch. 12, art. 1.

5. Campanella, *De Sensu Rerum*, bk. II, ch. 13.

6. Campanella, *De Sensu Rerum*, bk. I, ch. 4.

7. Campanella, *Realis Philosophia*, bk. I, ch. 12, art. 1.

time, the object would consequently be stripped of its own form like naked matter or would be totally corrupted.[8] The difficulty for the sensing subject would be as great. Since all information supposes total destruction of the previous form and the introduction of a new form, the subject would successively become all the forms that it is called to receive, which again is absurd. Therefore, sensation does not occur by information of the subject.

It remains true that sensation consists of a simple modification of this subject. Every sensation is an alteration. When the sensible conserves or perfects the symmetry of the constituent parts of the sense, it is agreeable and pleases. When the sensible destroys that symmetry, it is painful and displeases. In all cases, the sensible acts through modification of the spirit. For example, the light that a stone reflects traverses the eye, touches the spirit, and impresses upon it the figure that it has received from the stone. The spirit is not informed by the stone. Otherwise, it would become the stone itself. But it feels itself modified by the light that the stone reflects, and that suffices for the spirit to form a judgment on the nature of the object that modifies it. Likewise, the spirit knows the sun and fire when they modify it. After the feeble modification the spirit experiences, it measures the strength of the fire by a judgment and estimates that it is considerable. Accordingly, sensation always supposes not only a passion but also a simultaneous reasoning, which is so rapid that it is not perceived, but it is nevertheless true reasoning, since recognizing fire according to part of its heat supposes a genuine syllogism.[9] Consequently, after sensation we see reasoning about nature occur, upon which we will have to insist. Let us note for the moment only that all sensation is reducible to perception of a passion accompanied by reason.

Such is the nature of the external sense from which we see all human knowledge develop. Otherwise, it would be necessary to recur to other powers of the soul distinct from it. In the first place comes memory. Memory resides in the sentient spirit, which is identical to the spirit that feels and remembers.[10] All sensation supposes the production of a movement in the spirit, and the movement remains there as we see something stay in the air because of its extreme mobility. But other things that the spirit perceives determine an infinite number of other movements. This

8. Campanella, *De Sensu Rerum*, bk. II, chs. 12 and 15.

9. Campanella, *De Sensu Rerum*, bk. II, chs. 15 and 21. Cf. bk. I, ch. 4.

10. Campanella, *De Sensu Rerum*, bk. II, ch. 20.

engenders the illusion that the spirit has forgotten the earlier things. However, it always knows them, and the moments determined by the objects' actions remain in the spirit as if asleep. If one of these moments is never awakened again by the same object or by some similar object, inevitably, it is completely forgotten. The spirit that had been modified is exhaled and exits the body without communicating to the newly engendered spirit other movements than those it currently possesses. But the memory is preserved when the spirit has perceived the same thing several times, has received a single but strong impression of it, or frequently perceives similar objects. Therefore, memory is enfeebled sensation.[11] In this way, seeing a ship, we remember the seasickness we suffered on a voyage. Although we are far from experiencing it with the same force, it is still very certain that one and the same power of the soul feels and remembers.

We will be led to the same conclusion in regard to the faculty of imagination, and it is easy to admit it after the previous considerations. The more a spirit has perceived things and has conserved memories of them, the easier it can imagine others by uniting and dividing the movements that these things have left in it.[12] Imagining is nothing but picturing the unknown by means of the known, as one might imagine what England could be by looking at Sicily or could imagine a centaur by picturing the horse and his rider as just one thing. Because material things are the most evident and best known of all, the imagination easily represents all others in a corporeal fashion, the way poets symbolize virtues by images of women.[13] Accordingly, imagination is also identified with the faculty of feeling.

Imagination is also wholly identified with understanding. If we have an idea of human being, it is because we have previously perceived human beings. No universal natures exist in the world, and when I think of *human being* instead of thinking of Peter or Francis, it is because I have perceived Peter, Francis, and other similar beings. Their particularities have gone out of my spirit, which they moved only once or a few times. By contrast, what they have in common remained there because the spirit has been frequently impressed by it. That is why we retain the general

11. Campanella, *Realis Philosophia*, bk. I, ch. 16, art. 3.

12. Campanella, *De Sensu Rerum*, bk. II, ch. 21.

13. Campanella, *Realis Philosophia*, bk. I, ch. 16, art. 8.

better than the particular.[14] Consequently, there is intellection when the spirit receives a common thing in abstraction from its particularities. In considering Peter, Paul, and Socrates, I see that it is human to feel, speak, have a figure, a nose, and so forth, but I also discover what each of them has in particular, and this is why every individual receives two names, *human being* and *Peter*, for example. The understanding does not stop there and by the same procedure forms the most general ideas of animal, living, body, and finally the most general idea of all, that of *being*. All these operations, apparently so complex, are therefore reduced to memory, which itself is reduced to sensation.[15]

All knowledge, therefore, springs from sensation. Ascertaining this fact will allow us to make value judgments about our different orders of knowledge and to discover the way that leads to truth.

There is a very widespread opinion that only universal knowledge is valid. Genuine science would not have the particular as its object. Anyone who reflects upon the considerations we have just set out cannot fail to see how poorly supported such a proposition is. The widely accepted conception must be overturned, and we must recognize the superiority of particular knowledge by establishing the inferiority of intellectual knowledge in relation to sensible knowledge.

What is it to know? Knowing is having inner certainty about what things are that excludes the slightest doubt. If that is true, it is impossible to deny that in human beings sensible knowledge is surer than any intellectual knowledge. Any knowledge of memory, imagination, or understanding arises out of the senses. When those kinds of knowledge have a need to confirm their certainty, they recur to the senses to be corrected or be established more solidly. No reasoning holds against perception. Even after philosophers have deduced their conclusions about things without looking at them, the first rustic who arrives that has seen the things corrects the learned syllogisms. Augustine and Lactantius denied the existence of the antipodes, but the two eyes of Christopher Columbus destroyed their reasoning beyond any possible dispute.[16] Obviously, we cannot know all things by perceiving them, and we must be content with

14. Campanella, *De Sensu Rerum*, bk. II, ch. 22.

15. Campanella, *Realis Philosophia*, bk. I, ch. 16, art. 6.

16. Campanella, *De Sensu Rerum*, bk. II, ch. 30.

the belief by which we assent to the testimony of those who have directly seen and perceived things. To believe in Adam's existence, the existence of Rome, or the new world, we must believe the eyes of those who have seen them. Believing is perceiving by the senses of another instead of perceiving by one's own senses.[17] It is to accept as true what is proposed to us by another when neither reasoning nor, above all, our own experience contradicts it. When an affirmation conflicts with some sensation or contradicts some reasoning, we only accept it through opinion. On the contrary, we consider to be absolutely true what all our sensations confirm: *Quando omnes sensationes praesentes praeteritaeque concordant, nostrae atque alienae, certa fit scientia.*[18]

The value we can assign to reasoning in the presence of the absolute certainty that concordant sensations give us is simply relative and subordinated. Human beings do not waste time discoursing and arguing about what they are certain of. We only reason in matters where certainty is lacking, and if we want to establish the reasoning on a sure foundation, it must be sought from the sense that alone can provide it. Human beings only reason about what they do not know, and the only point of solid support for their reasoning is in the sensation. The senses are preeminently the light that permits us to see what is hidden in the shadows.[19] Every reasoning is uncertain. Any experience repeated several times is worth more than any discursive argument.[20]

Accordingly, Aristotle was mistaken in declaring that the senses cannot permit us to assign the cause in question, as reason does, and in concluding that sensible knowledge is inferior to rational knowledge. Assigning a cause is to explain where that about which we are uncertain comes from. The senses are certain and require no proof. They are the proof. By contrast, reason is uncertain knowledge, which requires a proof because of this very uncertainty. The proof we attain by assigning the cause of that about which we are not certain must always be sought in a sensation.[21] We also see that the more skilled a person is, the briefer his reasoning is, and the closer he is to the direct sight of things. The perfect

17. Campanella, *Realis Philosophia*, bk. I, ch. 16, art. 4.
18. Campanella, *Realis Philosophia*, bk. I, ch. 16, art. 2. Cf. bk. I, ch. 16, art. 4.
19. Campanella, *De Sensu Rerum*, bk. II, ch. 30.
20. Campanella, *De Sensu Rerum*, bk. II, ch. 31.
21. Campanella, *De Sensu Rerum*, bk. II, ch. 30.

knowledge that God possesses is not discursive. It grasps everything in one single perception.

This is to say that general knowledge is inferior to particular knowledge, of which it is a schematic summary and an impoverishment. The form I perceive from a distance appears to me simply as human. If I see it closer, I know it is Peter. Children call all the women they see *mother*. When they know them better, they no longer fall into that error.[22] All of a hen's eggs are the same to us. For the hen, who knows them better than we do, this is not so. Accordingly, genuine science does not deal with the general. We resign ourselves to the general, but it is a last resort. Physicians know well that knowledge of fever in general is useless. In practice, what helps is knowledge of this or that kind of fever. Better yet, it is knowledge of each particular fever. Still, we are far from the end when we have determined the special nature of a fever. It is necessary to know when and how it began, what are the patient's particular complexion, his strength, and his temperature. It is necessary to know remedies, not in general, as for example the nature of rhubarb, but the nature of this particular rhubarb that must be administered at this point to this particular patent.[23] This is genuine science, something a mind incapable of retaining anything but generalities would be hard-pressed to give us. Knowledge is more perfect insofar as it approaches sense knowledge and takes greater notice of what is particular.

This kind of theory of knowledge might seem to have its logical outcome in a philosophy completely based on observation and experience, concerned above all with leading human thought along prudent, sure paths to knowledge of things. Considered from this point of view, Campanella would take his place among the philosophers who made the effort to establish a philosophy in the most perfect possible agreement with the new data science had just provided. Unquestionably, this tendency, which finds its complete expression in Bacon and Descartes, appears in Campanella's philosophy. It comes directly from Campanella's teacher Telesius, whose physics, at least in its general lines, seems to Campanella to provide the only possible explanation of the universe. Galileo designates the philosopher from Cosenza *venerable father of philosophy*, and

22. Campanella, *De Sensu Rerum*, bk. II, ch. 22.

23. Campanella, *De Sensu Rerum*, bk. II, ch. 22.

Bacon calls him *first of the new men.*[24] Telesius had already insisted on the necessity of philosophers observing nature before explaining it. He reproaches his predecessors, and above all Aristotle, for having devoted so many sleepless nights in meditations upon the structure of the world and the nature of things the world contains without ever dreaming of looking at the world. At the beginning of *De Rerum Natura*,[25] Telesius sums up his philosophy's program: *Mundi constructionem corporumque, in eo contentorum magnitudinem naturamque non ratione, quod antiquioribus factum est inquirendam sed sensu percipiendam et ab ipsis habendam esse rebus.* From his teacher, Campanella inherited this respect for observation and the concern not to reconstruct the world arbitrarily according to the incorrect method of the ancients who, when they failed to discover the causes and principles of the universe, did not hesitate to fabricate an imaginary universe.[26] Evidently, he is excessively credulous and, in his zeal to gather facts from which explanations of the nature of things will flow, he accepts real observations and the most fantastic legends. He believes that a rooster can terrorize a lion and that an angry bull stops and suddenly calms down if he passes under a fig tree.[27] For all the beliefs of this kind that abound in the Middle Ages and from which Renaissance philosophers did not manage to free themselves,[28] Campanella insists on supplying a rational explanation in which no hidden virtue or Aristotelian faculty is involved. But, if he applies his principle uncritically, his intentions are clear. All his works exude lively curiosity about natural phenomena and a constant desire to be alert for observation. We can imagine no fact so humble or particular that a lesson cannot be drawn from it. If there are no useless facts, there are no common or contemptible facts either. Everywhere, in the least and lowest detail of creation,

24. We know that Telesius's influence on Bacon deserves to be taken into account. See Bacon, *De Principiis atque Originibus secundum Fabulas Cupidinis et Coeli*, in *Philosophical Works*, edited by Robert Leslie Ellis and James Spedding, with translations of the principal Latin works by Spedding, 3:63–118.

25. Telesio, *De Rerum Natura*.

26. Telesio, *De Rerum Natura*, bk. 1, proemium. See the introduction published by Giovanni Gentile, *Bernadino Telesio* (Bari: Laterza, 1911), appendix, 122–24.

27. Campanella, *De Sensu Rerum*, bk. 1, ch. 8.

28. The source of these beliefs is quite easily located in medieval bestiaries and lapidaries. See, for example, Langlois, *La connaissance de la nature*. We see them reproduced not only in Telesius and Campanella but even in Mersenne, and some are found in Bacon.

we find the same laws and the same wisdom.[29] Also, particular facts and even personal anecdotes frequently appear in his demonstrations.[30] He knows how to make medical observations about himself and orient them if necessary as genuine experiments.[31] He frequently analyzes his own states of consciousness,[32] but he also draws lessons from the spectacle of others as well.[33] It cannot be denied that Campanella's philosophy is consistent on this point with his theory of knowledge and assigns a major role to observation.

However, it is equally certain that reading Campanella's work does not leave the impression that observation is important. The facts this philosopher has carefully collected and arranged disappear almost completely under the interpretations and explanations his exuberant imagination supplies for them. This thinker, who only recognizes sense knowledge as certain and who forcefully reproaches the ancients for substituting their free-ranging fantasy for observation of phenomena, guides us across a world inhabited by mysterious forces like an enchanted forest. Stones, plants, and animals are endowed with soul and knowledge. The world itself has an immortal soul, and this soul explains everything everywhere. To account for the movement of the planets, we find an instinct of conservation that pushes them to be moved. By transmitting their light, the stars communicate their thoughts to each other and thus can understand each other. Air, water, and all liquids perceive and experience sympathies and antipathies like us. This is why rain flows to the sea as to its common source. The ocean follows the movement of the moon and the sun. Liquids invade bread and sponges in opposition to the laws of weight.[34] These animate forces are manifested everywhere. It is impossible not to return to them when we attempt to explain the world. How

29. This is what justified Campanella's real coarseness and the frequently vulgar examples he chooses. Cf. *De Sensu Rerum*, bk. I, ch. 4; bk. II, ch. 29; bk. IV, ch. 14.

30. We note in passing that Campanella closely observed subconscious psychological phenomena. On this point, see also a very interesting passage, *De Sensu Rerum*, bk. II, ch. 25.

31. Campanella, *De Sensu Rerum*, bk. IV, ch. 8.

32. Campanella, *De Sensu Rerum*, bk. III, ch. 10; bk. IV, ch. 9; bk. IV, ch. 17.

33. For example, he notes that the prohibition against the marriage of priests is excellent, because priests and philosophers are cerebral, and it is preferable that men of this kind should not procreate, being incapable of producing anything other than dullards. By way of proof, consider the son of Telesius, *De Sensu Rerum*, bk. IV, ch. 19.

34. Campanella, *De Sensu Rerum*, bk. III, chs. 1–13.

can a philosophy that does not agree with any means of knowledge but sensation lead to this poetic phantasmagoria?

To understand him, it is necessary to pay attention to what is perhaps the most important element of this philosophy and will give us the key to the whole system. We mean the concept of likeness and reasoning by analogy.

The preface of *Realis Philosophia* informs the reader at the outset that if Francis Bacon of Verulam, Chancellor of England, ever brings to successful completion his *Instauratio Magna*, a work eminently worthy of receiving assistance and consideration, it will appear that the two philosophers move toward the same goal. Both propose to follow the footprints of things, advancing by means of the senses and by experience. However, there is no doubt that, by means of inductions that are more complete than Bacon's, we can draw a large number of conclusions and deeper ones than he has reached.[35] This warning allows us to foresee that Campanella's philosophy reserves a major role to reasoning and acknowledges its considerable value. Although sensible knowledge is incomparably more certain than other kinds, it has the defect of being limited in scope and only bearing upon a restricted circle of objects. The things our senses can perceive are minute in proportion to those that we will never perceive, either because they are not presented to us or because their nature is such that our senses cannot deal with them. Accordingly, we should try to discover them by another mode of knowledge, unless we accept being forever ignorant about them. Reasoning is what provides this mode of knowledge.

First, let us recall as an established thesis that discursive knowledge is inferior in certainty to sensible knowledge. It must be added, however, that, in compensation, it is broader and that it is legitimate to acknowledge its value, which, although relative, remains comparable to that of perception. In fact, reasoning is a kind of perception itself, and discursive knowledge can be briefly defined as *sensus similis in simili*.[36] Each time that we reason, we grasp the like in the like. Instead of perceiving a thing in itself, we perceive it in another thing that resembles it and in the aspect that resembles it. Evidently, this mode of perceiving is imperfect, because it only allows us to grasp things outside of themselves. Yet this is how God allows us to inquire about most things and discover them indirect-

35. *Realis Philosophia*, *Proemium* of Tobias Adami.

36. Campanella, *De Sensu Rerum*, bk. I, ch. 4.

ly.[37] When we cannot apprehend an object in itself, it generally remains possible for us to apprehend it in another that is like it, and this very thing is what we call reasoning. *Cognoscere et sentire in simile est ipsum discurrere, hoc est per aliud sentire.*[38]

Consequently, we reason when we pass from things known by sense to unknown things, and this passage is only accomplished by likeness. We imagine the majesty of God through the pope's majesty, the tenuousness of angel through the tenuousness of wind, and so for all other cases. We will thus have likeness of origin, time, place, matter, action, passion, form, situation, figure, color, and so on.[39] Between two things, there can even be likeness of difference, because we know the contrary of the contrary. So, if it is established that heat is white, we infer that cold is black. Moreover, when we have more likeness of likeness, there will be a proportion, and we will be able to deduce new conclusions. Reasoning of this kind establishes that six is to three as two is to one, that flesh nourishes a wolf as grass nourishes a sheep. One who knows these likenesses will thereby know how to reason and easily understand all things by going from known likenesses to unknown likenesses. The more the senses can grasp the things upon which reasoning is based and the more similar they are to unknown things, the more perfect and certain is the knowledge that we have of these unknown things. These are the two conditions that determine the value of discursive knowledge. For example, we know the parts of the human body better by learning the anatomy of a pig than of a plant, and better also by seeing this anatomy with our eyes than reading its description in a medical textbook. The first of these instances of knowledge outweighs the second in its degree of certainty and closeness of likeness.[40] Therefore, sensation always remains the criterion of certitude, but with the addition that we can perceive one thing in another by reason of their similarity. In this way, Campanella opens up a new mode of knowledge that allows us to attain that which, since it is beyond sensible experience, would escape our investigation.

At the same time, we see the antinomy that puzzled us being dissolved, and most of Campanella's solutions to philosophical problems achieve their true meaning from this viewpoint. The apparent oddities

37. Campanella, *De Sensu Rerum*, bk. II, ch. 30

38. Campanella, *De Sensu Rerum*, bk. II, ch. 21.

39. Campanella, *De Sensu Rerum*, bk. I, ch. 20. Cf. *Realis Philosophia*, bk. I, ch. 16, art. 5.

40. Campanella, *Realis Philosophia*, bk. I, ch. 16, art. 5.

and childishness of his discussions, the purely imaginative character of his proofs are explained by his conception of discursive knowledge. Any likeness or proportion is a beginning of explanation in Campanella's eyes. Any accumulation of likenesses or concordant proportions is a demonstration.

Let us consider some of the proofs destined to establish that "the world is a living animal," which F. Bouillier attacks. They are based on the analogy of natural phenomena with the constitution or operations of human beings. The world is an animal, since all its parts seem to stay closely united, as is evident by nature's horror of a vacuum. Just as in us the arm does not want to be separated from the shoulder, nor the head from the neck, nor the legs from the trunk, so the division that is produced when emptiness is introduced between the parts of bodies horrifies the whole world. If air did not experience some fear or pain when emptiness arises and takes away its contact with any other body, it would not precipitate itself so rapidly as it does to regain the contact it has lost.[41] Therefore, the world is an animal. But, if it is an animal, it is endowed with feeling. We cannot deny this consequence under the pretext that the world has no eyes, ears, feet, or hands. Such sense organs correspond to the spirits of animals like humans, not to thick, coarse matter like the world, which needs orifices to feel what happens outside it. As for movement, it is enough for the world to be round for it to move easily. Its hands are rays and the forces that gush out of it and extend around the world to act without burdening it with bulky arms like ours. Its eyes are the stars, the moon, and the sun, which see and allow us to see. To deny that things can feel, because they do not have sense organs would be as absurd as to say the wind does not move because it does not have legs, or that fire does not devour things since it has no mouth or teeth.[42] If this conclusion is true, a simple proportion will let us further establish that the world must be provided with a soul. Since the corporeal spirit is not enough for beings like humans, and since we still find immortal souls in humans, with much greater reason we must suppose that the world has this kind of soul. A work of supreme goodness, the very beautiful and very good soul must not only contain within itself parts that are endowed with feeling but also have a soul higher than any angel. This soul is the first instrument of the first wisdom. The world has a spirit that is the sky, a coarse

41. Campanella, *De Sensu Rerum*, bk. I, ch. 9.

42. Campanella, *De Sensu Rerum*, bk. I, ch. 13.

body that is the earth, blood that is the sea, and the soul that we have just allotted it. Constituted in this way, the world is not inferior to the humans it contains.[43] The whole is not inferior to its part.

Such are the inductions by analogy through which Campanella intends to establish his conclusions. We may ask what he thinks is the basis that guarantees some value to these conclusions. Above all, this reasoning supposes that there is likeness in the world. It supposes that, but does not suffice to establish it. More precisely, it does not establish whether objective likeness, which the reasoning shows us, rests or fails to rest on objective likeness within things themselves, likeness that is a constituent of the reality of things. To resolve this problem, after we show how Campanella's logic is tied to his theory of knowledge, we must recur to consideration of another order that permit us to show the profound connection that binds his logic to his metaphysics.

Almighty God, best and wisest, eternally delights in himself in the infinity of his glory and wishes to create the world in order to produce a statue or live image simulating his infinite goodness. Since the Holy Trinity, or to express ourselves most suitably, the *Monotriad*, saw that beneath its own infinity it can give existence to finite being, its goodness did not want to begrudge its power the production of beings made in its own likeness. This is why God created the universe, but at the same time that we find the reason why God created it, we discover the general law that presides over its constitution. The world, whose only reason for being is to express divine perfection under a finite mode, must necessarily be constituted in each part by power, goodness, and wisdom. Upon this condition, the world will reproduce as much as possible the characteristics of the divine Monotriad from which it gets existence.[44]

Accordingly, the universe must appear to us as created in the image and likeness of God. This affirmation's repercussions upon Campanella's philosophy are absolutely general. It immediately accounts for Campanella's universal animism. If all things are endowed with feeling, it is because all things resemble God who created them and consequently possess some faculty that recalls God's perfect wisdom, at least from afar. It is difficult to conceive a world that would be the image of an omniscient God

43. Campanella, *De Sensu Rerum*, bk. II, ch. 32.

44. Campanella, *Realis Philosophia*, bk. I, ch. 1, art. 1.

but whose parts do not possess the faculty of knowing in some degree. In things, science is only wisdom itself or at least a spark of divine wisdom.[45] Campanella quite logically strives to demonstrate the omnipresence of a sensing principle, as much in stones, minerals, and plants as in animals and humans. God owes himself this perfection of his universe.

The same reason logically explains the necessity of giving things and beings the necessary forces for their own conservation. Each thing has the power of existing as long as God permits it to last, because just as the thing is wisdom, it is likewise power. Once these forces are conferred upon the world, it maintains itself in existence alone and unfolds the regular chain of its causes and effects to the infinite. All that must happen is prepared in its causes from the origin of the world, and every antecedent is the cause, condition, or sign of its consequences.[46] Therefore, philosophers who attempt to explain the world will encounter the image of divine power fragmented and disseminated throughout the universe. But the philosopher will discover divine power nowhere more clearly than in humans, who not only possess understanding derived from divine wisdom and will derived from divine love, but also a whole set of powers derived from the power of God. *Cum Mens ex Potestativo essentietur, et intellectivo et volitivo, spiritusque ei deserviens has primalitates participet, organa ipsorum triplicia erunt. Alia enim Potestataria, alia Sensoria, alia Appetitoria formaliter.*[47] In Campanella's philosophy, the singular theory of the *Potestative* follows from this. It proposes to reestablish the equilibrium broken by the Scholastics by connecting to the soul's cognitive and appetitive functions, equally important functions that complete the likeness of creature to creator. Just as there are as many senses as sensibles, there will be as many powers as objects for the animal to overcome in order to assure its being and conservation. The first obstacle that the animal has to overcome is the weight of its own body, which of itself tends toward the earth. The animal rises above this tendency thanks to the sustaining power it has from God.[48] However, the body is a composite that perpetually threatens to dissolve by letting the humors it contains escape.[49] It overcomes this perpetual obstacle through an appropriated

45. Campanella, *De Sensu Rerum*, bk. II, ch. 30.

46. Campanella, *De Sensu Rerum*, bk. III, ch. 9.

47. Campanella, *Realis Philosophia*, bk. I, ch. 11.

48. Campanella, *Realis Philosophia*, bk. I, ch. 11, art. 2, *De sustentativo potentatu.*

49. Campanella, *Realis Philosophia*, bk. I, ch. 11, art. 3, *De potentatu contentivo.*

power of contention. Accordingly, the vital power again will provide the fire of life that is perpetually in danger of being extinguished.[50] The combative power, whose preeminent organ is the hand, will guarantee it against the attacks of its enemies.[51]

Made in the image of Supreme Power, the world is also made in the image of supreme love. Hot and cold, the two active principles, allow us to understand the formation and constitution of all beings, if we take love into account, which each principle experiences toward itself, and the hate it experiences for the opposite principle. Their self-love, which is the source of their mutual enmity, engenders a multitude of good things in the universe. After the hot active principle concentrated a large part of the primitive matter into smoke, it first extended the smoke over a vast area. Then, after agitating the smoke in a circular fashion and scattering it upon the firmament, the hot active principle formed the heavens out of the most tenuous part. Out of the part that was a little thicker it formed the air. The sea is from the coarsest part. By contrast, cold felt itself surrounded on all sides and threatened by its enemy heat. It concentrated itself in the center of the firmament with its own portion of matter. It united its parts into a single round globe, just as everything surrounded by enemies tends to do. To remain as far away as possible from its enemy heat, it remained where it was, hard and dense. This was the earth.[52] On the other hand, since heat felt threatened by cold packed tightly in this way, it concentrated itself in the higher regions at a certain number of points from which stars were born.[53] Accordingly, at every degree of creation, we meet original love and its inevitable corollary, hatred. Without the pleasure and pain that flow from them, things and beings would remain perpetually inactive. These are the two spurs, the two guides of good and evil, whose disappearance would entail the disappearance of the being or the animal.[54] From there come all the demonstrations where Campanella invokes attractions and repulsions, sympathies and antipathies, harmony of beings and discord.

Thus, the universe appears as the living image and likeness of the Trinity. But in the collection of beings that God leads to their natural

50. Campanella, *Realis Philosophia*, bk. I, ch. 11, art. 4.
51. Campanella, *Realis Philosophia*, bk. I, ch. 11, art. 8.
52. Campanella, *Realis Philosophia*, bk. I, ch. 1, art. 4.
53. Campanella, *Realis Philosophia*, bk. I, ch. 1, art. 5.
54. Campanella, *Realis Philosophia*, bk. I, ch. 19, art. 1.

actions with immutable perfection, one occupies a special place, the human being. The freedom God has given human beings as the condition of their merit and demerit allows them to turn away from the universal end of things if they want.[55] However, it is evident that the first obligation of humans is to try as much as they can to introduce a perfect divine likeness into the universe. This is why society, whose structure directly depends upon the human will, must be informed according to this principle. The utopias of the *Civitas Solis* express the ideal of a society that wants to be in perfect harmony with the essential structure and last end of the universe. Each of us continually hears this prayer echo in the secret ears of our souls, which supreme justice whispers to us:

> O souls that I sow in human bodies, when you fall into the evils with which bad societies are riddled, imagine establishing a republic in the image of the one that I myself rule with my ministers in sovereign perfection in the heaven of heavens. If you do not succeed in discovering in your own needs the idea that would serve as model, consider the government established in the universe by my universal wisdom. With sovereign skill it tempers the hot and the cold without subjecting them to violence, in order that they may act spontaneously for the common goal at the same time as they assure their own good. Wisdom inserts into each portion of the universe the seed suitable to it, knowing how to use what is lowly to secure what is noble. Therefore, make just one leader, as there is just one sun and just one God. Have only one and the same Father, teacher, shepherd, and priest. If, falling away from this perfection, you cannot attain such harmony, give yourselves two leaders so there are two active principles, hot and cold, and moderate one by the other. Is this analogy still too exalted? At least look at your body. See how each member serves the head for its sake and for its own utility, and unites as these members are united. Accordingly, have a religion that will be the *soul* of the mystical body constituted in this way. May the law of justice be its spirit and humans be its body. Laborers and soldiers will be its hands; the learned its eyes; the ignorant will be its more humble parts. Among the latter, the most skilled will fulfill the function of liver and heart, that is, they will be caretakers and guards of the public storehouses. This immense body's feet will be the merchants and sailors. Be careful that one who is a laborer by nature should not become king, and that one who is king by nature, should not become

55. Campanella, *De Sensu Rerum*, bk. I, ch. 7.

> an artisan. Chance rather than wisdom would govern then. You would be like a man who walks on his hands or a herder who follows his goat. Know that it is not I who made Nero emperor and Socrates a simple citizen. It is your ignorance. Caiaphas was not high priest but a laborer. He occupied the high priesthood covered by a mask. When I showed you Emmanuel, true King of the Jews, all the chance kings rose against me. Likewise, today all the chance kings conspire against royal natures, like actors in their masks. But when the end of time comes, it is I who will change everything as God who knows the underside of the universal comedy, with masks off and the stage cleared.[56]

The voice of wisdom proclaiming legal justice in the name of natural justice and divine justice is nothing more than the faithful interpretation of the fundamental intuition that guides Campanella, the intuition of universal analogy.

His theory of reasoning by likeness is now based in reality. The structure of the universe is such that it gives a foothold to analogical induction everywhere. Everywhere the image of the divine Monotriad must offer itself to one who knows how to look. In things, as in God, the elements imply each other reciprocally. So many forces and different operations, all those colors and lights, the infinite number of astonishing properties, are all produced solely by cold and heat. These two principles are themselves ruled by pleasure and pain and therefore by love and hate. Love and hate, in their turn, emerge from wisdom, because nothing hates or loves except when it knows the evil that destroys it and the good that conserves it. In this way, all power comes from love and all love comes from wisdom. But all wisdom comes from the First Wisdom, all love from the First Love, and all power from the First Power.[57] Nature taken as a whole is a participation in the eternal law, as the light of the public square is borrowed from the sun's light.[58] This means that the word's diversity always leads us to God's unity. But to travel this road, we cannot dispense with discursive knowledge. Less certain than sensation, whose weakened echo it is, discursive knowledge still raises human nature to such a point that it almost seems to deify human nature. Consider that, with a little circle and a quadrant, human reason measures the movements of the heavens,

56. Campanella, *Realis Philosophia*, bk. III, ch. 16, art. 3. Cf. bk. III, ch. 5, art. 7.

57. Campanella, *Realis Philosophia*, bk. I, ch. 13.

58. Campanella, *De Sensu Rerum*, bk. I, ch. 6. Cf. likewise, bk. I, ch. 7, and bk. II, ch. 26.

the size of all things, and their distances. Whereas animals, limited to sensible knowledge, only know a small number of likenesses, humans, who are endowed with reason, can aspire to knowledge of the universe, because everything is alike. This is so because everything depends upon the same very powerful and very good cause that is God: *Discurrimus facile ad objecta omnia quoniam similia omnia sunt invicem. Similia autem sunt, quoniam ab eadem pendent causa potentissima optimaque.*[59]

Such we believe is Campanella's viewpoint. We should adopt it if we want to discover his work's unity and understand its details. Viewed in this perspective, it offers a collection of inductions, which though eminently imaginative and poetic in nature, are still oriented in one direction and controlled by a common principle. The harmonious diversity of this universe is explained by one and the same origin, all of whose parts are subject to the law of analogy. Those parts inevitably lead thought toward the creating Trinity. The universe cannot be known either by abstract reason, incapable of inventing and creating the world anew, or by sensible knowledge limited to our immediate perception. A close alliance of sense and reason is necessary. The former supplies the necessary point of support, without which the meanderings of reason would be lost in a vacuum. The latter, through perpetually renewed inductions, lifts us from what we see to what we could not attain by grasping it directly. In this way, the philosopher leads us from likeness to likeness onward to the knowledge of the omnipresence of a feeling principle, and on to affirm in the name of sensible perception the existence of a universal, immortal soul of the universe. Perhaps the affirmations are rash, but it would be imprudent to label them absurd. Two centuries after *De Sensu Rerum*, in a phrase that we might believe to be a translation of Campanella, Ernest Renan wrote: "After we see, we certainly have no choice but to try to construct the theory of what we do not see, or else we are like the animal inclined toward the earth, who only is concerned with the object closest to its senses and its appetites." Again, it is the author of *Avenir de la science* who writes: "We feel an immense universal *nisus* to accomplish a plan to fill a living matrix, to produce a harmonic unity, a conscience. The conscientiousness of the whole so far is very obscure. It does not seem to exceed the consciousness of an oyster or polyp. But it exists. The world

59. Campanella, *De Sensu Rerum*, bk. II, ch. 30.

moves toward its ends with sure instinct. The mechanistic materialism of scientists of the end of the eighteenth century seems to me one of the greatest errors that can be made."

The apparent sterility of Renaissance philosophers perhaps stems from our inability to see where their real posterity is found.

SIX

Theology and Cartesian Innatism

Recent research on Descartes leaves little doubt about the influence certain theological movements had upon his thinking. The Cartesian concept of divine freedom, his teaching about evil, error, and judgment, and lastly his notion of human freedom are not completely explained if we fail to consider his education at la Flèche, his reading of St. Thomas, and his contacts with Neoplatonic members of the Oratory. The case is not peculiar to the Cartesian doctrine of freedom; the doctrine of innate ideas also has theological origins. Our purpose here is not to expound Cartesian innatism for is own sake, nor do we claim to offer a complete explanation of the doctrine. We consider that we will achieve our goal if we can dispel some surprises that are sometimes occasioned and in some measure specify innatism's real meaning.

Descartes's Adversary

If we refer to St. Thomas's genuine doctrine, human beings are constituted by a composite, the union of soul and body. This is not an accidental union resulting from the juxtaposition of two essences whose nature does not require that they be united, but a substantial union that makes a complete being arises by uniting two beings that are incomplete when considered separately. Matter and form, incomplete realities, become a single complete substance at the moment when form is insinuated into matter, which for its part receives it. The knot that secures them is the substantial union itself. This union constitutes the human composite.

It means that a human being includes two incomplete beings within himself, matter that is the body and form that is the soul. The body is not a complete being, whether by *body* we designate prime matter, which is pure potency, or rather indicate the organized body, that same matter provided with the organs necessary for life. In order to be body and not simply matter, it requires the act that its union with the form will supply. Nor is the soul a complete being. That must be said not only about the vegetative and sensitive soul but also about the rational soul itself. Within the soul there exists an inclination toward the body to the point that the soul separated from the body, as it is between human death and resurrection, is in a state that, though not violent, is not natural. Because the soul is destined to constitute the complement of another essence, whether united to the body or separated from the body, it always remains an incomplete substance.[1]

By contrast, it is apparent that a complete being must arise from these two incomplete substances. Between soul and body there is a natural relation and a sort of proportion that destines them to constitute a substantial unity. Their relation is not analogous to that of two drops of water; that is, the relation is not just a negative absence of repugnance to be united. It is a natural and mutual inclination, whose object is the constitution of the *unum per se* that is called human being. An important consequence follows regarding the nature of our knowledge. When we speak of human beings or their operations, these terms do not designate just operations of the soul but operations of the human composite, that is to say of something intrinsically one, which soul and body constitute.[2]

1. Aquinas, *Summa Theologiae*, pt. I, q. 75, art. 7, reply to obj. 3: "Corpus non est de essentia animae, sed anima ex natura suae essentiae habet, quod sit corpori unibilis, unde nec proprie anima est in specie sed compositum"—*Summa Theologiae*, pt. I, q. 90, art. 4, body of the article: "Anima autem, cum sit pars humanae naturae, non habet naturalem perfectionem, nisi secundum quod est corpori unita."—*Summa Theologiae*, pt. Ia IIae, q. 4, art. 5, reply to obj. 2: "Animae humanae remanet esse compositi post corporis destructionem."—*Summa Theologiae*, pt. I, q. 76, art. 1, reply to obj. 6: "Anima humana manet in suo esse cum fuerit a corpore separata, habens aptitudinem et inclinationem naturalem ad corporis unionem."

2. Aquinas, *Summa Theologiae*, pt. I, q. 75, art. 2, reply to obj. 1: "Dicendum quod *hoc aliquid* potest accipi dupliciter. Uno modo pro quocumque subsistente, alio modo pro subsistente completo in natura alicujus speciei. Primo modo excludit inhaerentiam accidentis et formae materialis. Secundo modo excludit etiam imperfectionem partis; unde manus posset dici *hoc aliquid* primo modo, sed non secundo modo. Sic igitur, cum anima humana sit pars speciei humanae potest dici *hoc aliquid* primo modo, quasi subsistens, sed non secundo modo; sic enim compositum ex anima et

Clearly, the soul and not the body is the principle of all operations of life. The soul is that by which we move and nourish ourselves and also that by which we feel and know. But if the first principle by which we know is the soul, it is equally true that the soul is the form of the body, such that it is properly soul only in the measure in which it constitutes a substantial union with the body. Therefore, the act of knowing does not belong to the soul but to the human being. Besides, everyone can experience that it is certainly himself who knows, not some part of himself. An action can be attributed to a subject in three manners. A thing is said to act and move either according to its total being like a physician who cures, or else according to some part of itself, as someone sees by his eyes, or lastly by an accident, as the white builds if the builder is white. It is evident that the act of knowing does not belong to Socrates or to Plato by an accident. It is attributed to them insofar as they are human beings and *qua* essential predicate. It is equally certain that Socrates knows according to his total being and not according to some part of himself. It is certain that human beings are not their rational souls but rather that the soul is only a part of the human being. It is the human being who grasps himself as perceiving by the senses and knowing by the intellect. The exercise of the senses is not conceivable without the body. The body is an integral part of the human being.[3]

The final hypothesis is that according to which Socrates's intellect is a part of Socrates, the mode of union between Socrates's soul and body being such that it is certainly Socrates, and not only his intellect, that knows. For this condition to be fulfilled, it is necessary that the soul should not be united to the body as the motor to the thing moved or the pilot to his ship. If that Platonic position is admitted, we cannot say that Socrates knows. The action of the motor is not attributed to the thing moved except accidentally, as we attribute the carpenter's action to the saw. On this account, the act of knowing would only be attributable to Socrates as an instrument his soul uses. Moreover, the instrument would be corporeal, for, since the soul is the motor, it would be necessary that the body is what moves. But we know a corporeal instrument does not carry out that intellection. Therefore, the soul does not unite to the body as motor to thing moved.[4]

corpore dicitur *hoc aliquid*."

3. Aquinas, *Summa Theologiae*, pt. I, q. 75, art. 4.

4. Aquinas, *Summa Theologiae*, pt. I, q. 76, art. 1, body of article, paragraph 4: "Actio motoris nunquam attribuitur moto nisi sicut instrumento, sicut actio carpentarii

Likewise, although the part's action can be ascribed to the whole, as seeing can be ascribed to the human being, this action is never attributable to another part except by accident. We do not say that the hand sees because the eye sees. Accordingly, if Socrates and his intellect are two parts of the same whole, it follows that the action of his intellect is not, properly speaking, ascribable to Socrates. If, on the other hand, Socrates is a whole composed of the union of his intellect with the rest of what constitutes Socrates, without this intellect being united to the rest other than as motor, it follows that Socrates is not one and that, consequently, he is not even being, since everything possesses being only in the measure in which it possesses unity.[5] This consequence is as absurd as the previous one.

A conclusion becomes unavoidable. The soul is the form of the body. Because it is the form of the body, every intellectual operation that is really an operation of the union supposes the involvement of the body. This does not mean that the act of knowing is a corporeal act. The cognitive faculty is not the act of a corporeal organ as sight is the act of the eye. Moreover, this is why the cognitive faculty can attain the immaterial and universal. The soul is both separated and in matter. It is separated insofar as the act of the intellect is exercised without a corporeal organ. It is in matter insofar as the soul endowed with intellect is the form of the body.[6] However, we must never lose sight of both terms of the relation. That is the mistake Plato commits when he claims to discover innate knowledge in the soul. His reasoning always supposes that human beings are pure intelligences, like angels, or that human beings enjoy in this life the beatific vision that God reserves for his elect.

The cognitive power is proportioned to the knowable. The angelic intellect, totally separated from the body, has as its proper object the intelligible substance separated from the body. It knows the natural by a pure intelligible. By contrast, the human intellect, which is naturally

---

serrae. Si igitur intelligere attribuitur Socrati, quia est actio motoris ejus, sequitur quod attribuatur ei sicut instrumento, quod est contra Philosophum (I *De Anima*, textu 12) qui vult quod intelligere non sit per instrumentum corporeum."

5. Aquinas, *Summa Theologiae*, pt. I, q. 76, art. 1, body of article.

6. Aquinas, *Summa Theologiae*, pt. I, q. 76, art. 1, reply to obj. 1: "Anima humana est quidem separata, sed tamen in materia. Separata quidem est secundum virtutem intellectivam, quia virtus intellectiva non est virtus alicujus organi corporalis, sicut virtus visiva est actus oculi. Intelligere enim est actus, quo non potest exerceri per organum corporale, sicut exercetur visio; sed in materia est, inquantum ipsa anima cujus est haec virtus, est corporis forma et terminus generationis humanae."

united to the body, has as its proper object the quiddity that is the nature existing in corporeal natures, and the intellect can rise to certain knowledge of invisibles only through such natures of visible things. It pertains to these sorts of natures to exist in individuals, which does not occur without some corporeal matter. Thus, the nature of stone or horse can only present itself to us in a determined stone or horse. The nature of stone or any other corporeal object can only be truly and completely known *qua* the nature existing in a particular being. We apprehend the particular by sense and imagination, and therefore, the intellect cannot comprehend its proper object in act without turning toward corporeal species. Only by this means will it contemplate the universal natures existing in particular objects. On the other hand, when we admit with Plato that the forms of sensible things subsist in themselves, outside particular objects, it is clear that the intellect no longer needs corporeal species to attain its object. Although the soul is totally separated from matter, it can then apprehend an immaterial object by itself. The relation of faculty to object is safeguarded here.[7] But that will be the state of future life; it is not the state of our present life. Here below there is no intelligible truth without a conversion of the soul toward the *phantasmata*, that is to say, without participation of the body in the acquisition of knowledge.[8]

With this observation we reach the point of distinction of the two doctrines. The Platonists who admit that the human intellect is naturally full of all the intelligible species must explain how this intellect does not always consider them immediately with clear knowledge. Their doctrine

7. Aquinas, *Summa Theologiae*, pt. I, q. 84, art. 7: "Potentia cognoscitiva proportionatur cognoscibili. Unde intellectus Angeli, qui est totaliter a corpore separatus, objectum proprium est substantia intelligibilis a corpore separata, et per hujusmodi intelligibile materialia cognoscit. Intellectus autem humani, qui est conjunctus corpori, proprium objectum est quidditas sive natura in materia corporali existens, et per hujusmodi naturas visibilium rerum, etiam in invisibilium rerum aliqualem cognitionem ascendit. De ratione autem hujus naturae est quod in aliquo individuo existat, quod non est absque material corporali . . . Particulare autem apprehendimus per sensum et imaginationem, et ideo necesse est, ad hoc quod intellectus actu intelligat suum objectum proprium, quod convertat se ad phantasmata speculator naturalem universalem in particulari existentem. Si autem proprium objectum intellectus nostri esset forma separata, vel si formae rerum sensibilium subsisterent non in particularibus, secundum Platonicos, non oporteret quod intellectus noster semper intelligendo converteret se ad phantasmata."

8. Aquinas, *Summa Theologiae*, pt. Ia IIae, q. 6, art. 1, reply to obj. 2: "Homini secundum statum praesentis vitae est connaturalis modus cognoscendi veritatem intelligibilem per phantasmata sed post hujus vitae statum, habet alium modum connaturalem."—Cf. *Summa Theologiae*, pt. I, q. 84, art. 7, and q. 89, art. 1.

of reminiscence leads to an explanation: When the soul is united to the body, it drinks a brew of oblivion that makes it lose all its innate knowledge, and thereafter the only goal of the soul's efforts is to recover the lost knowledge. In such a doctrine the body plays the role of a veil interposed between our faculty of knowing and the object of our knowledge. But, if the soul's very essence includes the propensity to be united to the body, as we have posited, it will be difficult to admit that the soul's natural operation, which is to know, is totally hindered by something in conformity to its nature, namely its union with the body.[9] This means that intrinsically, in the being constituted by the human composite, no place could be left for innate knowledge. The soul acquires knowledge with the cooperation of the body, not in spite of the body, and it is certainly the human being, not the soul alone, that knows.

It would be incorrect to claim that there is absolutely nothing innate in our faculty of knowing. If our intellect naturally contains no actual knowledge, it at least contains the seeds of knowledge that are the first principles by which we judge all things.[10] These principles, known by themselves, that we discover in the natural light with which God has endowed us, are to our active intellect what tools are for a workman.[11] But we must not conclude that with the aid of these principles alone we can raise ourselves to the contemplation of eternal, invisible realities. Initially, the rational soul only knows in potency. Like a blank slate on which nothing is written, the soul offers no material to the intellect to which the first principles might be applied.[12] The rational soul must be led from potency to act by the intelligible species, as the sensible soul is led from potency to act by the action of the sensible upon the senses. This amounts

9. Aquinas, *Summa Theologiae*, pt. I, q. 84, art. 3: "Praecipue autem hoc videtur inconveniens si ponatur esse animae naturale corpori uniri, ut supra habitum est, quaestione 76, articulo 1. Inconveniens enim est quod naturalis operatio alicujus rei totaliter impediatur per id quod est sibi secundum naturam."

10. Aquinas, *De Veritate*, q. 11, art. 1, body of article: "Praeexistunt in nobis quaedam scientiarum semina."

11. Aquinas, *De Veritate*, q. 1, art. 4, reply to obj. 5: "Veritas secundum quam anima de omnibus judicat est veritas prima. Sicut enim a veritate intellectus divini effluunt in intellectum angelicum species rerum innatae secundum quas omnia cognoscit, ita a veritate intellectus divini exemplariter praecedit in intellectum nostrum veritas primorum principiorum secundum quam de omnibus judicamus. Et quia per eam judicare non possumus nisi secundum quod est similitudo primae veritatis, ideo secundum primam veritatem de omnibus dicimur judicare."

12. Aquinas, *De Veritate*, q. 11, art. 3, body of article.

to saying that the intellect does not contain innate species within itself, but that by nature it is in potency to all species of this kind.[13] As for the mind's first conceptions, which are the principles, they are only known in the light of the agent intellect through the cooperation that is established between our innate natural light and the forms that our intellect abstracts from sensible matter.[14] Even when the soul tries to rise to the knowledge of its innate contents, left to itself, it cannot do anything.

Let us apply this doctrine to the problem of knowledge of God. Must we say that human beings naturally possess innate knowledge of him? If by that we understand actual knowledge that human beings would encounter completely formed in their intellects, it must be affirmed that they possess nothing of the sort. But it can be said that human beings know God naturally as they desire him naturally. Human beings desire God naturally insofar as they naturally desire happiness, which is a likeness of divine goodness. Accordingly, God considered in himself is not what human beings naturally know, but only his likeness. It is also with the help of the likenesses of God found in God's effects that human beings can rise by reasoning to the knowledge of their creator.[15] Applying to this difficulty the solution we offered for the knowledge of principles, we can say that what is innate in human beings is not the knowledge of God's existence, but only the means of acquiring it.[16]

With that, at the same time that the necessity of the *a posteriori* demonstrations of God's existence through his effects is imposed upon our minds, we discover the root of St. Anselm's error. It is not enough to posit innate knowledge of God's existence for the *a priori* affirmation

13. Aquinas, *Summa Theologiae*, pt. I, q. 84, art. 3: "Et propter hoc Aristoteles posuit quod intellectus quo anima intelligit, non habet aliquas species naturaliter inditas, sed est in principio in potentia ad hujusmodi species omnes."

14. Aquinas, *De Veritate*, q. 11, art. 1, body of article: "Primae conceptiones intellectus, quae statim lumine inellectus agentis cognoscuntur per species a sensiblibus abstractas."

15. Aquinas, *Summa contra Gentes*, bk. I, ch. 11: "Sic enim homo naturaliter Deum cognoscit, sicut naturaliter ipsum desiderat. Desiderat autem ipsum homo naturaliter, in quantum desiderat naturaliter beatitudinem, quae est quaedam similitudo divinae bonitatis, Sic igitur non oportet, quod Deus ipse, in se consideratus, sit naturaliter notus homini, sed similitudo ipsius. Unde oportet quod per ejus similitudines in effectibus repertas, in cognitionem ipsius homo ratiocinando perveniat."

16. Aquinas, *De Veritate*, q. 10, art. 12, reply to obj. 1 [Translator: there are two series of replies to objections in this article, and this passage is from the first reply of the first series]: "Cognitio existendi Deum dicitur omnibus naturaliter inserta, quia omnis naturaliter insertum est alquid unde potest perveniri ad cognoscendum Deum esse."

of his existence to become legitimate. Even if some idea of the perfect being were naturally granted to us, it would still remain to be demonstrated that this perfect being, whose necessary existence *in intellectu* we acknowledge, possesses this existence *in re*.[17] But, if we do not have the idea of perfect being at all, it is quite evident that the proof fails at its foundation. We do possess some natural knowledge of God in the sense that God constitutes the terminus of our desire without our knowing it. Human beings aspire to happiness, and, since God is human happiness, it turns out that human beings desire God. If we apply the adage *nil volitum quin cognitum* here, we will admit that human intellects are directed confusedly toward God. But that leaves us far from knowledge properly speaking, of the sort we would have if we found a perfect idea within us, that is, an idea of a being *quo majus cogitari non potest*. Just as certain people believe that happiness resides in wealth and others in pleasure,[18] some are found who believe that God is identified with the universe and, moreover, that he is corporeal in nature.[19] Given that the fool says in his heart, "There is no God,"[20] how can we claim that the existence of a perfect being is a truth known by itself without demonstration? After all, the concept of God upon which the assertion is based lacks the necessary, universal character of first principles. However deeply we enter into our souls, we never find there two principles of innate knowledge: *God is the supremely perfect being* and *God exists*. Nevertheless, we will find there a natural light not provided with intelligible species—which distinguishes this light from angelic knowledge—but capable of receiving all species.[21] Here below, the light is unable to grasp the divine essence directly but capable of rising to the knowledge of God by the knowledge of his effects. These three theses imply each other reciprocally: we are denied any *a priori* knowledge of God; we are denied any knowledge of this kind because we have no innate knowledge; we possess no innate knowledge

17. Aquinas, *Summa Theologiae*, pt. I, q. 2, art. 1, reply to obj. 2: "Dato etiam quod quilibet intelligat hoc nomine, Deus, significari hoc quod dicitur, scilicet illud quo majus cogitari non posset, non tamen propter hoc sequitur quod intelligat, id quod significatur per nomen, esse in rerum natura, sed in apprehensione intellectus tantum."

18. Aquinas, *Summa Theologiae*, pt. I, q. 2, art. 1, reply to obj. 1.

19. Aquinas, *Summa Theologiae*, pt. I, q. 2, art. 1, reply to obj. 2.

20. Ps 53:1 (52 in Vulgate).

21. Aquinas, *Summa Theologiae*, pt. I, q. 84, art. 3, reply to obj. 1: "Intellectus angeli est perfectus per species intelligibiles secundum suam naturam; intellectus autem humanus est in potentia ad hujusmodi species."

because such a way of knowing is at odds with the substantial union of soul and body with the inherent unity of the human composite.

When Descartes undertakes the reconstruction of metaphysics upon a new foundation, many difficulties turn him away from St. Thomas's doctrine. In 1629[22] (the date of the elaboration of Descartes's metaphysics), though his doctrine is not definitively completed, Descartes puts forward negative positions that nothing can shake. Already in 1619–1620 Cartesian physics is established in method and spirit.[23] Evidently, Descartes did not introduce unchanged into his definitive physics the explanations he proposed to his friend Beeckmann or that he recorded in his *Cogitationes Privatae*. But the spirit is the same as the one that will animate *The World* or *The Principles*. He already knows how to treat the problems of physics by the method of mathematics.[24] Although he does not yet seem to be aware of the metaphysical consequences that the application of such a method might entail, he already resolves all difficulties without involving any occult qualities or substantial forms within matter. The most significant passages from this point of view during this period are perhaps two notes composed by the philosopher: *Lapis in vacuo versus terrae centrum cadens quantum singulis momentis motu crescat*, and especially *Aquae comprimentis in vase ratio reddita*. At the beginning of the second note, the young physicist (Descartes was twenty) excuses himself for being unable to deal completely with the questions put to him because he would need to give long explanations about the foundations of his mechanics.[25]

From the first, we are transported far from Scholasticism's substantial forms and real accidents. Despite the syllogistic form that Descartes still retains for his argumentation, it is easy to see that in his thinking, physics is already based on a method that radically separates it from Scholastic metaphysics. For example, consider the definitions that Descartes posits at the start of his demonstrations, notably the definition of

22. Descartes, Letter to Mersenne, April 15, 1630, in Adam, *Vie et oeuvres de Descarte* (hereafter AT), 1:144.

23. This is what Isaac Beeckmann's journal seems to indicate. See AT, vol. 10, pp. 68, 226, 242–43.

24. AT, vol. 10, p. 52: "Hic Picto cum multis Jesuitis aliisque studiosis virisque docta versatus est. Dicit tamen se nunquam hominem reperisse, praeter me, qui hoc modo, quo ego gaudeo, studendi utar, accurateque cum Mathematica Physicam jungat. Neque etiam ego, praeter illum, nemini locutus sum hujusmodi studii."

25. AT, vol. 10, pp. 67–68: "Ut plane de propositis quaestionibus meam mentem exponerem, multa ex meis Mechanicae fundamentis essent praemittenda, quod, quia tempus non sinit, breviter, ut jam licet, conabor explicare."

what he calls a body's weight. It is obvious how careful he is to refrain from an appeal to any idea that fails to be clear and distinct. To understand what the term *weight* means we must imagine that the heavy body moves downward and consider it at the first instant of its movement. The impelling force that this movement receives at the first instant constitutes weight. It is important not to confuse it with the force that during the whole movement draws the body down, because this second force can be entirely distinct from the first. Accordingly, we define the body's weight as the force against the surface immediately underlying the heavy body.[26]

The methodological certainty revealed in this definition is no less manifest in demonstrations. Descartes has the sense of offering something new and original in these matters.[27] He is no longer satisfied by verbal explanations provided by Scholastic physics about semi-material, semi-spiritual beings: *gravia et levia ab insita gravitate et levitate moventur*. From here on, everything happens as if Descartes already knows that matter is defined by extension alone. In 1626 he no longer has to discover this thesis but simply achieve clear awareness of a principle he has been applying for a long time.

The metaphysical demonstration of that principle is the reason for being and the essential object of the *Meditations*. If we read Descartes's confidential declarations to Mersenne, his treatise was supposed to have the effect of preparing readers to receive his physics favorably and "to establish a bridge."[28] This is why the *Meditations* are entirely oriented toward a double conclusion: the soul is only thought, and the body is only extension. Beyond the *cogito*, God's existence, and the doctrine of clear and distinct ideas, Descartes journeys toward the fundamental thesis summed up by the title of Meditation Six, the real distinction between the human soul and body. This, indeed, is the main metaphysical foundation of the genuine science whose acceptance Descartes seeks. Once we admit that the body is only extension and movement, substantial forms, real qualities, occult forces, and other beings of reason are eliminated. Descartes does not direct violent, open criticism against them. He does better; he replaces them. According to Descartes, all these entities

26. AT, vol. 10, p. 68: "Dicemus igitur gravitatem esse vim qua proxima superficies corpori gravi subjecta ab eodem premitur."

27. The principle of clear and distinct ideas is affirmed from this moment on, AT, vol. 10, p. 70.

28. Letter to Mersenne, January 28, 1641; AT, vol. 3, pp. 297–98. [Translator: Descartes actually says *ford* rather than *bridge*.]

originate in the generalized confusion between what belongs to the nature of the soul and what belongs to the nature of the body. In this way, we represent weight as the tendency of some soul or other that lodges in heavy bodies.[29] All such things disappear on their own, when we admit the distinction between soul and body in the Cartesian sense.

Furthermore, this radical distinction makes possible not only exact knowledge of physical phenomena but also the clear and distinct explanation of everything that occurs in living bodies like our human bodies. To account for it, we consider the body solely as an animal to the exclusion of the soul. Consequently, the vegetative soul, the locomotive soul, and the organic faculties whatever they may be, are suppressed, and what emerges from the *Meditations on First Philosophy* are the *Principles of Philosophy* and the *Treatise on Man*. Descartes's immediate disciples perceived that clearly. Armed with the real distinction between body and soul, they affirmed the uselessness and obscurity of the principles Scholasticism employs to explain nature,

> uselessness in which it is impossible to resolve by their means the slightest difficulty of physics, and obscurity, since obviously terms must be considered obscure when no idea in the mind corresponds to the meaning given them. Speaking generally, we have the ideas of only two sorts of beings. We know about what is extended, which is called body, and what thinks, which is called mind. So, when we speak of any other being that cannot be related to either of these or to some one of the properties or accidents that the ideas of either of them include within itself, such as those beings that are called substantial forms of bodies, qualities that are real, imprinted, intentional, occult, sympathetic, or the digestive, relative, or expulsive faculty, and so forth, it is impossible that any idea could respond to these terms in the mind or that what we say then has any sense that we can conceive.[30]

Eliminating such beings of reason relieved physics from a cumbersome burden. But it would also leave a void in the Thomist doctrine of knowledge, which Descartes perceives.

29. Cf. Gilson, *Index scolastico-cartésien*, entry for "Pesanteur."

30. Forge, *Traité de l'esprit de l'homme*, 9–10. Cf. completely similar affirmations in *L'Homme de René Descartes*, Clerselier's preface. Cf. likewise Cordomoy, *Le Discernement du corps et de l'âme*, 60–61.

According to St. Thomas, all knowledge requires the involvement of the body in order for it to be attributable not just to the soul but also to the human being. Therefore, it becomes difficult to explain the act of knowing without appealing to some of those entities that are at once material and spiritual, something Cartesian philosophy intends to condemn. This is why the notion of *phantasmata* acquires a central place in a doctrine like that of Aquinas. They are certainly not enough to explain the act of knowledge or at least provide its complete explanation. The real cause of the intellectual operation is situated in the active intellect, which by rendering the *phantasmata* intelligible in act confers the power of modifying the passive intellect upon them. Accordingly, they are not the cause of knowledge properly speaking but rather the matter upon which this cause is exercised.[31] They play the role of *agentia instrumentalia* in actual knowledge,[32] but they are absolutely indispensable for the intelligible included within the real to be apprehended as such by a human understanding.

Thomas seems to define the role that ought to be assigned to these *phantasmata* more precisely than he defines their nature.[33] What we know is that the act of knowing is not accomplished by means of reception of the things themselves in the intellect or in the senses. Real identity cannot be established between the knowing subject and the known object. Thomas wants to express this when he affirms that the object does not come to us according to its real being (*esse reale*), but only according to its intentional being (*esse intentionale*).[34] In this way he excludes the error of the ancients mentioned by Aristotle τὴν ψυχὴν τὰ πράγματα τιθέντες.[35] However, the concept of intention remains purely negative.

Thomas tells us further that the object's *species* must not be understood as Democritus understood the εἴδολα. The act of knowing is not reduced to the simple influx of some atoms into the patient intellect, because it is all too evident that material images cannot penetrate into

31. Aquinas, *Summa Theologiae*, pt. I, q. 84, art. 6, body of article: "Phantasmata non sufficiunt immutare intellectum possibilem, sed oportet quod fiant intelligibilia actu per intellectum agentem; non potest dici quod sensibilis cognitio sit totalis et perfecta causa intellectualis cognitionis, sed magis quodammodo est materia causae."

32. Aquinas, *Quaestiones Disputate de Veritate*, q. 10, art. 6, reply to obj. 7.

33. On this question, see Baron, "Die Bedeutung der Phantasmen," 5–13, and Sertillanges, *Saint Thomas d'Aquin*, 2:113ff.

34. Cf. Baeumker, *Witelo*, 470 and 478n1.

35. Aristotle, *De Anima*, bk. I, ch. 5, 409 b 27.

a spiritual intellect. Furthermore, the action of the sensible itself upon the sense does not consist of projecting a small version of itself upon the subject. We cannot invoke *idola* and *defluxiones* either for the sense or for the intellect. Consequently, it is completely correct to affirm that in the Thomist system the species must not be considered the object's material double. The agent's species is only received in the patient according to its spiritual being.[36] The sensibles are found in the sense, or in the medium that separates them from it, according to the same mode of incorporeal being. If species met according to their material being, it would make no sense that the species of contraries could be received in the same part of the medium and simultaneously, as they are.[37]

We can specify further the mechanism of the sensitive soul's operation. In the *Summa Theologiae*, St. Thomas notes that the sensible's impression upon the sense does not occur *per modum defluxionis, ut Democritus posuit, sed per quamdam operationem* (in the mode of an emanation as Democritus claims, but through a certain operation).[38] As for the nature of this operation, it seems we must distinguish according to cases.[39] Sound, for example, delivers a transferal in place, since it results from a collision and a commotion in the air. Therefore, it is a kind of *defluxio* produced between object and sense. By contrast, sight supposes a purely spiritual modification. Form and color are received in the pupil without changing it and without determining any alteration in the milieu. So the impression of objects upon the senses works according to their different natures and according to whether we are dealing with light, sound, order, or taste. We cannot assign general explanations for this fact. Whatever diversity of relations can be established between the

36. Aquinas, *In Libros Sententiarum*, bk. IV, dist. 19, q. 1, art. 3, reply to obj. 1: "Species agentis recipitur in patiente secundum esse spirituale ut intentio quaedam, secundum quem modem res habit esse in anima sicut species lapidis recipitur in papilla."

37. Aquinas, *Quaestiones Disputatae de Anima*, q. 4, art. 5: "Sed sensibilia ad hoc quod moveant sensum non indigent aliquo agente, licet secundum esse spirituale sint in sensu, qui est susceptivus rerum sensibilium sine materia, ut dicitur in III, *De Anima* (Comment. 38); et in medio quod recipit spiritualiter species sensibilium; quod patet ex hoc quod in eadem parte medii recipitur species contrariorum, ut albi et negri."—This passage, although taken from an objection, expresses the philosopher's thought well. The response will bear upon the assimilation of the intelligible species to the sensible species.

38. Aquinas, *Summa Theologiae*, bk. I, q. 84, art. 6, body of article.

39. Aquinas, *Summa Theologiae*, pt. I, q. 78, art. 3, body of article. See also Sertillanges, *Saint Thomas d'Aquin*, 2:119–21.

sensorial organs and the sensibles, at the end of the operation the result is that the intermediary between the material being and intellectual knowledge is established. This intermediary is the *phantasma*.

The *phantasmata* are neither material nor intelligible. If they were material, absolute identity would exist between the senses and objects. For instance, the eye would become color. But if they were intelligible, disproportion would be established between the senses and their objects. The colors have the same mode of existence in the visual power, that is, in a corporeal organ, as in the individual matter of the objects that affect us.[40] The proper object of the senses is the particular, the form existing in corporeal matter. Power and object are proportionate, since the sense itself, unlike the intellect, is the act of a corporeal organ.[41] Accordingly, we must be able to re-encounter in the *phantasma* the mark of the particular that it represents, the individuating, material conditions from which the agent intellect abstracts the intelligible, universal species.[42]

We must understand, therefore, St. Thomas's expression in its full literal sense: *phantasmata sunt similitudines individuorum*.[43] Matter introduces a difference of kind between the sensible and the intelligible (*sunt alterius generis*).[44] This difference is sufficient for the sensible as such to remain incapable of being raised to the intelligible order. The illumination of the sensible by a light that falls from above, that of the agent intellect, is still necessary. The *phantasma* is a spiritual being and yet representative of the object's individuating material conditions. It is

40. Aquinas, *Summa Theologiae*, pt. I, q. 85, art. 1, reply to obj. 3: "Ad tertium dicendum, quod colores habent eumdem modum existendi prout sunt in materiali corporali individuali, sicut in potentia visiva, et ideo possunt imprimere suam similitudiem in visum; sed phantasmata, cum sint similitudines individuorum, et existant in organis corporeis, non habent eumdem modum existendi quem habet intellectus."

41. Aquinas, *Summa Theologiae*, pt. I, q. 85, art. 1, body of article: "Quaedam enim cognoscitiva virtus est actus organi corporalis, scilicet sensus, et ideo objectum cujuslibet sensitivae potentiae est forma, prout in materia corporali existit."

42. Aquinas, *Summa Theologiae*, pt. I, q. 85, art. 1, body of article: "Et hoc est abstrahere universale a particulari, vel speciem intelligibilem a phantasmatibus, considerare scilicet naturam speciei absque consideratione individualium principiorum quae per phantasmata repraesentatur."—Moreover, this is why the human intellect only apprehends the universal directly. *Quodlibet* XII, 8–9, art. 11: "quia cognitio fit per similitudinem cogniti in cognoscente, et haec est in intellectu nostro per abstractionem a conditionibus individuantibus et a materia, et ideo, cum recta cognitio per speciem fit, non cognoscit directe nisi universale."

43. Aquinas, *Summa Theologiae*, pt. I, q. 85, art. 1, reply to obj. 3.

44. Aquinas, *Quaestiones De Anima*, q. 4, reply to obj. 5.

laden with the *species intelligibilis* that it contains in potency and that only the agent intellect will render intelligible in act, and it is situated between matter and spirit, at the mysterious limit where the soul enters into contact with things without ceasing to be itself. The rational soul is immersed in matter, since it is the form of the body, but emerging from matter, since it exercises operations in which the body does not share (*non totaliter immersa*). The soul constitutes a kind of frontier where the spiritual and material meet: *Anima humana abundat diversitate potentiarum, videlicet quia est in confinio spiritualium et corporalium creaturarum. Et ideo concurrunt in ipsa virtutes utrarumque creaturarum.*[45]

Consequently, the mixed nature of the *phantasma* expresses first of all the necessary condition for a point of connection between these heterogeneous realties to be possible.

Though coherent from the point of view of the metaphysical principles on which it is based, St. Thomas's doctrine, nevertheless, presents many difficulties. To be more precise, it lacks a solid physical and physiological substructure to safeguard the metaphysical theses it ought to support. After justifying the intrinsic possibility of sensible knowledge, the medium of the reception of the sensible in the sense remains to be explained. It does not really resolve the problem to invoke the singular *medium quo*, about which we are not told how it can represent a material object although it is not at all perceptible in itself. Nor are we told how it is formed in the medium, or how it transverses the medium to pass from object to organ, or how it penetrates the organ. St. Thomas gives only scattered, fragmentary answers to all these questions. As they stand, insufficient as they may be, they show that our philosopher has perceived the problem's complexity, since he admits, as we have indicated, the possibility of diverse explanations according to different sensible and different senses. Visual images, among others, harmonize more easily with his metaphysical point of view since he sees in the action of light only a purely qualitative, spiritual modification of the medium.[46] But he needs to demonstrate this thesis for itself in order to extend his research to the other senses. Above all, it is necessary that other philosophers should take up the problem at the point where Thomas leaves it. That was not to be, and the only evolution we can observe on this issue in Scholasticism is a regression. In Thomas's contemporaries as in Thomas himself,

45. Aquinas, *Summa Theologiae*, pt. I, q. 77, art. 2, end of body of article.—Cf. *Quaestiones de Anima*, q. 1, reply to obj. 18: "Esse animae est quodammodo corporis."

46. See Baeumker, *Witelo*, 357–433, on the metaphysics of light in the Middle Ages.

we hardly find more than unproved affirmations.[47] Bonaventure teaches that the species are formed in the medium, pass into the external sense organ, then into the common sense, and from there into the apprehensive power. He gives no indication how this phenomenon occurs. Duns Scotus, who takes up this problem again after these two masters, seems to believe that by simply affirming progressive dematerialization of the sensible species between object and sense, we account sufficiently for the mysterious power of material bodies to act spiritually upon our organs.[48] In the absence of a clear doctrine on this point, thinkers little by little lean toward a crude, simplistic solution of the problem. Instead of pushing research in the directions that have been indicated to them, they fall back without being clearly aware of it into the εἴδολα of Democritus that Thomas had explicitly rejected. When they do not purely and simply deny the *species intentionalis*, as William of Ockham does, they transfer it into a singular entity that its adversaries and even its partisans more and more insist on considering as a material subject transporting a spiritual quality.

In 1609, when Descartes studied philosophy at the College of La Flèche, he may have read the definition of intentional species in the textbook by Eustachius of St. Paul: *Speciem intentionalem hic apellari signum aliquod formale rei sensibus objectae sive qualitatem quamdam quae ab objecto immissa et in sensu recepta vim habeat ipsum objectum repraesentandi, licet ipsa sensu minime sit perceptibilis.*[49] The contradiction is now plainly situated at the very heart of the definition. It is difficult to understand how corporeal images present the extraordinary character of being both material and representative. On the other hand, so many arguments seemed to weigh in favor of this doctrine that it was preferable to retain it, even at the cost of a contradiction. It is astonishing but true: *Tertia* [difficultas est] *quomodo species illae repraesentant objecta? Respondetur eam esse, et quidem stupendam penitus, illarum specierum*

47. Cf. Bonaventure, *Itinerarium*, ch. 2, number 4: "[Sensibilia] intrant, inquam, non per substantias sed per similitudines suas, primo generatas in medio et de medio in organo et de organo exteriori in interiori et de hoc in potentiam apprehensivam; et sic generatio speciei in medio et de medio in organo, et conversio potentiae apprehensivae super illam facit apprehensionem omnium eorum quae externus anima apprehendit."

48. Duns Scotus, *De Rerum Principio*, q. 14 (Wadding edition, vol. 3, p. 124): "Habet species sensibilis esse tripliciter, scilicet, in objecto extra, quod est esse materiale; in medio, et hoc esse est quodammodo spirituale et immateriale; habet esse in organo, et hoc adhuc magis spiritualiter et immaterialiter quam in medio."

49. Eustachius a Sancto Paulo, *Summa Philosophiae*, vol. 2, pt. 3, p. 330.

conditionem, quod cum sint materiales, utpote in subjecto corporeo inhaerentes, modum tamen spiritualem in repraesentando servent.[50] Sometimes it is necessary to admit what one cannot explain.

When Descartes was confronted with this problem, his attitude was completely different. Far from considering such beings as constituting necessary intermediaries between intellect and things, Descartes found himself compelled by the fundamental principles of his physics to deny all beings of this kind. In his view, there is no reason to maintain these intentional species that amazed the people who did maintain them. That is why we see him politely endeavor to distance himself as little as possible from received opinions,[51] but to eliminate species firmly wherever he finds them.[52] The *Dioptrics* offers a good occasion. Descartes declares: "It is necessary to be careful not to suppose, as our philosophers usually do, that in order to feel, the soul needs to contemplate some images that objects send to the brain. At least, the nature of these images must be conceived differently from the way the philosophers conceive them. Insofar as they consider nothing in them but the resemblance the species must possess to the objects they represent, it is impossible for them to show us how they can be formed by these objects and received by the organs of the external senses and transmitted by the nerves to the brain."[53] Still more explicitly, Descartes writes:

> As a consequence that you will have the occasion to judge that it is not necessary to suppose that something material passes from the objects to our eyes to make us see colors and light, or even that there is anything in these objects that is similar to the ideas or feelings that we have about them, just as nothing comes out of the things that a blind person feels that would have to pass all through his cane up to his hand, and that the resistance or movement of these bodies, which is the only cause of the feelings he has of them, is in no way similar to the ideas that he conceives about them. By this means, your mind will be freed of all those little images flitting about in the air, called

50. Eustachius a Sancto Paulo, *Summa Philosophiae*, vol. 2, pt. 3, p. 332.

51. AT, vol. 6, p. 112, lines 28–29. He is a good pupil of the Jesuits. The *Ratio Studiorum* of 1596 recommended to the Jesuits: "Enixe quoque studeant communiores magisque nunc approbatas philosophorum sententias tueri."

52. On this point see the references to all the passages of this sort in Gilson, *Index scolastico-cartésien*, for the entry, "Espèces."

53. Descartes, in AT, vol. 6, p. 112, lines 5–17.

> *intentional species*, which so much exercise the imagination of philosophers.[54]

The consequences of this attitude go far beyond the collection of problems studied by Dioptrics. If intentional species are eliminated from our cognition, it follows that they cannot play any role in the elaboration of our ideas. Since we can literally say, *puram intellectionem rei corporeae fieri absque ulla specie corporea*,[55] it must also be true regarding knowledge of immaterial substances like our souls, particularly as regards knowledge of God. Our soul is more known to us than our own body. Against the teaching of St. Thomas, this signifies that, in order to reach knowledge of our soul, we have no need to learn anything that shares in the nature of the body.[56] Liberated from subjection to corporeal species, our knowledge will now be *directa*, no longer necessarily *reflexa*. The same holds for knowledge about God. We will no longer be forced to affirm that it necessarily requires a *conversio ad phantasmata*.[57] We will not consider it certain that, because our natural knowledge has its origin in the senses, it cannot reach beyond what the sensibles permit us to know comparatively.[58] Quite to the contrary, such affirmations present themselves as difficult to reconcile with what we know about the necessary conditions of our knowledge. When the absolute distinction of soul and body, of extension and thought, is posited, as natural philosophy requires, it is necessary to acknowledge a proper, valid content in thought outside any sensible material element or else definitively to condemn our thought to be empty. The soul must be able to be introduced to the knowledge of God without going out of itself or to pay the whole cost of this beginning of a violation of the radical distinction between body and

54. Descartes, in AT, vol. 6, p. 85, lines 13–27.

55. Descartes, in AT, vol. 8, 2nd part, p. 363, line 20 to p. 363, line 3.

56. Aquinas, *Summa Theologiae*, pt. I, q. 87, art. 3, body of article: "Est autem alius intellectus, scilicet humanus, qui nec est suum intelligere, nec sui intelligere est objectum primum ipsa ejus essentia, sed aliquid extrinsecum, scilicet natura materialis rei. Et ideo id quod primo cognoscitur ab intellectu humano est hujusmodi objectum, et secundario cognoscitur ipse actus quo cognoscitur objectum, et per actum cognoscitur ipse intellectus cujus est perfectio ipsum intelligere."

57. Aquinas, *Summa Theologiae*, pt. I, q. 12, art. 12, reply to obj. 2: "Dicendum quod Deus naturali cognitione, cognoscitur per phantasiam effectus sui."

58. Aquinas, *Summa Theologiae*, pt. I, q. 12, art. 12: "Dicendum quod naturalis nostra cognitio a sensu principium sumit. Unde tantum se nostra naturalis cognitio extendere potest, inquantum manuduci potest per sensibilia. Ex sensibilibus autem non potest usque ad hoc intellectus noster pertingere, quod divinam essentiam videat."

soul. Accordingly, in order to establish that the new physics is compatible with the fundamental truths of religion, Descartes tries to establish that a Catholic apologetic is possible without involving the body, without going beyond the soul. The demonstration of this thesis could only be accomplished on the condition of abandoning Thomas's point of view about the origin of our knowledge and of replacing it with another than did not make all *a priori* demonstrations of God's existence impossible. The doctrine of innate ideas would offer Descartes this point of view.

Theological Origins of Cartesian Innatism

We already know that, for Descartes, innatism cannot be a discovery or an accidental revelation. No philosophy student was unaware of this well-known doctrine that Thomas summed up and then combated, and that the entire faculty at the school presented and refuted in almost the same way as Thomas.[59] Strictly speaking, we could admit that Descartes took a criticized, abandoned doctrine that he got from Thomas's teaching, but that he needed and suited him. This hypothesis does not square with what we know about Descartes's character and the project he proposed to carry out. He wrote the *Meditations on First Philosophy* to give rational grounding and effective cover to his physics. Would it not have been a miscalculation to support the physics on unanimously rejected conceptions? He could only abandon Thomas's philosophy and retain the hope of making himself understood on the condition of providing himself with authorities who were, if not superior or even equal, at least sufficient for his orthodoxy to remain above suspicion. If Descartes could maintain the doctrine of innate ideas, we can infer that with some likelihood other philosophers and theologians of his time did maintain it.

59. Later, when it was time for Descartes's philosophy to be considered for the school curriculum, St. Thomas's simple refutation would be opposed to Cartesian innatism and to the *a priori* proofs of God's existence. Manuscript Course of Jean Courtillier (given 1679 and 1680 at the Montaigu School in Paris), Tours Municipal Library, Manuscript 1717, folio 215: "Objicies secundo: cognoscimus naturaliter Deum esse, ergo haec propositio: *Deus est*, nobis est in ipso lumine naturali nota. Dico: an cognoscimus confuse et cum discursu, concedo. Distincte et per se, nego. Quanquam enim Deus sit ens essentialiter existens, non tamen sine examinis circuitu id novimus: quod et si supponamus, videndum praeterea supererit, deturne ens essentialiter existens. Quodquidem resolvere licet Cartesio sit levis operae, non tamen aliis adeo est facile, sed difficillimum quod sufficit ut propositio haec: *Deus est*, seu *ens essentialiter existens existit*, non sit nota per se quoad nos."

All during the Middle Ages, the authority of Pseudo-Dionysius and of St. Augustine led some theologians to accept conceptions at odds with Aristotle's philosophy. For example, it is easy to find in John of La Rochelle a theory of our knowledge of God much closer to Descartes than to St. Thomas.[60] This is not a historical accident. Before and after Thomas, there is a whole school of theologians that explicitly taught the doctrine of innate ideas and extended its application to the central problem of the proofs of God's existence.[61] This Platonically-minded current is sometimes observable in a direct appeal to innatism, either extended to the whole fabric of our knowledge or restricted to part of it. More often, it shows up in the more or less fundamental rejections of the doctrine of Aristotle and Thomas. Countless adjustments can be made and in fact have been made between the Aristotelian theses of the intellect's receptiveness in regard to the intelligible forms and the Platonic thesis of spontaneity of the intellect.[62]

One of the most interesting cases of harmonization, which seems to have enjoyed considerable popularity, was suggested to the theologian by certain passages in Augustine and in the pseudo-Augustinian *De Spiritu et Anima*. Instead of considering the object image as introduced into the sense by the material object itself, this thesis admits that the soul instantaneously forms the image of this object in itself. Here the sense only plays the role of an excitant, of a messenger who announces the object and invites the soul to represent the object to itself.[63] There is more than one concession to Platonism here, and Thomas sees nothing but Plato's own pure doctrine.[64] We continually meet this thesis, deformed and

60. Johannes a Rupella, *Summa de Anima*, pt. II, 35 (Domenichelli edition, Prato, 1862): "Forma vero qua cognoscitur Deus, est similitudo vel imago primae veritatis impressae animae a creatione. Propter quod dicit Damascenus: omnibus cognitio existendi Deum ab initio naturaliter insita est. Imago autem impressa primae veritatis dicit in cognitionem ipsius cujus est imago."—See the interesting article by Manser, "Johann von Rupella, Ein Beitrag zu seiner Charakteristik mit besonderer Berücksichtigung seiner Erkenntnislehre."

61. On this point, see Grunwald, *Geschichte der Gottesbeweise in Mittellalter*.—Cf. Baeumker, *Witelo*, 286–316 and 467–503; Baumgartner, *Die Erkenntnislehre des Wilhelm von Auvergne*, 1; finally, Palhories, *Saint Bonaventure*, 81–84.

62. Baeumker, *Witelo*, 471–72.

63. Augustine, *De Genesi ad Litteram*, XII, 16, 35. *De Spiritu et Anima* (Migne, *Patrologia Latina* 40), 798.

64. Aquinas, *Summa Theologiae*, pt. I, q. 84, art. 6, body of article: "Et quia incorporeum non potest immutari a corporeo . . . sensum etiam posuit [Plato] virtutem quamdam per se operantem, . . . nec ipse sensus, cum sit quaedam vis spiritualis,

adapted, even in circles that are deeply imbued with the Thomistic and Aristotelian spirit.[65] We should expect it even more from a theologian influenced by Augustinianism. Duns Scotus notably seems to have retained some of it.[66] Perhaps its influence explains, on the one hand, that we find it in the sixteenth century in the *Commentarii Collegii Conimbricenses*,[67] and even in the *Metaphysical Disputations* of Suárez, paradigms of the philosophical spirit with which young Descartes's teachers were imbued.

For Suárez, just as for St. Thomas, it is quite true to say that the intellect never forms any intelligible species without being determined by the sensible species.[68] However, by reason of the natural form of the *phantasma*, and since it subsists in a lower power, the phantasm cannot cooperate with spiritual power like the intellect: *phantasma . . . cum sit materiale non potest cooperari ad actum spiritualem*.[69] It must be supposed, not that the agent intellect illuminates the species to elevate it to the intelligible order, but that there are in the passive intellect, species of things that it knows by the senses without the sensible knowledge itself cooperating in any way as the efficient cause of the action. In still other words, the *phantasma* does not determine the intellect through some kind of impression or influence but *materiam et quasi exemplar intellectui agenti praebendo* (as providing matter and a sort of exemplar to the agent intellect).[70]

What does not seem to have been noticed is the change of attitude in regard to the problem of God's existence that this suspension of St. Thomas's fundamental principles would entail. If the sensible species is no longer the result of a transformation of the sensible species supplied to the soul by the senses but the work of the agent intellect, and if the agent intellect instead of illuminating and transforming something given from

---

immutatur a sensibilibus: sed organa sensuum a sensibilibus immutantur. Ex qua immutatione anima quodammodo excitatur, ut in se species sensibilium formet. Et hanc opinionem tangere videtur Augustinus XII super Genesim ad Litteram (capitulo 24) ubi dicit quod corpus non sentit, sed anima per corpus, quo velut nuntio utitur ad formandum in seipsa quod extrinsecus nuntiatur."

65. On this point and for what follows up to the doctrine of Suárez inclusive, see the interesting article by Lechner, "Die Erkenntnislehre."

66. Cf. Lechner, "Die Erkenntnislehre," 132.

67. See *Commentarii Collegii Conimbricensis*, on *De Anima*, bk. III, ch. 5, q. 6, art. 2.

68. Suárez, *Disputationes Metaphysicae*, IV, 2, 1; quoted by Lechner, 128n6.

69. Suárez, *Disputationes Metaphysicae*, III, 1, 9; Lechner, 129n3.

70. Suárez, *Disputationes Metaphysicae*, IV, 2, 12; Lechner, 129n5.

the outside creates and draws the intelligible species out of itself, which it forms in the likeness of the *phantasma*, it follows that at least within certain limits, innatism becomes true again. The agent intellect encounters, if not content of actual knowledge, at least a natural faculty of building it within itself when certain external conditions are fulfilled. Perhaps we have found the reason why, although Suárez does not admit that God's existence is known with immediate evidence, he still acknowledges that such a truth is in close relationship of suitability with the natural light and universal human agreement, to such a degree that it is difficult for us to conceive that someone does not know it.[71] This knowledge evidently does not emerge in all human beings through logical demonstration, since not all are capable of that. But neither does it come from the mere evidence of the terms with which we are confronted. Supposing that *God* means, as St. Anselm has it, the being that is necessary of itself and such that nothing greater can be conceived, it is not immediately evident whether the content of this term is something simply known by our understanding or some genuine, actually existent being.

Accordingly, we must assign a double origin to this knowledge. First, the tradition transmitted to us by the ancients, which we receive from our parents, as in general the ignorant receive it from the more learned. This is the most likely origin of this belief among ordinary people. Moreover, knowledge about God is presented to us perfectly proportioned and suited to our nature. Once given the proposition *Deus est*, and once the terms that compose it are explained, although not absolutely evident, it immediately appears satisfactory to reason, and everyone who is not entirely corrupted willingly consents to it. Nothing in this truth makes it impossible or difficult to believe. On the contrary, it provides us with many motives for assent, not only metaphysical or physical but also moral, not only external, but internal. If a person reflects about himself, he cannot fail to acknowledge that he does not hold his existence from himself and that he does not suffice for his own perfection, and that, moreover, no creature is self-sufficient. Creatures are very far from being self-sufficient; even human beings, who are superior to those creatures, are still imperfect in their degree and acknowledge themselves to be weak and infirm both in knowledge of what is true and love for what is good.

71. Suárez, *Disputationes Metaphysicae*, XXIX, 3, 34: "Addiderim tamen, quamvis non sit notum nobis, Deum esse tanquam omnino evidens, esse tamen veritatem hanc adeo consentaneam naturali lumini et omnium hominum consensioni, ut vix possit ab aliquo ignorari."

From that, human beings are easily convinced that they need some higher nature from which they get their origin and by which they are ruled and governed. Considered from this perspective, knowledge of God presents itself to ordinary folk with evidence that is certain, practical, and moral, sufficient to make them obey, obliged not only to give their assent to the truth *God is*, but also to render cult to God. This allows us to understand what we read in the doctors about innate knowledge of God that we are supposed to have.[72]

Obviously, it will be disputed and rightly, that we have self-declared innatism here. Nonetheless, in the doctrine of Suárez we have a suppler and more conciliatory doctrine of the sources of our belief in God than in St. Thomas. The way is open to accommodation. The breech has been made. Innatism will slip through in its entirety.

Many causes seem to have come together to foment a renovation of Platonic innatism in the first years of the seventeenth century. It is very true that at the heart of Aristotelian scholasticism and particularly in Jesuit theology, as we have just seen, a movement in that direction had been long noted. We would exaggerate its importance if, with certain historians,[73] we searched within that movement for the immediate origin of the Platonism and Augustinianism that will reach full development after 1650. But it has been correctly observed that the Jesuit current is one of its forerunners. It foretold the Oratory's Augustinianism, as will be seen in Thomassin, du Hamel, and Malebranche. But before coming to this point, Platonism and innate ideas will have passed through the *Meditations*.

Consequently, in Descartes's time at La Flèche, he may already have been exposed to an intellectual current favorable to innatism. But it is difficult to think that the philosopher did not meet this doctrine several

72. Suárez, *Disputationes Metaphysicae*, XXIX, 3, 36: "Multa sunt quae statim inclinant ad assentiendum illi veritati; multa, inquam, non solum metaphysica vel physica, sed etiam moralia; nec solum externa, sed etiam interna. Nam, si homo in seipsum reflectatur, cognoscit se non esse a se, neque sibi sufficere ad suam perfectionem . . . Unde facillimo negotio homo sibi persuadet indigere se superiori natura a qua ducat originem et a qua regatur et gubernetur . . . Unde haec notitia majori ex parte videtur fuisse per humanam fidem praesertim apud vulgus potiumquam per evidentiam rei; videtur tamen fuisse cum quadam evidentia practica et morali, qua sufficere poterat ad obligandum tum ad assentiendum huic veritati, quod Deus sit, tum etiam ad colendum ipsum Et juxta haec facile intelliguntur omnia quae de cognitione Dei naturaliter insita a Doctoribus dicuntur."

73. Lechner, "Die Erkenntnislehre," 133.

years later, perhaps even upon leaving the school, in an explicit, self-conscious form, intending either to complete the Thomistic doctrine of knowledge or even to replace it. This goal of replacement would certainly seem to have been that of the moralists who had been working from the beginning of the sixteenth century to revive Stoicism by Christianizing it. We know that Descartes was familiar with their doctrine and that he was very influenced by it. His correspondence with the Princess Elizabeth bears conclusive evidence to this.[74] We must believe that Descartes encountered in Justus Lipsius the Stoic doctrine of innate ideas. This ethics may have contributed to introduce a doctrine into Descartes's mind that was presented as closely linked to it. Certain terminological details invite us to think so. However, Descartes could re-encounter this innatism that he found in the Christianized Stoics within Catholicism in orthodox theologians who possessed authority. Furthermore, Descartes could not help constantly meeting the doctrine of innate ideas, as it sprung up abundantly around him in the philosophical and theological environment where we find him around 1628.

Among the first theologians won over to this doctrine and with whom Descartes associated, we must include Cardinal de Bérulle, founder of the Oratory and his disciple Fr. Gibieuf. We know about the close relations Descartes maintained with them for some time.[75] It is difficult to believe that the spiritual director of the young philosopher did not make an effort to incline his penitent toward a doctrine so dear to his heart. Bérulle was a Platonist,[76] not simply an indirect Platonist by way of some accidental reflections. Perhaps he was all the more resolute in that his Platonism was spontaneous and almost instinctive. One cannot be a Platonist without holding the doctrine of innate ideas. Perhaps Descartes heard his spiritual director recall that God's grace wills us to be more happy than Plato and his disciples, since we are "brought up in a better school, educated in a higher philosophy, illuminated by a much more luminous Sun and endowed by itself with an infused light which is supernatural and divine."[77] As de Bérulle conceived it, professing Christianity "is an art of portraiture, which teaches us to paint, but in ourselves and not on a different background, and to paint a single object." This object

74. Strowski, *Pascal et son temps*, 1:113–20.

75. On this point we remit to our *La Liberté chez Descartes et la Théologie*, pt. 1, ch. 4.

76. Gilson, *La Liberté*, pt. 1, ch. 4.

77. Bérulle, *Oeuvres complètes*, col. 284.

is none other than the sun of the intelligible world, Jesus Christ. We do not need to go out of ourselves to form his image. "We have to spend our life in this beautiful and noble exercise in which we express and form in ourselves him whom the eternal Father expressed in himself and that he has expressed into the world and into the Virgin's womb by the new mystery of the incarnation. And in this noble and divine exercise, our soul is the artisan, our heart is the canvass, our mind is the brush, and our affections are the colors that must be employed in this divine art and in this excellent portraiture."[78] Better still Jesus himself will come to paint himself within us. Descended into us, he is going to rise up in our soul the memory of himself.

> Because entering into the world to save the world and die for your sins, he wanted to be united to human nature . . . And now he rises up and addresses God his father in the excellent prayer, asking him to be established in the usage, in the exercise, and in the possession of the clarity due him, of which he has the principle in himself, divinely and personally united to his humanity. Neither more nor less than the rational soul, if it were existent before the body, as the Platonists hold, being infused into the body of the little child, who has the life of the soul but not the light of the soul, and being stripped for a time of this light and knowledge of its state, the soul without doubt will rise up to its author who had infused it into the body and will ask him to be fully established in the usage, in the exercise, in the actuality of its knowledge and of its proper light owed to its essence.[79]

In this way, God is manifested in us because he is imprinted in the deepest part of our soul, "if this excellent and adorable being is not visible in his nature, he is sensible in his effects, and not to know him would be to lack sense, in so far as he is brightly painted on everything and engraved long before in our hearts. We would recognize this principle of principles by principles born in ourselves, if we were not always outside ourselves."[80] It will be enough to erase the world from our soul to see God appear there.

In Fr. Gibieuf, who is more of a philosopher than his superior, the doctrine of innate ideas is affirmed clearly, without any of the allegorical mystique and theological transposition under which we have just encountered it. To establish the existence of the freedom whose nature Gibieuf

78. Bérulle, *Oeuvres*, col. 287.

79. Bérulle, *Oeuvres*, col. 303.

80. Bérulle, *Oeuvres*, col. 417.

proposes to explain, he only asks that the inner witness of his conscience, the testimony of our freedom, be found among the great number of other things known that our reflection can discover. What is true of freedom is equally true of all the first and most universal notions of qualities and things. They are neither fabricated by human artifice and industry nor constructed at the whim of philosophers. We find them inscribed by nature in the depth of our souls. He who achieves calm in himself or better, he who would consult the truth present in himself that responds to those who interrogate it, discovers these first notions buried in his soul as in a deep well.[81]

Such language is not at all unorthodox, though it takes us far from St. Thomas. The tradition upon which it was based was universally respected in the church, something of which Descartes could not fail to be aware. By following the doctrine of innate ideas, he did not stray in the slightest from what is probable and safe in faith, *probabile et tutum in fide.* He substituted Augustine for Thomas.

This is an understatement. It is not enough to say innatism raised no suspicion. At the moment when Descartes was about to elaborate the *Meditations,* some philosophers and theologians saw a necessary element of Catholic apologetics in this doctrine.[82] We have seen the position St. Thomas adopts regarding the problem of God's existence. For him, the only two ways by which knowledge of God can come to us are supernatural revelations that the church transmits and *a posteriori* demonstrations that we construct starting from God's effects. Strictly speaking, it follows that, as to actual content, the human soul has no natural knowledge of God. Perhaps there is some imprudence in repeating that the human soul, which is the genuine breath of God, the reflection that the light of the divine image has left upon us (*signatum est super nos lumen vultus tui, Domine*), has nothing within it itself by which it might rise to the knowledge of its Creator. The imprudence is all the more serious in that at the beginning of the seventeenth century, the "fool" mentioned in the

81. Gibieuf, *De Libertate Dei et Creaturae,* bk. 1, p. 1: "Primae et universalissimae rerum qualitatum notiones non concinnantur hominum arte et industria, nec ad arbitrium etiam philosophorum effinguntur, sed mentibus nostris reperiuntur a natura consignatae. Qui autem animo ad tranquillitatem composito naturam audiunt, vel si paulo dignius loqui mavis, qui veritatem intus presidentem et responsa dantem consiliunt, illas tanquam in alto puteo ibi delitescentes percipiunt."

82. Here, we reason from the historical seventeenth-century perspective that is quick to interpret the Augustinian doctrine of illumination in an innatist key. We do not accept this interpretation as our own.

psalm seemed to have multiplied extraordinarily. He abuses the right or, rather, the possibility granted to him, to say in his heart, "There is no God." This is why a metaphysician like Suárez is visibly concerned to justify the compelling necessity of the truth that *God is* and concerned to bestow upon it sufficient practical, moral evidence as to oblige everyone to accept it and render unto the creator the worship due him. If innatism makes real progress from St. Thomas to Descartes, it is perhaps because atheism has progressed too. There is less and less resignation to undertaking the struggle against the atheists with a diminished apologetics. An adequate response is needed to the arguments of nonbelievers who claim that by nature they lack any idea of God. It is necessary to close this way out to them so that the harsh phrase of the apostle was justified, "that they should be inexcusable," *ut sint inexcusabiles.*[83] We find it used by Descartes himself in the dedication to the *Meditations.*

Jean de Silhon is a philosopher whose practical objectives are clear.[84] He wants to defeat a formidable enemy, the atheists, who in practice are mixed up with the libertines. Every dialectical means to obtain this result is good. Silhon would gladly recur to means of another order. Accordingly, he does not hesitate to condemn Plato and Aristotle successively, leaving the possibility that they both may be accepted in the end.[85] Philosophy only interests Silhon secondarily. Beyond truths like God's existence and the soul's immortality, anything we may be able to learn about the universe has little importance.[86] These central truths are attacked on all sides and so savagely that they seem ready to crumble. "Faith never had great need of being vivified. Never has there been more dangerous sinning against religion. The attack is not against the roof or the defenses. The base of the wall is threatened. The foundations are undermined. They want to blow up the whole building."[87] To come to the aid of Religion thus threatened, Silhon collects all the proofs of God's existence. He forms a

83. St. Paul, Romans 1:20.

84. For the relations of Silhon and Descartes and in general on everything concerning the influence of the Neoplatonic movement on Descartes, see the very interesting article by Espinas, "Pour l'histoire du cartésianisme."

85. He even accepts Descartes before the *Discourse on Method* appears. Silhon proposes the *Cogito* as the foundation of philosophy and states that we can rise from it to the knowledge of God. Experience points out this very curious development that clearly constitutes an anticipated loan and seems to indicate that Descartes and Silhon had established philosophical relations.

86. Silhon, *De l'immortalité* (in quarto, Paris: Billlaine, 1056 pp.), p. 3.

87. Silhon, *De l'immortalité*, bk. 1, p. 66.

compact bundle in which we find not only "the decisive and evidently conclusive truths" but also those that are "conjectures and probabilities rather than rational."[88]

Silhon argues against skeptics in general and atheists in particular: "that the consent of all ages and natures concludes that this belief in general, namely *that there is a divinity*, is born out of the light of nature and consequently trustworthy."[89] Moreover, the universality of this knowledge finds its basis in the immediate evidence of such a proposition, and in the impossibility in which we find ourselves of thinking the opposite: "Idolatry was a deluge that in less than no time almost inundated the earth, but since Jesus Christ dried up the floodwaters by his arrival, the devil changed weapons and instead of an infinity of gods that he introduced into the world in a short time, he has not been able to render in sixteen hundred years, I will not say half the world or a kingdom, but not a town, not a whole family susceptible of the other extreme, *that there is no God*, and that comes from this contradiction and repugnance toward this belief with which we are naturally imprinted, which is an unquestionable sign that it is false."[90] Everything calls us to assent to this knowledge, *that there is a God*. It comes to the philosophers by the light of reason and the force of discourse, and to ordinary people by the tradition of their fathers, by the example of their fellow men, by the authority of their superiors and of the sages, and by external things and the traces of God's hand that are scattered throughout the world.[91]

Yet, one cannot resist certain astonishment, after having pointed out the previous assertions, when we encounter a radical critique of innate ideas by Silhon.[92] It is even more surprising when Silhon energetically battles Platonist innatism:

> Now let us see whether the species that comes out of sensible objects first of all enters the external senses. Having undergone examination there and scrutiny, and having begun to be dematerialized and, so to speak, to be *decorporealized* there, they penetrate into the internal organs where they undergo other examinations and more scrutiny, and they become more subtle and more detached, until they arrive at the organ of the

88. Silhon, *Les deux verités*, 27–28.
89. Silhon, *Les deux verités*, 21.
90. Silhon, *Les deux verités*, 23.
91. Silhon, *De l'immortalité*, 106.
92. Silhon, *Les deux verités*, 393.

> imagination where they are refined still further and acquire the last degree of subtlety in which they can climb without changing order and remaining in the ranks of material things. That the so-called agent intellect intervenes after that, that it takes hold of these species, elaborates them, gives them another kind of refinement, which strips them of their sensible conditions, in a word, which completely purges them of everything corporeal and elementary, and makes them spiritual forms and objects suited to terminate what is called the passive intellect, which can know nothing material or nothing out of its order. If this is not the case, at least it is the ordinary Scholastic jargon and most common meaning of Aristotle's interpreters. If you ask me, this opinion has dazzling language and beautiful verbiage, but I see nothing solid or necessary in it.[93]

We will not follow the pointed critique that Silhon directs against the detail of the Scholastic doctrine he has constantly employed and that he now destroys acrimoniously.[94] He ties it up in dilemmas and sometimes in ponderous quadrilemmas: "What passes into the soul from the side of the organ . . . is either something spiritual or something material . . . If it is something material . . . how can it be applied to a spiritual being and to an indivisible nature like the soul?"[95] But if it is the soul that impresses these images upon the internal sense, the same two questions are posed again. The discussion is sharp, dense, and carried on in a flippant tone that contrasts remarkably with the discrete irony Descartes uses in the same questions. Silhon reconciles this attitude and the radical condemnation of innate ideas with complete simplicity: what he has written on innatism is only a manner of speaking and does not prejudge the question in any way.

> Let us find out now whether the soul naturally possesses and comes into the world carrying infused within it the species of certain knowledge and whether, when our soul has the intelligence unfettered and reason opened up, it is inclined by certain general species to act and to open up certain knowledge to encounter objects that are presented to the species by means of the eternal senses. That may be so, although it is not the opinion of Aristotle, although the Scholastics do not commonly agree, and although I have spoken otherwise in certain places in this

93. Silhon, *De l'immortalité*, 996–97.
94. Silhon, *De l'immortalité*, 996–1056.
95. Silhon, *De l'immortalité*, 1002.

> work to go along with the current and speak in the usual way. It may be that Adam's sin has not done such general damage to the souls of his descendents and has not stripped him so much of all the gifts of nature that good remainders of them are still present . . . And accordingly, it may be that Aristotle's opinion that there is nothing in the understanding that has not entered by the senses is not absolutely and generally speaking trustworthy.[96]

Such is the state of mind of this friend of Descartes. Starting from a formal condemnation of *Christianisme platonisé*,[97] Silhon is led to introduce Platonism into his own system. Innate ideas had become one of the necessary foundations of these two truths, *first God, second the soul's immortality*. The two theses,[98] and the foundations on which they rest will be found again in the *Meditations*.

In adopting this posture, Silhon had predecessors. At this moment, the Augustinian movement was very widespread, and the needs of the movement are too pressing for Catholic apologists, living in the same environment and addressing the same adversaries, to be able to adopt radically different points of view on the same question. From 1623, Descartes's closest friend Mersenne, who would remain his most faithful correspondent, was openly giving legitimacy to the doctrine of innate ideas in his *Quaestiones in Genesim*.[99] Doctrines easily achieved this legitimacy from a benevolent eclecticism. However, it must be admitted that Mersenne grants innatism an important place, and that by making this one of the surest proofs of God's existence, he assigns it a role of the greatest relevance. Like Silhon, Mersenne finds himself inclined to this by circumstances.

We know who Fr. Mersenne's adversaries were: the deists, the libertines, and the atheists. These three kinds of impiety were combined into one in our theologian's sharp eyes. The deists are dangerous because they lead imperceptibly to atheism. An excellent Minim confrere of Mersenne warmly praised him for having turned faithful souls away from this peril.[100] As for libertines and atheists, who join science and religion in the

96. Silhon, *De l'immortalité*, 956–60.

97. Cf. Gilson, *La Liberté*, pt. 1, ch. 4.

98. Descartes, *Meditations*, dedicatory letter, AT, vol. 9, p. 4.

99. Mersene, *Quaestiones Celeberrimae in Genesim*.

100. Ode by Fr. Nicholas Girault, Minim, on the laudable plan of the venerable Fr. Mersenne to write against the impiety of the deists:

same contempt, it is necessary to fence them in by a circle of arguments so tight that no escape remains open. The problem is not to confront them with a rigorously coherent system of apologetics from which they would escape simply by denying one of the principles, but to meet each one of their objections by opposing an appropriate refutation. At least this seems to have been Mersenne's tactic, which moreover easily suits the encyclopedic turn of mind that he perhaps acquired from the Renaissance philosophers.[101] Among the arguments his adversary directs at the existence of God, no less than sixteen are based on the affirmation that our intellect contains no actual notion of divinity. Even if one did not conclude God's nonexistence from that impious affirmation, it would still be a ready-made basis for the atheist who wanted to deduce the conclusion. This would not be the first time that heresy led to atheism.[102] Faced with the thesis that we have no notions of God, *quod nullas de Deo notitias habeamus*, Mersenne will immediately strive to demonstrate the opposite. In this way, more than thirty columns of *Quaestiones in Genesim* are dedicated to maintaining the doctrine condemned by St. Thomas that innate ideas, and especially the idea of God, are present in human beings.

A first proof that the idea of God is naturally innate is found in universal consent. All peoples have formed a more or less confused

The new hemlock plant
That grows close by the lettuce
Can easily deceive the eye
Of one who in the salad
Eats it as if it were chervil.
This makes him fall ill
Or lays him in the grave.

In Mersenne, *L'Impiété des déistes*, (Paris, 1624, 2 vols., in octavo).

101. Mersenne, who provokes such astonishment when we come to him through Descartes, seems much more normal when we come to him by way of Telesius and Campanella. He is very far from feeling the scorn toward them that Descartes will exhibit. They and the other Renaissance philosophers represent science in Mersenne's eyes. It is a point of honor to show them that a Catholic theologian knows as much as they do. Mersenne, *Quaestiones*, preface to the reader: "plurimas vero quaestiones quae alioquin curiosae videri possint etiam agitasse, ut ostenderem Campanellae, Bruni, Telesii, Kepleri, Galilaei, Gilberti et aliorum recentiorum discipulis, falsum esse quod aiunt, Doctores videlicet catholicos et theologos solum Aristotelem sequi et in ejus verba jurare, licet experientiae atque phaenomena contrarium evincant."—He goes so far as to show them open sympathy and believes that they have been condemned too quickly. The doctrine of the world soul and that things possess sensation, among others, seem very reasonable to him. Mersenne, *Quaestiones*, 938–39, 947.

102. Mersenne, *Quaestiones*, 233.

representation of the existence of a perfect being upon whom human beings are dependent in their being as well as in their actions. This knowledge is natural to the human understanding.

> Illud intellectui naturale videtur, quod minime situm est in videri et non videri, sed conceditur apud omnes, quale est jus naturale; at manifestum est omnes Deum aliquem sibi constituisse aut saltem concepisse; omnis enim congregatio Deum aliquem semper coluit. [That seems natural to the intellect, which is least in seeing and not seeing, but everyone grants what constitutes natural justice. But it is manifest that everyone has established some God for themselves or at least conceived one. For every gathering always worshipped some God.]

This natural knowledge, moreover, is neither inexplicable nor mysterious in its origin. Its foundation is in the very idea of God. If we analyze its content, we will see that it comes down to the concept of an absolutely perfect being. St. Anselm clearly demonstrated that the concept of perfect being necessarily involves the concept of an actually existent being. On this point, it is sufficient to reproduce his argument literally.[103] Evidently, we can ask whether ordinary minds are capable of developing such a proof spontaneously. How could ordinary people conceive that by the term *God* we designate a being such that a greater cannot be conceived?[104] How would they understand that having posited the definition, it follows that God really exists, because what really exists is greater than what is merely conceived? The fact is that to perceive the argument's conclusive force, it is useless to develop the complete argu-

103. Hauréau, *Histoire littéraire de Maine*, sees in the passage of St. Anselm reproduced by Mersenne, the source of the Cartesian argument that proves God's existence by the idea of Perfect Being. Unlike Tennemann and Cousin, who consider this coincidence merely accidental, Hauréau sees a dependence on the *Proslogion* through the intermediary of Mersenne's book (Hauréau, 8:130–31). The issue of whether there is dependence and not accidental coincidence is not in doubt. But it is useless to invoke the *Quaestiones in Genesim* to explain how Descartes knew St. Anselm's argument. All philosophy and theology students knew it by the exposition and classic refutation in Aquinas's *Summa Theologiae*, bk. I, q. 2, arts. 1 and 2; *Summa contra Gentes*, bk. I, chs. 10 and 11; and *De Veritate*, q. 10, art. 12. That is not to claim that Mersenne played no role in this doctrinal dependence. If he did not provide Descartes with St. Anselm's argument, he surely contributed to making Descartes accept it. By openly defending the argument, Mersenne became a theological authority for Descartes on the issue.

104. Mersenne replies here to St. Thomas's distinction between the things that are *per se notae omnibus* and those that are *per se notae sapientibus tantum, qui rationes terminorum cognoscunt, vulgo ignorante* (Gilson, *Index scolastico-cartésien*, text 126).

ment. It immediately appears that God is known of himself in the sense that the opposite cannot be thought. When the proof is reduced to its essence, its core consists of making apparent that the predicate *existence* is necessarily included in the subject *God*. God *qua* perfect necessarily includes being in his essence. More precisely, his essence is his being (*esse*). Therefore, St. Thomas is right to conclude that for someone who places himself in this perspective, the question *quid est* (what is it) is identified with the question *an est* (whether it is). The affirmation of God's existence becomes a superlatively known proposition (*notissima per se*), because by saying "God is," the understanding simply apprehends the identity of one predicate with the essence of its subject.[105] Even admitting that not all human beings are capable of immediately apprehending God's existence in a simple intuition and a simple glance, it must be admitted that at least all can conceive it by an imperceptible syllogism. Each of us, perceiving that there exist some creatures more noble than others, comes to rest his thought in the Supreme Being who is called *God*. From there, the common notion is born in the human soul that there is something we ought to adore.[106] Universal consent thus finds its basis in the very idea of God.

However, St. Anselm's argument requires that the idea of God should be naturally present in the thought of every human being, that the idea of God should be innate. Otherwise, the objection of Illyricus recovers its force. God's existence can be offered to thought as the result of long, subtle dissertations, or as the content of a tradition, or as a belief imposed on us by external authority, but it will remain true that we have no natural knowledge of God. In order to avoid this consequence, we must suppose that the idea of God is imprinted in the soul of every human being or that at least everyone's soul contains something out of which to form the idea. Mersenne does not try to avoid this consequence. On the contrary, he develops it and strives to confirm it.

105. Mersenne, *Quaestiones*, ch. 1, v. 1, rat. 8, col. 41: "Nec certe mirum est si per se notum sit Deum esse, cum praedicatum in subjecto includatur et cum eo penitus sit idem. Addo quod illud intellectui naturale videtur, quod minime situm est in videri et non videri, sed conceditur apud omnes, quale est jus naturale: at manifestum est omnes Deum aliquem constituisse, aut saltem concepisse: omnis enim congregatio Deum aliquem semper coluit."

106. Mersenne, *Quaestiones*, ch, 1, v. 1, rat. 8, cols. 41–42: "Et quamvis non statim quilibet simplici intuitu Deum esse apprehendat, illud saltem imperceptibili syllogismo concipit, ut Aureolus, d. 2 primi, advertit cum enim inter creaturas aliis alias nobiliores esse dependet, in quodam summo mens finitur, quod Deum appellat, unde nascitur illa notio communis, aliquid adorandum esse."

At first sight, the demonstration of such a thesis may give the impression of a wager. The objective is to prove that everyone naturally has the idea of God to those who claim not to have any such idea. Is not the fact that just one person affirms he does not find within himself any knowledge of a perfect being enough to settle the question? That would be the necessary conclusion, if we did not take account of the blindness in regard to spiritual things into which human beings can fall, like animals that only believe the testimony of their senses.[107] Thinking that all questions related to philosophy and theology are chimerical, they refuse to pay attention to them. How then would they see that toward which they do not wish to turn their gaze? Furthermore, this natural knowledge of God in our souls is obliterated by original sin. All our sins, all the perverse movements of our will, which are so many rebellions against the divine law, contribute to erase an idea that He from whom all knowledge comes had originally placed in us. How can we be surprised that many people upon sincerely consulting their consciences fail to discover within themselves the slightest trace of the image that ought to shine in them in all its purity? Therefore, to someone who tells us that no idea of God remains in him, we ought to respond:

> If anything human remains in you, listen to me and make that innate knowledge reappear in the core of your soul, which the crime of our revolt has erased. Far from being surprised that the idea of God has disappeared from your soul, be surprised rather about the indulgence divine goodness shows, which in all justice could have not only refused you grace but also any natural light and finally could destroy even that nature itself.[108]

However, in his infinite mercy, the creator has decided otherwise. His image has to have been thoroughly obscured in our soul for us no longer to be able to restore it by an effort of reflection. We can recall the story of the missionary, who, in order to confound the most learned priests of a savage people, simply interrogated in their presence an old peasant whom they acknowledged to be completely ignorant. By skillfully directed questions, the missionary led him to confess the necessity of a creator of the world, since it is necessary that the least object have its author. He had no difficulty in making the peasant admit that the true God is none other than the creator of the immense and magnificent vault

107. Mersenne, *Quaestiones*, ch. 1, v. 1, art. 3, col. 231.

108. Mersenne, *Quaestiones*, ch. 1, v. 1, art. 4, obj. 1, reply to objection 10, col. 258.

of the heavens above us. Once this point was proved, established, and granted by all, the missionary demonstrated successively the commandments of the Decalogue, which are engraved in the hearts of all human beings; and he set forth these truths in a discourse so clear that the old peasant recognized that he already knew all these things, but had never imagined them.[109] Therefore, the fact that such knowledge is not actually present in the heart of a man does not authorize the conclusion that he really lacks it. We can have innate ideas in us that we do not know how or do not want to develop.

It is not necessary to consider the innate ideas as actual knowledge that we already possess in our mother's womb or that is impressed on us at the instant of birth.[110] The innate knowledge, which we designate by the name of speculative principles or the practical principles imprinted in us by God, is not really distinguished from our faculty of willing or our faculty of knowing. These do not constitute special entities that God has to add after the fact. If we consider things rightly, innate knowledge, the cognitive faculty, and our natural light are the same thing. When God creates the human soul, he makes it like himself. This resemblance constitutes the first natural light, or more exactly, the natural light flows from this resemblance. When the understanding apprehends the terms of some truth and comprehends it without the slightest effort or any reasoning, the faculty that it possesses of comprehending this truth—for example, that the whole is greater than the part or that the same thing cannot be and not be at the same time constitutes the natural light itself. The same occurs in the will. In the will, there is, as it were, a certain weight that carries it toward good and turns it from evil; this weight is nothing but the seeds of virtue that are innate in each of us.[111] We see by that how these

109. Mersenne, *Quaestiones*, ch. 1, v. 1, art. 4, obj. 1, cols. 261–62: "At solo rustico te revincere velim, qui satis apud Indos nuper ostendit, quantum divinae cognitionis valeret innata notitia . . ."

110. Mersenne, *Quaestiones*, ch. 1, v. 1, art. 4, reply to objection 15, Illyr. Arg., col. 272: "Verumtamen, non inde sequitur nos nihil de Deo cognoscere posse, sive, quod nunc idem est, ullas de Deo notitias nobis impressas non esse; nec enim hic de aliquo habitu loquor, quo nobis in utere matris, vel statim atque in lucem prodimus, imprimatur."

111. Mersenne, *Quaestiones*, ch. 1, v. 1, art. 4, obj. 1, reply to objection 16, col. 278: "Cum autem de notionibus cognitionis divinae nobis innatis et impressis hactenus tam multa disserimus, paucis accipe quid de illis sentiendum existimem, et quid sit lumen illud naturale, quo prima quondam principia tam practica quam speculativa scire dicimur. Illas ergo notiones, naturaeque lumen nihil aliud esse arbitror praeter ipsam vim intellectivae et appetitivae facultatis. Enimvero, cum Deus creat animam,

words ought to be understood: every human being has innate knowledge of God in his soul. If it is objected that this doctrine is Platonic, we will answer that the point is not to find out what Aristotle and Plato think about it, but what is true in reality. If we keep the previous affirmations within the limits in which we have proposed them, they are compatible with the doctrine of either philosopher. Whether learning only consists of remembering or whether our soul resembles an empty slate, it remains equally true that God has left innate truths within us. Here we affirm no more than what the psalm and the apostle say: *signatum super nos lumen vultus Dei*. In creating us, God has imprinted in our soul the power and faculty of rising to the knowledge of the divine being each time the soul wishes.[112] This is enough for atheism to be unpardonable.

Such is the doctrine taught by a Catholic theologian in 1623, whose vast knowledge was always allied with an orthodoxy above suspicion. Moreover, we know that he was not the only one to hold it. There was Silhon, that other friend of Descartes; there were Gibieuf and Bérulle, the first of whom gladly conversed with Descartes about philosophical subjects, while the second was Descartes's spiritual director; there was the metaphysician Suárez, whose thought reached young Descartes through his teachers at la Flèche. They had all just reintroduced something of Platonic innatism into Catholic apologetics. Certainly, Platonic reminiscence was not accepted with all the consequences it had in Plato's own mind, but it had become clear then that the doctrine of the clean slate, taken strictly, presented serious disadvantages. By adopting the doctrine of innate ideas, Descartes did not take a personal initiative; he assumed his place within a party with many adherents.

---

eam sibi similem efficit; in qua similitudine lumen naturae situm est, vel ex ea resultat. Cum igitur intellectus alicujus veritatis terminos apprehendit et hanc sine ullo labore aut ratiocinatione comprehendit, vis illa qua veritatem, verbi gratia, totum sua parte majus esse, idem non posse simul esse et non esse, et similia cognoscit, est ipsum lumen naturale; praeterea habet in voluntate pondus aliquod quo fertur in bonum vel a malo deflectet, quod pondus idem esse puto ac semina veritatis unicuique indita."

112. Mersenne, *Quaestiones*, ch. 1, v. 1, art. 4, reply to objection 13, col. 263: "Non querimus quid Plato vel Aristoteles senserint, sed quid rei veritas doceat, tametsi ex ambobus istis philosophis eas notitias comprobare possim; enimvero, sive discere nostrum sit reminisci, sive anima sit instar tabulae rasae, hasce Dei notitias in homine ponendas esse dicimus. Quid enim aliud nos docere putas, ubi affirmamus cum Psalte et Apostolo: signatum est super nos lumen vultus Dei, nisi quod hanc Deus mentis nostrae vim et energiam indidit, ut, quoties vellet, ad divini numinis conditionem exurgere posset, adeo ut nullus possit esse locus excusationi."

Consequently, it is impossible to determine the historical antecedents that prepared the advent of Cartesian innatism. We can discern philosophical and more properly theological precedents. From the strictly philosophical point of view, the Thomist doctrine of knowledge had become unacceptable for most thinkers. Clearly, in the mind of its author, it did not involve the conception of intentional species that were corporeal and spiritual at the same time, with which its commentators would burden it. But in fact, the Thomist school had certainly ended in this contradictory consequence. In Descartes's time, the critique of intentional species was complete. We have seen how timidly the partisans of intentional species presented the doctrine. We have seen Silhon deny it in the same work in which he maintained it earlier. As for its adversaries, they had more than sufficiently demonstrated its uselessness and ridiculousness. Coming after Campanella, for example, Descartes could fairly present his criticism as extremely courteous and moderate. In Descartes's mind, as in that of all the philosophers who abandoned Scholasticism during this period, innatism benefitted by the criticisms under which the opposite thesis succumbed. It finds its place naturally in the vacuum that the departure of intentional species had just set up. We have tried to show, from the point of view of Cartesian physics, what other particular difficulties arise the Scholastic doctrine of knowledge. In his own system, Descartes found intrinsic reasons to prefer Platonic innatism to a conception that was already objectionable in itself.

Furthermore, a very powerful religious movement of the moment contained it. Encouraged by philosophical speculation, innate ideas found favor among several theologians. Against the libertines, who denied the necessity of religious or moral principles, some were able to invoke the irrefutable testimony of conscience bearing these principles deeply engraved in it. Favorable to the mysticism of someone like Bérulle that opened up an inner path of the soul toward God, innatism furnished the apologist with a weapon against unbelievers from which very few theologians of the time could deprive themselves. In the measure in which the *Meditations* can be considered a new defense of the most essential religious truths, it must have seemed natural that their author should adopt the doctrine of innate ideas like the most famous apologists of the period.

If we proposed to do a complete study of Cartesian innatism, we would have to determine what our philosopher was able to add to the many elements his environment provided him, and what new orientation he was capable of giving a movement that oriented him in some measure and carried him along. We do not intend this kind of research, and we feel that any effort in this direction would lead to the conclusion that Hamelin so energetically expressed and supported: "Innateness is independence, aseity, and sufficiency of thought."[113] Let us add that it is also and perhaps primarily independence, aseity, and sufficiency of the extended. This addition must eliminate some useless criticisms and liberate the historian from some surprises. Francisque Bouillier calls the theory of innate ideas "incomplete and vague."[114] Others see in it one of the weakest points of the Cartesian system.[115] That is certainly interesting to record. But perhaps it is more interesting to discover why Descartes was satisfied with it. The fact is that as it stood, vague and incomplete though it was, it nevertheless was sufficient for what the philosopher wanted to do. By affirming the aseity of thought, his intention was surely not to ground idealism, and this is why the realist structure that still remains in his thought is not surprising.[116] Nor did Descartes seek to elaborate his doctrine in a perceptionist or even occasionalist sense. From the strictly historical point of view, we should look at Descartes before, not after, Cartesian innatism, in order to understand him. By taking into account Augustinian exemplarism, with which so many thinkers were deeply imbued even in Descartes's immediate circle, we would understand more easily realism, idealism, and even the occasionalism found in his thinking. They are interconnected, though we cannot perceive that across centuries of philosophy. Better, they are at the stage of originary indifferentiation. This is why a host of difficulties must arise when we try to get Cartesian innatism in the form of metaphysics more elaborated than its author's was. But if we really want to take this doctrine as it was in Descartes's own mind, it is essentially meant as the prohibitions against thought penetrating the realm of what is extended and for the corresponding prohibition intended against what is extended penetrating the realm of thought. That perhaps show why Cartesian innatism is not developed with a single stroke as a metaphysical principle unfolding under the impulse of some internal principle, but fragmentarily and in successive stages. Descartes completes those previous affirmations

113. Hamelin, *Le système de Descartes*, 176.

114. Bouillier, *Histoire de la philosophie cartésienne*, II, c. 2.

115. Zimmermann, "Arnaulds Kritik der Ideenlehre Malebranche," 3.

116. Hamelin, *Le système*, 178.

according to the difficulties presented him and the objections that the doctrine provoked.

If we add the consideration of the sources of Cartesian doctrine to this reflection, the sketchy character of Cartesian innatism on particular points will no longer surprise us. Hamelin writes that Descartes "tied the idea of innateness to that of the faculty of producing ideas. But the idea of faculty is rather obscure."[117] The fact is simply that, once Descartes achieved the end he was pursuing, he had no reluctance to leave the problem at the point where he had found it. If we juxtapose Mersenne's affirmations with the solution Descartes proposes, we can only notice how similar the positions adopted by the theologian and the philosopher are. When Descartes teaches that the innate idea of God, as well as the natural light that grasps it, are only the mark the workman stamps on his work, the likeness left in us by our creator,[118] he repeats claims we have met in Mersenne. To be still more precise, saying that innate knowledge is not actual knowledge that would be stamped in us from our mother's womb, is to repeat what is very explicitly affirmed in the *Quaestiones in Genesim*.[119] When Descartes denies that the soul has innate ideas distinct from the faculty of thinking,[120] or when in order to refute an objection that Hobbes takes from St. Thomas,[121] Descartes affirms that these innate ideas are not permanently within the sight of our natural light,[122] because their innateness is reduced to our power of producing them, he is still accepting Mersenne's position pure and simple.[123] The positive content of such an affirmation certainly seems to be just the elimination of a traditional objection. This power of producing ideas expresses nothing more than the refusal to admit innate ideas that would always be present and actually realized in the soul. In short, the philosopher Descartes and the

117. Hamelin, *Le système*, 178.

118. Descartes, *Mediations*, in AT, vol. 3, p. 9, line 41. See above p. 116 n112 in this chapter.

119. Cf. Descartes, in AT, vol. 8, p. 358, lines 6–11; and see quotation from Mersenne, *Quaestiones*, p. 165 n110 above. Observe that if Descartes speaks like Mersenne here, he does not take the expression from him. Regius provides it to Descartes in his objection.

120. Descartes, AT, vol. 8, p. 357, lines 26–28: "Non enim unquam scripsi vel judicavi mentem indigere ideis innatis, quae sint aliquid diversum ab ejus facultate cogitandi."

121. Cf. p. 136 n9 in this chapter.

122. Third objections; AT, vol. 9, p. 147.

123. See p. 166 n112 above in this chapter.

theologian Mersenne want to obtain the benefits of innateness without putting up with its disadvantages.

Moreover, the historian goes beyond his role by reproaching Mersenne for having proposed this solution and Descartes for having accepted it. As it stands, it is enough to satisfy their purposes: Mersenne crushed atheism, whose foundations he undermines, whereas Descartes can base his proofs of the existence of God solely on the content of thought radically different from extension. Seen from this standpoint, Cartesian innatism perhaps would not appear to be a shapeless rudiment or a group of indications to be developed and coordinated. It would be exactly what its author wanted: the adaption of a Platonic doctrine, given a place of honor by certain theologians, to mechanistic physics of extension and movement.

SEVEN

Descartes, Harvey, and Scholasticism

The explanation of the movement of heart and arteries is one of the parts of Descartes's philosophy of which he felt proudest. To establish it, he not only studied the best contemporary anatomists, but he personally observed and dissected as a professional anatomist might have done. In the fifth part of the *Discourse on Method*, when he wants to present a sample of what his method can do for medicine, he gives a brief but substantial summary of his theory of the movement of heart and arteries. Descartes considered that his purely geometrical and mechanical explanation of such an important phenomenon would make apparent to everyone the deeply original character of the new science he was in the process of establishing.

Today this part of Cartesian philosophy lies in the same oblivion as the rest of his physics. Historians of Cartesianism do not discuss it, and the commentators upon the *Discourse on Method* prudently skirt the pages where Descartes compares his solution of the problem to the one offered by Harvey. We think, however, that even out of concern for Descartes, the comparison should not be avoided. The glory of the illustrious English physician has nothing to lose, since he completely controls and directs the debate. But Descartes's attitude can be seen in a rather surprising light. Still, if we want to give the Cartesian theory of movement of heart and arteries the real significance its author attributed to it, we must first bring it out of the historical isolation in which the historians of Cartesianism have left it. All the passages of Descartes and indeed of Harvey himself on this question are related to the Scholastic doctrine of the movement of heart and arteries that everyone in the period knew but that is completely unknown today. Accordingly, the aim of the present study is to explain Descartes and Harvey's theories and their relation to the medicine of their time.

Scholasticism and Fernel

To understand the Scholastic theory of the heart, it is helpful first to forget most of what we know today about the subject. It is certainly necessary to convince ourselves that for Descartes's teachers, the problem of the movement of heart and arteries was closely tied, not to the problem of the circulation of the blood (about which they were ignorant), but to the problem of breathing that enormously concerned them. We can form a fairly precise notion of what Descartes was taught on this point by directing ourselves to the *Parva Naturalia* of the Coimbra school.[1] Given the character of popularization that this commentary had to adopt, since it was composed for the schools, it is useful to complement it by a more profound scientific work when we want to get certain technical details that are indispensable to understand the doctrine. The great authority to whom the Coimbra commentators refer is a Renaissance physician, Jean Fernel. Descartes also knew him and cites him as a medical authority, *ut auctoritatem etiam auctoritate refellam*, an expert who, moreover, is consequently right about the subject on which he is disputing (namely, intermittent fevers).[2] Therefore, from this common source of Descartes and the Scholastics we discover the state of question about the heart at the moment Descartes's philosophy is established.[3]

Respiration is a vital function that depends on a dual cause. First, it has a principal efficient cause, which is the soul. Next, it has an

1. *Commentarii Collegii Conimbricensis, in Libros Aristotelis qui* Parva Naturalia *Appellantur.* See especially *In Librum De Respiratione*, 56–57, *In Librum De Vita et Morte*, 81–95.

2. Letter of Descartes to Plempius, February 15, 1638; AT, vol. 1, p. 532, line 28, to p. 533, line 12.

3. See Fernel, *Universa Medicina.* Fernel was born at Clermont in Beauvoisis in 1490. He died at Paris in 1558. His work sets out a medicine and anatomy dominated by Galen, whose doctrine Fernel defends against the *juniores.* His general spirit is rather that of a Renaissance man than a Scholastic properly speaking. In the exposition that follows, the Scholastics accept everything Fernel holds. The differences always involve questions of detail. The core of the explanation of the movement of heart and arteries is identical in the two works, as will become clear.

instrumental cause, which is a certain motor force inherent in the body (*vim motricem corpori inhaerentem*). The instruments through whose service movement is effectuated are the parts of the body that bring external air to the heart or receive it from outside, because respiration, as we will see in greater detail, is simply attracting outer air toward the heart.

The organs in charge of supplying and expelling air are heart, lungs, diaphragm, the venous artery, and the windpipe artery. The lung[4] is a light rare body, whose substance is similar to a sponge. It is eminently suited to drink in air and be permeated with it and is composed of a triple network of intertwined vessels. The first comes from the arterial vein. Starting from the right cavity of the heart, it penetrates into the lung and branches into its least particles. The heart feeds the lung through it. The second network comes from the venous artery, whose many small ducts, similar to little roots dispersed through the lung, are then gathered into a single trunk to empty out into the heart's left cavity. The third network is that of the arterial windpipe, which starts from the windpipe, then separates into branches and subdivides through the whole lung to bring external air into it. The extremities of those ducts branch out gradually to be lost in the lung, so that we cannot see that they are continuous with each other anywhere. The air absorbed by inspiration across the arterial windpipe spreads into the lungs and undergoes a process that makes it subtler and the heart inhales it.

The diaphragm is situated under the lung; it is a simple round muscle that serves as a wall between the heart and lungs on one side and the liver and spleen on the other. The diaphragm is the first instrument of respiration, but given that the heart plays a certain role in respiration, we must first describe it.

The description of the heart in late sixteenth-century Scholastic treatises still suffered from the difficulty into which erroneous teaching of Aristotle had led physicians. According to Aristotle, and Pliny, who followed him here, the heart, at least in large animals, is subdivided into three ventricles. The large ventricle is located on the right, the small on the left, and the middle is between the two. By contrast, Galen followed by physicians and anatomists, teaches that the heart is divided into two ventricles only, of which the left is noticeably larger than the right. Galen was followed, but Aristotle was still cited. On the other hand, Galen is the cause of some uneasiness among the Scholastics regarding the heart's

4. According to the usual description of the *Commentarii Collegii Conimbricensis*, *De Respiratione*, ch. 1, p. 55; and Fernel, *De Partibus Corporis Humani*, I, 8, p. 47.

exact location. Aristotle,[5] followed by Pliny,[6] situated the heart in the middle of the chest, but he added that, at least in humans, the tip of the heart is prolonged toward the front of the chest just under the left breast.[7] The Coimbra professors adopted this solution mainly because the clear observation of pulsations underneath the left breast seems generally decisive, but also because Aristotle demonstrated the necessity of the inclination of the tip of the heart toward the left. The left part of the body is passive in carrying out movement. In some way, it serves as the point of support, while the right part is active and carries out the movement. The right side of the body brings along the left, supporting itself upon it. The result is that the right side is naturally warmer than the left side, and that the heart, which is eminently hot, must be inclined a little bit toward the left in order to warm it.[8] The same does not hold for animals for whom walking is almost their only movement. By contrast, human beings, beside the movements of walking, carry out movements that different activities require: painting, writing, weaving, and countless others of the same kind, in which the right part of their bodies is especially involved. The right part must be provided with more heat, since heat is the principal instrument of moving. Therefore, it is admitted with Aristotle that the heart is inclined toward the left, but Galen's argument is still taken into account,[9] along with several others, that the heart is in perfect equilibrium in the middle of the chest and that it is easy to perceive this through anatomical observation. Allowing for the possibility that Galen might be right against Aristotle, the latter is excused beforehand for having committed this error at a time when dissection was not yet cultivated. *Quod si ita est, danda venia erit Aristoteli, quia nondum ejus aetate membrorum dissectio vigebat.*

According to Fernel the heart is pyramid-shaped. Its base is designated *caput* and its top is referred to as *mucro*. The heart is made of extremely strong, resistant, and dense flesh. It cannot be otherwise for a

5. Aristotle, *Historia Animalium*, I, 17.

6. Pliny, *Natural History*, XI, 37.

7. Aristotle, *Historia Animalium*, I, 17.—Pliny, *Natural History*, XI, 37: "Cor animalibus caeteris in medio pectore est; hominis tantum infra laevam papillam turbinato mucrone in priora eminens."—Fernel, *De Partibus Corporis*, 44: "Caput quod et basin recte nuncupes (est enim figura pyramidis) sub osse pectoris ad quintam costam consedit, turbinato autem mucrone infra laevam papillam in priora thoracis eminet."

8. *Commentarii Collegii Conimbricensis, De Vita et Morte*, ch. 4, p. 85.

9. Galen, *De Usu Partium*, bk. VI, ch, 7.

continually burning organism that is the location of natural heat and agitated by a movement that is indispensable to the body's life. This movement is not under our control. It is a natural movement that does not depend on us. It is not a movement subject to our will, like the movement of our muscles. It follows from this that the heart is not a muscle or an organ composed of muscles.[10] In reality, it is composed of fibers extended in all directions that allow the heart to have every kind of movement. Moreover, these fibers are much more resistant than muscles, and we will see below how they cooperate in the heart's double movement of contraction and dilation. To nourish this sort of substance, thick blood, not yet thinned out, is necessary. This is supplied to the heart by a branch of the vena cava, which goes from the vena cava into the heart's outer covering before penetrating into the right ventricle.

The heart has two ventricles. The right ventricle is of a not very pronounced concave shape. It contains only blood that is denser and thicker than the spirits, in the amount necessary to nourish the lungs. This is why only a fairly thin wall surrounds the right entrance. The left ventricle goes further toward the heart's end point. Since it contains a great quantity of very rarefied and subtle spirits whose origin is the heart, it is wrapped in a thicker membrane.[11]

Each of the heart's cavities receives two conduits. On the left, the vena cava, which has traversed the diaphragm, sends out from its left wall a short but large branch. From another part of the same cavity comes another vein that empties into the lungs and brings a rarefied blood suited to nourishing them. It is precisely because this vein already carries and contains more subtle blood that nature provided it with a double covering, so that rarefied blood does not leak through the vein as it might with a single covering. That is why it is called the arterial vein. Since its content is similar to that of the arteries, its structure likewise approximates that of the arteries. In this regard, we should note that the arterial vein cannot be considered a prolongation of the vena cava, because what is double does not prolong what is single. It originates in the heart itself, and the general rule is that all the conduits that run into the heart have a simple covering, while all those that start from the heart have a double covering.

10. Fernel, *De Partibus Corporis*, I, 8, p. 44: "Ex quo perspicuum evadit, cor neque musculuum esse, neque ex musculis compluribus coagmentatum."

11. Fernel, *De Partibus Corporis*, I, 8, p. 45; *Commentarii Collegii Conimbricensis, De Vita et Morte*, ch. 4, p. 86.

If we now consider the heart's left cavity, we see that a conduit comes to it that starts from the lungs, through which the cold spirits contained in the air pass to the heart. Since this conduit contains air or spirits, it receives the name *artery*, but, on the other hand, since we are dealing with rather thin air that has not yet been converted into vital spirits, a single covering is sufficient. By content an artery, it is therefore a vein by structure. This is why it is the venous artery.[12] From the same left cavity the large aorta artery emerges, which branches off and spreads through the whole body. Since it is intended to preserve and transport the subtlest spirits, it is naturally furnished with a double garment and does not prolong the venous artery. At the point of origin of this large artery, certain large animals like deer and fallow deer have a bone that serves as a sort of foundation or root of the artery. Galen describes how it is found in all animals: in small ones in the form of a membrane, in medium animals as cartilage, and in large animals (like elephants, bovines, and humans) in the form of a cartilaginous bone.

We said that the base of the heart, its largest part, is called *caput*, the head of the heart. This is why the two nervous membranes placed around the entrance to the two ventricles, are called *ears*. That is why the heart is said to have ears, or that two ears are placed on its head.[13] The main function of these membranes is to supply the arterial vein and venous artery, which would be too weak to withstand directly the impact of pulsation. They are in perpetual movement, and they swell up and sink back in alteration, like bellows. The ears must aspirate blood and pure spirits toward the heart more quickly than it would do by itself, and provide for its aeration and ventilation.

We come next to a wonderful secret of nature: the heart valves.[14] The valves are membranes placed at the end of the veins and arteries that they close by dilating themselves and open by withdrawing. In conduits that bring something to the heart, these membranes have the function of preventing what has entered the heart from being able to go out again. In this way, three membranes enclose the vena cava, and two the venous artery. On the other hand, if we consider the conduits that leave the heart, their structure will appear different. They open toward the exterior, and

12. Fernel, *De Partibus Corporis*, I, 8, p. 45

13. Fernel, *De Partibus Corporis*, I, 8, p. 45: "Cor auritum esse multi praedicant, huicque utrinque a capite auricula eminere."

14. Fernel, *De Partibus Corporis*, I, 8, p. 45: "Caeterum mirificum hic naturae arcanum contemplamur in appellatis valvis positum."

once anything leaves the heart, it cannot return. We find this sort of valve, each composed of three membranes, in the aorta artery and in the arterial vein. These ventricles function as follows. Nature has willed that when, by the sequence of the contraction of its fibers and vertical threads (the movement that the Greeks call *diastole*), the heart dilates, by the very dilation, it attracts into the right ventricle the blood of the vena cava and into the left ventricle air from the lungs. At this moment, the valves of the first two conduits fall back and yield to the pressure of the materials aspirated by the heart. By contrast, the valves of the last two conduits stretch and spread so that the heart does not reject what it has received. However, due to the contraction of its transversal fibers (what is called *systole*), the heart soon contracts and expels from itself the materials it has received. The spirits pass from the left ventricle into the aorta artery. The blood that has become more tenuous passes through the arterial vein from the right ventricle into the lung. At this point also, the valves of these conduits open and withdraw when the valves of the others dilate and close.

To examine the question of the heart's movement in itself, we must specify the nature of the veins and arteries, which are inseparable from the heart. As can be observed in the preceding explanation, the difference between veins and arteries depends much less on structure than on their content. The veins are conduits composed of a single wall, all of whose fibers extend longitudinally. A single wall suffices, because they only contain thick blood, and there is no need to prevent leakage.[15] Where veins must contain spirits, they are covered by a double wall like the arteries we have already seen. Furthermore, the arteries are rather similar to the veins. They constitute the channels and conduits by which the vital spirits are spread throughout the body, branching out everywhere. Nevertheless, the subdivision of arteries is much less frequent than that of the veins, because the blood is too thick to reach the smallest and furthest parts, if the veins did not lead it there. By contrast, the vital spirits are much more tenuous and subtle than blood. They escape from the extremities of the large arteries and arrive in the most distant parts by hidden conduits, without the help of the arteries that brought them there. We have also seen that when the arteries only contain thicker air instead of spirits, which is the case of the venous artery, they assume the appearance of veins, since leaks are not to be feared, given the thickness

15. Fernel, *De Partibus Corporis*, I, ch. 11, p. 63.

of their content. Consequently, we can conclude that veins always contain blood and arteries spirits, except the arterial vein, which contains blood loaded with spirits, and the venous artery, which contains cold and rather thick spirits taken from the air in the lungs.[16]

We now possess the necessary elements to understand our lungs' respiration, the heart's beating, the pulsation of the arteries, their respective behavior, and their relations.

The heart's movement can only be understood if we know its purpose. This purpose is dual, to be cooled and to be ventilated. The heart, which is the locus of continual heat and effervescence, has been endowed by a benevolent and provident nature with movement that continually agitates it and is, furthermore, transmitted to certain other parts of the body less boiling than it. The heart's pulsation must introduce outer air into it and empty it of the filthy excretions that fill it up. This is why we cannot explain the movement of the heart without taking into account the movement of the arteries and of the lungs, because the same end regulates these three movements.

Let us first examine the common behavior of this triple moment. The motor force or faculty, which agitates the heart to ventilate and cool it, is propagated along the arteries, dilates and contracts them alternately in order to refresh and get rid of the impurities in the areas these arteries traverse. Each time that the faculty pulsates along the covering of an artery, it stimulates and dilates the artery. The artery is opened, and it opens its extremities. At that moment, the artery aspirates external air at the same time as a small amount of surrounding blood.[17] The arteries are furnished with openings, some of which open up under the skin, others in the intestines and viscera, and others in veins. The proof is that if the large artery is cut, the animal loses all its blood. When the pulsating faculty that comes from the heart decreases and contracts the arteries, they expel through the skin or other parts of the body all kinds of excretions, which come from the combination of vapors and spirits.[18]

The heat that sets the heart on fire is so intense that the movement of the arteries alone is insufficient to cool it. Accordingly, a special organ

16. Fernel, *De Partibus Corporis*, ch. 12, p. 73.

17. Fernel, *De Partibus Corporis*, p. 73: "Arteriae autem ex eodem (scilicet laevo cordis ventriculo) in pulmones ejectae, simplicique tunica venarum modo conditae . . . ductum de coelo haustumque in pulmones spiritum cordi subministrant."

18. Fernel, *De Functionibus et Humoribus*, VI, 17, p. 293. Cf. *Commentarii Collegii Conimbricensis, De Respiratione*, ch. 6, p. 63.

is attached to it to accomplish the function of ventilator or bellows (*cor majore quodam adminiculo quasi flabello indiget*). This is the lung's task in warm-blooded animals and the gills' job in fish. Since the heart is inflamed and is incapable of refrigerating and ventilating itself by its own movement (prolonged by the movement of the arteries), it stimulates and irritates the lung and in some way compels the motor faculty to impress a rapid up and down movement upon the diaphragm, the thorax, and the lungs, which are attached to it. When the lungs are roused, air and spirit are introduced as in a bellows. By contrast, they are expelled when the lungs subside and fall back upon themselves.[19] In this way, cold air drawn in by inspiration rapidly penetrates the deepest recesses of the body and permits its refrigeration. Consequently, just as the arteries' pulse serves to regulate the heat of other parts of the body, likewise the heart's burning is tempered by inspiration. The arteries are to the body what the lung is to the heart. Inversely, expiration cleanses the heart of its sooty excretions, as the contraction of the arteries purges them from the rest of the body.

Therefore, there is a correspondence between the movement of heart and arteries and that of respiration. Inspiration can be compared to diastole and expiration to systole. Respiration and lungs have been given to animals for the same end.[20] The surrounding air penetrates through mouth and nose into the arterial trachea at the moment of inspiration. It not only fills the branches of this artery but also the whole mass of the lungs so that, inflated and swollen by air, they occupy the whole thoracic cavity. The air drawn from the outside undergoes a first elaboration in the lung. The lung's flesh is extremely tenuous, soft, and rarefied and subjects the air to a kind of preparation and concoction. The thick, cold, and impure external air cannot provide suitable nutrition to the interior spirits, and the air must not penetrate abruptly and directly from the outside into the heart. It must be first digested like food and be transformed little by little to achieve a kind of relationship with the interior spirit that it must provide for and feed.

19. Fernel, *De Functionibus*, VI, 17, p. 293: "Dum enim cor ardoris incendio flagrat, nec satis valet pulsationes agitationesque sua refrigerationem consequi et sibi adsciscere, tum temporis pulmones ipsamque sentiendi vim premit et irritat, efficitque necessitate quadam, ut movendi facultas diaphragma et thoracem hincque annexos pulmones, crebro tollat deprimatque."

20. Fernel, *De Functionibus*, p. 294: "Ergo unius ejusdemque usus causa respiratio et pulsus dati sunt animalibus."

When the spirit contained in air has been carefully elaborated, it passes into the left ventricle of the heart, a kind of furnace and secret workshop, in which it is going to undergo its most characteristic transformation. At this moment we have together the blood's vapor that comes from the right ventricle, an innate faculty of the heart, the spirit that it contains naturally, and the intense heat located in it. By the cooperation of these varied factors, the vital spirit is elaborated in the left ventricle in the same way as in a cauldron, to spread out afterwards into the whole body through the arteries and confer salutary heat upon the body.[21] The movement of this concoction is naturally accompanied by the emission of torrid vapors that are expelled by the pulse of heart and arteries and the lung's expiration.

The complete process of these operations is as follows. While the thorax is stimulated, the arterial trachea and its ramifications are filled with air. On the other hand, the venous artery and its ramifications are filled with excreted fumes that are expelled from the heart's left ventricle so that its natural heat is not smothered. The arterial veins are replenished with light blood that the right ventricle sends to the lungs in order to feed them. In this way, thanks to the three different conduits whose interconnection constitutes the lung, the lung is filled at the moment of inspiration with external air, excretions of the left ventricle, and blood from the right ventricle.[22] When the lungs fall back on themselves and expiration takes place, the smoky excretions are expelled through the arterial trachea. The air that has been prepared and elaborated in the lung passes through the venous arteries into the left ventricle of the heart. The lighter and subtler blood that is in the lung flows back a little toward the

21. Fernel, *De Functionibus*, VI, 18, p. 296: "Non enim externus aer, rudis, rigidus et impurus et derepente irruens fieri potest interioris spiritus conveniens pabulum, sed hunc quemadmodum et alimenta necesse est paulatim mutari et familiarem innato spiritui qualitatem, longiuscula mora recipere. Posthaec autem elaboratus diligenter spiritus, in sinistrum cordis ventriculum arripitur, ex quo accedente etiam sanguinis vapore, qui ex dextro ventriculo permanavit, vi cordis insita, ejusque innato spiritu et ingenti caloris incendio, haud secus atque in fornace spiritus procreatur vitalis, qui demum in omne corpus per arterias effusus, salutarem impertit toti calorem."

22. It is absolutely necessary to purge the heart of vapors that result from the production of vital spirits "cooked up" in the left ventricle. The heart's heat can be extinguished either by excess of external cold (as occurs to those who have traveled through snow or drank too much ice water all at once), but the heat can also be extinguished because of lack of fresh air and absence of ventilation, In such a case the heart's heat is snuffed out like the flame in a glass. *Commentarii Collegii Conimbricensis, De Respiratione*, 58–59.

heart through the venous artery by reason of the lung's contractions but it mostly serves to nourish the flesh.

The movement of the lung is assisted by the beating of the heart and of the arteries that cooperate to assure the same results. At the moment of the diastole, the heart aspires elaborated air from the lung by the content of the venous arteries and draws it into its left ventricle. Lastly, it draws blood taken from the vena cava into the right ventricle. The valves of these various conduits are open at this moment. During the systole, the heart sends the blood from the right ventricle through the arterial vein into the lung. From the left ventricle it sends the vital spirits it has just elaborated into the aorta artery and the small arteries. At this moment all the arteries must expand. Lastly, it sends back the excretions by which its heat could be smothered through the aorta and through the lungs.[23]

The relation of cardiac and arterial pulsations remains to be determined. As was usual, Fernel properly recalls the remarkable agreement between the beating of the heart and the beating of the arteries, but he departs from the usual doctrine on one important point. According to the Coimbra professors, the arterial and cardiac pulsations correspond exactly. Following Galen, they observe the simultaneity of the two pulses in order to justify their affirmation. Moreover, this affirmation must have seemed very natural, giving the exact correspondence of functions assigned to heart and arteries. The arteries are only a kind of elongated heart. By dilating, heart and arteries aspire exterior air destined to the ventilation of the heart. By being compressed, heart and arteries send back vital spirits and excretions. Nothing is more natural than to see them dilating and contracting at the same time.[24] By contrast, Fernel insists on the fundamental difference between the two pulsations. The arteries dilate when the heart is in systole, and they relax when the heart is in diastole. In fact, the arteries dilate at the instant when the heart by contracting, sends to them the vital spirits it has just elaborated.[25] However,

23. Fernel, *De Functionibus*, 296–97. *Commentarii Collegii Conimbricensis, De Respiratione*, ch. 6, 64–65.

24. *Commentarii Collegii Conimbricensis, De Respiratione*, ch. 6, 64: "Consentiunt et cordis pulsatio, quatenus eodem tenore et concentu sibi respondent; cum enim sese cor explicat explicantur arteriae: dum se contrahit, subsidunt: id quod facile deprehendet ut Galenus, libro III de praesagiis pulsum, capitulo II ait, qui altera manu cordis pulsationem, altera motum arteriarum exploraverit."

25. Fernel, *De Functionibus*, 297: "Hae [*scilicet*, arteriae] tamen dilatantur in systole cordis, committuntur autem in diastole. Dilatantur enim dum compressum cor in eas spiritum immittit. At non solius influentis spiritus et sanguinis in vapores extenuati

Fernel immediately restricts the scope of the last conclusion. Although the arteries dilate when the animal spirits penetrate them, the spirits and vapors of the blood do not suffice to fill them. If the arteries were dilated by vapors and spirits, they would only dilate at the precise moment when vapors and spirits reached them. Consequently, they would not all be seen beating simultaneously, but we would see the pulse being propagated up to the extremities of the body, in the measure in which spirits arrived there. However, since the pulse of all arteries is simultaneous, it must be admitted that a single force is the cause of all these movements of diastole and systole, namely, the same forces that cause the movement of the heart. It resides in the substance of the arteries, but owes to the heart its origin or at the very least its conservation.[26]

The Scholastics knew the explanation Aristotle had proposed of the nature of this pulsifying faculty (*vis pulsans, vis pulsifica*). By a remarkable twist we will find it again coming from Descartes's pen. But it was not accepted. According to Aristotle, the heat of the blood in ebullition in the heart explains the pulsifying of heart and arteries.[27] However, this affirmation rests on a philosophical error (*sed non recte philosophantur*). Heat is a principle of alteration, but at least directly and inherently cannot determine a movement. Heat is the necessary condition of all movement. It is the immediate cause of none. Besides, the vital faculty that engenders the vital spirits and vital heat in the heart has its seat located in the heart. By contrast, the pulsifying faculty is common both to the heart and arteries. The vital faculty extends its influence over bones, cartilage, flesh, and the smallest parts of the whole body. On the other hand, other than heart and arteries, and perhaps also the brain, no part of the body undergoes the influence of the pulsifying faculty. Consequently, this faculty is obviously different from the vital faculty. In some way, this faculty is the servant. Its functions consist in distributing spirits and heat of the

---

copia implentur: non enim fieri tum posset ut omnes uno eodemque memento pulsarent, quod nequeat puncto temporis spiritus per arterias in corporis extrema pervadere. Ergo quum simul omnes pulsare deprehenduntur, quaecumque hosce diastoles et systoles motus effecit causa, eadem sane est quae cor movet."

26. Fernel, *De Functionibus*, 297: "Eas [scilicet vis pulsifica] est in arteriarum corpore posita, sed quae tamen suam originem aut certe conservationem cordi acceptam referat."

27. *Commentarii Collegii Conimbricensis, De Respiratione*, ch. 6, 64: "Primum quod utraque [arteriarum et cordis pulsatio] sit a facultate vitali, hoc est a virtute quadam motrice, quae in corde quod vitae fons est, ortum habet. Hanc vim sunt qui putent non esse aliud quam calorem sanguinis in corde ebullientis."

vital faculty throughout the body, yet it follows the innate heat through a movement that serves to increase it.[28]

Accordingly, as the explanation of "cardiac revolution," a Scholastics expression that is still used, although the original meaning has been forgotten,[29] Descartes received information that completely coincided with what he might find in the works of the most distinguished seventeenth-century physicians. With the exception of the synchronism of the cardiac and arterial pulsations, Fernel and the Conimbricenses ended with the same conclusion, the first using more physiological arguments and the second more philosophical ones. The movement of heart and arteries is explained by a special pulsifying faculty, subordinated to the vital faculty that produces heat and spirits in the heart and consequently different from the vital faculty. The movement's end is to bring air to the heart that this heat will transform into spirits, to regulate the excessively violent heat, and to clean the heart of sooty vapors that could suffocate it.

Harvey against Scholasticism

When Harvey published his treatise on the movement of the heart in 1628, a treatise[30] composed several years earlier (*libellum per aliquod*

28. Fernel, *De Functionbus*, 298: "Ex quibus profecto perspicuum fit, vim illam pulsantem plurimam a vitali discrepare, esseque tanquam ancillulam et ministram, tum spiritus ejus et caloris distribuendi, tum et innate calori motus quidam adhibeatur, certaque in ratione gubernetur."—*Commentarii Collegii Conimbricensis, De Respiratione*, ch. 6, 64: "Illa autem vis motum ciens naturalis quaedam facultas est a secundo qualitatum genere ad id munus particulariter adminstrandum delegata. Micant autem jugi motu arteriae ob id tantum quod tunicis cordi adhaerentibus constent: alioqui oporteret etiam venas omnes, quas intermedio venae cavae cordi copulantur, una concitari; sed quia ita cum corde uniuntur, ut ingenitam ad talem motum potestatem habeant a corde tamen dependentem."

29. Cf. *Commentarii Collegii Conimbricensis, De Respirati*one, ch. 7, 65–66: "Quamobrem motus cordis coelestium sphaerarum conversioni assimilis perhibetur?" Answer: Since the movements of the body depend on the movement of the heart as the sublunary movements depend on celestial movement, it was necessary that the movement of the heart be continuous and similar to the conversion of the celestial sphere.

30. Harvey, Guglielmi Harvei, Angli, medici regii, et in Londinensi medicorum collegio professoris anatomia, *De Motu Cordis et Sanguinis in Animalibus, Anatomia Exercitatio* (Frankfurt, 1628). We cite the edition published by Arnold Leers, Rotterdam, 1661, which also contains the *Exercitationes Anatomicae Duae de Circulatione Sanguinis*, 1649, which must be consulted if we want to discover Harvey's attitude toward Aristotelians and Galenists. For Harvey's biography and bibliography, see the *Encyclopedia Britannica* article.

abhinc retro annis alioquin factum), he had already made and taught his discovery for some time. For more than nine years, Harvey had not only presented the discovery in private, but he had dared to teach it publicly in his anatomy classes. He had demonstrated it in the presence of his colleagues and student by experiments; he had illustrated it by every kind of reason and argument; and lastly, he had defended it against the objections of the anatomists.[31] By publishing the discovery, Harvey had simply yielded to his friends. He still refused to turn it into a large book of the kind that was published in the period. The short exposition of the discovery and of the proofs that justified it was enough for Harvey. *De Motu Cordis* is a model of concision and clarity. Stripped of all unclear development it does not waste the time of author or reader reviewing the opinions of ancient anatomists on the question. This demand for objectivity is based on one of the most overriding features of Harvey's thinking, that of a strictly experimental method.

Anatomy can be taught and learned by dissection, not through books. Knowledge of anatomy must be sought in the study of the body's structure, not in philosophical doctrines. In such areas, the decisive method consists in seeing for oneself how organs are constructed and what goes on in them. When we arrive at the direct observation of the works of nature and, in a word, *autopsy*, we no long need the authority of the ancients. We no longer have to be afraid of their opinions. However ancient they are, nature is still more ancient. However high their authority is, nature's is still higher. *Natura enim nihil antiquius majorisque auctoritatis.*[32] Accordingly, it is necessary either to look oneself or believe those who have looked. We should leave those who are unwilling to do either to their own devices. No argument can convince someone blind from birth that the sun is brighter than the stars. But neither are the blind person's arguments of any worth against the observation of facts by the senses and their interpretation by reason.[33] It is all the more interesting to find that the treatise, which is so concise and lacks any scholarly appa-

31. Harvey, *De Motu Cordis*, dedication and ch. 1, pp. 1 and 24.

32. Harvey, *Exercitationes Anatomicae*, II, 242.

33. Harvey, *Exercitationes Anatomicae*, II, 258–60. See also 266–67: "Haec collectio mea demonstrativa et vera est et necessaria si vera sint praemissa; illa autem vera esse vel falsa, sensus nos facere debet certiores, non recepta ratio, αὐτόψια, non mentis agitatio." Again, 267–68: "Denique hoc est, quod enarrare et patefacere per observationes et experimenta conabar, non ex causis et principiis probabilibus demonstrare, sed per sensum et experientiam confirmatam reddere, anatomico more, tanquam majori auctoritate, volui."

ratus or any Scholastic disputation, commences with a formal critique of Aristotelian and Galenic doctrines of the movement of heart and arteries. We will have to view the treatise first from this viewpoint.

The generally accepted opinion combines pulse and respiration.[34] That is false and contrary to experiment. Furthermore, it is unlikely that pulse and respiration should be matched either in regard to their end or to their way of movement. In fact, the movements and structure of heart and arteries are different from the movements and constitution of the lungs. Consequently, it is extremely likely that the purposes of heart and lungs are very different. Some anatomists went so far as to say that if nature constructed lungs around the heart, it is simply because the pulse of heart and arteries would not be enough to ventilate and refrigerate the heart. By contrast, Harvey proposed to establish in regard to the cardiac pulse, first, that two organs are different in structure as heart and lungs could not have the common function of respiration.

Let us start by examining the question of arterial pulse.[35] Taken in its pure form, the commonly accepted doctrine admits that the arteries only contain spirits and that the moment of dilation and contraction is similar to the moment of inspiration and expiration of air from the lungs. Regarding the first point, we must begin by observing that ancient anatomists willingly offer some restrictions to their theory. Some find only spirits in the arteries. Others find blood there too, and Galen's great authority is on their side. Lastly, others affirm that the arteries contain blood, but an extremely light blood, different in nature from venous blood, because it is penetrated and loaded with spirits. Harvey observes that if the arteries are full of blood, as it is easy to prove by experiments, it matters little whether this blood is loaded with spirits or not. To admit that the arteries transport blood loaded with spirits is to admit that their function is to transport blood thought the whole body. As to the spirits themselves, it is not necessary to take them into account because they are mixed with the blood. Blood loaded with spirits is still blood, and the spirits constitute one single body with the blood in which they reside.

34. Harvey, *De Moto Cordis*, 1–21: "Proemium quo demonstratur quod, quae hactenus scripta sunt de motu et uso cordis et arteriarum minus firma sunt."

35. We reconstruct Harvey's critique not only with the help of his preamble which is especially devoted to that task, but also with the assistance of passages taken from the body of the work and even from the *Exercitationes Anatomicae*, which are posterior to Descartes's publications. Harvey depends only on himself in the whole critique and all the subsequent texts only develop and specify what the previous passages already clearly indicate.

They stand in the same relation to it as serum and butter to milk or heat and water to hot water.[36] Therefore, starting with *De Modu Cordis*, Harvey's position on this is perfectly clear. Against the theory attributed to Erasistratus, according to which the arteries would only contain spirits, Harvey puts forward Galen's authority confirmed by experiment. Against the customary theory of a specify difference between arterial blood and venous blood, Harvey affirms that the spirits are not independent bodies but a simple property of blood, a quality, as it were.

In his *Exercitationes* against Riolan, Harvey will take up this double thesis again to develop it.[37] Not only can it be demonstrated by experiment that the arteries are full of blood, but we can also explain why certain thinkers believe they only contain spirits. It is because the heart continues to beat and to expel arterial blood after the lungs have ceased to send it to the heart. If the heart ceased to beat at the same time as the lungs cease to breathe as happens in those who drown in cold water or who die of syncope, we would find the arteries as full of blood as the veins.[38] Here Harvey returns to the subject of how the spirits are separable from blood to give it his definitive treatment. If we ask the ancient authors what sort of spirits exist, what is their nature, what they consist of, whether they are separate and distinct from blood and from the solid parts, or whether they are mixed and combined with them, there are so many and so diverse opinions that we understand how the spirits, whose

36. Harvey, *De Moto Cordis*, 7–8: "Quamvis in arteriis sanguis uberiori spirituum copia turgeat, tamen existimandum est hos spiritus a sanguine inseparabiles esse, sicut illi qui in venis; et quod sanguis et spiritus unum corpus constituant (ut serum et butryum in lacte, aut calor et aqua in calido) quo replentur arteriae." Harvey mentions veins, because, p. 7: "Etiam sanguinem, prout sanguis, et qui in venis fluit spiritibus imbui nemo negat."

37. Harvey, *Exercitationes*, II, 235: "Sed levissimis argumentis conantur adstruere sanguinem arteriosum, specie differentem esse, sed aeriis hujusmodi spiritibus repletas esse arterias et non sanguine, contra ea omnia quae Galenus adversus Erasistratum, tum ab experientia, tum a ratione petita attulit."

38. Harvey, *De Motu*, ch. 9, 94: "Haec res forsan antiquis dubitandi praebuit occasionem et existimandi spiritus solos in illis concavitationibus contineri dum vitae superstes animal esset. Cum enim expiraverint pulmones et moveri desiverint de venae arteriosae ramulis in arteriam venosam et inde in sinistrum ventriculum cordis sanguis permeare prohibetur; cumque una cum pulmonibus cor non desinat moveri sed postea pulsare et supervivere pergat, contingit sinistrum ventriculum et arterias emittere in venas ad habitum corporis sanguinem et per pulmones non recipere ac proinde inanitas ire." Harvey takes this up again in *Exercitatio* II, 224: "Vacuitas arteriarum in corporibus mortuis (quae forsan imposuit Erasistrato, ut arterias spiritus tantum aereos continere existimaret) inde evenit . . ."

definition remains uncertain, have become a simple means of hiding their ignorance. When the cause of an effect is unknown, spirits explain it. The spirits do everything and they are made to appear on stage as bad poets make the *deus ex machina* appear to make an escape at the end of their works.[39]

Fernel and others suppose that the spirits are airy, invisible substances. They suppose that there are animal spirits—exactly as Erasistratus demonstrated that there are spirits in the arteries—because we find cells in the brain, and since nothing remains empty, those cells must be filled with spirits while the animal is alive. Moreover, all physicians (*tota schola medicorum*) agree in admitting the existence of three species of spirits, natural spirits in the veins, vital spirits in the arteries, and animal spirits in the nerves. Beside these mobile spirits, the physicians recognize as many sedentary spirits.[40] Harvey, however, never found any kind of spirit in veins, nerves, arteries, or any other part of the animals he

39. Harvey, *Exercitatio* II, 226: "Fernalius et alii spiritus aereos et invisibles substantias supponunt."—Cf. Fernel, *De Spiritu et Innato Calido*, IV, 143–44: "Atqui cum nequeat simplex calor in qualitatis genere consituto, sine sede et vehiculo in omne corpus permeare, huc illucque momento diffundi, qualiter tamen hunc a corde per omnes arterias partibus singulis impartiri cernimus, fuit, opinor, necessarium hunc corpore aliquo fluxo et profluente contineri. Caeterum nullus humor ad hoc aptus erat et habilis, ut tanta celeritate corpus omne trajiceret; quocirca necesse fuit calori materiam susteni substantia tenuissimam, pernicitate velocem, quae simul fovendo calori familiaris esset et amica. Atque cum ejus modi sit aerea, aut si rectius appellare velis aetherea, optima ratione debuit talis calori subjici quae semper aetheris modo incensa ardet, cuique perpetuo talis calori subjici, quae semper aeteris modo incensa ardet, cuique perpetuo calor insidet, ut mentem possit ab altero dirimi . . . Aristoteles crebro spiritus est dictus non nunquam calidum, atque naturalis calor; alias quidem a tenuitate et velocitate alias a viribus et effectu ratione nominis desumpta."—Harvey directly opposes this argument, *Exercitatio* II, 233–34.

40. On the spirit as *vinculum animae*, cf. Fernel, 145: "Hanc corporis atque animi comunionem confirmans Alexander Aphrodiseus, spiritum quem proposuimus ait perquam idoneum vinculum illis interponi, qui adversas naturas interjectu suo conciliet atque contineat."—From that we get the complete definition of spirit, pp. 145–46: "Est igitur spiritus corpus aethereum, caloris facultatumque sedes et vinculum, primumque obeundae functionis instrumentum. Quisquis illius substantiam et statum nondum plene sit assecutus, corporis nostri structuram contemplatus, arterias adeat, in cordis sinum et in cerebri ventriculos introspiciat, quos dum inanes ac nullius prope humoris participes videbit, neque tamen frustra ac temere tantos a natura conditos, haec quidem mente contrectans, mox opinor cogitatione comprehendet praetenuem auram eos tum implevisse, dum in vivis fuit animal, quae tamen eo animam agente levissima cun esset, sine sensu evanuerit."—For the different kinds of spirit, see ch. 6, 165: "Unde intelligitur praeter innatos spiritus qui stabilis et in unaquaque parte fixi sunt, tres insuper errantes et vagos influentesque existere."

dissected alive.[41] Some declare that the spirits are corporeal. Others claim they are incorporeal. Those who maintain they are corporeal make them out to be the most tenuous part of the blood and suppose them to be carried in a suspension in the blood. Those who declare that the spirits are incorporeal do not know where to place them, but they distinguish these spirits by faculties and recognize as many spirits as there are faculties or organs. Consequently, there are digestive, "chylific," and procreative spirits, and so on. The Scholastics go even further. They enumerate the spirits of strength, prudence, and patience. They have spirits for every virtue without forgetting the very holy spirit of wisdom. They suspect that there are good and bad spirits that help some and possess others, since they abandon them and wander here and there. They believe that evil spirits are the cause of sickness.

In fact, it must be acknowledged that the spirits that circulate through the veins and arteries do not separate themselves from blood any more than a sherry is separated from the spirit it contains. Blood and spirit are the same thing—*sanguis et spiritus unum et idem signficant*—and just as a wine that no longer contained a spirit would no longer be wine but vinegar or a flat liquid, blood without any spirit could no longer be called blood, *sanguis*, but by equivocation, *cruor*. Therefore to say that blood has become *spiritus* does not mean it is transformed into something airier or that it has become like vapor, but simply that there is a greater vital force. This difference in intensity of their vital force is all that distinguishes arterial blood from venous blood.[42]

41. Harvey, *Exercitationes*, 226: "At nos neque in venis, nervis, arteriis, aut caeteris partibus vivorum dissectionibus explorando ullos invenimus."

42. Harvey, *Exercitationes*, 230: "Idem itaque sanguis, in arteriis, qui venis inest, licet spirituosior agnoscatur et majori vi vitale pollere, non autem quid magis aërium convertitur, aut vaporosior redditur."—Let us indicate again the very ingenious arguments by which Harvey confirms his opinion (pp. 231–32), his hypothesis in relation to the lung's function (p. 233, expiration purifies blood, inspiration moderates heat); also the observations that demonstrate that the spirits are inseparable from blood (a frozen part of the body regains its heat at the same time as its normal color due to the rush of blood); the experiment that would reveal spirits, even supposing them to be invisible if they were separated from blood (the open end of a severed artery is plunged into water or oil, and we do not see any bubble of air escape from it); pp. 236–37: "hoc enim modo, crabrones, vespas et hujusmodi insecta in oleo demersa et suffocata, ultimo aëris bullulatas e cauda, dum moriuntur, emittunt: unde ita respirare vivos non est improbabile: the affirmation of the identity in nature of the normal and the pathological" (p. 238: "ne quis tandem eo confugiens dicat haec ita esse cum libere natura et praeternaturaliter constituta sit, non vero cum sibi relicta libere agat. Quandoquidem in morbosa et praeternaturali constitutione, eodem apparent, quae in naturali et sano statu . . .").

A second point remains to be clarified. Does the movement of dilation and contraction of the arteries belong to the same order as the lung's respiratory moment? Many objections can be directed against this hypothesis, and Harvey accumulates them in the preamble to his first book. First, if we admit that pulse and respiration serve the same purpose, that the arteries absorb air during diastole and return exhalations of air through the pores during systole, it is difficult to challenge the authority and experiments of Galen, who demonstrated that the arteries contain blood and nothing else, to the exclusion of any other exhalation or spirit? In such a hypothesis, the stronger the pulse, the more air the arteries ought to absorb through the pores of the skin. Therefore, if we plunge into a bath of water or oil a person whose pulse is very strong, his pulse ought to diminish and slow down immediately, through the removal of surrounding air. But that does not occur. If the arteries expel sooty excretions in their systole, why do they not expel the spirits they contain at the same time, which are much subtler than these vapors? If the arteries absorb and return external air in diastole and systole as the lungs do in respiration, why do they not continue to do so in the case of trachea arteriotomy? When a wound sections the trachea, we clearly see air enter and leave. By contrast, if an artery is sectioned, we clearly see the blood that gushes out in continuous movement, but we do not see air that penetrates into it or exits from it. Could we admit that the arteries are full of air but nevertheless capable of also receiving surrounding air? But if the arteries absorb air during the diastole, at what point will they draw blood from the heart? If that happens during the systole, we will admit something impossible, that the arteries fill up at the moment when they contract, or that they fill up without being dilated. If it is during diastole, the arteries will carry out the same movement for two opposite uses, aspirating simultaneously blood and air, the hot and the cold, which is improbable. Furthermore, the arteries dilate because they are filled, as a skin would do; they do not fill up because they dilate, as bellows would do. If an artery is cut, we see the blood gush forth violently, now further, now less, alternatively. The artery always gushes further during diastole and not systole. Consequently, it is certainly the rush of blood that distends the artery because if the artery were distended by itself, instead of expelling blood with greater force, it would aspirate through its orifice as it ought to do according to the most common account.[43] Accordingly, the arteries definitely have a certain movement, but it only consists in coming back

43. Harvey, *De Motu*, preamble, 2–10.

to their natural state after having been dilated by the rush of blood. The heart dilates them, and they contract by themselves.[44] Therefore, we must shift to the consideration of the heart's movement in order to obtain the primary explanation of their movement.

The movement of the heart takes place as follows. First, the auricle contracts and by contracting sends blood, with which the auricle is full, into the ventricle of the heart. Once the heart is filled, the heart contracts, immediately strains all its nerves, contracts the ventricles, and produces the pulsation that drives into the arteries the blood sent by the auricle. The right ventricle drives the blood into the lungs by the vessel called the arterial vein, which by its constitution and function is an artery. The left ventricle sends the blood into the arteries, and by means of the arteries throughout the whole body. The two movements (of the auricle and the ventricle) occur consecutively, but in a constant harmony and invariable rhythm in such a way that they seem to be produced simultaneously and that we might believe is a single movement, especially in warm-blooded animals whose pulse is very rapid.

Things occur in the heart as in a machine where one wheel moves another in such a way that everything seems to be moved simultaneously, or as in the mechanical disposition that is applied in muskets. One presses the trigger, the flint drops, strikes the steel, produces the spark that falls into the powder, and sets it on fire. The explosion takes place; the ball departs and penetrates into the target. All the operations, by dint of their rapidity, seem to occur in the blink of an eye and simultaneously. Such is the heart's movement, whose peculiar action is the transfusion of blood and its propulsion to the extremities of the heart by means of the arteries; the pulse that we feel in the arteries is only the pulse of the blood projected into the arteries by the heart.[45]

When the heart's movement is described this way, we still have to explain the origin of considerable amounts of blood that the heart receives from the veins and sends into the arteries. In order to explain how the veins do not wear out and do not empty quickly and also how the arteries do not burst under the pressure of the blood that the heart continually sends into them, Harvey wonders whether blood does not return by some path from the arteries to the veins and to the right ventricle of the heart. He conceives the hypothesis of a circular movement of blood, a hypothesis he subsequently can verify. The blood sent through the left

44. Harvey, *Exercitatio* II, 220.

45. Harvey, *De Motu*, ch. 5, 48–51.

ventricle into the lungs returns through the small veins into the vena cava and to the right auricle in the same way that it returns from the lungs to the left auricle through the venous artery. Harvey calls this moment circular, as Aristotle called the movement circular by which air and rain imitate the movement of the heavenly spheres. Humid earth heated by the sun evaporates. The vapors rise from the earth and condense. Having condensed, they descend again in the form of rain, humidifying the earth so that the sun's circular movement, going away and coming closer, engenders storms and meteors. Plausibly, the same occurs in the body. All parts of the body are nourished and fed by the circulation of warm blood loaded with spirits. In certain places the blood becomes cool again, thickens, and loses its power, but it returns toward the heart in order to regain its prior perfection there, to be reheated and re-impregnated with spirits. The heart, whose movement is at the origin of this circulation, is therefore certainly the principle of life and the sun of the human microcosm, as the sun is the heart of the world.[46]

This movement of the heart, the cause of all circulation of the blood, comes from the heart's being a muscle. Hippocrates affirms this already in his treatise *De Corde*. Furthermore, all anatomists, following Galen, think that the heart is composed of ventricle, horizontal, and transversal fibers. Accordingly, the heart is a muscle by its structure and function, which is to contract, and by contracting to move. It moves by contracting in itself the blood it contains. This movement of contraction is the only movement that is found in an animal. Each time that there is dilation and contraction, it can be admitted that only the contracting is action. The usual concept of a heart that dilates and by dilating attracts something to itself is wrong. Only contraction is active in pulsation, not dilation.[47]

46. Harvey, *De Motu*, ch. 8, 80–85.

47. Harvey, *De Motu*, ch. 17, 160–61: "Quin etiam contra vulgarem opinionem, quia neque cor neque aliud quidquam seipsum extendere sic potest, ut in seipsum attrahere sua distole quicquam possit (nisi ut spongia ei prius compressa, dum reddit ad constitutionem suam) sed omnem motum localem in animalibus primum fieri et principium sumpsisse constat a contractione alicuius particulae . . ."—*De Motu*, ch. 17, 165–66: "Omnes anatomici cum Galeno annotarunt, cordis corpus fibrarum ductu, videlicet recto, transfero et obliquo fabrefectum esse. At in corde elixo, aliter se habere deprehenditur fibrarum structura: omnes enim fibrae in parietibus et septo circulares sunt, quales in sphinctere; illae vero qua sunt in lacertulis secundum longitudinem exporrectis, obliquae. Sic fit, dum omnes fibrae simul contracta sunt, ut contingat et conum ad basim a lacertulis adductum esse, et parietes in orbe circumclusas et cor undique contractum esse et ventriculos coarctari, proinde, cum ipsius action sit contractio, functionem ejus esse sanguinem in arterias protudere existimandum est."

If, as frequently happens, we encounter the old expression *vis pulsifica* in Harvey's writings used to characterize the heart's movements, we must not let ourselves be misled about the real meaning he gives the expression.[48] This pulsifying faculty indicates contractivity of the muscles, but it disturbs Descartes, so susceptible and quick to become concerned when faced with such phrases.

Descartes as Harvey's Defender

Descartes reads Harvey's *De Motu Cordis* in 1632. He is composing the *Treatise on Man*, the part of *The World* that must explain the principal human functions, but he becomes directly acquainted with Harvey after having written the part of his work that deals with this issue. To be precise, Mersenne had spoken to him "previously" about Harvey's book. Since the adverb is employed in 1632, it seems that Mersenne indicated the work to Descartes at a date close to its appearance. Mersenne not only reported the book's title to Descartes but also the great discovery of the circulation of blood, whose explanation is contained in the book. This account would be plausible enough in itself, but it becomes a certainty, if we link the following facts to it. In the part of the work composed in 1632 before reading Harvey, Descartes affirms the circulation of blood. In all subsequent passages, where he mentions Harvey, Descartes attributes the honor of the discovery to him. Descartes, therefore, admits the circulation of blood and sides with Harvey even before reading his book by reason of his own observations that seem to him to confirm his conclusions decisively. From his initial reading of Harvey's book, Descartes indicates to Mersenne that he is not in agreement with Harvey on all points. This simple reservation immerses Descartes in a controversy whose extension is still unforeseeable but that would leave several seventeenth-century anatomists and physicians in doubt, men who were equally impressed by the reasons and authority of Descartes and Harvey.[49] Since the

48. To be sure, in *De Motu*, preamble V, p. 10: *facultas pulsificativa* is used in regard to Galen, but also *Exercitatio* II, 218: "sed quo clarius, quod in dubio est, appareat, pulsificam vim non per arteriarum tunicas a corde manare." and *Exercitatio* II, 219: "interceptio facultatis pulsificae,"—See, above all, in Harvey's summary of his doctrine, *Exercitationes*, 264: "unde auricula dilatata, sua facultate pulsifica se contrahens, propellit cum confestim in dextrum cordis ventriculum . . ."

49. Before reading *De Motu Cordis*, Descartes wrote (*The World, Treatise on Man*; AT, vol. 11, p. 127, lines 3–13): "Besides, there are very few parts of blood that could be

philosopher does not differ from the physician on the question of the circulation of the blood, the disagreement can only refer to the question of the movement of the heart. Indeed, we will see that this will always be Descartes's attitude toward Harvey. Descartes will be totally committed to defending the circulation of the blood and its discoverer. But he will obstinately maintain a theory of the moment of the heart contrary to Harvey's. Let us now consider the first of these attitudes.

In 1637, in the *Discourse on Method*, Descartes openly favors the circulation of the blood, grounding the doctrine's necessity for the same reasons we have seen Harvey invoke: "But if it is asked how the blood in veins is not exhausting by running continually in this way into the heart, and how the arteries are not filled up too much since everything that passes through the heart is returned to them, I need to answer only what has been already written by an English physician (Herveius, *De Motu Cordis*), to whom the credit must be given for having broken the ice here and for being the first who taught that there are several small passages at the extremities of the arteries through which the blood they receive from the heart enters into the little branches of the vein so that the blood's trajectory is nothing but perpetual circulation."[50] The most frequent demonstrations that Descartes borrows from Harvey are "the ordinary experience of surgeons who, having bound an arm moderately tightly, above the place where they open a vein, make the blood come out more abundantly than if they had not previously bound it up." Then there is the existence of valves that only permit the venous blood to move itself from the extremities toward the heart. Lastly, there is the experience that shows that all of an animal's blood goes out of its body in a short time if an artery is tied very close to the heart, and one cuts it between the heart and the place where it is tied.[51]

---

united each time to the solid members in the way I have just explained. But most blood returns into the veins through the extremities of the arteries, which at several places are joined to the extremities of the veins. Perhaps it also happens that some parts pass into the nourishment of some members, but the majority return into the heart, since it goes from there directly into the arteries, so that the movement of blood into the body is only perpetual circulation."—Immediately afterward, Descartes writes, Letter to Mersenne, November or December 1632, AT, vol. 1, p. 263, lines 8–12: "I have seen the book *De Motu Cordis* about which you spoke to me previously, and I find myself differing slightly from his opinion, although I have only seen it after writing on the subject."

50. Descartes, *Discourse on Method*, pt. 6; AT, vol. 6, p. 50, lines 19, to p. 51, line 1.

51. Descartes, *Discourse on Method*, pt. 6; AT, vol. 6, p. 51. —Harvey, *De Motu*, ch. 11, 113–14: "Hinc apparet qua de causa in phlebotomia, quando sanguinem longius

Descartes never waivers on this point. From the beginning he takes Harvey's side and to the end he never ceases to acknowledge his rightful merit, both in public and in correspondence with private individuals. He is in complete agreement in regard to the circulation of blood, and he considers Harvey the first to make this fundamental discovery: *ipsumque ut praestantissi illius inventi, quo nullum majus et utilius in medicina esse puto.*[52] Speaking of the circulation, Descartes reminds the Marquis of Newcastle that an English physician, *Herwaeus* "very felicitously discovered it [circulation of the blood]."[53] Descartes celebrates Harvey's triumph and his merit in being the first to discover circulation, which makes him worthy of high honor in medicine. Descartes also inquires about other treatises that Harvey seems to promise, because "those short works are more worthy of seeing the light of day than many thick books that only soil paper."[54]

In the description of the human body dating from 1648, Descartes returns once more to the demonstration that he had already reported in the *Discourse on Method.*

> This circular movement of the blood was first observed by an English physician named *Herwaeus*, who cannot be praised enough for such a subtle discovery. Although the ends of veins

---

prosilere et majori impetu exire volumus, supra sectionem ligamus, non infra; quod si per venas inde effluerет tanta copia a partibus superioribus, ligatura illa non modo non adjuvaret, sed impediret; etenim inferius ligandum verisimilius esset, quo sanguis inhibitus uberius exiret, si ex partibus superioribus eo per venas descendens emanaret. Sed quia aliunde per arterias impellitur in venas inferiores in quibus regressus per ligaturam praepeditur, ideo vena turgent, ei distentae ipsum majori impetu per orificium elidere et longius ejicere possunt; soluta vero ligatura, viaque regressus aperta, ecce sanguis non amplius, nisi guttatim decidit; et quod omnes norunt, si vel vinculum solveris in administranda phlebotomia, vel infra ligaveris, vel stricta nimis ligatura membrum constrinxeris, tum tanquam ablato impetu non exit: quia scilicet via ingressus et influxus sanguinis per arterias intercepta est stricta illa ligatura: aut regressus liberius datur, per venas ligatura soluta."—On the function of the venous valves, discovered by Fabricius of Aquapendente, see ch. 13, 119–31. Those who discovered these veins did not understand them.—For the third proof see ch. 9, 91ff.

52. Letter to Beverwick, July 5, 1643; AT, vol. 4, p. 4, lines 7–11.

53. Letter to the Marquis of Newcastle, April 1645; AT, vol. 4, p. 189, lines 16–19.

54. Letter to Boswell (?), 1646(?): AT, vol. 4, p. 700, lines 3–10: ". . . sed quantum ad circulationem sanguinis, ipsique honor debetur quod fuerit primus inventor, in quo Medicina et multum debet. Is promittebat alios quosdam tractatus, sed nescio an quippiam postea ediderit; talia enim opuscula magis digna sunt quae lucem aspiciant, quam magnus numerus crassorum voluminum, quibus charta innutiliter commaculatur."—Cf. likewise *Passions of the Soul*, pt. I, art. 7; AT, vol. 11, p. 332, lines 1–18.

> and arteries are so slender that the openings through which the blood passes from the arteries into the veins cannot be seen with the naked eye, we nevertheless see it in some places. And there are very evident reasons to prove that blood passes from the arteries into the veins, so evident that they leave no room for doubt.[55]

Among those reasons Descartes mentions first the experiment of arteriotomy immediately adjacent to the part and the experiment of bandaging the arm in the case of this operation and he concludes:

> This manifestly shows that the ordinary path of blood is to be carried toward the hands and other extremities of the body by the arteries and to return from there toward the heart by the veins. That has already been so clearly proved by *Herwaeus* that it can no longer be doubted by those who are so attached to their prejudices or so accustomed to dispute about everything that they are unable to distinguish real, certain reasons from false and probable ones.[56]

Descartes does not limit himself to offering theoretical judgments in support of Harvey's discovery of the circulation of the blood. He immerses himself in the controversy and acts in support of Harvey. It was already a great contribution to the cause for Harvey to be supported by an ally whose stature grew daily after the publication of the *Discourse on Method*, but Descartes did more. Everyone considered him to be definitively involved in the controversy about circulation. Descartes's friends sometimes complained that in the controversies about Harvey, Descartes appeared to be uselessly taking on enemies.[57] "The Louvain physician"

55. Descartes, *Description of the Human Body*, art. 17; AT, vol. 11, p. 239, lines 12–18. — Concerning the cutting of the aorta close to the heart, see line 9, to p. 240 line 11.—On phlebotomy, see AT, vol. 11, p. 240, lines 12–23.

56. Descartes, *Description of the Human Body*; AT, vol. 11, p. 240, line 24, to p. 241, line 2.

57. Letter to Mersenne, February 9, 1639; AT, vol. 2, p. 500, line 21 to p. 501, line 24: "You write me that an Italian physician has written against Harveus's *De Modu Cordis*, and it troubles you that I am involved in writing on the subject."—A rather mediocre refutation of Harvey had just appeared. The work consisted in cutting up Harvey's text into fragments that were linked by long Scholastic refutations. The argumentation, sprinkled with indignant or comically scandalized exclamations, did little more than maintain old viewpoints and for the most part is purely verbal. See G. *Herveii, De Motu Cordis et Sanguinis in Animalibus, Anatomica Exercitatio, cum Refutationibus Aemylii Parisani, Romani Philosophi ac Medici Veneti, et Jacobi Primirosii, in Londinensi Collegio Doctoris Medici* (Leyden: Jean Maire, 1639).

Plempius held Descartes responsible not only for his own theory of the heart's movement but also for the theory of the circulation of the blood and directed three objections against him in 1638.

First, if blood circulates, arterial and venous blood must be absolutely similar or even identical, since the same blood travels through the whole body. Yet that is contrary to the results of autopsy. Arterial blood is redder and shinier. Venous blood is darker and duller.

In the second place, when febrile matter is in the small veins far from the heart, so as to cause only intermittent fever, several attacks ought to be produced per day, namely each time the blood and the febrile matter that the blood carries return through the body. According to Descartes's own calculations, there ought to be two hundred attacks per day.

Third, if the majority of veins that go toward the leg are bound in a living animal, while the arteries are left free, the leg should soon be considerably inflated, since arterial blood continues to arrive into the veins. But the opposite occurs. If the veins are left tied up for a long time, the member shrinks through lack of nourishment. Accordingly, it seems that experiment decides against circulation of the blood rather than in favor of it.

In regard to the first objections, Descartes might have maintained the circulation of the blood while refusing to take Harvey's side. The first objection bears rather on the explanation Harvey offers for circulation than on circulation itself. In the *Discourse* Descartes indicates (and we will return to this point) that from Harvey's viewpoint we cannot understand the difference between arterial and venous blood, and that blood does not undergo transformation in the heart, and it exits as it entered. By contrast, from Descartes's point of view, the blood swells and comes to a boil, which apparently suffices to explain the difference between arterial and venous blood. The objection only bears upon the circulation of the blood as Harvey, not Descartes, conceives it.[58]

As for the objection based on intermittent fevers, it rests on a false conception of fevers' origin. Against this baseless opinion, Fernel demonstrated in his *Pathology*[59] that febrile matter does not reside in the veins. Without taking into account the personal arguments that he might offer or explaining his opinion on fevers, which would take him too far afield,

58. Letter to Plempius, February 15, 1638; AT, vol. 1, p. 531, line 15, to p. 532, line 5.

59. Fernelius, *Pathologia*, bk. 4, ch. 9: "Intermittentium febrium continentem proximamque causam non esse in habitu corporis."

Descartes limits himself to recalling one of Fernel's demonstrations that is sufficient all by itself. If the matter of intermittent fever comes from the veins, either there would never be double third day fevers or else, on the contrary, every third day fever would be double, and the same would hold for fourth day fever.[60]

There remains the experiment that consists of binding the majority of the veins of the leg, leaving the arteries free. Here, we must distinguish. As long as the veins are free in this way, there is no doubt that they will swell somewhat, and that if one of the veins is opened above the biding, all or almost all of the blood will flow out through the opening. Surgeons observe this every day. This does not just make circulation of the blood merely probable; it is an evident demonstration. But if the vein remains bound for a long time it is very possible that the member will atrophy, because blood that stagnates in the vein rapidly becomes thick and incapable of nourishing the body. Therefore, new arterial blood will be introduced constantly into the veins, because of all the openings and ducts. Both arteries and veins are obstructed by this thick blood and no longer let new arterial blood pass through. Perhaps the veins can even

60. It is difficult to understand in isolation Descartes's allusion to Fernel's demonstration, which is the following. According to the doctrine to be refuted, the matter of fever is corrupted blood that passes from an organ into the large veins, from the large into small veins, and from the small veins into the whole body. When the fever comes into contract with the higher organs, which are very sensitive, they harden and shake. The blood mixed with corrupted humor is heated; it is corrupted in its turn; it is dissipated in sweat, which ends the attack until the arrival of the next one—*De Febribus*, 484–85: "Quartans continua omnium est febrium rarissima. Quandoquidem (ut etiam Avicennas animadvertit) melancholia admodum raro peccet in vasis majoribus, rariusque multo putrescat; quartana autem intermittens admodum frequens ac saepe popularis. Jam si admodum raro melancholia vitiosa est in venis, quomodo ex his potest tam copiosa suffici, aut tam crebro in corporis habitum pelli, quae tot gignendis intermittentibus quartanis sit satis? At nunc obsecro opinio haec rationem reddat compositarum febrium, et cur in tertiana duplici, bilis (quae ejus una censetur antecedens materia in venis majoribus) portio quaedam quotidie in omnem corporis habitum propellitur. Si copia id efficit, tertiana omnis vehemens, ut quae ab exsuperante bile fit, in tertianam duplicem, omnisque quartana ferocior in duplicem triplicemque quartanam facesset. His quasi laqueis ita sese irretiunt opinionis hujus interpretes, ut se nunquam extricare possint."—A simple fever comes from the corruption of a single humor. A composite fever revolves into several simple fevers, each of which is produced by a different humor. Since intermittent fevers are daily, or every third day, or every fourth day, we see the combinations that can occur. Double third day fever (very common) is composed of daily attacks by two fevers, one producing attacks on even days, the other on odd days (*De Febribus*, XV, 497–99).

deflate a little, if the blood that they contain escapes by unobservable transpiration. But that is no proof against circulation of blood.[61]

It is noteworthy that for once the discussion between Descartes and Plempius reaches a positive outcome, at least on this point. Plempius declares himself satisfied and ready to be placed among Harvey's supporters: *Caetera quae dicis pro circulatione sanguinis satis bene se habent, neque ea sententia valde displicet.*[62] Descartes does not insist, and Plempius who began by opposing the circulation of the blood in his lectures and his writings, publicly abjures of his errors, which makes him become an example to all Harvey's adversaries, as a model of good faith and submission to the truth.[63] Baillet is not wrong when he affirms:

> Monsieur Descartes' opinion about the circulation of blood contributed marvelously to reestablish William Harvey's reputation on this subject, which had been mistreated by satires and the disparagement of different physicians in the Low Countries, the majority ignorant or bogged down in the old maxims of their faculties. This made the public receive rather badly what two physicians named Parisanus and Primerosius caused to be printed by le Maire at Leyden in mid-September of this year regarding the circulation of blood, against Harvey's opinion.[64]

More importantly, we have Harvey's own grateful testimony: "Ingenio pollens, acutissimus vir, Renatus Cartesius cui ob mentionem mei nominis honorificam plurimum debeo . . ."[65] Consequently, Descartes's situation is perfectly defined. He immediately understood the immense value

61. Letter to Plempius, February 1, 1638; AT, vol. 1, p. 531, line 15, to p. 534, line 5.

62. Letter of Plempius to Descartes, March 1638, AT, vol. 2, p. 54, lines 28–29.

63. Plempius, *De Fundamentis Medicinae*, bk. II, ch. 7: "Primum mihi inventum hoc non placuit, quod et voce et scripto publice testatus sum, sed dum postea ei refutando et explodendo vehementius incumbo, refutor et ipse et explodor, adeo sunt rationes ejus non persuadentes, sed cogentes. [Descartes uses this same expression with Plempius: *non . . . probabiliter persuadet, sed evidenter demonstrat*, letter to Plempius, February 15, 1638; AT, vol. 1, p. 533.] Diligenter omnes examinavi et in vivis aliquot canibus eum in finem a me dissectios, verissimum comperi."—Plempius is cited as an example of conversion by Zacharias Sylvius of Rotterdam in his preface to the 1661 edition of *De Motu Cordis*. It is true that Plempius attributes his conversion to Waleus rather than Descartes, but we have just seen that Descartes had contributed to it. On Jean de Wale, Harvey's supporter, and Wale's *Disputatio Medica quam pro Circulatione Sanguinis Harveiana Proposuit Waleus*, 1640, see AT, vol. 3, p. 70n1.

64. Baillet, *La vie de M. Descartes*, 2:36.

65. Harvey, *Exercitatio*, 2:280.

of Harvey's discovery. He did everything to make it known and for all the credit to be given to its true author.

Descartes against Plempius and Harvey

By contrast, just as Descartes shows himself to be a firm defender of the circulation of blood, he insistently marks the disagreement that separates him from Harvey on the heart's movement. We see Descartes indicate to Mersenne in 1632 that, having read *De Motu Cordis* after writing out his own theory of the heart's movement, he found himself differing somewhat from Harvey's opinion.[66] In the circulation of blood, Descartes depends entirely on Harvey, both in regard to the thesis itself and to the demonstrations that he gives of it. It is notable that in the version of *The World* prior to reading *De Motu Cordis*, Descartes affirms the circulation without demonstrating it. However, Descartes offers a totally different theory for the heart's movement that is his own, which he has elaborated with data from contemporary authorities and thanks to his own method, against Scholastic doctrine that he was taught. Consequently, the history of Descartes's explanation of the heart's movement includes the two periods: elaboration of the new theory where Descartes opposes earlier medicine alone, and second, the reading of *De Motu Cordis* and discovery of his disagreement with Harvey.

The affirmation of Descartes's disagreement with Harvey is no less clear and constant than his approval of the circulation of blood. Starting with the *Discourse on Method*, Descartes indicates that the real cause of movement of the blood is what he has described.[67] In the *Description of the Human Body*, Descartes notes that Herveus has not "succeeded in regard to the heart's movement as he has in what involves circulation."[68] Sometimes Descartes even seems impatient in his correspondence at seeing that he is taken for a mere defender of Harvey without consideration of the important point that separates them, "because, although those who only look at the surface judge that I have written the same thing as Harvey on the issue of the circulation of blood, which is the only thing they see, I, however, explain everything about the motion of the heart in a way

66. Letter to Mersenne, November or December 1832; AT, vol. 1, p. 263, lines 9–11.

67. Descartes, *Discourse on Method*, pt. 5; AT, vol. 6, p. 52, lines 3–5.

68. Descartes, *Description of the Human body*; AT, vol. 11, p. 241, lines 3–4.

completely opposite to Harvey's."[69] Let us examine the discovery of which Descartes is so proud and why he believes he is justified in defending it obstinately against Harvey.

The only principle employed in the Cartesian explanation of the heart's movement is the heat of the heart and the arrangement of organs and vessels into which the blood passes: *omnem motum sanguinis ex solo cordis calore ac vasorum conformatione deduxi.*[70] In what regards the arrangement of the organs, we meet no difficulty. Descartes has anatomized a great deal and passionately. He never claims to have invented anything in the anatomy of the heart or the arterial and venous systems. He accepts the doctrine of his epoch or at least that of the best contemporary anatomists. Like Harvey and before reading him, Descartes knows that blood cannot filter from one ventricle to another, that the venous artery is a vein, and that the arterial vein is an artery. He knows the arrangement of the heart valves and their use. His novel supposition is that the human body is a kind of machine. His novel contribution is an explanation of how the machine works. As for the structure of the parts that make up the machine (nerves, muscles, veins, arteries, heart), Descartes simply urges us to "make some scholar of anatomy show them."[71] He only declares that he has not supposed "anything new in anatomy or in any way controversial among those who write about it." Moreover, this is easily verified by following his controversies with different adversaries, notably Harvey.

Descartes's peculiar conception of cardiac heat remains the point of departure of his personal theory of the heart's movement. We will see that all his errors come from there. Descartes considers the heart as a kind of furnace with a very intense heat. The fire heats blood as it passes through, which keeps up the heat in the whole body. To give life to the

69. Letter to Mersenne, February 9, 1639; AT, vol. 2, p. 501, lines 1–6.—See likewise letter to Beverwick, July 5, 1643; AT, vol. 4, p. 4, lines 10–11, "circa motum cordis omnino ab eo dissentio," and letter to Boswell?, 1646?; AT, vol. 4, p. 700, lines 10–11: "Equidem de motu cordis nihil dicit, quod in aliis jam non extaret, neque illi per omnia assentior."

70. Letter to Beverwick, July 5, 1643; AT, vol. 4, p. 4, lines 5–6. The three essential explanations of the heart's movement are found in *Discourse on Method*; AT, vol. 6, pp. 47–55; in *Description of the Human Body*, numbers XVII–XVIII; AT, vol. 11, pp. 239–45; and the summary of Descartes's doctrine in the letter to Beverwick, July 5, 1643; AT, vol. 4, pp. 3–6, cited above.

71. Descartes, *Treatise on Man*, ch. 18; AT, vol. 11, p. 120, line 25 to p. 121, line 3. *Discourse*, pt. 5; AT, vol. 6, p. 47, lines 1–27. Cf. letter to Mersenne, June 14, 1637; AT, vol. 1, p. 378, lines 20–25.

human body, God does not have to add a vegetative or sensitive soul to it, but simply to stimulate the heat in the walls of the heart. This heat is at the origin of all functions of the human body. As for its exact nature, it is evident in the last analyst that it comes down to a certain kind of movement. Nevertheless, Descartes enjoys designating it by images. He considers it "one of those fires without light" that is really no "different from the fire that heats the hay when it is stored before drying or that makes new wines boil when they are allowed to ferment on grated cheese." He considers that this "kind of fire that is without light" is similar to what is caused in *aqua fortis* when a large quantity of powdered steel is put into it, and is like the fire of all fermentation.[72] The location of this heat is "the heart's flesh" whose walls are always boiling and ready to volatilize liquids that fall into it.

This singular conception may seem remarkable today, but we recall that Descartes worked out his explanation of the heart's movement without having read Harvey and under the influence of the Scholastic conceptions that Harvey combated. Once again, Descartes strives to give a rational explanation for a fact that does not exist. The heart beats. That is indisputable. The Scholastics explain this by a pulsifying faculty, but Descartes first and foremost wants to explain the mechanical phenomenon. He conceives the heart as a kind of internal combustion engine. He is sure that this mechanical explanation is suggested by a Scholastic concept of the heart as the furnace from which heat radiates and is transmitted throughout the whole body. A Scholastic pseudo-fact is the immediate origin of this Cartesian doctrine. Descartes, who trusts his teachers more than he imagines, believes like them that the heart is an organ in which, "there is more heat than in all the rest of the body."[73] When we explained the Scholastic doctrines, we saw why the heart is eminently hot, *calidissimum est*.[74] It must be like a furnace in order to be able to distill blood into vital spirits and heat the body by means of them.[75] Descartes even

72. *Description of the Human Body*, AT, vol. 11, p. 123, lines 12–13; *Discourse on Method*; AT, vol. 6, p. 46, lines 7–12; letter to the Marquis of Newcastle, April 1648?; AT, vol. 4, p. 189, lines 11–16.

73. Descartes, *Description of the Human Body*, XVIII; vol. 11, p. 244, lines 25–26.

74. *Commentarii Collegii Conimbricensis, De Vita et Morte*, ch. 4, 85.

75. See Fernel above and *Commentarii Collegii Conimbricensis, De Vita et Morte*, ch. 5, 86–87: "Ad calorem vero servandum reficiendumque oportuit, ut Aristoteles 3 de Partibus animalium, capitulo VII, et Galenus in libro de Formatione foetus aiunt, locum in animali esse aliquem veluti focum, qui naturae fomites et primordia ignis nativi contineret foveretque, et eumdem totum esse veluti arcem corporis totius. Hic

holds with the Conimbricenses that the left ventricle of the heart is hotter than the right, and that the organ's form and structure prove this, since the left cavity "is much larger and rounder and the surrounding flesh is thicker."[76] This Scholastic notion of an extremely hot heart that maintains the whole body's temperature by means of blood or spirits is the idea that Descartes will maintain against Harvey and against everyone's objections.

Once it is granted that the heart is a warm organ and that the anatomists correctly describe its structure, its movement is explained mechanically. Flameless fire in the heart's walls makes its flesh "so hot and burning" that when blood enters, the liquid immediately swells, expands, and boils. What happens then is exactly what happens when blood or milk is poured drop by drop into a very hot glass:

> And the fire that is in the hart of the machine I am describing to you serves for nothing but to dilate, heat, and make the blood subtler in this way, as it falls continually drop by drop, through a tube of the vena cava into the concavity of its right side, from which it is exhaled into the lungs, and from the lung's vein, which the anatomists call the venous artery, it goes into its other concavity, from which it is distributed throughout the body.[77]

The blood expelled from the right ventricle in the form of vapors passes into the lung whose flesh is sparse and soft and is permanently refrigerated by the air in respiration. There, the vapors that have gone through the arterial vein "thicken and are converted into blood once again. Then, from there, they fall drop by drop into the left concavity of the heart. If they entered the concavity without being thickened again in this way, they would be insufficient to serve as nourishment for the fire that is in it."[78] In this sense, respiration, whose only function is to refrigerate and condense the vapors of blood, is indispensable to the heart's movement.

---

autem locus cor est; habet enim cor insitum a natura calorem, cujus opera quamdam sanguinis portionem sibi a jecore transmissam exactius decoquit, et in vitales spiritus attenuat, quorum vehiculo in omnes partes corporis quasi subsidio calorem mittit, quo membra omnia servantur et voventur vitaeque munia exercent."

76. Descartes, *Description du corps humain*, ch. 14; AT, vol. 11, p. 237, lines 21–28. —*Commentarii Collegii Conimbricensis, De Vita et Morte*, V, 86–87: "sinister ventriculus est officina spirituum vitalium, siquidem multo . . . calidior in illo sanguis deprehenditur, unde et illum natura, ut vitae magis necessarium, duplici membrana contexit."—As in Descartes, this is in order to prove "sinistrum ventriculum multo esse praestantiorem dextro."

77. Descartes, *Description of the Human Body*, XIV; AT, vol. 11, p. 123, lines 9–28.

78. Descartes, *Description of the Human Body* XIV; AT, vol. 11, p. 124, lines 3–7.

Despite the antiquarian survivals that we nowadays perceive in Descartes's explanation, its novel character was too evident to the partisans of the old medicine for it not to be immediately resisted. Liber Froidmont and his disciple Plempius would send Descartes their explanations after reading the *Discourse*, and Plempius, who capitulated so readily in the matter of the circulation of blood, will never surrender in the area of the heart's movement.[79] Arguing from the Scholastic viewpoint, Froidmont observes the substitution of simple fermentation for the sensitive soul and the substantial forms, and he first objects that noble operations like sensation cannot come from such a crude cause as fermentation. Also, if animals' vegetative and sensitive souls are eliminated in this manner, the door is opened to atheists who attribute the rational soul's operations to the same kind of cause and will give us a material soul instead of the spiritual soul that we have. As for the abrupt evaporations of drops of blood, he finds it to be a bit fast and implausible, unless the heart's heat is equal to that of a genuine furnace (*nisi aestus cordis aequet fornacis ardorem*). Descartes answers quite adroitly that in his philosophy, animals feel completely differently from the way we do. They see as we see when we do not know what we see. They see without thinking. Consequently, they are always in the situation in which we are when the images of external objects brush against our retina and our members carry out various moments without our being aware of it, as if we were automata. Nobody ever considers this kind of activity as too noble to be caused by heat. As for opening the way to atheists, Descartes defends himself like a true theologian. He cites Leviticus and Deuteronomy in the places where they say that animals have no soul but blood. In the name of these passages we must mercilessly condemn those who attribute substantial forms to animals or anything more than blood, heat, and spirits.[80] To the difficulty

---

This concept of a *pabulum* that is necessary to maintain the fire contained in the heart and furnished by the humid is Scholastic in origin, Fernel, *De Spiritu et Innato Calido*, bk. IV, 161: "quod plane argumentum est humorem insitum, non minus atque calorem ad naturae opera conferre. Huc pertinet quo humidum tanquam fomentum et pabulum est caloris, calor autem illius beneficio sustinetur."—The Cartesian concept of the lung's function of refrigeration is similarly Scholastic. See above in this chapter, pp. 173–74.

79. Letter of Plempius to Descartes, September 15, 1637; AT, vol. 1, p. 400, lines 3–6. See the note on Plempius, p. 401. See also the letter of Froidmont to Plempius, September 13, 1637; AT, vol. 1, pp. 402–3.

80. Letter to Plempius, October 3, 1637; AT, vol. 1, pp. 413–16. See also p. 416 on Descartes's profound line of argument about the difficulties of the Scholastic theory. It

of abrupt dilation of blood, Descartes answers that dilations of boiling liquids which are slow at the beginning and abrupt at the end, are not rare, and these dilations do not necessarily require intense heat, since there are liquids that inflate as soon as they have been warmed.

Plempius's objections are anatomical and medical. They are also much stronger and more dangerous. Descartes cannot help feeling respect for their author.

In the first place, Plempius objects against Descartes in a way that for a modern reader is most unexpected, but which can be anticipated from some medieval or Renaissance physicians: Descartes's doctrine of the movement of the heart is not new but ancient, indeed Aristotelian. Descartes embraces Aristotle's party against Galen and perfects Aristotle's theory of heart movement. Aristotle taught that boiling blood is the real cause of heartbeat.[81] Descartes seems to have been a bit disconcerted by this critique. He certainly had been acquainted with Aristotle's theory against which the Scholastics always argued in favor of Galen, but he had probably forgotten it.[82] He immediately insists on the differences between his opinion and Aristotle's. First, there is an imaginary difference. Aristotle would have spoken about a humor originating in food, while Descartes speaks about blood, although it is quite clear that the humor about which Aristotle talks is nothing but blood. The second difference is more real, but was implicitly recognized by Plempius. Aristotle affirms the swelling of the heart without indicating the mechanism of ventricles, veins, arteries, and valves that cause it. Accordingly, Aristotle speaks rightly, but without knowing why. From the Cartesian viewpoint, Aristotle's theory is no more worthy than if it had been false. If two men arrive at the same point, one by following the right road, the other by mistaking the way,

---

shows us what a direct Cartesian critique of Scholasticism would have been.

81. Aristotle, *De Respiratione*, XV; AT, vol. 11, p. 245; cited by Plempius: "Pulsatio cordis fervori similis est; fit enim fervor, cum humor caloris opera conflatur; nam humor propterea se attolit, quod in molem adsurgat ampliorem. In ipso autem corde tumefactio humoris, qui semper e cibo accedit, ultimam cordis tunicam elevantis, pulsum facit: atque hoc semper sine ulla intermissione fit, nam semper humor, ex quo natura sanguinis oritur, continue influit. Pulsatio igitur est humoris concalescentis inflatio."—Plempius adds, letter to Descartes, January 1638; AT, vol. 1, p. 497, lines 15–20: "Haec Aristoteles, quae a te ingeniosius et pulchrius explicantur. Galenus noster contra a facultate aliqua cor moveri docuit, et omnes hactenus id docemus medici, a quibus quod adhuc stem haec faciunt ratiunculae."

82. See above for the passage from the Conimbricenses, its reference to Aristotle's doctrine, and the refutation of that doctrine that it gives.

we cannot really say that one follows the tracks of the other.[83] Despite the protestation on principle, Descartes, who in his subsequent editions takes maximum notice of Plempius's observations, reserves an honorable place for Aristotle's idea alongside his own.

> This is why, although it was known always that there is more heat in the heart than in the rest of the body and that blood can be rarified by heat, I have the greatest admiration for the fact that hitherto, however, there was no one who noticed that this rarification of blood alone is what causes the heart's movement. Because, although it seems that Aristotle thought of it when he said in chapter 20 of the book on respiration, that this moment is similar to the action of a solution that heat makes boil. And also he says that what makes the pulse is the juice of foods that have been eaten, entering continually into the heart, and raise its last skin. However, because in this place he makes no mention of blood or of the tissue of the heart, we see that it is only by chance that he blunders into saying something approaching the truth and that he has no certain knowledge of this. Also his opinion has not been followed by many in this, despite the fact that he had the fortune to be followed by several in making other less plausible things.[84]

These explanations do not keep Plempius from numbering Descartes along with Aristotle and Harvey, among the adversaries of the pulsifying faculty and supporters of the boiling of blood. The error is serious in regard to Harvey, who had to reestablish the truth in his fashion by counting, in his turn, Descartes among the followers of Aristotle and criticizing the very doctrine Plempius incorrectly attributed to him.[85]

Plempius's grouping is only a prelude to his objections properly speaking. The first, and one of the stronger ones, focuses on Descartes's thesis that the heart continues to beat for some time after it has been removed from the body, and even that, if it is cut into pieces, each of the

83. Letter to Plempius, February 15, 1638; AT, vol. 1, p. 522, lines 5–28.

84. Descartes, *Description of the Human Body*, XVIII; AT, vol. 11, p. 244, line 24, to p. 245, line 13.

85. Cf. Plempius as quoted in note AT, vol. 1, p. 535, line 3 from bottom: "Motus cordis fit a facultate pulsifica, non a fervore sanguinis, contra Aristotelem, Cartesium, Harveum."—In what concerns Harvey, *Exercitationes Anatomicae Duae, De Circulatione Sanguinis ad J. Riolanum, I. Filium Exercitatio* II, p. 282: "Neque mihi arridet causa efficiens pulsus quam posuit (secundum Aristotelem) eamdem fore tam systoles quam diastoles, nempe effervescentiam sanguinis, tanquam ebullitione factam."

particles beats for some time, although blood neither enters nor leaves. Therefore, the boiling of blood does not cause the heart's movement. In his reply, Descartes declares that the phenomenon does not escape him, but that he explains it by the presences of little drops of blood falling on the parts that are seen beating. It is enough for a very small bit of blood to fall from a less hot part onto a hotter part for pulsation to be produced. Moreover, two causes facilitate the phenomena. The smaller the quantity of liquid we consider, the more easily it boils and is rarefied. In the second place, the more times a member carries out a movement, the more easily it carries it out. Consequently, we understand that the heart, which has never stopped beating since the first moment of its formation, continues to do so when it receives the least impulse. Lastly, in his depiction of the heart, Descartes continues to admit the presence in the corners of the heart of a sort of liquid ferment capable of heating the blood with which it is mixed.[86] Accordingly, he too feels the need to appeal to something other than the heart's heat to explain blood's effervescence. Descartes consoles himself by thinking that Plempius's objection is still stronger against the doctrine of the pulsifying faculty, because since the rational soul is indivisible it cannot explain the movement of those pieces, and as faith requires that we believe that the sensitive and vegetative souls are not other souls beside the rational soul, it is impossible to see how the soul could make the fragments from a heart divided thus, beat.[87]

A second objection by the Scholastic physician is taken from one of Galen's experiments. If we introduce a pipe into an artery, and the artery is bound onto the pipe, it will no longer beat below the binding. Accordingly, pulsation does not come from the blood flowing in the artery, but from something that is transmitted in the artery's own wall. Descartes answers that he has never done this difficult experiment. Happily, it is

86. Letter to Plempius; February 15, 1638; AT, vol. 1, p. 523, lines 16–20.

87. Letter of Plempius to Descartes, January 1638; letter to Plempius, February 15, 1638; AT, vol. 1, p. 497, lines 20–23; p. 522, line 29, to p. 523, line 28. Plempius will respond that the higher parts of the heart upon which blood cannot fall, also continue to beat. Cf. AT, vol. 1, p. 534 note. He adds, letter of Plempius to Descartes, March 1638; AT, vol. 2, p. 52, line 8 to p. 53, line 16, that if the objection is still stronger against the pulsifying faculty, that simply proves that perhaps both theories are false, not that Descartes's theory is true. Furthermore, he will try to save the usual theory by noting that if the soul does not reside in the fragments in question, the spirit, instrument of the soul, resides there, and that is enough to explain the phenomenon.—See letter to Plempius of March 23, 1638; AT, vol. 2, p. 63, lines 1–21, for Descartes's very complicated answer to Plempius on the first question and his evidently easier response on the second; AT, vol. 2, p. 64, line 22 to p. 65, line 14.

completely useless to do it, because if we admit the cause assigned to arterial pulsation by Galen's experiment, the laws of mechanics (that is to say physics) teach that everything must take place as Plempius affirms that things do. If the pipe floats freely in the artery, evidently everything happens as if nothing had been introduced into the artery. If, on the other hand, we bind the artery onto the pipe, the blood pressed into the pipe loses some of its force at the moment when it emerges again from the pipe into the artery, because every liquid loses some of its force by passing from a narrow conduit into a larger one, and it will exert its last force in the direction of length rather than of width. Therefore, the artery will still be full of blood below the binding, but the blood that fills it will not have enough force to strike its walls and effectuate pulsations there.[88] Evidently, this conception is opposed to that of Galen, who holds that the arteries do not dilate like other skins, because they are full, but that they are full like bellows because they dilate. However, Descartes wants to redo an experiment already indicated by Harvey, which demonstrates the opposite. If the aorta is cut, we see blood gush out in the moment that it dilates, whereas, according to Galen, the aorta ought to aspirate air during diastole and only emit blood during systole.[89]

Plempius's third objection concerns the duration of diastole. If the heart's dilation comes from the blood's rarefication, diastole would last much longer than it does. The amount of blood that is introduced into the heart is large enough so that it could not be rarefied as quickly and suddenly as would be necessary if that were produced in diastole. Time is necessary for all the blood to be changed into vapor, all the more because the heart is warm, but less than fire, and fish, whose heat is weak and are rather cold, have a pulse as rapid as ours. Descartes affirms that this is a very explicable case of *rarifactio in momento*, and that this is proved precisely by the fact that diastole takes place *in momento*.[90] As for fish,

88. Letter of Plempius to Descartes, January 1638; AT, vol. 1, p. 497, line 24, to p. 498, line 14; and letter to Plempius, February 15, 1638; vol. I, p. 523, line 29, to p. 527, line 7.

89. Letter to Plempius, February 15, 1638; AT, vol. 1, p. 526, line 12, to p. 527, line 7. See Plempius's answers, AT, vol. 1, p. 535, note; letter of Plempius to Descartes; March 1638; AT, vol. 2, p. 53, line 30, to p. 54, line 14; and Descartes's answer, letter to Plempius, March 23,1638; AT, vol. 2, p. 65, line 21, to p. 66, line 5.

90. Here is Descartes's answer, letter to Plempius, February 15, 1638; AT, vol. 1, p. 529, lines 15–24: "Fit denique rarefactio in momento, juxta philosophiae meae fundamenta, quoties liquoris particulae, vel omnes, vel certe plurimae hinc inde per ejus molem dispersae, simul tempore mutationem aliquam acquirunt, ratione cuius locum

it is true that we do not feel much heat in them, but their hearts' relative heat compared to whole body heat is what matters. The heart of fish is much hotter than their other organs. Consequently, the rapidity of their pulsations is explained. It remains for us to find out whether blood is a liquid capable of boiling and of dilating instantly, which is not doubtful, and chemistry furnishes many analogous examples. Furthermore, it can be directly observed by seeing how blood dilates after it is heated. But above all, we must realize that dilation of blood is explained by a somewhat more complex cause than simple heat of the heart. Each time that rarefied blood is expelled into the arteries, a little remains within the inner folds of the ventricles, where it acquires a new degree of heat and takes on a nature analogous to that of leavens. When the heart deflates, it immediately receives new blood from the vena cava and the arterial vein, and the remainder of the old blood is mixed with it and makes it inflate until it flows into the arteries, leaving a little leaven in the heart. In this way, without very intense heat, whose degree can vary according to the nature of blood of different animals, blood can be rarefied and fermented, as is wine under the action of dregs for wine or of leaven for bread. Plempius, it should be said, is not satisfied on any of these points. Although the heat of our hands is greater than that of the hearts of fish, it is not enough to dilate blood. How, then, is their hearts' heat sufficient? As for the *fermentum cordale*, even supposing that it is not a pure and simple fiction, how does it explain the abrupt rarefication of blood? In general, fermentations are much less rapid.[91]

One last objection, the weakest, remains. If the arteries are inflated by blood that the heart sends to them, the closest part of the heart ought to beat alone, since it is the first to receive blood, and the others should only beat later, at the moment blood comes to them. Yet, all the arteries of the whole body beat simultaneously, which means that their movement does not come from the rush of blood that they receive, Descartes easily shows that, since the arteries are always full of blood, there is no need for

notabilitar ampliorem desiderunt. Ultimum autem hunc modum enim esse, quo sanguis rarefit in corde, res ipsa indicat; ejus enim diastole fit in momento."—Descartes automatically relapses into his explanation and justifies it in the same way.—"Ad hoc enim tota cordis fabrica, ejus calor, atque ipsa sanguinis natura ita conspirant, ut ullam rem sensibus usurpemus, quae certior esse mihi videatur."

91. Letter of Plempius to Descartes, January 1638, AT, vol. 1, p. 498, lines 15–26; and letter to Plempius, February 15, 1638; AT, vol. 1, p. 528, line 1, to p. 531, line 10; and note AT, vol. 1, p. 535; and letter of Plempius to Descartes, March, 1638; vol. II, p. 54, lines 13–20.

blood that leaves the heart to spread instantaneously into the whole body for all the arteries to beat together. It is enough for the heart to push the blood it contains to the immediately adjacent part of the artery for all blood contained in the rest of the artery to be agitated: *quod fit absque mora, hoc est, ut Philosophi loquuntur, in instanti.* Plempius, unimpressed, publishes his own objections in his *De Fundamentis Medicina* along with extracts from Descartes's answers, commenting that these answers are worthless. Descartes then has Regius accuse Plempius of mutilating his answers. To this Plempius responds by publishing Descartes's two letters in the second edition of the work. The controversy remains there.[92]

While Descartes defends himself against Plempius and supervises the endeavors of Regius, who was engaged in the controversy on Descartes's behalf, he parts ways with Harvey on the issue of the heart's movement.[93] The composition of the *Treatise on Man*, which dates from a period when Descartes had not yet read *De Modu Cordis*, contains no objection to Harvey's theory. By contrast, the *Discourse on Method*, after giving credit to Harvey regarding the circulation of blood and without engaging in any direct polemic with Harvey, establishes that the true causes of movement of blood is not what Harvey assigns. In support of his own thesis, Descartes offers the mathematical evidence of his explanation, but also, the ease with which his explanation accounts for phenomena that remain inexplicable within Harvey's thesis. The most important is the difference between arterial and venous blood.

> The difference that is observed between the blood that comes of our veins and what comes out of arteries, can only stem from the fact that being rarified and distilled, as it were, while passing through the heart, the blood is more subtle and brighter and

92. On the last objection, cf. letter of Plempius to Descartes, January 1638; AT, vol. 1, p. 498, line 27, to p. 499, line 3; and letter to Plempius, February 1636; AT, vol. 1, p. 524, line 16, to p. 525, line 15; and note, AT, vol. 1, p. 534; and letter of Plempius to Descartes, January 1638; AT, vol. 2, p. 53, lines 17–29; and letter to Plempius, February 15, 1638; and letter to Plempius, March 23, 1638; AT, vol. 2, p. 65, line 15, to p. 66, line 5.—See passages from Plempius, AT, vol. 1, p. 536. Descartes complained for a long time about Plempius's bad behavior. — Cf. Letter to Beverwick, July 1643; AT, vol. 4, p. 6, lines 6-16.

93. See particularly the letter of Descartes to Regius, November 1641; AT, vol. 3 pp. 440–42. We set aside the whole affair of Regius, which, despite enormous historical interest, adds nothing to what we know about Descartes's ideas on the circulation of blood and movement of the heart. On Regius, Marinus Johannes Antonie de Vrijer's recent work may be consulted, *Henricus Regius, een "Cartesiaansch" hoogleeraar aan de Utrechtsche hoogeschool* (s-Gravenhage: Martinus Nijhof, 1917).

> hotter immediately after having emerged (this is to say, when it is in the arteries) than it was only a little before entering there, that is to say when it was in the veins.[94]

Taking things rightly, if it is not the heart that modifies blood by distillation, we are obliged to recur to Scholastic expedients. Either there are faculties that change the blood's quality while it is in the heart, or else its transformation is explained by "the heat that everyone acknowledges to be greater in the heart than in all other parts of the body.[95] Between these mechanical explanations and those occult qualities, there cannot be an instant's hesitation.

The source of Harvey's mistake, as Descartes supposes it to be in the *Description of the Human Body*, resides in his describing inexactly the heart's movement itself. Against the common opinion of other physicians and against the ordinary judgment of sight, "Harvey imagines" that when the heart is stretched, its concavities are widened, and that when it contracts, they become narrower.[96] By contrast, Descartes, like traditional physicians, intends to demonstrate that at the moment the heart contracts, its ventricles become wider. Two very different conceptions of systole and diastole are present here. For Harvey, the heart is straightened at the moment of systole. Its point then touches the chest, and the pulse can be felt from the outside. At the same time, the heart contracts everywhere, but most of all laterally. Therefore, it appears smaller and compact.

> The reasons that lead to this opinion are that he [Harvey] has observed that the heart, when contracting, becomes harder[97] and that even in frogs and other animals that have little blood, it becomes whiter or less red than when it expands.[98] Also, if we make an incision that penetrates into its concavities, the blood exits through the incision at the times when the heart has con-

94. *Discourse on Method*, pt. V; AT, vol. 6, p. 52, lines 3–12.

95. *Description of the Human Body*, XVIII; AT, vol. 11, p. 243, line 22, to p. 244, line 10.

96. *Description of the Human Body*, AT, vol. 11, p. 241, lines 3–10.

97. *Description of the Human Body*, AT, vol. 11, p. 241, lines 11–13; Harvey, *De Motu* [?], II, p. 28: "Comprehensum manu cor eo quo movetur tempore, duriusculum fieri: a tentione autem illa durities est, quemadmodum si quis lacertos in cubitu manu comprehendens, dum movet digitos, illos tendi et magis renitentes fieri percipiet."

98. Harvey, *De Motu* [?] II, 28: "Notandum insuper in piscibus et frigidioribus sanguineis animalibus, ut serpentibus, ranis etc., illo tempore quo movetur cor, albidioris coloris esse; cum quiescit a motu, coloris sanguinei saturum cerni."

> tracted in this way and not at the time when it is expanded.[99] From this he believed he might well conclude that since the heart becomes hard, it tightens, and since it becomes less red in some animals, this shows that blood goes out of it; and since we see this blood exit by the incision, we must believe that it comes from the space that contains it being made narrower.[100]

Descartes even proposes a supplementary exercise that Harvey might have invoked in favor of his thesis. If the point of the heart of a living dog is cut, and one puts his finger through this incision into one of the dog's ventricles, he will clearly feel that finger pressed by blood each time the heart contracts, and that finger will cease to be pressed each time that the heart expands.[101]

The old conception is completely opposed to this new one. At the moment when the heart strikes the chest and when the pulse makes itself felt outside, it is imagined that the heart's ventricles dilate and are filled with blood, when the reverse explanation is true, since the heart empties by contracting. The heart's peculiar movement, which the Scholastics, Fernel, and Descartes have described under the name of diastole, is really systole. Consequently, when the Scholastics see the heart dilate to aspirate blood and spirit, and when Descartes sees it dilate under the action of blood distilled by the heat of the heart, Harvey sees its walls contract, harden, and thicken to expel the blood and empty. The diastole alleged by Fernel, Descartes, and the Conimbricenses that is explained by the contraction of the heart's vertical fibers, by the rarefaction of blood, or by aspirated spirits, for Harvey is related to the swelling of a muscle that contracts. It is obvious that the two descriptions of the heart's movement are exactly the reverse of each other. According to the ancient doctrines that Descartes follows, the heart is in diastole and fills up at the exact moment when according to Harvey it is in systole and empties.[102]

99. Harvey, *De Motu* [?] II, 29: "Verum nemo amplius dubitare poterit, cum usque in ventriculi cavitatem inflicto vulnere, singulis motibus sive pulsationibis cordis in ipsa tentione, prosilere cum impetu foras contentum sanguinem viderit."

100. *Description of the Human Body*; AT, vol. 11, p. 241, lines 11–24.

101. *Description of the Human Body*; AT, vol. 11, p. 241, line 25, to p. 242, line 31.

102. Harvey, *De Motu* [?], 31: "Hinc contrarium, vulgariter receptae opinioni apparet, secundum quam eo tempore quo cor pectus ferit, et pulsus foris sentitur, una cor distendi secundum ventriculos, et repleri sanguine putatur: quanquam contra rem se habere intelliges, videlicet cor, dum contrahitur, inaniri. Nam qui motus vulgo cordis Diastole existimatur, revera Systole est. Et similiter motus proprius cordis Diastole non est, sed Systole; neque in Diastole vigoratur cor, sed in Systole; tum enim tenditur,

The attitude Descartes adopts in the face of Harvey's description is extremely interesting. He never denies that Harvey's description is coherent and capable of accounting for the phenomenon. On the contrary, Descartes sees this is one of the cases where two different explanations account for the same phenomenon in an equally satisfactory way. Everything can happen according to the explanation provided by either Descartes or Harvey:

> However, that proves nothing but that the same experiments give us the occasion to be mistaken when we do not sufficiently examine all the causes that they may have. Because, although, even if the heart tightens from within, as Hervaeus imagines, that might make it become harder and less red in animals with little blood, and though the blood that is in the concavities may come out by the incision that has been made, and finally the finger placed in this incision may be pressed there, that does not keep all these same effects from being able to proceed from another cause, namely, from the dilation of the blood that I have described.

It is necessary to recur to experiments of another kind to determine the real cause of the movement of blood. In the *Discourse on Method*, Descartes speaks about experiments such "that their outcome is not the same if it must be explained in one fashion than if it is explained in an other," or as Descartes says now, it is necessary to recur to experiments "that cannot admit both of the two causes."[103]

The transformation undergone by blood in the heart, which is inexplicable from Harvey's viewpoint and very explicable from the Cartesian perspective, is already one of those experiments.[104] But Descartes proposes two others that seem to him equally appropriate to decide the

---

movetur, vigoratur. Neque omnino admittendum (tametsi divini Vesalii adductor exemplo confirmatum de vimineo circulo scilicet ex multis juncis pyramidatim junctis) cor in Systole secundum fibras rectas tantum moveri, sic et dum apex ad basin appropinquat, latera in orbem distendi, cavitates dilatari, ventriculos cucurbitulae formam acquierere, et sanguinem introsumere. [This is the thesis taken from Vesalius by Fernel, as we have seen.] Nam secundum omnes quas habet fibras, cor eodem tempore tenditur, constringitur, incrassatur et dilatur, potius secundum parietes et substantiam quam ventriculos . . . Sicut omnes musculorum fibrae, dum contrahuntur et in longitudine abbreviantur, ita secundum latera distenduntur eodem modo quo musculorum ventres incrassantur."

103. Descartes, *Discourse on Method*, pt. VI; AT, vol. 6, p. 63, lines 3–8, and vol. XI, p. 242, lines 17–20.

104. Descartes, *Description of the Human Body*; AT, vol. 11, p. 243, lines 22–25.

question. The first is that if the heart becomes hard because its fibers contract, that ought to diminish its thickness. On the other hand, if the heart becomes hard because blood dilates it, the heart ought to become larger instead of smaller. "Now we see by experiment that it [the heart] loses nothing of its thickness but rather increases it," which makes other physicians and Descartes judges that it swells at this moment. Another experiment likewise shows that "when the heart contracts and is hardened, its arteries do not become narrower because of that but wider." In fact, if we cut the point of the heart of a young still living rabbit (because the phenomenon is less apparent in a dog or a more vigorous animal), we observe visually that its ventricles stretch at the moment when the heart hardens and that they expel blood then. Even when they do not throw off more than a few drops, because the animal has lost almost all its blood, the ventricles conserve the same length. What prevent the ventricles from dilating more under the pressure of the blood are the fibers "extended like ropes from one side to the other of their cavities and which constrict them."[105] Accordingly, in Descartes's explanation the heart must thicken and its ventricles widen, when it pushes blood into the arteries, and this is what in fact happens. In Harvey's hypothesis, the heart must become smaller and its ventricles contract, which is the opposite of what we observe. The experiment, therefore, proves Descartes's explanation and refutes Harvey's explanation.

Harvey against Descartes

Of all Harvey's opponents, the only one that he judges worthy of an answer was the anatomist Jean Riolan, whose fame was universal and who had written against the circulation of the blood,[106] expecting that Harvey would pronounce himself against Pecquet's discoveries. Riolan was a biting polemicist, and the treatise he wrote on the circulation of blood was a formal declaration of war, not only against Harvey but all those who took his side. However, Riolan does not completely reject the new idea

105. Descartes, *Description of the Human Body*; AT, vol. 11, p. 242, line 17, to p. 243, line 21.

106. We quote from the London edition: Flesher, 1649, *Opuscula Anatomica Nova Quae Nunc Primum in Lucem Prodeunt. Instauratio Magna Physicae et Medicinae per Novam Doctrinam de Motu Circulatorio Sanquinis in Corde. Accessere Notae in Joannis Wallaci Duas Epistolae de Circulatione Sanguinis.* Authore Joanne Riolano, Professorum Regiorum Decano.

but tries to repair it and give it a correct formulation. The circulation of blood according to Harvey and his followers, prominent among whom was Jean de Wale, would transform Galen's whole medical theory. Riolan is faithful to Galen. He accepts a circulation of the blood that leaves Galenic medicine intact, and he thinks he finds it in a reduced circulation that involves only half of our blood, circulating only two or three times per day.[107] Furthermore, after having refuted general circulation, Riolan takes on the followers of Harvey in succession to demonstrate their error, first Walleus, then Conrigius, and then Cartesius, who immediately precedes the convert Plempius. Riolan judges Descartes's theory unkindly. He labels it new, unheard of, and completely absurd. To expound it is to refute it.[108]

Responding to Riolan, *quotquot sunt hujus saeculi Anatomicorum facile princeps et Coryphaeus*, Harvey takes advantage of the opportunity to reply to the objections Descartes had raised against him and to criticize in turn the philosopher's doctrine. When we read attentively the *Exercitatio Anatomica Altera ad J. Riolan*, we come across at least one passage where Descartes is under consideration without being named, in expectation that at the end of the work, Harvey would address him directly.

One of the errors that Harvey most vigorously reproaches is his adversaries' failure to understand that systole and diastole must be explained by two different causes. The dilation of the heart has one cause

107. Riolan, *Monitio ad Lectorem, Opuscula Anatomica*: "Deinde demonstro circulari, non totam sanguinem, sed ferme dimidium dumtaxat, alterum dimidium contineri in vena porta, et canalibus minoribus venae cavae et aortae qui nullo modo naturaliter circulatur. Is tantum circulatorius est, qui intra canales majores venae cava et aortae, a jugulo ad extremos artus extensos includitur, in corde per septum medium a dextra cavitate in sinistram illabitur, sine transitione per pulmones, Idque fit bis terve intra diem naturalem, sanguinem tam venosum quam arteriosum in suo excursu omnibus partibus largiendo. Per hanc circulationem sanguinis Medicina Galeni non mutatur, ut accidit in altera Harvei."

108. Riolan, *Opuscula Anatomica*, ch. 9, p. 44: "Renatus Cartesius, Philosophus in Batavia non ignobilis, sanguinis circulationem necessariam esse judicat ad motum cordis . . . Nova est ac inaudita et prorsus absurda haec opinio de circulatione sanguinis . . . talem mecum agnoscent qui in rebus Anatomiae mediocriter versati fuerint: ipsam patefacere refutare est . . ."—A briefer refutation follows in which Riolan supposes that blood changes in air according to Descartes. When he refutes Regius's theory (*vir non indoctus*), Riolan does not seem to grasp that he is meeting Descartes's theory again. In this same chapter see Riolan's refutation of Cornelius de Hogelande, ch. 12, 49: "Veram ejus cogitationes de cordis diastole et systole mihi non placent, quia sunt obscure descriptae per Mechanicam illam Philosophiam novam Hollandicam."

and its contraction has another. If we want, we can attribute the dilation of blood and of the heart to a kind of ferment that makes blood expand little by little and leads it to pass out into the heart, but that requires two explicit conditions. The first is that we do not mix up this raising of blood with any consideration of vapors, spirits, or anything of the kind. The second is that we consider this heat to be natural and internal to blood instead of viewing it as the effect of some external agent. The heart is not a heater or a fireplace, or like a kind of warm vat that communicates heat to blood. To the contrary, blood communicates heat to the heart, just as it does to all other parts of the body. The heart is warm only by reason of the blood it contains.[109] Accordingly, we must conceive blood contained in veins and especially in the vena cava so close to the base of the heart and to the right auricle of the heart, as little by little heating up by its internal heat (*sensim ab interno suo calore incalescens*), inflating and raising up as ferments do (*et attenuatus turget et attollitur fermentantium in modum*). The right auricle swollen by blood contracts by reason of its pulsifying faculty (*unde auricula dilatata sua facultate pulsifica se contrahens*), and immediately pushes it into the heart's right ventricle. Once filled, the ventricle gets rid of the blood it has received by sending it by its systole into the arterial vein that it dilates. Therefore, the operation's first principle is blood's own heat that disgorges into the heart and not the heart's heat that would dilate blood.[110]

Harvey owes much to that powerful and penetrating thinker René Descartes for the laudatory mention Descartes makes in the *Discourse of Method* of him (and of others along with him). Descartes, however, seeing that the heart of a fish extracted and placed upon a table extends and opens at the moment when it rises up, turns up, and hardens, concludes that its ventricles increase in capacity then. This is the opposite of the truth. When the heart is curled up upon itself, all its cavities are shrunken, and it is certainly in systole, not in diastole. Nor, certainly, is it in its diastole and its period of distension when it falls back upon itself and relaxes, and its ventricles are certainly not wider at that moment. We do not say that the heart of a dead body is in diastole because it has relaxed from its systole and lacking movement falls back upon itself

109. Harvey, *Exercitationes* [?], 276: "Neque cor (ut aliqui putant) tanquam anthrax, focus (instar lebetis calidi) caloris origo est et sanguinis, sed magis, sanguis calorem cordi (ut reliquis omnibus partibus) tribuit, quam reficit, utpote omnium in corpore calidissime."

110. Harvey, *Exercitationes* [?], 264–65.

without swelling. The heart swells and is in diastole properly speaking when it fills with blood thanks to a contraction of the auricles, as is easy to observe by vivisection.

Our perspicacious Descartes did not suspect what difference there is between simple relaxation of heart and arteries and the authentic distension of diastole. Nor does he see that the cause of the heart's dilation is not the same as that of its relaxation or of its constriction, while all anatomists know that movements of adduction and extension are caused in each member by antagonistic muscles, and that contrary effects or moments must have different causes. For contrary or different movements, nature had to fabricate active organs that are contrary and different.

Finally, the efficient cause that Descartes and Aristotle assign to pulse does not satisfy Harvey. For Descartes, the same cause, the effervescence of blood resulting from a kind of boiling, explains systole and diastole. But the heart's movements are abrupt blows and rapid beating, and there is nothing that could inflate itself and fall back in this way, almost in the blink of an eye, through fermentation and boiling. What recedes little by little can only swell slowly. This is all the more true because in dissection we see by autopsy that the heart's ventricles are dilated and filled by constriction of the auricles, and that the ventricles grow in the measure in which they are filled. Lastly, let us add that dilation of the heart is a violent movement that can only result from impetus and not from some attraction. For all these reasons, the Cartesian conception of the heart's movement must be rejected.[111]

The last objection that Harvey makes to Descartes is rather surprising, and it is difficult to see what it corresponds to. The two drops of blood that must dilate in the heart fall into it by their own weight without requiring any attraction. The force exerted upon the walls of the heart by blood in ebullition resembles an impulse much more than a dilation. Accordingly, it does not seem that Harvey's objection is justified. But all the others, by contrast, are justified, and it certainly seems that Descartes's contemporaries grasp that immediately.[112] Descartes regards this theory

111. Harvey, *Exercitationes Anatomicae*, II, 280–82. Cf. the appendix at the end of this chapter.

112. See especially Back, *Dissertatio de Corde*, especially appendix, 231–32: "Anne Harveius sentiat cordis ventriculos in systole dilatari, ut sanguinem recipiant, et in diastole constringi ut eumdem extrudant; tale e Cartesii suppositis sequi; cujusnam potior de systole et diastole sit sententia."—This appendix contains an excellent comparison of the two doctrines.

as very important and presents it as evidence that his philosophy can teach us in the area of medicine. He declared that if the theory is false, so is the rest of his philosophy.[113] The theory was antiquated and had been left behind even before seeing the light of day. Once more, Descartes had taken Scholastic conceptions as facts and spent all the powers of his genius to interpret false data geometrically and mechanically.

Harvey attacks Descartes for the claim that the heart is an organ endowed with particularly intense, specific heat, and indeed Descartes commits a fundamental error in admitting this imaginary datum through faith in his teachers and the ancient physicians. Again, Descartes admits without discussion that the heart's active movement corresponds to diastole, that the blow struck by the heart against the breast at the moment of diastole causes cardiac pulse, that blood undergoes a transformation in the heart by which it is laden with spirits. All these ancient survivals persist in the new doctrine permitting us to understand the very peculiar nature of the errors in which Descartes gets entangled. If the heart is warm, if blood is distilled in it, and if the heart actively dilates, the mechanical solution that Descartes proposes imposes itself. But if the heart gets its heat from the blood, if the blood goes out of the heart just as it came in, if its moment is one of contraction, then Descartes's solution no longer makes sense.[114]

Descartes's failure to establish a valid natural science, despite his personal certainty about flawlessly handling an infallible method, is therefore not only observable, but can be historically explained. From the standpoint of the explanation of phenomena, Descartes was clearly the thinker of his time most totally liberated from Scholastic influence. It is possible that subsequently, and even in our own time, few thinkers were as completely liberated as he. Descartes is suspicious about it and sees it reappear almost everywhere. He thinks he finds it even in Harvey himself upon whom he imposes by his own authority two specific faculties, one to explain the heart's movement, the other to explain the transformation of blood in the heart.[115]

However, while mathematics liberated Descartes from the influence of the ancients in the realm of ideas, it exposed him to that influence by encouraging him to *a priori* deductions in the realm of fact. Neither

113. Letter to Mersenne of February 9, 1639; AT, vol. 2, p. 301, lines 15–24.

114. Cf. Back, *Dissertatio de Corde*, 185, 187, 189.

115. *Description of the Human Body*; AT, vol. 11, p. 243, lines 25 and 27.

nature, as Descartes ended by acknowledging, nor his Scholastic education, nor his mathematical genius predisposed him to be an observer or an experimenter. Only anatomy, which he practiced and loved, could have subjected his mind to the discipline of facts. But he practiced anatomy too late, and in philosophy. He did so more in order to verify deductions already framed in order to seek the point of departure for new deductions. This weakness was only the reverse of his genius. It permits us to understand how such a new powerful and fertile way of thinking did not succeed in becoming completely free from the past, even in the realm in which it was aware of being most deeply novel.

APPENDIX TO CHAPTER 7

William Harvey's Critique of the Cartesian Theory of the Movement of the Heart

Ingenio pollens, acutissimus vir, Renatus Cartesius (cui ob mentionem mei nominis honorificam plurimum debeo) et alii cum ipso, cum extractum cor piscium super planam tabulam expositum, pulsum aemulari, colligendo seipsum vident; quando erigitur, attolitur et vigoratur, ampliari, aperiri, ventriculosque suos exinde capaciores esse autumant; quod haud recte mecum observant.

Collectum enim cum est, tunc temporis coarctari potius capacitates ejus omnes et in sua systole esse, non diastole certum est; ut neque est, quando tanquam enervatum collabitur et relaxatur, in sua diastole et distentione, neque ventriculi exinde ampliores sunt; sic in mortuo, non dicimus in diastole esse cor, quia a systole coincidit relaxatum, collapsum, omni motu destitutum et requietum, non distentum: distenditur enim et in sua diastole proprie est, cum ex impulsione sanguinis per contractionem auricularum impletur, ut in vivorum anatome evidenter satis apparet.

Latet acutissimum virum, quantum differant relaxatio et relapsus cordis et arteriarum, a distentione vel diastole; et quod eadem casa distentionis, relaxationis et constrictionis non sit; sed potius contrariorum effectuum causas contrarias, diversorum motuum diversas, sicut adductionis et extensionis, in quovis membro, oppositos esse musculos antagonistas, sat omnes anatomici norunt; sic contrariis motibus, aut diversis, contraria et diversa activa organa, a natura necessario fabricata.

Neque mihi arridet causa efficens pulsus quam posuit (secundum Aristotelem) eamdem fore tam systoles quam diastoles, nempe effervescentiam sanguinis, tanquam ebullitione factam. Sunt enim cordis motus subitanei ictus, celeresque percussiones; nihil vero ita quasi nictu oculi, fermentatione vel ebullitione assurgit et collabitur, sed lente sufflatur, quod affatim deprimitur. Praeterquam quod in dissectis, autopsia cernere liceat ventriculos cordis, ab auricularum constrictione, distendi et repleri, et prout magis vel minus replentur, augeri; distentionem etiam cordis, motum quemdam violentum esse, ab impulsione, non ab attractione aliqua factum.[1]

1. Harvey, *Exercitationes Anatomiae*, II, 280–82.

8

Cartesian and Scholastic Meteors

Meteors are a task that occupies Descartes's mind quite early. He conceived the idea in 1629, on the occasion of the phenomenon of perihelia. Mersenne had spoken to him about them, and one of Descartes's friends had described them two months earlier, requesting an explanation. Since Descartes never found anything except through a long chain of different considerations, and since he felt compelled to devote himself to a whole subject when he wanted to examine some part of it, he interrupted the sketch of *Meditations on First Philosophy*, on which he was working, and examined all *meteors* in order, before finding a satisfactory explanation. Still Descartes succeeded: "I now think that I can give some account of them, and I am decided to make up a little treatise that will contain the reason for colors of the rainbow, which have been more trouble for me than everything else, and generally all sublunary phenomena."[1]

From that moment, Descartes concerned himself with meteors almost unceasingly until the moment of his work's publication. The winter of 1629–1630 was so warm in Holland that neither ice nor snow was seen, and Descartes complained about being unable to make "some remarks" regarding his meteors. However, it must be added that he was able to observe hexagonal snowflakes. "For the rest, if Gassendi has some other remarks about snow than what I have seen in Kepler, and observed again this winter, *De Nive sexangula et Grandine acuminata*, I would be very ready to learn them. For I want to explain meteors as exactly as I can."[2] He

1. Letter to Mersenne, October 8, 1629; AT, vol. 1, p. 22, line 9, to p. 23, line 12.
2. Letter to Mersenne, March 4, 1630; AT, vol. 1, p. 127, lines 6–19.

was curious about the observations of others and desirous to make some himself. Sometimes he called them "remarks," others "observations," sometimes even "experiments," as is the case for two coronas that he saw around a candle while crossing the Zuyderzee at night on a journey from Frisia to Amsterdam. In fact it is there that he observed that colors do not form in the air but in the humors of his right eye, "and just by putting a finger between my eye and the flame of the candle, they disappeared entirely. I think I can account for this sufficiently, and the experiment pleased me so much that I do not want to forget it in my *Meteors*."[3]

During the printing of *Dioptrics*, Descartes conceived the plan of adding the *Meteors* to the *Discourse on Method*. He had been occupied the first two or three months of the summer of 1635 in solving several difficulties that he had not yet examined and that he took pleasure in straightening out. But he could not resolve to make a fair copy of his treatise or to write the preface he wanted to add to it at the point when he no longer had to learn anything about the matter.[4] However, in 1636, the *Meteors* was ready for the printer, and along with the *Dioptrics* and *Geometry* was to accompany the "project of universal science that can raise our nature to its highest degree of perfection."[5]

The collection of these treatises converges in the same project. They all have the goal of "preparing the way and establishing the access" for the treatise on physics that Descartes will publish if the world desires it, and if he finds his "accounts and his security" in it. But each treatise is distinguished from the others by its peculiar character. The first teaches a method whose worth was proved by the following three. Of the next three treatises, the first has "a mixed philosophical and mathematical subject" (*Dioptrics*). The second is "pure *Philosophy* in its totality," and the third is "pure mathematics in its totality" (*Geometry*).[6] Consequently, the subject of meteors falls within pure *philosophy*. In this treatise (and the point is important for the present study), mathematics need not be involved. This treatise without mathematics, so new in the method it employs, is not at all new in the subject it studies. In the valuable pages that Charles Adam devotes to meteors,[7] he rightly insists on the fact that with the treatise,

3. Letter to Golius, May 19, 1635; AT, vol. 1, p. 319, line 19, to p. 320, line 5.

4. Letter to Huygens, November 1, 1635; AT, vol. 1, p. 329, line 28, to p. 330, line 11.

5. Letter to Mersenne, March 1636; AT, vol. 1, p. 339, line 16, to p. 340, line 10.

6. Letter to . . . , April 27, 1637; AT, vol. 1, p. 370, lines 2–15.

7. Adam, *Descartes, Sa vie et ses oeuvres*, AT, vol. 12, pp. 197–208.

Descartes returns to a traditional subject of Scholastic philosophy. The mere perusal of the summary of the *Meteors* of Eustachius a Sancto Paulo, a rather brief chapter in his *Summa Philosophiae*, and of the topics that the *Course* by Abra de Raconis situates under this heading, is enough to give the clear impression that in writing his work, Descartes wants to offer an example that demonstrates the crushing superiority of the new philosophy over the old.[8] This is why, when Descartes is reproached for the weakness of his explanation, we see him ask that his *Meteors* be compared with those of the Scholastics, and that which side possesses the most fertile principles be investigated.[9]

> If one compares what I have deduced from my supposition regarding vision, salt, winds, clouds, snow, thunder, rainbows, and other similar things, with what others have gotten out of theirs regarding the same topics, I hope that will be enough to persuade those who are not too preoccupied that the effects that I explain have no other causes than those from which I have deduced them.[10]

The mere publication of this essay would inevitably be seen as an act of defiance against Scholastic philosophers. Henceforth one would have to take sides for or against the new philosophy. Short of pretending to be unaware of the work, one could no longer teach in schools Aristotle's *Meteors* without first demonstrating the falsity of Descartes's. Descartes had to be refuted or followed. Descartes wrote to Fr. Noël in October 1637:

> For the rest, there is no one who seems to me to have more interest in examining this book than those of your company [i.e., the Company or Society of Jesus], because I already see that so many persons are led to believe what it contains that (particularly for Meteors) I do not know how they can teach them henceforth as they do every year in most of your schools, if they do not refute what I have written or they do not follow it.[11]

8. See these summaries in Adam, *Descartes*, 204–5.

9. Letter to Plempius, October 3, 1637; AT, vol. I, p. 430, lines 9–15: "Sed si velit enumerare problemata, quae in solo tractatu *De Meteoris* explicui, et conferre cum iis quae ab aliis de eadem materia . . . hactenus tradita fuere, confideo ipsum non adeo magnam occasionem reperturum pinguiusculam et mechanicam philosophiam meam contemnendi."

10. Letter to Regius, January 1642; AT, vol. 3, p. 504, line 28, to p. 505, line 2. See also letter to Morin, July 13, 1638; AT, vol. 2, p. 200, lines 13–21.

11. Letter to Fr. Noël, October 1637; AT, vol. 1, p. 455, lines 18–26.

It was also because Descartes counted on the *Meteors* to introduce his philosophy into the Jesuit schools[12] that it was difficult for him to forgive Fr. Bourdin for publicly attacking the *Meteors*. The Reverend Father's precipitous judgment alone was enough to keep all those who taught the subject every year in the schools of the Society of Jesus from reading Descartes's *Meteors*.[13] Consequently, perhaps it would be interesting to compare Descartes's *Meteors* with one of the Scholastic treatises he used in the course of his studies at La Flèche and to find out whether the concern about opposing the philosophy of his old teachers did not leave traces in his work that would be interesting to bring out. We will take as the base of comparison one of the rare scholastic textbooks that we are sure Descartes knew, that of the Conimbricenses,[14] which is the most notable of all for the wealth and beautiful order of its contents.[15]

If we compare the subjects treated in the Scholastic *Meteors* and Descartes's *Meteors*, we cannot help but observe a certain similarity between the content of the two approaches:

Conimbricenes *In Librum Meteorum*	Descartes *Meteors, Principles*
Tractatus I Quaenam sit materia (scilicet vapores et exhalationes), quae causa efficiens meteorum impressionum. De locis in quibus elementariae impressiones contingunt. Quaedam apparentia quae portenta dicuntur.	*Meteors*, Discourse 2 Vapors and exhalations

12. See on this point Gilson, *La liberté chez Descartes et la théologie*, 319–32.

13. *Meditations on First Philosophy*, Seventh Objections, note; AT, vol. 7, p. 573: "Jamque mihi videor ejus rei fecisse experimentum circa Tractatum quem edidi de Meteroris; cum enim partem Philosophiae contineat quae, nisi admodum fallor, accuratius et verius in ipso explicatur, quam in ullis scriptis aliorum, nullam puto esse causam cur Philosophi, qui Meteora singulis annis in unoquoque ex vestris Collegiis docent, illum praetermittant, quam quia forte de me R.P. [namely Bourdin] judiciis credentes, nunquam legerunt."

14. Letter to Mersenne, September 30, 1630; AT, vol. 3, p. 185, lines 11–12: "I now only remember the Conimbricenses, Toletus, and Rubius . . ." Further on he adds the summary of Eustachius a Sancto Paulo, the Feuillant, whose name he has forgotten.

15. Conimbricenses, *Commentarii in libros Meteorum Aristotelis Stagyritae*, Coimbra: 1598, in quarto.

Conimbricenes *In Librum Meteorum*	Descartes *Meteors, Principles*
Tractatus II De meteoris ignitis particulatim. De tonitru. De fulgure. De fulmine. De fulminum effectis.	*Meteors*, Discourse 7 Storms, about lightning and all the other fires that illuminate the air.
Tractatus III De cometis	"And in order that I tried to explain curiously their production and their nature [i.e., of comets] and that I do not believe that they belong to meteors any more that tremors of the earth and minerals that many writers attach there" VI, 323, lines 18–22.
Tractatus IV De spectris et imaginibus quae sub astris aliisve locis in sublimi apparent De circulo lacteo, seu via lactea. De coloribus in aere apparentibus De voragine, hiatu et area seu corona. De virgis et parheliis.	On the Milky Way, nothing On the colors that we see in the air, *Meteors*, Discourse 9, p. 345, line 1 to p. 348, line 6. On area or corona, p. 318, line 6 to the end. On perihelia, see last Discourse On the apparition of several suns
Tractatus V De iride seu arcu colesti	Discourse 8 On the rainbow
Tractatus VI De ventis	Discourse 4 On the winds
Tractatus VII De aqueis concretionibus. De nubibus et pluvia. De pluviis extraordinariis et prodigiosis. De presagiis temporum. De nebula seu caligine. De nive. De grandine. De glacie. De rore et pruina. De melle. Antiquorum saccharum non esse quidpiam e colesti rore concretum ut quidam putant. De manna.	Discourse 5 On the clouds Discourse 6 On snow, rain, and hail. For extraordinary rains, see Discourse 6, p. 321, line 16–21. On forecasting weather, Discourse 6, p. 310, line 23 to p. 311, line 24. On dew and frost, see p. 309, line 17 to p. 310, line 14. On honey, see p. 310, lines 14–22.

Conimbricenes *In Librum Meteorum*	Descartes *Meteors, Principles*
Tractatus VIII De mari. De maris ortu situque. Varii motus quibus mare cietur. Reciprocum maris aestum non ubique sui similem esse. Variae philosophorum sententiae de effectrici causa aestus marini. Eorum sententia qui causam marini aestus in Lunae vim conferunt. Quamobrem mari datus a natura motus. De maris et terrae permutationibus De diluviis.	In *Meteors* nothing *Principles of Philosophy*, part 4, articles 49–56. "I have touched upon something of this in my *World*, where I very particularly explained the origin of fountains, and the tides of the sea, which is the reason that I have not wanted to put anything about it in my *Meteors*." II, p. 430, lines 15–24.
Tractatus IX De fontibus et fluminibus	In *Meteors* nothing. See previous section. *Principles of Philosophy*, part 4, articles 64–66.
Tractatus X De aquarum qualitatibus De quarumdam aquarum excellente fragore et de aquis calidis. De aquarum sapore et odore. De salsedine. De salsedine maris variae philosophorum sententiae. Explicatio verae opinionis de maris salsedine. Quaenam aquae salubrioris praestantioresque sint.	Discourse 3 On salt *Principles of Philosophy*, part 4, articles 67–70.
Tractatus XI, XII, XIII De terraemotu. De ignis subterraneis. De metallis.	In *Meteors,* nothing. See the passage from Descartes cited in regard to Tractatus III. *Principles of Philosophy*, part 4 Earthquakes, articles 77–79. Subterranean fires, article 94. Metals, articles 57–63, 72–75, 136–44, and so on.

There are striking similarities, between the content of these two works, beside differences that should not be ignored. Perhaps the most notable difference is that Descartes removes the explanation of comets from the *Meteors*. Scholasticism considered comets as sublunary phenomena, not as heavenly bodies. The matter attributed to them was a thick, fatty exhalation, composed of parts pressed tightly together and consequently capable of easily catching fire and burning for a long time.[16] Comets move in the upper region of air much higher than the highest meteors, but they do not retreat further into the heavens. For Descartes, comets are heavenly bodies and no longer meteors. Since, along with the Scholastics, Descartes defines meteors as "sublunary phenomena," he has to eliminate comets from them.

Similarly, Descartes removes minerals and the tremors of the earth from the *Meteors*, topics several authors packed into it. The title of the Scholastic treaties on meteors does not exactly correspond to its content. After a preliminary study of elements, the work's real object is to study mixtures. Some mixtures are imperfect; the elements that constitute these mixtures retain within them their original qualities. Such are dew and frost and all the imperfect mixtures of the kind where we still easily discern the hot, the cold, the dry, and the humid. Beside these imperfect mixtures, others exist in which the mixture of elements has been perfect, so that beyond a certain proportion of the four elementary qualities, we also discover in them a specifically proper form, distinct from the form of its qualities. Some mixtures are animate, like plants; others are inanimate, like stones and minerals. Aristotle eliminates the animate perfect mixtures. Accordingly, the Scholastic treatise will bear the title *De Mixtis Inanimatis*. Sometimes it is asked why Aristotle used the title *Meteors* (a name that designates *quae in sublimi mundi sublunaris regione oriuntur*) for his treatise in which he also discusses things that occur in subterranean places and in the bosom of the earth. Whatever reasons may be invoked to justify this anomaly,[17] the very existence of the question shows that the combinations of meteors and metals in the same treatise does not stem from a confusion but from a plan that is firmly rooted in the Scholastic mind. Both are inanimate mixtures, whether perfect or imperfect. By contrast, Descartes retains from the Scholastic treatise on meteors only what concerns imperfect mixtures, that is to say, meteors

16. Gilson, *Index scolastico-cartésien*, text 77, p. 47.

17. Gilson, *Index scolastico-cartésien*, text 284, p. 181.

properly speaking. Nevertheless, it is notable that the existence of perfect mixtures in Scholastic *Meteors* has left at least one testimony in the *Meteors* of Descartes. The philosopher wants to show, at least by a typical example, that the forms of mixture are as explicable by his philosophy as those of meteors. This is why Descartes inserts into his treatise between vapors and winds, the study of salt:

> For, because these vapors, rising from the water of the sea, sometimes form salt along the surface of the sea, I take to occasion to stop a little in order to describe it and to check whether we can know the forms of this body that the Philosophers say are composed of elements in a perfect mixture, as well as those of meteors, which they say are only composed of imperfect mixtures.[18]

The explanation of salt by the principles of Cartesian philosophy is a powerful demonstration of the definitive replacement of substantial forms by mathematical reasons in the explanation of the natural properties of bodies.[19] To that end, Descartes allows, in behalf of salt, a suspension of the rule he has expressed excluding perfect mixtures.

The difference in the structure of the two works is very important, and it relates to the most fundamental difference that separates the two philosophies, their methods. The Scholastic treatises classify meteors according to the four elements, fire, water, air, and earth. They examine fiery, aqueous, earthen, and airy meteors in succession.[20] Descartes, on the other hand, structures his consideration in one of those "long chains" of reasons geometers are accustomed to employ. He first explains the earthen bodies in general, which prepares the explanation of exhalations and vapors. Then he examines salt deposited on the sea by vapors. He follows these vapors in the aerial ascent and explains wind; then, by the gathering of winds, he comes to clouds. He dissolves these clouds in rain, hail, or snow. Lastly, he clarifies the nature of storms, thunder, lightning, the different fires that flare up in the air, and the lights that are seen in it. Above all, Descartes tries to thoroughly explain the nature of

18. Descartes, *Meteors*, I; vol. 4, p. 232, lines 4–12.

19. Letter to Regius, January 1642; AT, vol. 3, p. 506, lines 15–20: "Ergo formae ad causas actionum naturalium reddendas ullo modo sunt inducendae. Contra autem a formis illis essentialibus, quas nos explicamus, manifestae ac Mathematicae rationes redduntur actionum naturalium, ut videre est de forma salis communis in meis *Meteoris*."

20. Adam, *Vie et oeuvres*; AT, vol. 12, p. 205.

the rainbow, its colors, and consequently all the colors, to which he adds the explanation of colors that we ordinarily see in clouds, of the circles that surround heavenly bodies and finally "the cause of the suns or the moons, several of which sometimes appear together." The solution of the problem whose consideration gave birth to the *Meteors* is therefore also its conclusion.

Descartes's general intention is clearly indicated from the start of his work: "We naturally admire more the things above us than those at the same height or below." This is a common reflection and the Scholastic philosophers revisit it.[21] Descartes wants to show precisely that there is nothing so admirable on earth that its cause cannot be found and its explanation provided. He affirms this explicitly from the beginning of his First Discourse. In the conclusion to his treatise, he goes further and declares that he hopes to have eliminated all subjects of admiration. "Because I hope that those who have understood all that has been said in this treatise, hereafter will see nothing in the clouds whose cause they cannot easily understand or that is the subject of admiration for them."[22] To attain this goal, it is first necessary to explain the nature of earthly bodies in general.[23] However, since Aristotle commits the error of treating proximate matter before remote matter, delaying the study of the four first qualities to book 4, Descartes repairs the order by first setting out his new concept of matter. This is a point on which he definitely opposes his teachers. He wants neither Gasendi's atomism, nor the substantial form or real qualities of Scholasticism. He wants only particles that can always be subdivided in an infinite number of ways and that differ among themselves "only as the stones of several different figures that had been cut out of the same rock."[24] Some are long and united, they are those of water. Others are irregular and unequal; these compose hard bodies. In

21. *Commentarii Collegii Conimbricensis*, preface: "Ea quae in sublimi apparent majorem conspicientibus amirabilitatem movent."

22. *Dioptrics*; AT, vol. 6, p. 636, lines 23–28.

23. Descartes, *Discourse* I; AT, vol. 6, p. 232, lines 1–4. This is the remainder in Descartes's work, of the distinction between proximate matter and remote matter of the meteors. *Commentarii Collegii Conimbricensis* I, 1, p. 5: "Sciendum igitur meteorologicas impressiones duplicem habere materiam unam remota alteram proximam. Materia remota est potissimum terra et aqua; haec enim materiam propinquam, ex qua fiunt Meteora, de suo dant. Materia propinqua est vapor et exhalatio." — It is likely that this First Discourse is only a transformation of the preface that Descartes originally wanted to give his treatise.

24. Descartes, *Discourse* I; AT, vol. 6, p. 238, lines 28, to p. 239, line 12.

the intervals within these particles, subtle matter moves perpetually; its parts are always very small but of varying thickness, and they are moved at different speeds. These suppositions suffice to account for water, earth, air, and all the bodies that surround us, and for the hot and cold and all qualities. They are going to be revisited throughout all the meteorological problems posed by Scholasticism in order to provide new solutions to them.

It is first necessary to deal with the vapors and exhalations, the proximate matter of meteors.[25] Descartes considers them analogous to the clouds of dust raised by the feet of an individual or a crowd in the countryside. The parts of bodies that are small and easy separable detach themselves when they are violently agitated by the sun and rise in the air:

> not by some particular inclination they have toward rising, or that the sun has itself some force that attracts them, but only because they find no other place in which it is easy for them to continue their movement. Thus the powder of a country road rises when it is only beaten and agitated by the feat of some passerby.[26]

There is no need to suppose that the heat of heavenly bodies, by dissolving air and water, confers on them the lightness that everything thin and hot possesses. By this purely mechanical action, we do away with the supposed *lightness inherent* in exhalations.[27]

Vapors and exhalations must not be confused. In general lines, Descartes's distinction between them is the same as the Scholastic distinction. Vapors are aqueous in nature. Exhalations are composed of those irregular parts of which we mentioned that hard bodies like earth are composed.[28]

25. Descartes, *Discourse* II, *On Vapors and Exhalations*; AT, vol. 6, p. 239.

26. Descartes *Discourse* II; AT, vol. 6, p. 239, line 24, to p, 240, line 7.

27. *Commentarii Collegii Conimbricensis* I, 1, p. 9: "Hoc vero maxime praestant sua vi et influxu corpora coelestia . . . Causa vero instrumentaria, qua corpora coelestia ad haec effecta utuntur, est potissimum calor, qui aquam, ac terram pervadit, easque attenuando in halitus solvit; quos pariter in sublime effert interventu levitatis, quae calorem ipsum et raritatem consequitur, ut in superioribus elementis conspicimus." —Scholasticism knew about an explanation similar to that of Descartes but rejected it. —"Sunt tamen qui putent vapores et exhalationes haudquaquam in se recipere levitatem, cujus impulsu in altum ferantur, sed trudi extrinsecus a calore, quem sol in hac infima regione reciprocantibus in se radiis congeminant. At non recte philosophantur. Primum quia clamor non est virtus per se loco movens. Secundo quia cum praedicti halitus sint tenues et calidi, qua ex complicatione levitas oritur, cur non habeant levitatem sibi in haerentem, cujus vi sursum commeent?"

28. *Discourse* I; AT, vol. 6, p. 231, lines 1–2.

> But note that these little parts that are lifted into the air by the sun must for the most part have the figure that I attributed to water because there are no others that could be so easily separated from the bodies where they are. I will give the particular name *vapors* to these alone, in order to distinguish them from more irregular figures, for which I will retain the name exhalations, because I know no other that is more distinctive.[29]

Scholasticism also defines vapors as warm and humid respirations that come from liquid, while exhalations are warm and dry puffs that come sometimes from more fatty earth, sometimes from drier earth.[30] Besides, Descartes agrees with Scholasticism on the point that certain exhalations can be set ablaze. That is why he excludes from vapors those composed of parts analogous to the parts of water, but subtler and easily inflammable; because of the latter characteristic, he places them among the exhalations.[31] Again, Descartes excludes air from exhalations to avoid introducing a body that is only distinguished from them by its extreme subtlety, but that had never been counted among exhalations.[32] He includes several exhalations whose parts are smooth like those of water, but which can be set on fire, namely the spirits, but he eliminates air, whose parts are divided into branches because of its extreme subtlety. To round out the class of exhalations, there remain distilled alcohols, aqueous but subtle and inflammable, and those whose parts, being of terrestrial nature, are more crass and entangled in bodies, but that fire can hunt down in smoke

29. *Discourse* II; AT, vol. 6, p. 240, lines 20–29. Descartes does not like this term, because it keeps the idea of *halitus* or *anhelitus*, which does not fit well with a mechanical explanation of the phenomena by the sun's action upon the subtle body's movement.

30. *Commentarii Collegii Conimbricensis* I, 1, p. 5: "Est autem vapor, halitus sive spiratio calida et humida, quae ex humore aqueo prodit, qualem videre est ascendentem ex aqua, quae in olla subjecto igni effervescit . . . Exhalatio est anhelitus terrae calidus et siccus, continetque sub se duas quasi species . . . Prior e terra pingui oritur . . . posterior ex aridiori terra."

31. *Discourse* II; AT, vol. 6, p. 240, line 29, to p. 241, line 2: "However, I will also include among exhalations those that have almost the same figure as parts of water but, being more subtle, compose spirits or distilled alcohol." Descartes here even seems to make inflammability the distinctive characteristic of exhalations. For Scholasticism, cf. *Commentarii Collegii Conimbricensis* I, 1, p. 6: "exhalationem potestate proxima ignem esse." See also, ibid.: "Exhalatio . . . continet sub se duas quasi species, unam quam parvo negotio flammam concipit, et in ignem mutatur . . . alteram quae non ita facile incenditur, ex qua proxime venti existunt.

32. *Discourse* II; AT, vol. 6, p. 241, lines 2–5.

or that water can carry off with itself. Moreover, vapors and exhalations most often rise up together to be separated thereafter, with exhalations stopping in a region either higher or lower than vapors, according to the greater or lesser coarseness of the parts that make them up.

Whatever that coarseness is, there is none that stops lower than the parts of which common salt is composed: "And although they are not properly exhalations or vapors, because they never rise above the surface of water, still, since it is by evaporation of this water that they come into it and since there are several very remarkable things that can by easily explained here, I do not want to omit them."[33] For Descartes, salt is nothing but "the thickest part" of seawater that cannot be bent like other parts by the action of subtle matter nor even be agitated without the intervention of the parts of water that are smaller than they are. This alone is enough to resolve all the problems that Scholasticism poses regarding the salinity of the sea. Descartes explains the biting taste of salt,[34] why salt prevents the corruption of food,[35] why seawater is heavier than sweet water,[36] why the thickest and heaviest parts that constitute salt do not fall to the bottom of the water,[37] why springs and rivers, not being composed of waters that have been lifted up as vapors or else have passed through a great deal of sand, should not be salty.[38] But Descartes is not mistaken in thinking that his presentation of salt is clearly superior to that of the Scholastics. He deals with a very considerable number of particular problems, and without saying a word, he eliminates the rather naïve finalistic considerations developed by the Scholastics to account for the salinity of the sea. He does not think the sea is salty to allow saltwater fish to live in it and be nourished by the salt it contains: *Est autem aqua salsa ad marinos pisces suo modo alendos, idonea, quia habet admistam quasi olei pinguedinem.*

33. *Discourse* II; AT, vol. 6, p. 248, lines 17–26. Cf. *Commentarii Collegii Conimbricensis,* X, 3–5, pp. 112–16.

34. *Discourse* III; AT, vol. 6, p. 250, lines 10–19. *Commentarii Collegii Conimbricensis,* X, 3, p. 112.

35. *Discourse* III; AT, vol. 6, p. 250, line 19, to p. 251, line 1.

36. *Discourse* III; AT, vol. 6, p. 251, lines 1–5. *Commentarii Collegii Conimbricensis,* X, 9, p. 114.

37. *Discourse* III; AT, vol. 6, p. 251, lines 5–27. *Commentarii Collegii Conimbricensis,* X, 9, p. 114: "Cur superius mare salsius et calidius sit, quam inferius? . . . quamquam esse e contrario debuit: gravius enim quod salsum." Note, however, that although the two problems are related, they are not the same.

38. *Discourse* III; AT, vol. 6, p. 254, lines 21–29. *Commentarii Collegii Conimbricensis,* X, 9, p. 114.

Nor does he think that, if the sea is saline *propter aquatilium commoda*, it is also saline with a view to facilitating navigation.[39]

Setting aside the consideration of salt in order to return to vapors, Descartes examines how vapors move in air and how they cause winds there. He defines wind as, "any agitation of air that is perceptible."[40] In so doing, Descartes takes the side of Hippocrates against Aristotle, because the former maintains, *nihil aliud esse ventum quam aerem commotum*. If Descartes adds the clause *that is perceptible* to the definition rejected by Aristotle, it is precisely in order to remove any force from the Greek philosopher's objection that it is absurd to identify wind with any agitation of the air, since many commotions of the air are not winds. For example, the commotions of air that cymbals produce are not winds, because they are not perceptible. Nothing more.[41]

Aristotle proposes a different definition of wind that makes it a hot and cold exhalation, *spirationem calidam et siccam*. Descartes chooses a definition that is close to that of Scholasticism, because he declares, "Every invisible and impalpable body is called air."[42] With that Descartes accepts that vapors and certain exhalations fall under the definition of air. If Aristotle defines wind as an exhalation, the Conimbricenses complete Aristotle by adding vapors to exhalations, whose movement causes wind. For his part, Descartes is disposed to acknowledge a real role for exhalations in the production of winds, although a very modest one, and notes that exhalations accompany winds often. Here the two philosophies make concessions to each other. Scholasticism insists on exhalations as the matter of winds, while conceding about vapors. Descartes insists on the role of vapors, although he grants a subordinate role to exhalations. "The vapors of which they [the winds] consist do not rise only from the surface of water but also from humid land, snow, and clouds."[43] Ordinarily, these most extensive winds . . . are nothing other than the movement of vapors that, in dilating pass from the place where they are into some other where they find it easier to extend themselves."[44]

39. *Commentarii Collegii Conimbricensis*, X, 9, p. 115. Despite the arbitrariness of the explanations that Descartes offers, a new spirit really animates this whole treatise.

40. *Discourse* IV; AT, vol. 6, p. 265, lines 3–4.

41. X, 6, 1 and 2, p. 51 [translator: my surmise is that this is a reference to Conimbricenses]. Cf. Gilson, *Index scolastico-cartésien*, text 480.

42. *Discourse* IV; AT, vol. 6, p. 265, line 4.

43. *Discourse* IV; AT, vol. 6, p. 266, lines 25–29.

44. *Discourse* IV; AT, vol. 6, p. 265, lines 1–17.

> When vapors pass from one place to another in this way, they take away or push along all the air that is in their part, and all the exhalations that are among them, so that, although they alone cause almost all the winds. Still they are not alone in compositing the winds. Also, even the dilation and condensation of this air can help the production of these winds, but that is so little in comparison with the dilation and comparison of vapors, that they almost should not be taken into account.[45]

As for the problem of the cause of winds, Descartes dwells upon it with all the more relish in that Scholasticism recognized itself incapable of resolving it. The Conimbricenses propose a certain number of those *rationes probabiles* that Descartes wants to eliminate from physics, and they modestly conclude by remitting to Jeremiah and Psalm 135 [Psalm 134 in the Septuagint enumeration]: *Haec sunt quae de ventorum causis probabilius dicuntur a philosophis. Verum ut ingenue fateamur, hoc unum est ex iis quae in naturae contemplatione magna ex parte latent. Adeo ob id Psalmi CXXXIV et Jeremiae X dicatur Deus producere ventos de thesauris suis, id est de occultis naturae causis.*[46] Descartes sets aside the mysterious causes to which appeal was made, as for example the influence and conjunction of certain heavenly bodies and insists on the phenomena of condensation and rarefaction. But he does not completely abandon the notions Scholasticism had transmitted to him and makes dilation and condensation of vapors the center of his explanation.

This is why, although Cartesian explanations are completely new in spirit, they frequently recall Scholastic explanations. The persistence in Descartes's doctrine of the distinction between vapors and exhalations is the cause of this. With his teachers, Descartes observes, "Vapors that come from water are much more humid and much thicker than those rising from land, and among them there is always much more air and

45. *Discourse* IV, AT, vol. 6, p. 268, lines 12–22.—Cf. *Commentarii Collegii Conimbricensis*, VI, 2, p. 52: "Verum enim vero minime nobis displicet ea sententia, quae asserit ventorum materiam non esse puram exhalationem, sed interdum ac frequenter etiam vapores exhalationibus permixtos. Primum quia aliquando per integros menses spirant venti e mari, quod etiamsi mutum habeat exhalationum ob terrenae concretionis admixtionem, ut ejus salsedo testatur, atque adeo non solum vapores, sed exhalationes quoque egerat, tamen non est verisimile tantam exhalationum vim ab eo nasci. Item quia non est cur vapores ad mediam regionem provecti, non etiam inde pellantur et resiliant, ut exhalationes sicque flatum edant."—Let us add that the definition of wind as agitation of air was not only attributed to Hippocrates, but also to the Stoics, Vitruvius, Isidore, and St. John Damascene. It was a commonplace.

46. *Commentarii Collegii Conimbricensis*, VI, 3, p. 49.

exhalations."[47] He deduces the reasons that make the north wind dry and cold,[48] the south wind hot and humid,[49] and the wind from the west humid.[50] He appeals to vapors rather than air to explain the birth of winds, "because air, being dilated, only occupies two or three times more space than when condensed in an average way, while vapors occupy two or three thousand times more space."[51] Similarly, Descartes is no longer interested in the conjunction of heavenly bodies, but he still interprets mechanistically the action upon vapors and consequently upon winds that is attributed to conjunctions. The action exerted by each heavenly body must be proportional to the intensity of the light with which it strikes our eyes. It is weak for the stars in proportion to the moon, and weak for the moon in proportion to the sun, but is nonetheless real: "Moonlight, which is quite unequal according to how far from or close the moon is to the sun, contributes to the distribution of vapors, as does the light of the other heavenly bodies."[52]

After having explained how vapors cause winds by dilating, Descartes examines how they compose clouds and fogs "by condensing and tightening."[53] If they remain very low and "extend to the earth's surface,"

47. *Discourse* IV; AT, vol. 6, p. 275, lines 23–26: "ad generationem motumque ventorum multum conferre peculiarem quorumdam astrorum influxum . . ."

48. *Discourse* IV; AT, vol. 6, p. 270, line 17. *Commentarii Collegii Conimbricensis*, VI, 5, p. 56: "Septentrionales [venti] qui per loca nivosa et frigida transmeant, frigidissimi sunt et sicci."

49. *Discourse* IV; AT, vol. 6, p. 272, lines 29, to p. 273, line 4. *Commentarii Collegii Conimbricensis*, VI, 5, p. 56: "oppositi vero qui per mare et loca humentis et calida, ut per Zonam torridam ad nos perveniunt, calidi et humidi."

50. *Discourse* IV; AT, vol. 6, p. 269, lines 11–18; *Commentarii Collegii Conimbricensis*, VI, 5, p. 56.

51. *Discourse* IV; AT, vol. 6, p. 268, lines 23–26.

52. *Discourse* IV; AT, vol. 6, p. 278, lines 8–12. *Commentarii Collegii Conimbricensis*, VI, 3, p. 49: "ad generationem motumque ventorum multum conferre peculiarem quorumdam astrorum influxum . . ."

53. *Discourse* V; AT, vol. 6, p. 279, lines 3–6. Cf. *Commentarii Collegii Conimbricensis*, VII, 1, pp. 59–60: "Materia nubium est vapor. Causa efficens est tum sol et reliqua astra vaporem ipsum calore suo e locis humentibus ad mediam aeris regionem evocantia, tum etiam frigus circumstans et cogens. Generantur ergo nubes in hunc modum: posteaquam vapores ad mediam regionem pervenerunt, adventitium illic calorem deponunt, partim quia emersere jam ex aëre terras incubanti, qui ob solariorum geminationem calidior est atque ita remota causa calefacienti se ad nativum frigus revocant; partim quia illa ipsa media regio algore jam suo eos refrigerat. Itaque premente frigore concrescit paulatim vapor, ac tandem in nube attenuator. Quo fit ut nihil aliud sit nubes quam addensatus vapor."

they are called fog.[54] The clouds resolve into rain, though by different processes according to the two philosophies. Only the basic outlines of those processes correspond, namely, the resolution of the cloud into rain and congealing of this rain into snow or hail before it touches the ground.[55] When fog touches the ground, "it changes into frost if composed of already frozen vapors," or rather vapors that freeze as they touch the ground.[56] Other meteors are more peculiar: "There are also exhalations that compose manna and others like juices that descend from the air during the night. Vapors cannot change into anything but snow or ice. The juices are not only different in different countries, but also some only attach themselves to certain bodies, because the parts are obviously of such a figure that they do not take hold of other bodies enough to stop."[57] Descartes agrees with Scholasticism in assigning the origin of manna to exhalations,[58] although Scholasticism assigns an important role to vapors in its production. As for the "others like juices," which Descartes does not enumerate, everyone in the seventeenth century was aware that he meant both honey, which bees gather but do not produce and evidently another extraordinary sugar that the ancients harvested. Both juices are understood to be produced by vapors mixed with very subtle earthy parts, like manna itself. If Descartes declares them to be "different in different countries," it is because, in describing their properties, honeys were distinguished as coming from the Hymette Mountains, the Cyclades, and Sicily, which were the sweetest. The honey of Sardinia is better because the bees gather the dew on absinth. Some other honeys are poisonous, because just as nature equips bees with stingers, it has mixed venom in

54. Descartes, *Discourse* V; AT, vol. 6, p. 279, lines 3–6, and *Commentarii Collegii Conimbricensis*, VII, 4, *De Nebola seu Caligine*: "Interdum namque vapores crassi e locis humentibus proxime efflantur, atque ob suam spissitudinem et crassitiem in sublime efferi nequeunt, sed vicinum terris aërem occupant, et nebulosa caligine circumfundunt."

55. *Discourse*, VI; AT, vol. 6, p. 293, lines 13–29. *Commentarii Collegii Conimbricensis*, VII, 5, pp. 65: "Cum nubes in media aeris regione ob vehementem irrigiditatem, antequam in aquam solvatur, gelascat, nix efficitur." See also 7, p. 67: "Generatur enim grando, cum aqua pluviae, priusquam terram pertingat, in gelu cogitur."

56. *Discourse*, VI; AT, vol. 6, p. 309, lines 17–23. *Commentarii Collegii Conimbricensis*, VII, 8, p. 70: "Roris et pruinae materia est vapor exiguus et subtilis . . . Causa proxima efficiens, est frigus serenae noctis, quod si temperatum sit, vaporem in rorem cogit; si vehemens, congelat in pruinam." [Translator: I have corrected Gilson's *dew* to *frost* in the text.]

57. *Discourse*, VI; AT, vol. 6, p. 310, lines 14–22.

58. *Commentarii Collegii Conimbricensis*, VII, 11, p. 75.

the honey that tempts us by its sweetness, in order to make humans less greedy and more prudent.[59]

Descartes also wants to give his opinion on weather forecasting, but he holds to traditional empirical rules. If fog appears in the morning, it is a sign of rain,[60] along with other indications of the same kind that he labels very uncertain. It is even something about which he prefers not to speak, and these are obviously predictions that are drawn not only from the sun, but from the moon, the stars, the sea, frogs (*ranae ultra solitum vocales*), cranes, geese, crows, and many other objects,[61] or "the wind that makes the cinders and wisps of straw at the corner of the fire play and excites them like little whirlwinds, which quite amaze those who are ignorant about their cause and which are ordinarily followed by some rain."[62] But he does not insist on these matters and proceeds to the study of storms, of lightning, and of all the other fires that light up the air.

Descartes explains storms by the abrupt fall of a cloud violently pushing out all the air underneath. The Conimbricenses see them as exhalations enclosed in a cloud that they violently burst in order to escape. That explains sudden, violent storms at sea around the equinox.[63] Certain

59. *Commentarii Collegii Conimbricensis*, VII, 9, p. 72: "Philosophi autem mellis generationem hoc pacto se habere docent. Quando una cum vapore illo tenui, ex quo ros generatur, efferuntur, potissimum sublucanis temporibus, partes quaedam terrae subtiles; ex varia ejusmodo partium cum humido tenui commixtione, si humidum aqueum non multum dissolvatur, gignitur succus praedulcis qui herbis, foliis, flosculis et terrae solo excipitur: atque hic vel vocatur." Regarding the sugar of the ancients and the controversy about it, see VII, 10, pp. 74–75.

60. *Discourse* VI; AT, vol. 6, p. 310, lines 23–31. *Commentarii Collegii Conimbricensis*, VI, 4, p. 64: "Haec nebula . . . si confestim ascendat et, ad aerem frigidum evecta, una cum vaporibus concrescat, saepe in pluviam vertitur."

61. *Commentarii Collegii Conimbricensis, De Presagio Temporum*, VII, 3, pp. 61–64. When Descartes finds an intelligible and rationally explicable predictor of weather, he indicates it and provides the explanation. This is the case of swallows (*Discourse*, VII, p. 312, lines 12–21; *Commentarii Collegii Conimbricensis*, VII, 3, p. 63).

62. *Discourse*, VII; AT, vol. 6, p. 312, lines 21, to 313, line 3. Cf. *Commentarii Collegii Conimbricensis*, VII, 3, pp. 62–63: "Domesticus ignis pallens murmuransque tempestatem . . . spondet. Cum ignis contectus e se favillam discutit, cum cinis in foco concrescit, cum carbo vehementer pelucet, aquarum significatio est."

63. *Discourse*, VII; AT, vol. 6, p. 313, line 26, to p. 314, line 4: "In as much as other clouds are hardly ever seen in those places [Cape of Good Hope], as soon as the sailors see one that is beginning to form . . . they rush to lower their sails and prepare for a storm that always follows immediately."—*Commentarii Collegii Conimbricensis*, VI, 7, p. 58: "Hi ergo flatus procellam gignunt . . . Eam nautae Lusitani sub Aequinoctiali nonnunquam experiuntur. Quare suis jam periculis edocti, ubi eo loco nubem

exhalations mixed with the vapors that make up these clouds, separate from them according to Descartes because of the agitation of the air, and coming to attach to the ships' ropes and masts, are gripped by this violent agitation. "They make up what are called St. Elmo's fires, which console the sailors and make them expect good weather."[64] Descartes does not limit himself to indicating the existence of meteors whose descriptions were transmitted by the ancients; he also wants to account for the details of the description given. The Conimbricenses repeat with some skepticism the pagan navigators, who perceived two lights and labeled them Castor and Pollux, concluding that the end of the storm was near. When they perceived only one light, they named it Helen and anticipated a bad outcome. But this distinction of one or two lights and the forecasts that were drawn from them seem pointless and physically unjustified to Scholastic philosophers despite all the efforts made to account for them.[65] Descartes does not share this skepticism and seems to believe that rational justification is possible for what the Conimbricenses despaired of explaining. Since there can be several superposed clouds, there can be a fire of this kind above each of them: "If they only saw one of them, they ancients called it the star of Helen . . . they thought it a bad omen, as if they still had the worst of the tempest ahead. By contrast, when they saw two of them, they called that Castor and Pollux and took them for a good omen."[66]

---

conspicantur, confestim vela dejiciunt, ni faciant, vibranti impetu demergendi."

64. *Discourse*, VII; AT, vol. 6, p. 315, lines 1–4.

65. *Commentarii Collegii Conimbricensis*, II, 2, pp. 17–18: "Nona est Castor, Pollux, Helena. Haec concretio provenit ex halitu admodum viscoso et pingui. Inflammatur antiperistasi [in opposition to the surrounding cold] circumfusi aëris frigidi, vel per collisionem. Nonnunquam navigantibus tempore tempestatum apparere solent ex his luminibus duo, interdum unum tantum. Ethnici ut erant infinitis implicati superstionibus cum istiusmodo inflamationes binae conspiciebantur, credebant esse Castorem et Pollucem; cum una dumtaxat, Helenam; et unam quidem infaustum exitum significare, binas prosperum; 'graves, inquit Plinius, libro 2, capitulo 37, cum solitariae venere, mergentesque navigia, etsi in carinae ima deciderint, exurentes; geminae autem salutares, et prosperi cursus praenuntiae, quarum adventu fugari diram ac minacem, appellatamque Helenam ferunt; et ob id Pollucio et Castori id nomen assignant eosque in mari deos invocant.' Hae ille. Quae distinctio duorum luminum, vel unius, quoad fausti, vel infausti eventus significationem, vana videtur, nec ejus ulla Physica ratio satis ideonea afferri solet etsi eam nunnulli redere conati sint. Certe cum hae concretiones huc illuc discurunt, tempestatis vim et turbulentos ventorum flatus, quibus agitantur, indicant; si vero in antennis, aliisve navium partibus insideant, futurae serenitatis signa habentur; quia argumentum est frangi tempestatem et desinere ventos, qui jam exhalationi quietem dant."

66. *Discourse*, VII; AT, vol. 6, p. 315, lines 4–26.

As for the storms accompanied by thunder, flashes, whirlwinds, and lightning, Descartes has been able to see some examples on land. They are like avalanches, but instead of a fall of snow, there is a fall of clouds. When a cloud is on top of the other, if it falls abruptly on the lower cloud, a loud noise is produced, which is thunder:

> Note that the noise produced above us must be heard better because of the resonance of air and be louder because of the snow falling, which is not that of avalanches. Then, note also that from the simple fact that the parts of higher clouds fall altogether or one after another or more quickly or more slowly than lower ones, are larger or smaller or more or less thick, and resist more or less strongly, all the different sounds of thunder can be caused easily.[67]

The Conimbricenses prefer to admit what Aristotle offers as the fundamental cause of thunder, the noisy ripping of certain clouds by the exhalations enclosed within them. They also attribute the different noises of thunder to different possible agitations by exhalations within clouds. But they also admit the possibility of an explanation that does not involve the eruption of vapors. Lucretius and Seneca[68] explain thunder by the collision of several clouds, and this explanation has value. If clouds can produce noise by being ripped, why would they not do so when they collide violently and break?[69]

We still need to account for flashes, whirlwinds, and lightning. The difference among these phenomena "only depends on the nature of the exhalations that are in the space between two clouds, and the way in which the upper cloud falls upon the other one."[70] The flash occurs

67. *Discourse*, VII; AT, vol. 6, p. 317, lines 11–20.

68. Lucretius, *De Rerum Natura*, bk. VI, lines 96ff. Seneca, *Naturales Quaestiones*, II, 17.

69. This is the origin of the Cartesian theory of thunder. *Commentarii Collegii Conimbricenses*, 1, 3: "Quarto sciendum ex quorumdam sententia posse etiam absque exhalationum erruptione et conflictu magna inter se nubium collisione tonitrum effici, quod Lucretio et Senecae locis antea citatis placet. Nec id certe alienum videtur a ratione. Si enim nubes cum a spiritu derumpuntur sonum excitant, cur non idem inter se magno impetu colisae et fractae efficient? Nec obstat, ait Seneca, quod nubes impactae montibus sonum non edant; primum quia non quocumque modo impulsae tonant, sed si apte sint compositae ad sonum edendum; sicut nec aversae inter se manus cum colliduntur, ita magnum plausum edunt; sed cum palma palmam percutit. Deinde quia mons non scindit nubem, sed sibi eam circumfundit."

70. *Discourse*, VII; AT, vol. 6, p. 317, lines 20–25.

when the fall of the higher cloud sets on fire the very subtle and eminently flammable exhalations that are between the clouds after periods of heat and dryness. The Scholastics also explain flashes by the exhalations catching fire.[71] Both positions admit that there can be flashes without thunder and even thunder without flashes, depending on the nature of the exhalations present.[72] As for lightning, according to Descartes, its position is connected to the formation of a whirlwind. The whirlwind's origin is similar to what the Scholastics attribute to lightning. When the upper cloud, whose fall causes thunder, drops all at once, its edges touch the edges of the lower clouds before the centers of the two clouds meet. An air pocket is formed in this way, which, pressured and pushed out by the upper cloud that continues to descend, bursts the lower cloud to escape, descends violently toward the earth and climbs back spinning. "And so, it constitutes a whirlwind that cannot be accompanied by lightning or flashes, unless there are exhalations in this air that are of the right kind to be set on fire. But when there are such, they will assemble in a pile, and being pushed toward earth very energetically with this air, they constitute lightning."[73] The Conimbricenses do not involve whirlwinds in the generation of lightning, but they also consider lightning an exhalation set on fire that bursts the cloud in which it is enclosed with a frightful noise. If it bursts part of the cloud, the same impulse by which it has severed the cloud, hurls it toward the ground. The two explanations of the phenomenon are closely related,[74] as are the descriptions of their effects. Descartes judges:

71. *Commentarii Collegii Conimbricensis*, II, 4, p. 20.

72. *Discourse*, VII; AT, vol. 6, p. 318, lines 1–10: "So that we can then see such flashes without hearing any noise of thunder at all . . . as, to the contrary, if their are no inflammable exhalations in the air, we can hear the noise of thunder without any flash appearing for all that." —Cf. *Commentarii Collegii Conimbricensis*, II, 4, pp. 20–21: "Non semper autem haec deflagratio contingit, quia non semper materia ad ardorem concipiendum idonea est, quare nec semper ante tonitrum nubes fulgurant . . . Fit enim non raro, ut coruscatio detur absque ullo tonitruo; cum nubes adeo tenuis est, ut exhalationi discurrenti non valde obsistat, ex nihilominus eam habet concretionem, quae ad excitandum ignem sufficiat."

73. *Discourse*, VII; AT, vol. 6, p. 319, lines 5–11.

74. *Commentarii Collegii Conimbricensis*, II, 5, p. 21: "Fulmen est exhalatio ignita e nube magno impetu excussa . . . Incenditur vero talis exhalatio, quae admodum sicca esse debet, vel per motum, vel per antiperistasim; et quia accensa rarefit magnoque conatus exitum e nube frigida et densa ac diu reluctanti quaerit, dum eam tandem rupit horrendum edit tonitrum; quod si nubem per inferiorem partem, quam tunc tenuiorem invenit, frangat, eadem vi et impetu quo eam scindit, ad terras fertur; nec

> This lightning can burn clothing and shave off hair without harming the body, if these exhalations, which ordinarily have the smell of sulfur, are only fatty and oily, so that they constitute a light flame that only attaches itself onto bodies easy to burn. Since, by contrast, the lightning can break bones without damaging flesh, or melt a sword without damaging the scabbard, if these exhalations are very subtle and penetrating, and only participate in the nature of *sal volatile* or *aqua f*ortis . . . Lastly, lightning can sometimes be changed into a very hard stone that breaks and shatters everything it meets, if among the very penetrating exhalations, there is a quantity of others that are fatty and sulfurous.[75]

These explanations testify how the Scholastic chapter on meteors, *De Fulminum Effectis*, lives on in Cartesian physics, where we meet again the same odd phenomena described and commented.[76]

Similar observations could be made in regard to many details of Cartesian physics. By means of his principles, Descartes explains "that, if the cloud, is opened on the side, since lightning is hurled laterally, it seeks the points of towers and rocks more than low places," because according to Scholasticism, *fulmen plerumque oblique fertur*, and also *feriunt autem saepius fulmina summos montes et praealtas turres, quia cum oblique ferantur, celsissima quaeque eis obviam fiunt ideoque in ea frequenter*

---

in aere mox diffluit et dissipatur, ut pleraeque omnes exhalationes ignitae, tum quia velocissime erumpit, tum quia constat partibus bene coagmentatis et inter se cohaerentibus. Nonnunquam tamen fulmen, quia languidiore ictu vibratur, non pertingit ad terras, sed in aere extinguitur et evanescit."

75. *Discourse*, VII; vol. VI p. 319, lines 11–29.

76 *Commentarii Collegii Conimbricensis*, II, 6, pp. 23–24: "Sane experientia compertum est fulmen non eodem modo omnem materiam impetere et vexare: nam sacculis nullo modo combustis aurum, aes et argentum conflat intus: manente vagina, ensem liquat . . . integra carne, et interdum, nulla ignis, aut ictus nota exterius apparente, ossa comminuit, et universim firmiora vehementius dissipat obteritque, cum lapide, ferro, ac durissimis quibusque confligit teneris et rarioribus, licet flammis opportuna videantur, parcit . . . Cujus rei causa quia in his, quae ignis trajectu obsistunt, qualia sunt dura et densa, necesse est fulmen, dum certum contumaciam vincit, moram trahere, atque adeo in ea vim sua imprimere; cui tamen imprimendae motus celeritas locum non dat. In aliis vero quae tenuia et rara sunt, ubi fulmen vim sibi resistentem non invenit per poros et occulta foramina celerrime atque adeo sine injuria transcurrrit." —Concerning lightning that changes into stone, cf. *Commentarii Collegii Conimbricensis*, II, 5, p. 21: "Fulmen, ut Aristoteles, libro 3, capitulo 1, ostendit, est ignis, non lapis igni delatus . . . tametsi non sit negandum posse exhalationes intra nubem concrescere in lapidem, qui una cum fulmine tanquam bombardae globus tradatur."

impingunt.[77] He adds, "with reason, it is held that very loud noises like those of clocks or cannons, can diminish the effect of lightning," that when flashes occur without thunder, clouds can assemble "several exhalations from which they constitute not only those little flames that might be called stars that fall from the heavens or others that cross through them, but also fairly large balls of fire, which arriving where we are, make something like little lightning bolts." These little flames that might be called stars and fall from the heavens are only exhalations set on fire. "The Philosophers were right to compare the flame that we see travel along the smoke from a torch that has just been extinguished, when it is lit by another torch that is brought near it."[78] However, Descartes reproaches them for having attributed the same nature to comets and stripes of columns of fire that last immeasurably longer.[79]

Descartes also attributes the formation of prodigious rains to combinations of different exhalations. The Scholastics likewise maintain this theory:

> In as much as there are exhalations of several different natures, I do not judge it impossible that the clouds should squeeze them, constituting sometimes a matter that, according to the color and consistency it has, seems to be milk or blood or flesh, or else by burning becomes such that it is taken for iron or stones, or lastly that which by being corrupted engenders some small animals in a short time, so it is that we often read among prodigies, that it has rained iron or blood or grasshoppers or similar things.[80]

Once again, Descartes simply follows medieval traditions. It was admitted that some rains escaped the normal course of nature, and certain of them were taken for prodigies.

Frogs, little fish, blood, milk, stones, and iron fall mixed into rainwater. These phenomena are sometimes explained because God disposes

77. *Commentarii Collegii Conimbricensis*, II, 5 and 6, pp. 21, 23.

78. *Discourse* VII; AT, vol. 6, p. 321, lines 3–16, and p. 323, lines 5–12. —Cf. *Commentarii Collegii Conimbricensis*, II, p. 16: "Quarta sunt sidera discurrentia. Haec dupliciter accidunt: uno modo cum flamma in exhalatione ad longum protensa accenditur, et per successivam aggenerationem funditur, dum una pars alteri ignem celeriter communicat, invitante nimirium ab uno extremo ad aliud materia, sicuti contingit, cum duae lucernae, superior una, altera inferior, juxta se positae sunt, illa accensa, haec paulo ante extincta; et istius fumus ex illa adeo celeriter ignem corripit, ut illius flamma ad hanc descendisse videatur."

79. On the latter meteors, see *Index scolastico-cartésien*, 114–16.

80. *Discourse* VII; AT, vol. 6, p. 321, lines 16–26.

second causes so as to strike mortals with terror or in view of some other goal. But also sometimes we should not look for any miraculous meaning in the rains. Their cause is a mixture of different exhalations with humid vapor produced by the appropriate force of the qualities. In what concerns animals, just as serpents and worms are born in swamps, muddy places, and other sites where there is some rotting matter, likewise they can be born suddenly from rain, if the same causes of fermentation meet in the air or even on the ground. As for milk and blood, here we are only dealing with the appearance of milk and blood, because genuine milk and blood always suppose a living principle at their origin. Some also say that the sun can aspirate red or white humors that then fall again with rain or even that whirlwinds pick up fish or stones that they transport to other places.[81] Descartes, therefore, agrees with the Conimbricenses about the basis of the phenomena. As to its explanation, it is a matter of taste to choose between *varia commixtio exhalationum humido congruenti qualitatum*, and exhalations of several different natures from which the clouds, by compressing them, compose a matter similar to milk, blood, or flesh. The pressure exerted by the cloud perhaps has only apparent and purely intentional superiority over the mixture of qualities. Only in the last three discourses, dealing with the rainbow and perihelia, does Descartes return to mathematics and completely escapes Scholastic influence.

Descartes's radical independence from Scholasticism is regained for the same reason in what he says elsewhere about comets, but he loses it again in the *World* or the *Principles*, when he deals with other phenomena that Scholasticism placed among the meteors. Such are vapors, acrid spirits, and oily exhalations, which, by linking metallic particles, constitute all fossils and bring metals to the light of day.[82] As for the metals themselves, Descartes relates them to three fundamental bodies that take the place of the three principles commonly admitted by chemists, salt, sulfur, and mercury. He would gladly have described all metals that derive from them, if he had been able to do all the experiments necessary for their exact knowledge. But he does not doubt that those three can explain them all.[83] He frees himself from Aristotle only to undergo the

81. Cf. *Commentarii Collegii Conimbricensis*, VII, 2, pp. 60–61; and *Index scolastico-cartésien*, 234, text 363.

82. *Principles of Philosophy*, IV, 70–71; AT, vol. 8, pp. 247–48. [Translator: AT volume 8 has two independently numbered parts. *Principles of Philosophy* constitutes the first half.]

83. *Principles of Philosophy*, IV, 63; AT, vol. 8, pp. 9–22: "Atque sic tria hic habemus,

influence of the alchemists[84] with whose doctrine Albertus Magnus and Thomas tried to reconcile that of Aristotle. In both philosophies, earth tremors are explained by exhalations embedded in the ground, which shake the earth's crust. Descartes supposes that these exhalations, ignited by some spark, abruptly dilate and shake the earth. The Conimbricenses propose a number of explanations, the last of which is identical to Descartes's.[85] To explain the formation of springs and rivers, Descartes and the Conimbricenses appeal to subterranean vapors that condense into water. According to Descartes, these vapors come from subterranean water and eventually from the sea,[86] while for certain Scholastics, water comes from a subterranean agglomeration of vapors and water. These philosophers cannot admit that the original source of springs and rivers is sea water because, if that were so, rivers would never diminish, their water ought to be salty, and above all, come up from the sea to be elevated up to the mountains from which a large numbers of rivers arise. Descartes must at least take notice of these difficulties, and since he admits the constant circulation between the sea and springs, he must explain *cur mare non augeatur ex eo quod flumina in illud fluant* and *cur fontes non sint salsi, nec mare dulcescat*.[87] Furthermore, he has to insist on the fact that the vapors of which he speaks *usque ad exteriorem camporum*

---

quae pro tribus vulgatis Chymicorum principiis, Sale, Sulphure ac Mercurio, sumi possunt . . . Credique potest omnia metalia ideo tantum ad nos pervenire, quod acres succi, per meatus corporis fluentes quaedam ejus particulas ab iis disjungant, quae deinde materia oleagina involutae atque vestitae, facile ab argento vivo calore rarefacto sursum rapiuntur, et pro diversis suis magnitudinibus ac figuris, diversa metalla constituunt. Quae fortasse singula descripsissem hoc in loco si varia experimenta, quae ad certam eorum cognitionem requiruntur, facere hactenus licuisset."

84. *Commentarii Collegii Conimbricensis*, I, 13, p. 133: "Immo et illam etiam [opinionem], quam chymistae defendunt . . . pro qua stat D. Thomas . . . aiens eam ab Aristotelis placito non dissentire: sed Aristotelem facere materiam remotam halitum, chymistas vero materiam proximam sulphur et argentum vivum, quae ex predicto halitu, ut ex remota materia metallorum concrescant."

85. *Principles of Philosophy*, IV, AT, vol. 8, p. 77. Cf. *Commentarii Collegii Conimbricensis*, XI, 2, pp. 110–21: "Vera et peripatetica sententia statuit commotionem terrae fieri ab halitu seu spiritu terrae visceribus incluso, et foras exire contendente . . . Potiores autem modi quibus id contingit, hi ferme sunt . . . tunc enim, ut pulvis tormentarius igni correptus impositam turrim commovet et disturbat, sic incensa exhalatio terram quassat."

86. *Principles of Philosophy*, IV, 75; AT, vol. 8, p. 244, lines 5–7.

87. *Principles of Philosophy*, IV, 75, 67; AT, vol. 8, p.243, line 23, to p. 244, line 15.

superficiem atque ad summa montium juga proveniat.[88] Descartes's whole explanation of this question is guided by Scholastic doctrine,[89] and it remains partially cluttered with it. He still believes that water only reaches the peaks of mountains in the form of vapors. It is as if he dreaded seeing it (as the objection of the Conimbricenses puts it) *contra nativam propensionem et conatum subire montes.* By admitting this perpetual circulation between springs and sea, analogous, to the circulation of the blood in the veins and arteries of an animal, he rallies to the solution proposed by the Conimbricenses against Aristotle, from whom they depart only reluctantly.[90]

Accordingly, there is no doubt about the influence of Scholastic *Meteors* upon Descartes's thinking. The more the philosopher allows Scholasticism to impose the selection of subjects he must treat, the more the very concern to refute Scholasticism leads him to argue against it and consequently follow it. He ultimately remains enmeshed in its doctrines, which he limits himself to interpreting and rearranging. We have been able to see what a central role the Scholastic distinction between vapors and exhalations plays in Descartes's *Meteors.* However profoundly he has

88. *Principles of Philosophy*, IV, 74; AT, vol. 8, p. 243, lines 4–5.

89. *Commentarii Collegii Conimbricensis*, IX, 2–3, pp. 94–96, especially, p. 95: "Alii arbitrantur perennium fontium, fluviorumque originem e mari esse [notably, St. Thomas, *In II Sententiarum*, dist. 14, sole question reply to obj. 5, and Albertus Magnus, *Meteors*, II, 2, 11, etc.] . . . Nititur haec opinio hisce potissimum argumentis. Primum quia incredibile omnino videtur tantum aquae ex vaporibus et aëre in terrae sinu quotidie generari, ut ad tam magnum fontanae et fluvialis aquae defluxum, et ad tot scaturigines replendas sufficiat. Secundo quia non alia videtur posse reddi causa cur tot fluminum quotidiano accessu maria non crescant, nisi quia flumina e mari exeunt, sicque eorum regresssu tantundem eis rependitur quantum egressu detrahitur . . . At enim quoniam hanc sententiam ea maxime difficultas urget quod non videtur qua ratione aqua suopte ingenio gravis possit ascendere e mari in altissimo montes e quibus tam multa flumina erumpunt . . ."

90. *Commentarii Collegii Conimbricensis*, IX, 3, p. 96: "Alii volunt esse in terra quasi venas, quibus aquae humor prolectetur, ad eum fere modum quo sanguis animalium venas. Quam similitudinem late persecutus est Seneca, libro 3, *Naturalium Quaestionum*, capitulo 15."—*Commentarii Collegii Conimbricensis*, IX, 3, pp. 99–100: "Non solum absolute affirmandum est amplissima flumina et fontes de quibus paulo ante diximus provenire e subterraneis aquis et mari oriundis ob rationem illic propositam, sed probabilius existimandum etiam minores fluvios et fontes perennes ab eisdem illis aquis ordinarie seu majori ex parte derivari. Pro quo etiam facit auctoritas Patrum quos tertio capite commemoravimus, fontium et fluviorum perennitatem e mari per subterraneos meatus deducentium."—The Conimbricenses make a minor concession to Aristotle. Let us add that they do not accept Seneca's comparison taken over by Descartes, but it is compatible with the solution they propose.

recast it and whatever transformation he has made, it remains the umbilical cord that ties the new doctrine to the old. This explains the feeling of oddness that most of the ingenious and admirably constructed treatise produces on us today. It is worthwhile reflecting on why Descartes allows all this Scholastic material to be imposed on him.

Let us first observe that the *Meteors* produced an impression of Descartes's contemporaries not very different from our own. Everyone admired its rigor, but, although Fr. Fournier seemed to give allegiance to it in his *Hydrographics* of 1643,[91] many others reserve their judgments. If we ignore Fr. Bourdin's attacks, we see that Jean Chapelain was able to establish a fair distinction among the different essays that accompany the *Discourse on Method.* "His *Dioptrics* and his *Geometry* are two masterpieces in the estimation of the professors. His *Meteors* is arbitrary and problematic, but still admirable."[92] Fromond, himself the author of a treatise on meteors, declared that Descartes's philosophy is *nimis crassa et mecanica*,[93] which provoked the response from Descartes that to reproach his philosophy for being mechanical was to reproach it for being true.[94] Gilles de Roberval formed a judgment on the *Discourse*, the *Dioptrics*, and the *Meteors*, which agreed remarkable with Chapelain's:

> For a change of discourse, we need to read the book by Monsieur Descartes very attentively. It contains four treatises, the first of which can be assigned to logic. The second is a work of physics and geometry; the third purely physics, and the fourth purely geometrical. In the first three, he quite clearly deduces his particular opinions on the subject of each. He who knows all knows whether they are true or not. As for us, we have no demonstrations for or against, nor perhaps would the author himself, who would be thoroughly bogged down, it seems to us, if he had to demonstrate what he puts forward. He must find out that what in his mind passes as a principle to ground his reasoning, would seem very doubtful in the minds of others. Also, he seems to take very little care, being content to satisfy himself, in which there is nothing but human nature and how a father

91. Adam, *Vie et Oeuvres*; AT, vol. 12, p. 200ff.

92. Letter of Chapelain to Balzac, December 29, 1637, cited in AT, vol. 1, p. 485 note.

93. Letter of Fromond to Plempius, September 13, 1637; AT, vol. 1, p. 406, lines 15–16.

94. Letter of Descartes to Plempius, October 3, 1637; AT, vol. 1, p. 420, line 21, to p. 421, line 17.

> would make things appear every day in regard to his children. This would not be a small thing, if what Descartes says could serve as hypotheses from which conclusions could be drawn, which agree with experience. In that there would be considerable usefulness.[95]

To sum up, these three essays by Descartes (including the *Meteors*) contain only arbitrary suppositions and not demonstrations. This conclusion greatly displeased our philosopher, who judged that Roberval was amusing himself "by insulting [him] and babbling, because he has nothing good to answer." "These are very great impertinence," he adds.[96] But perhaps the judgment that most surprised him was what Huygens communicated to him, that his principles would not be accepted in Scholasticism, because they were not "sufficiently confirmed by experience."[97] The same objection reappears where one least expects it.

What did Descartes himself think about his *Meteors*, and what kind of demonstrations did he use? The problem is perhaps more complicated than might be supposed. When Descartes announced the content of his essays to Mersenne, he presents the *Meteors* as a subject that is "completely pure philosophy," in contrast with *Dioptrics* or *Geometry* that are mixed with mathematics or purely mathematical. There is no mathematics in *Meteors*, however, except in the analysis devoted to the rainbow. That is why Roberval, who moreover is in remarkable agreement with Descartes in his way of characterizing the essays, is right to declare the essay on meteors "almost completely purely physical."

On the other hand, we cannot neglect certain affirmations by Descartes that absolutely contradict the previous one. Let us set aside all his well-known claims about the purely mathematical and mechanical character of his physics. Against the extreme rigor, we can object that his general declarations admit an exception, which in Descartes's own opinion, would be precisely the treatise on meteors. But, in this hypothesis, how do we interpret the following statement?

> Moreover [Girard] Desargues places an obligation upon me by the care he has been pleased to take with me, in that he testifies that he is saddened that I no longer want to study geometry. But I have only resolved to quit abstract geometry that is to say, the

95. Roberval against Descartes, April 1638; AT, vol. 2, p. 113, lines 8–30.

96. Letter of Descartes to Mersenne, May 27, 1638; AT, vol. 2, p. 141, line 11–21.

97. Letter of Descartes to Huygens, June 1645; AT, vol. 4, p. 224, lines 24–25.

> pursuit of questions that only serve to exercise the mind. And I do this in order to have all the more leisure to cultivate another kind of geometry, which proposes to explain natural phenomena. Because, if it pleases him to consider what I have written about salt, snow, the rainbow, and so on, he will certainly lean that all my physics is nothing but geometry.[98]

Descartes's first declaration must be interpreted in the following way: the *Meteors* is an essay in which abstract mathematics are not involved. Rather, from beginning to end, it is only a particular geometrical explanation of the oddest natural phenomena.

If this particular geometry were identical in nature to abstract geometry, from which it differs only by the kind of objects to which it is applied, it would be difficult to conceive that Descartes could oppose physics to mathematics as he does in characterizing his essays. The truth is rather that abstract geometry and geometry applied to the explanation of phenomena do not use the same kind of demonstrations. The *Meteors* are entirely geometrical, but their geometry is not abstract geometry. This is why, although geometrical, they are not or are nearly not mathematical.

Can we specify this geometry's nature? It is not what geometers use ordinarily. If it were necessary to provide geometrical demonstrations of the Euclidean type in physics, we would never demonstrate anything, and it would even be necessary to say that nothing has ever been demonstrated in those subjects. Descartes affirms this in *Dioptrics*, in regard to his theory of refraction, a subject easier to submit to calculation than meteorological phenomena are. The only demonstration that can still be required in order for Descartes's essays to be above challenge is the metaphysical demonstration of the principles of his physics. But, envisaged from the viewpoint of geometry or physics, nothing is missing in them. His theory of refraction is a demonstrated "as any other question of mechanics or optics or astronomy or other subject that is not purely geometrical or arithmetic has ever been demonstrated." Descartes adds: "But to ask me for geometrical demonstrations in a subject that depends on physics is to want me to do the impossible. If we want to call only geometrical demonstrations *proofs*, then it is necessary to say that Archimedes never demonstrated anything in the mechanics or Vitellio in optics or Ptolemy in astronomy and so forth, something that nobody says."

Accordingly, what is the nature of the demonstration in these subjects? First of all, although Descartes does not refer to it, physical

98. Letter of Descartes to Mersenne, July 27, 1638; AT, vol. 2, p. 268, lines 3–14.

demonstration only involves extension and movement. Only under this condition will it be geometrical and mechanical in the measure in which it can be. Next, if we consider it from the point of view of its form and no longer of its content, we will see that it must satisfy two conditions and only two: not make suppositions that are manifestly contrary to experience and not commit logical fallacies in reasoning. Consequently, a demonstration in physics is as geometrical as it can be, when, without involving anything but extension and movement, it is correctly deduced starting from hypotheses that are compatible with experience.

> Because, in such subjects, one is content that other people, having presupposed certain things that are not manifestly contrary to experience, having also spoken consistently and without committing fallacies, even if their suppositions were not exactly true. As I could demonstrate that even the definition of the center of gravity that has been given by Archimedes is false, and that there is no such center, and other things that he supposes elsewhere are not exactly true. For Ptolemy and Vitellio, they have very much less certain suppositions, and still we cannot on this account reject the demonstrations that they have deduced from them.[99]

It is important to make clear the meaning of the expressions Descartes uses here. We do not see him claim that his hypothesis corresponds to experience. He is satisfied with hypotheses that are not manifestly contrary to experience. This voluntary moderation in expression stems from the completely particular conception that Descartes has formed of the relations of hypotheses and scientific fact. The fact constitutes the initial datum furnished by the senses, for which the physicist must account. The rainbow, the order of its colors, hexagonal snowflakes, or more simply yet, the most manifest properties of air and water are facts. Therefore, we have reason to demand that our principles of demonstration do not contradict what our experience permits us to observe. That is what has been done in the *Meteors*. The treatise begins with suppositions from which, in sound method, we do not yet have the right to ask anything except that they should be compatible with the facts. It would be opposed to experience to admit that water is composed of irregular, unequal parts, coupled with one another like the branches of a hedge, or that earth is composed of long, united, and slippery particles that can meet without ever being entangled. But nothing precludes our supposing that the first

99. Letter to Mersenne, May 27, 1638; AT, vol. 2, p. 142, lines 5–26.

kind of particles is what makes up earth and the second kind what makes up water. Moreover, in general, the simplest thing is always to suppose that what we do not see is analogous to what we see. Aristotle's error was precisely to suppose that what happens to the particles of bodies that are too little for us to perceive is of a different nature from what occurs to the big parts we perceive. In order to account for phenomena, Aristotle made the mistake of imaging things "that have no relation with the things we perceive," like prime matter, substantial form, and all that paraphernalia of qualities, themselves harder to explain than what they explain.[100]

At the beginning of a treatise like the *Meteors* or even the *Principles*, it follows that we must not request anything more of hypotheses than that they not contradict facts. But, of course, they are nothing but hypotheses at that moment, and the physicist's work is to prove them and transform these hypotheses into truths. To get there, it is necessary to deduce the consequences of these principles that are supposed to be true, in order and without committing fallacies. For example, if the particles of which water or earth are composed are as we have described them, we can deduce that different possible arrangements can produce this or that perceptible effect. If we observe with our senses that these effects are really given in nature, it follows that they may have been produced in this manner. In such a case, the hypothesis *may* be true. The deduction is pursued in the same manner, since experiment permits us to observe that an ever-increasing number of phenomena are precisely as they ought to be if the principles of our deduction were true. In the measure that the principles' explicative fecundity is made clear, we are more inclined to believe them to be effectively true. When we finally observe that they not only explain all that our eyes observe, but even that no other supposition could explain it, we declare that the principles are true.[101] Accordingly the demonstration of a hypothesis of physics consists in showing that its correctly deduced consequences agree with the facts. The only refutation that we might offer would consist of showing by experiment that the initial hypotheses are false, or pointing out the fallacies in the deduction of consequences that are drawn from the hypotheses.

100. *Principles of Philosophy* IV, art. 201; AT, vol. 8, pp. 324–25. See particularly the same passage in the original French translation, AT, vol. 9, pp. 319–20.

101. *Principles of Philosophy*, IV, art. 203; AT, vol. 9, p. 321. The text of the French translation has been retouched by what can only be Descartes's own hand.

> Know that there are only two ways to refute what I have written. The first of them is to prove by experiments or reasons that the things I have supposed are false. The other is that what I have deduced from it cannot be deduced. Monsieur Fermat understands this very well, because this is how he wanted to refute what I wrote about refraction, by trying to prove that there is a fallacy. But for those who are content to say that they do not believe what I have written, because I have deduced it from certain suppositions that I have not proved, they do not know what they ask for or what they ought to ask for.[102]

A demonstration of this kind is sufficient if we understand the connection it establishes between the hypothesis and the fact, between the principle and the experiment. If the hypothesis proved the facts, and inversely, the facts were also invoked to prove the hypothesis, as some critics seem to believe, then the demonstration would hang in a vacuum. But things take place quite differently. The only thing that can be required of a hypothesis is that it *explain* the facts, and all that the facts can do then is to *prove* the hypothesis. The totality, consisting of the hypotheses that explain the facts and the experimentally observed facts that prove the hypothesis, is called demonstration. Consequently, there is not a logical circle but, on the contrary, two equally necessary moments of every demonstration in physics: the principles making the phenomena intelligible and the existence of phenomena guaranteeing the truth of the principles.[103] Moreover, let us add that when the initial hypotheses have already

102. Letter to Mersenne, May 27, 1638; AT, vol. 2, p. 143, line 20, to p. 144, line 2.

103. This is the sense of the passage of *Discourse*, pt. VI, 76, lines 6–22: "That if some of these [things] of which I have spoken in the beginning of the *Dioptrics* and the *Meteors* are shocking at first, because I call them suppositions, and because I do not seem to desire to prove them, one should have the patience to read everything attentively, and I hope that will give satisfaction. Because, it seems to me that the reasons follow each other in such a way, that since the last are demonstrated by the first that are their causes, these first are reciprocally proven by the last, which are their effects. It must not be imagined that in this I commit the fault that the logicians call a circle, because, since experiment makes the majority of these effects very certain, the causes from which I deduce them do not serve so much to prove them as to explain them. But, completely to the contrary, those causes are what is proven by the effects."—This passage is commented by the letter to Morin, July 13, 1638; AT, vol. 2, p. 197, line 25, to p. 198, line 28: "For that, I do not confess that it is one [circle] to explain effects by a cause, and then to prove the cause by them; because there is a great difference between *prove* and *explain*. To this I add that we can use the word *demonstrate* to signify both, at least if we take it according to common usage, and not in the particular signification that Philosophers give it . . . And I put in *that they do not serve so much to prove them*,

been proven by certain effects, they can in turn not just explain them, but also prove others. This is what gives them inexhaustible fecundity.

By way of example, let us compare Cartesian explanations to Scholastic explanations in physics. Descartes makes only one supposition. It is that bodies are composed of imperceptible particles. This is really not a supposition, because "it is something we see with our eyes in several things and that we can prove by an infinity of reasons in others." This supposition is the only one of its kind, properly speaking, because if we concede that bodies are composed of parts, it is easy to demonstrate that the parts of this or that body are of this figure rather than that other one. Starting from this initial premise, Descartes deduces the explanation of all meteors without needing to recur to other principles. By contrast, the Scholastics invoke a considerable number of different suppositions, like *real qualities*, *substantial forms*, the *four elements*, and "an almost infinite number of similar things." Armed with these innumerable suppositions, they explain very little. They declare themselves unable to account for many phenomena and, in order to explain others, they often appeal to supplementary principles and explanations of circumstances like the *antiperistasis* of final causes. Descartes's principles explain all phenomena and are proved by all phenomena, and are therefore demonstrated perfectly. Scholastic suppositions do not explain phenomena and are not proved by them and are consequently arbitrary and without foundation.[104]

What, exactly, is an experiment? It is the agreement that is established between the observation of a phenomenon and a moment of the deduction. Scholasticism does not do experiments, even when it invokes phenomena, because it is satisfied with makeshift explanations, imagining a particular cause for a particular effect. In this case, the agreement of cause and effect proves nothing because it is artificially obtained. But, to find a single cause from which a great number of effects flow, or even one that clearly explains a certain extraordinary effect, as are each of the meteors, it is necessary to have discovered the true cause.[105] When we

---

instead of putting in *that they do not serve at all*, in order that it may be known that each of these effects can also be proved by this cause in the case that the effect is put in doubt and that the cause has already been proved by other effects."

104. Letter to Morin, July 13, 1638; AT, vol. 2, p. 200, lines 2–21. When Descartes reserves completely "demonstrating" his principles to another place, he means metaphysical demonstration.

105. Letter to Morin, July 13, 1638; AT, vol. 2, p. 199, lines 15–24: "But although

have discovered the true case, each of the phenomena that we observe becomes an experiment. Therefore, a treatise like the *Meteors*, taken as a whole, is only a fabric of experiments. The same goes for all Descartes's treatises of physics. He has demonstrated "nearly as many experiments as there are lines in his writings," with each line explaining phenomena by its principles and proving these principles by the phenomenon's very existence. Furthermore, Descartes has not only explained all possible experiments, done or yet to do. Once his initial suppositions are demonstrated to be true, we can be sure in advance that they will explain everything, so that Descartes's physics is the complete experimental demonstration of all phenomena of nature.[106] This astonishing affirmation in the *Principles* must be taken literally: *nulla naturae phenomena in hac tractatione fuisse praetermissa*, "that there is no phenomena in nature that is not included in what is explained in this treatise."[107] In fact, all possible experiments would always consist of explaining a given phenomenon by *dispositiones quasdam magnitudine, figura et motu consistentes*.

When we adopt this point of view, the problem of Descartes the experimenter, which is initially so disconcerting, is easily resolved. Also, we easily explain why the *Meteors* does not free itself from Scholastic influence. In physics of this kind, all the phenomena are of the same nature and can be judged by the same explanations. The only defense that we might introduce between them is that some are known and others unknown. But this difference, which is entirely relative to our knowledge about them, does not prevent their being explained by the same principles: *magnitudo, figura, motus*. The very widespread mindset of our times that measures the importance of an experimental discovery by how profoundly it reshapes the edifice of science is as foreign as can be to

---

there are really several effects to which it is easy to adjust different causes, one cause to each, it is not, however, so easy to adjust the same cause to several different effects, if it is not the true cause from which they proceed."—Note the perfect agreement of these passages with the passage from the *Principles* that we have cited above.

106. Letter to Fr. Picot, June 1645; AT, vol. 4, p. 224, line 26, to p. 225, line 7: "Because, I am surprised at the fact that although I have demonstrated in particular nearly as many experiments as there are lines in my writings and that having accounted generally, with my principles, for all the phenomena of nature, I have explained by the same reasons all the experiments that can be done concerning inanimate bodies, and that by contrast, nothing has ever been well explained by the principles of ordinary philosophy. Those who follow ordinary philosophy do not cease to raise the objection against me of lack of experiments."

107. *Principles of Philosophy*, IV, 199; AT, vol. 8, pp. 3–14.

Descartes's mentality. When a version of physics has already received all the confirmation from experience (in the sense Descartes understands it) that Descartes's physics has received, it no longer has anything to hope for or fear from new experiments, however numerous we please to imagine them. We expect no revelation from experimental research. It can teach us nothing about the depth of things that we do not already know. It only furnishes us with new occasions to apply our old principles and to extend our power over nature. This is why, despite everything he may say, Descartes shows so little curiosity about new facts. Before searching for unknown phenomena, it is necessary first to explain known phenomena, and Descartes's chosen area is what is known by all, what is most common, that which each of us can observe for himself.[108] This is what he calls the universal or again the things that are most common and simplest of all.[109] Therefore, before doing experiments in the material sense of the word, it is necessary "to use only those that present themselves directly to our senses and that we could not ignore, provided that we carry out the slightest reflection upon them."[110] By means of these experiments that are ready-made, examining the first "and most ordinary" effects that can be deduced from his principles, Descartes "has found skies, heavenly bodies, earth, and even on earth, water, air, fire, and minerals." He has found them and the experiments he prefers are there, the most common of all. As for "particular experiments,"[111] it is necessary to conceive them more or less as Bacon conceived them. "Because, for this, I do not know any expedient but to once again seek some experiments that are such that their outcome is not the same if we have to explain it one way as it is in the other."[112] However, their number clearly frightens him: "One man alone could not suffice to do them all."[113] He would need assistants, money, and also particular talents for experimental procedures, which, toward the end of his life, Descartes acknowledged he lacked. He always retained an open predilection for experiments that fell upon him ready-made from

108. Letter to Mersenne, December 18, 1629; AT, vol. 1, p. 85, lines 1–6: "I have undertaken to explain only what is universal and what everyone can experience. I never would have done particular experiments that depend on the faith of some people, and I have resolved never to speak of them at all."

109. *Discourse on Method*, pt. VI; AT, vol. 6, p. 64, lines 11–12.

110. *Discourse on Method*, pt. VI; AT, vol. 6, p. 63, lines 20–25.

111. *Discourse on Method*, pt. VI; AT, vol. 6, p. 64, line 22.

112. *Discourse on Method*, pt. VI; AT, vol. 6, p. 65, lines 3–8.

113. *Discourse on Method*, pt. VI; AT, vol. 6, p. 72, lines 21–22.

the clouds, like hexagonal snowflakes, for those that only required "eyes to know them," but such windfalls are rare and he ended by becoming discouraged.[114]

There is an explanation, first of all, for Descartes's supreme indifference toward brute facts. When he possesses the demonstrative reasons for a phenomenon, he is delighted to make it be observed by others, even if he has not observed it himself. That is what happens with the coronas that are seen around candles.[115] But in the same letter in which he asks someone to observe for him this phenomenon that he can explain, he dissuades his correspondent from experimenting on the delay caused by air, because he finds himself incapable of explaining it.

> In the hindrance of movements by air, it is not necessary to consider what follows and what proceeds, but only one of the two. As to the *quantum*, I do not know it, and although a thousand experiments could be done to find it roughly, still, for what the experiments cannot justify by reason, unless I could still attain it, I do not think that anyone should take the trouble to do them.[116]

Descartes greatly prefers phenomena that perhaps do not exist, but that he can explain (in the case that they did exist) to a real phenomenon that he could not explain if he knew it. Such are the bands of phantasms that fight in the air and that the Conimbricenses declare not to belong to the physical order but attribute to God, angels, or demons.[117] Here Descartes appears very different from his adversaries. The Scholastics believe

114. Letter to Chanut, March 6, 1636; AT, vol. 4, p. 377, line 20, to p. 378, line 4: "If you have sometimes cast an eye outside your frying pan, you perhaps will have noticed other meteors in the air than those about which I have written, and you will be able to give me good instructions about them. A single observation that I made of hexagonal snowflakes in 1635 was the cause of the treatise I made about it. If all the experiments I need for the rest of my physics could have fallen from the clouds in this way and only my eyes were necessary to know them, I would promise myself to finish in a short time. But, because hands are also necessary to do experiments, and I lack hands that are right for them, I am losing entirely the desire to do more."

115. Letter to Mersenne, December 18, 1629; AT, vol. 1, p. 98, line 18, to p. 99, line 19: "I very much excuse myself from speaking about something I have not seen, in front of those who have had the experience. But you will oblige me by informing me if I am mistaken . . . because if I speak rightly you will see at the same time that the two red circles . . ."

116. Letter to Mersenne, December 18, 1629; AT, vol. 1, p. 99, line 20, to p. 100, line 56.

117. Gilson, *Index scolastico-cartésien*, text 197.

in the phenomena and renounce finding an explanation. Descartes hardly believes, but he still indicates the causes that seem to him capable of producing them. "Even though I have never seen such a spectacle, and because I know how the reports made of it have habitually been falsified and magnified by superstition and ignorance, I will content myself with touching upon, in a few words, all the causes that seem to me capable of producing it."[118]

That is why Descartes's very vigilant criticism bears much less upon facts than upon explanation of them. He does not dispute the distinction between vapors and exhalations; he interprets it. He does not deny that lightning changes into stone, that shooting stars are simply exhalations on fire, or that thunder is produced by the collision of two clouds. He limits himself to explaining how that happens better than his predecessors did. Since these phenomena are comprehensible for Descartes, it does not occur to him that they might not be real. With greater reason, Descartes would not have dreamed of making a new choice of phenomena to be explained. The most common and the most universal phenomena are enough for him. The inventory drawn up by Aristotle, and maintained by Scholasticism, was suitable for his project. In renewing the Greek philosopher's attempt to achieve universal explanation, Descartes does not think of conserving anything of his conception of science. Nevertheless he conserves the illusion that science does not have to conquer the facts at the same time it conquers their interpretation. It is this very illusion that turns him away from completing his principles of mathematical and mechanical explanation through a method of empirical investigation more prudent than his. His universal mathematicism is truly a revolution in the history of science and of human thought. Nevertheless, there subsists something of Scholastic *apriorism* in the manner in which Descartes applies his mathematicism to reality.

118. Descartes, *Meteors*, *Discourse* VII; AT, vol. 6, p. 323, line 18, to p. 324, line 24.

Bibliography

In his Bibliographical Note, Gilson tells us that the first four chapters of *Studies in Medieval Philosophy* were unpublished. Chapters 5 and 6, on Campanella, had been published in 1913 in *Annales de philosophie chrétienne* and in 1914 in *Revue de métaphysique et de Morale*. Chapters 7 and 8 on Descartes and Harvey had been published in *Revue philosophique* in 1920 and 1921 and in *Revue néo-scolastique de philosophie* also in 1920 and 1921.

Gilson's Bibliographical Note consists of a few works for further study. The translator has compiled a Bibliography of works cited.

Abelard, Peter, St. *Petri Abelardi Opera*. Edited by Victor Cousin et al. 2 vols. Paris: Durand, 1849 and 1859. See especially:
Dialogus inter Philosophum, Iudaeum et Christianum, vol. 2.
Epistola ad Heloïssam, vol. 2.
Historia Calamitatum, vol. 1.
In Epistolam ad Romanos, vol. 2.
Introductio ad Theologiam, vol. 2.
Letter from Peter the Venerable to Heloise, vol. 1 appendix.
Theologia Christiana, vol. 2.
Tractatus de Intellectibus, vol. 2.

Adam, Charles. *Vie et oeuvres de Descartes*. Vol. 12 in *René Descartes, Oeuvres*. 12 vols. Edited by Charles Adam and Paul Tannery. Paris: Vrin, 1897–1910. (Hereafter AT).

Albertus Magnus, St. *De Animalibus*. Edited by Hermann Stadler. Münster: Aschendorff, 1916–1921.

———. *De Mineralibus*, vol. 5 in Borgnet, *Opera*.

———. *In Libros Sententiarum*. Vols. 25–30 in Borgnet, *Opera*.

———. *Opera Omnia*. Edited by Auguste Borgnet. Paris: Vivès, 1890–1895.

———. *Physica*, vol. 3 in Borgnet, *Opera*.

———. *Summa Theologiae*, vols. 31–33 in Borgnet, *Opera*.

Anselm, St. In *Patrologia Latina. Patrologiae Cursus Completus, Series Latina*. Edited by Jacques-Paul Migne. Vols. 158–159. Paris: Migne, 1844–1855.

Cur Deus Homo, vol. 158.
De Fide Trinitatis et de Incarnatione Verbi, vol. 158.
Epistola ad Falconem, vol. 158.
Proslogion, vol. 158.

Aquinas, Thomas, St. *In Boethii "De Trinitat."* In *Opuscula Theologica*, 2:293–389. 2 vols. Turin: Marietti, 1954.

———. *Quaestiones Disputatae de Anima*. Paris: Libraries de Saint-Paul, 1912.

———. *Quaestiones Disputatae de Veritate*. Paris: Bloud et Barral, 1883.

———. *Quaestiones Quodlibetales*. Edited by Raimundo Spiazzi. 8th ed. Turin: Marietti, 1949.

———. *Scriptum super Libros Sententiarum Magistri Petri Lombrardi*. 4 vols. Paris: Lethielleux, 1929–1947.

———. *Summa contra Gentiles*. Paris: Garnier, 1878.

———. *Summa Theologiae*. Sancti Thomae Aquinatis Opera Omnia 6. Turin: Marietti, 1891.

Aristotle. *The Complete Works of Aristotle*. 2 vols. Edited by Jonathan Barnes. A revised translation. Princeton: Princeton University Press, 1984. (Originally Oxford University Press, 12 vols. Gilson does not cite an edition.)
De Anima (*On the Soul*), vol. 1.
De Respiratione (*On Breath*), vol. 1.
Historia Animalium (*History of Animals*), vol. 1.

Augustine, St. In *Patrologia Latina*. Edited by Jacques-Paul Migne. Vols. 32–47. Paris: Imprimerie Catholique, 1844–1855.
De Genesi ad Litteram, vol. 34.
De Libero Arbitrio, vol. 32.
De Musica, vol. 32.
De Spiritu et Anima, vol. 40.
De Trinitate, vol. 42.
De Vera Religione, vol. 34.
Retractationes, vol. 32.

Back, Jacobus de. *Dissertatio de Corde*. Rotterdam: Leer, 1648.

Bacon, Francis. *De Principiis atque Originibus secundum Fabulas Cupidinis et Coeli: sive Parmenidis et Telesii et praecipue Democrati Philosophia Tractata in Fabula de Cupidine*. In *Philosophical Works*, edited by Robert Leslie Ellis and James Spedding, with translations of the principal Latin works by Spedding.

Baeumker, Clemens. *Witelo: Ein Philosoph und Naturforscher des XIII. Jahrhunderts. Beiträge zur Geschichte der Philosophie des Mittelalters* 3/2. Münster: Aschendorff, 1908.

Baillet, Adrien. *La vie de Monsieur Descartes*. Paris: Durand, 1691; Paris: Equateurs, 2012.

Baron, Johannes. "Die Bedeutung der Phantasmen für die Enstehung der Begriffe bei Thomas von Aquin: Ein Beitrag zur Geschichte des Erkenntnistheoretischen Dualismus." PhD diss., University of Münster, 1902.

Baumgartner, Matthias. *Die Erkenntnislehre des Wilhelm von Auvergne. Beiträge zur Geschichte der Philosophie des Mittelalters* 2/1. Münster: Aschendorff, 1893.

Bérulle, Pierre de. *Oeuvres complètes*. 2 vols. Reproduced Monstsoul: Maison d'Institution de L'Oratoire, 1960.

Bonaventure, St. *Doctoris Seraphici Sancti Bonaventurae Opera Omnia.* 10 vols. Ad Claras Aquas (Quaracchi): Ex Typographia Collegii Sancti Bonaventurae, 1882–1902.

Breviloquium, pp. 199–292 in vol. 5.

Collationes In Hexaemeron, pp. 327–54 in vol. 5.

Commentaria in Quatuor Libros Sententiae, vols. 1–4.

De Mysterio Trinitatis, pp. 43–116 in vol. 5.

De Reductione Artium ad Theologiam, pp. 317–26 in vol. 5.

Itinerarium Mentis in Deum, pp. 293–316 in vol. 5.

Bonaventure, St, et al. *De Humanae Cognitionis Ratione: Anecdota Quaedam, Seraphici Doctoris et Non Nullorum Ipsius Discipulorum.* Ad Claras Aquas: Ex Typographia Collegii Sancti Bonaventurae, 1883.

Bouillier, Francisque. *Histoire de la philosophie cartésienne.* 1st ed. Paris: Durand, 1854. http://gallica.bnf.fr/ark:/12148/bpt6k649072.

Brunwald, G. *Geschichte der Gottesbeweise in Mittellalter bis zum Ausgang der Hockscholastik, nach den Quellen dargestellt.* Beitrage zur Geschichte der Philosophie der Mittelalters 6/3. Münster: Aschendorff, 1907. http://gallica.bnf.fr/ark:/12148/bpt6k649072/.

Campanella, Tomasso. *De Sensu Rerum et Magia, libri quatuor.* Frankfurt: Apud Egenolphum Emmelium, 1620.

———. *Realis Philosophiae Epilogisticae, Partes Quatuor.* Frankfurt: Tobias Adami, 1623.

Chapelain, Jean. Letter to Jean-Louis Guez Balzac, December 29, 1637.

Chartularium Universitatis Parisiensis. Edited by Henri Denifle and assisted by Émile Chatelaine. Paris: Delalain, 1889–1897. Brussels: Culture and Civilization, 1964. Available electronically.

Alexander IV, 1255

Alexander IV, November 10, 1256

Gregory IX, 1227 Gregory IX to the theology masters of the University of Paris, July 7, 1228

Gregory IX November 26, 1229

Gregory IX, 1230

Gregory IX, Aril 13, 1231

Gregory IX, April 23, 1231

Gregory IX, February 1233

Guy de Bazoches, letter, 1185–1190

Honorius III, January 1225

Humbert of Romans, General of the Order of Preachers, June 1256

Innocent III, 1208–1209

Innocent III, January 20, 1212

Innocent IV, recommendations and regulations

John of Salisbury, 1164, 1167

John XXII, March 8, 1317

Nicholas IV, March 23, 1292

Ordinances of the University of Paris, Alexander III, 1163; Robert of Courçon,1213; Innocent III, 1219

Peter of Corbeil, Decree, 1210

Petrus Cellensis, 1164

Pierre de Blois, 1175
Stephen of Tournay
Thomas Becket to G. de Sense, November 1169
Clerselier, Claude. Preface to Descartes, *L'Homme de René Descartes*. Paris: Angot, 1664.
Commentarii Collegii Conimbricensis Societatis Jesu, in Tres Libros De Anima Aristotelis Stagiritae. Coimbra: Antoinij a Maris, 1598.
Commentarii Collegii Conimbricensis Societatis Jesu, in Libros Aristotelis qui Parva Naturalia *Appellantur*; especially *In Librum De Respiratione*, and *In Librum De Vita et Morte*. Lisbon: Lopes, 1593.
Cordemoy, Gérauld de. *Le Discernement du corps et de l'âme*. Paris: Lambert, 1666.
Courtillier. Manuscript Course of Jean Courtillier (given during 1679 and 1680 at the Montaigu School in Paris), Tours Municipal Library, Manuscript 1717.
Damian, Peter, St. *Opera*. Patrologia Latina 144–45. Paris: Migne, 1857–1866.
De Divina Omnipotentia, vol. 145.
De Perfectione Monachorum, vol. 145.
De Sancta Simplicitate, vol. 145.
Homily for the Feast of Saint Eleuchadius, vol. 144.
Descartes. *Description du Corps Humain*. AT 11:219–90.
———. *Dioptrice*. AT 6:584–50.
———. *Discourse de la Méthode*. AT 6:1–78.
———. *Dissertatio Methodi*. AT 6:540–83.
———. *La Dioptrique*. AT 6:79–228.
———. *Le Monde*. AT 11:1–118.
———. *Les Meteores*. AT 6:230–366.
———. *Les Passions de l'Âme*. AT 11:293–497.
———. Letter to Beverwick, July 5, 1643. AT 4:3–6.
———. Letter to A. Boswell (?). AT 4:694–701.
———. Letter to Chanut, March 6, 1636. AT 4:376–79.
———. Letter to Golius, May 19, 1635. AT 1:317–21.
———. Letter to Huygens, June 1645. AT 4:222–26.
———. Letter to the Marquis of Newcastle, April 1645. AT 4:188–92.
———. Letter to Mersenne, October 8, 1629. AT 1:22–32.
———. Letter to Mersenne, December 18, 1629. AT 1:82–105.
———. Letter to Mersenne, March 4, 1630. AT vol. 1:124–27.
———. Letter to Mersenne, April 15, 1630. AT 1:135–47.
———. Letter to Mersenne, November or December 1632. AT 1:260–64.
———. Letter to Mersenne, March (?) 1636. AT 1:338–42.
———. Letter to Mersenne, May 27, 1638. AT 2:134–53.
———. Letter to Mersenne, July 27, 1638. AT 2: 253–80.
———. Letter to Mersenne, February 9, 1639. AT 2:493–509.
———. Letter to Mersenne, September 30, 1640. AT 3:183–98.
———. Letter to Mersenne, January 28, 1641. AT 3:292–300.
———. Letter to Morin, July 13, 1638. AT 2:196–221.
———. Letter to Fr. Noël, October 1637. AT 1:454–56.
———. Letter to Fr. Picot, June 1, 1645. AT 4:222.
———. Letter to Plempius, October 3, 1637. AT 1:412–31
———. Letter to Plempius, February 15, 1638. AT 1: 521–36.
———. Letter to Plempius, March 23, 1638. AT 2:62–69.

———. Letter to Regius, November 1641. AT 3: 440–42.
———. Letter to Regius, January 1642. AT vol. 3, pp. 491-520.
———. Letter to ?, April 27, 1637. AT 1:368-371.
———. *Meditationes de Prima Philosophia.* AT 7:1–612.
———. *Méditations Metaphysiques de René Descartes Touchant la Première Philosophie.* AT 9: 1–244 (Clerselier's translation).
———. *Principia Philosophiae.* AT 8:1–348.
———. *Traité de l'Homme.* AT 11:119–215.
Duns Scotus, John. *De Rerum Principio.* In *Opera Omnia,* 4:267–717. Paris: Vivés, 1892.
Ehrle, Franz. "John Peckham über den Kampf den Augustinismus und Aristotelismus in der zweiten Hälfte des 13 Jahrhunderts." *Zeitschrift für katholische Theologie* 13 (1889) 172–93.
Endres, Joseph Anton. *Forschungen zur Geschichte der frühmittelalterlichen Philosophie. Beiträge zur Geschichte der Philosophie des Mittelalters* 17/2–3. Münster: Aschendorff, 1915.
Eriugena, John Scotus. *De Divisione Naturae, De Praedestinatione, Expositiones in Mystica Theologiam Sancti Dionysii, In Prologum Evangelii secundum Ioannem, Super Hierarchiam Caelestem Sancti Dionysii.* Patrologia Latina 122. Paris: Migne, 1853.
Espinas, Alfred. "Pour l'histoire du cartésianisme." *Revue de Métaphysique et de Morale* (1906) 265–93.
Eustachius a Sancto Paulo. *Summa Philosophiae Quadripartita de Rebus Dialecticis, Moralibus, Physicis & Metaphysicis.* Last edition prepared by author. Cologne: Zetznerus, 1629.
Fernel, Johannis Fernelii Ambiani. *Universa Medicina,* ab ipso quaedam author ante obitum diligenter recognita et justis accessionibus locupleta. 6th ed. Frankfurt: Marnius, 1607. Gilson mentions *De Functionibus et Humoribus,* pp. 227–98; *De Partibus Corporis Humani,* pp. 1–55; *De Spiritu et Innato Calido,* pp. 141–68; *Pathologia,* pp. 345–670, especially *De Febribus,* pp. 464–512.
Forge, Louis de la. *Traité de l'esprit de l'homme.* Geneva: Editorial de Genève, 1725.
Froidmont (Fromondus). Letter to Plempius, September 13, 1637; AT vol. 1.
Gauthier, Léon. *La théorie d'Ibn Rochd sur les rapports de la religion et la philosophie, Publications de l'École des lettres d'Alger.* Bulletin de Correspondance africaine 41, Paris: Leroux, 1909; Paris, Vrin-reprise, 1983.
Geyer, Bernhard, ed. *Abaelards philosophische Schriften. Beiträge zur Geschichte der Philosophie des Mittelalters* 21/1. Münster: Aschendorff, 1919.
———. *Die Sententiae Divinitatis. Beiträge zur Geschichte der Philosophie des Mittelalters* 7/2–3. Münster: Aschendorff, 1909.
Gibieuf, Guillaume. *De Libertate Dei et Creaturae.* Paris: Collereau, 1630.
Gilson, Étienne. *Index scholastico-cartésien.* Paris: Alcan, 1912; Paris: Vrin, 1979.
———. *La Liberté chez Descartes et la Théologie.* Bibliothèque de philosophie contemporaine. Paris: Alcan, 1913.
Grabmann, Martin. *Geschichte der scholastischen Methode.* 2 vols. Freiburg: Herder, 1909–1911.
Grunwald, Georg. "Geschichte der Gottesbeweise im Mittelalter bis zum Ausgang der Hochscholastik nach den Quellen dargestell." *Beiträge zur Geschichte der Philosophie des Mittelalters* 6/3 (1907).
Hamelin, Octave. *Le système de Descartes.* Paris: Alcan, 1911.

Harvey, William. Guglielmi Harvei, Angli, medici regii, et in Londinensi medicorum collegio professoris anatomia, *De Motu Cordis et Sanguinis in Animalibus, Anatomia Exercitatio.* Frankfurt, 1628. Gilson cites the edition published by Arnold Leers, Rotterdam, 1661, which also contains the *Exercitationes Anatomicae Duae de Circulatione Sanguinis*, 1649.

"Harvey, William." *Encyclopedia Britannica.* 11th ed. Cambridge: Cambridge University Press, 1910–1911.

Hauréau, Barthélemy. *Histoire littéraire de Maine*, volume 8. New ed. 10 vols. Paris: Doumoulin, 1876.

Heitz, Theodor. *Essai historique sur les rapports entre la philosophie et la foi: de Bérenger de Tours à Saint Thomas d'Aquin.* Paris: Lecoffre, 1909.

Jean, de la Rochelle. *Summa de Anima.* Edited by Teofilo Domenichelli. Prato: Giachetti, 1882.

John of Jandun. *Quaestiones in Libros Physicorum Aristotelis.* Venice: Sanctis & Santritter, 1488.

———. *Quaestiones super Tres Libros Aristotelis de Anima.* Venice: Hailbrun & Franckofordia, 1473.

Langlois, Charles-Victor. *La connaissance de la nature et du monde au moyen âge, d'aprés quelques écrits français à l'usage des laics.* Paris: Hachette, 1911.

Lechner, Matthias. "Die Erkenntnislehre des Suarez." *Philosophische Jarbuch* 25 (1912) 125–50.

Mandonnet, Pierre. "Chronologie sommaire de la vie et des écrits de Saint Thomas." *Revue des Sciences Philosophiques et Théologiques* 9 (1920) 142–52.

———. *Siger de Brabant et l'averroïsme latin du XIIIe siècle: analyse et documents inédits.* 2 vols. 2nd ed. Louvain: Institut supèrieur de philosophie de l'Université, 1908–1911.

Manser, Gallus Maria, OP. "Johann von Rupella: Ein Beitrag zu seiner Charakteristik mit besonderer Berücksichtigung seiner Erkenntnislehre." *Jahrbuch für Philosophie und speulative Theologie* 26 (1912) 290–324.

Martin, Raymond M. "Quelques premiers maîtres dominicains de Paris et d'Oxford, et la soi-disant école dominicaine augustinienne (1229–79)." *Revue des sciences philosophiques et théologiques* 10 (1920) 556–80.

Mersenne, Marin. *L'Impiété des déistes, athées et libertins de ce temps combattue et renversée de point en point par raisons tirées de la philosophie et de la théologie.* 2 parts in 1 vol. Paris: Bilaine: 1624.

———. *Quaestiones Celeberrimae in Genesim* (folio). Paris: Cramoisy, 1623.

Mirbt, Carl. *Die Publizistik im Zeitalter Gregors VII.* Leipzig: Hinrichs, 1894.

Palhories, Fortuné. *Saint Bonaventure.* La pensée chrétienne. Paris: Bloud, 1913.

Parisano, Emilio, and James Primrose. *G. Herveii, De Motu Cordis et Sanguinis in Animalibus, Anatomica Exercitatio, cum Refutationibus Aemylii Parisani, Romani Philosophi ac Medici Veneti, et Jacobi Primirosii, in Londinensi Collegio Medici.* Leyden: Jean Maire, 1639.

Plempius, Vopiscus Fortunatus. *Fundamenta seu Institutiones Medicinae, Libri Sex.* Louvain: Zegersius, 1638.

———. Letter to Descartes, September 15, 1637. AT 1:399–402.

———. Letter to Descartes, January 1638. AT 1:496–99.

———. Letter to Descartes, March 1638. AT 2:52–54.

Pliny the Elder. *Natural History*. 10 vols. Translated by H. Rackham et al. Loeb Classical Library. Cambridge, MA: Harvard University Press, 1938–1960.

———. *Registrum Epistolarum Fratris Johannis Peckham*. Edited by Charles Trice Martin. 3 vols. London: Longman, 1882–1885.

Riolan, Jean. *Opuscula Anatomica Nova Quae Nunc primum in Lucem Prodeunt. Instauratio Magna Physica et Medicinae per Novam Doctrinam de Motu Circulatorio Sanguinis in Corde. Accessere Notae in Joannis Wallaci Duas Epistolas de Circulatione Sanguinis*. Authore Joanne Riolano, Professorum Regiorum Decano. London: Flesher, 1649.

Schneider, Arthur. *Die Psychologie Alberts des Grossen: nach den Quellen dargestellt. Beiträge zur Geschichte der Philosophie des Mittelalters* 4, parts 5–6. Münster: Aschendorff, 1903–1906.

Sertillanges, Antonin Gilbert. *Saint Thomas d'Aquin*. 2 vols. Paris: Alcan, 1910.

Siger, of Brabant. *Quaestiones de Anima Intellectiva*. In *Siger de Brabant et l'averroisme latin, textes inédits*, by Pierre Mandonnet, 2:144–71. 2 vols. Louvain: Institute supérieur de Philosophie de l'Université, 1911.

Silhon, sieur de (Jean). *De l'Immortalité*. Paris: Billaine, 1634.

———. *Les deux vérités, l'une de Dieu et sa providence, l'autre de l'immortalité de l'âme*. Paris: Sonnias, 1626.

Strowski, Fortunat. *Pascal et son temps*. 3rd ed. Histoire du sentiment religieux en France au xvii siècle. Paris: Plon-Nourrit, 1907–1908.

Suárez, Francisco. *Disputationes Metaphysicae* (or *Metaphysicarum Disputationum*). Salamanca: Renaut, 1597.

———. *Opera Omnia*. Edited by André Michel and Charles Berton. 28 vols. Paris: Vivès, 1856–1878.

Telesio, Bernardino. *De Rerum Natura*. Edited by Vincenzo Spampanato. Modena: Formiggini, 1910.

Vrijer, Marinus Johannes Antonie de. *Henricus Regius, een "Cartesiaansch" hoogleeraar aan de Utrechtsche hoogeschool*. 's-Gravenhage: Nijhof, 1917.

Wulf, Maurice de. *Histoire de philosophie médiévale*. 4th ed. Louvain: Institut de philosophie, 1912.

Ziesché, Kurt. "Naturlehre Bonaventuras." *Philosophische Jahrbuch* 21 (1908) 156–89.

Zimmermann, C. "Arnaulds Kritik der Ideenlehre Malebranche." *Philosophisches Jahrbuch* 24 (1911) 3–47.

Index of Names and Subjects

Printed in the USA
CPSIA information can be obtained
at www.ICGtesting.com
LVHW042305140823
755251LV00028B/519

9 781532 655272